PETE BRISCOE

with Todd Hillard

experiencing Life today

PETE BRISCOE
with Todd Hillard

LIFE

experiencing Life today

Life: Experiencing Life Today
By Pete Briscoe
Edited by Todd Hillard
A Book from Pete Briscoe, Telling the Truth, and Dunham Books, LLC
ISBN: 978-1-934590-84-3
Second Printing

First published in the United States of America by Dunham Books, LLC

Unless otherwise indicated, Scripture is taken from the THE HOLY BIBLE, NEW INTERNATIONAL VERSION®, NIV® Copyright © 1973, 1978, 1984, 2011 by Biblica, Inc.™ Used by permission. All rights reserved worldwide.

Cover and Interior Design by: Hope Certalic

FOREWORD
by Pete Briscoe

If you and I had the chance to grab a cup of coffee and I were to ask you to describe your life for me, what would you say? If you said anything less than "abundant," good for you for being honest. And good for you for opening this book.

Somewhere along the line, you and I were fed the line that God's not actually for us. Yeah, we give lip service to the fact that God loves us, but deep inside we figure we have to march to a bunch of rules for Him to REALLY love us. It's much easier to believe that He's some cosmic buzz-kill whose sole intent is to make us fall in line and obey a list of rules.

Friend, that god (note the small "g") isn't God (note the big "G") at all. God sent His Son to give you and me LIFE. His LIFE living through us. He doesn't want to burden us down with religion and rules. To make us march to a bunch of to-do's and legalism. Nope, He wants us to DANCE!

Christ's passion is for us to allow Him to live His life through you and me. And in Scripture, He reveals just what that looks like.

So as you pick up this devotional, my prayer is that you won't see it as something else to add to your list of "to-do's." Instead, see it as a tool to help you experience the true, abundant LIFE that God wants for you. The LIFE of Christ living through you.

Do You Believe?

I want to know God's thoughts... —**Albert Einstein**

I'd like to start off the new year with some pretty bold thinking. I know that might be a little bit dangerous, since there's a good possibility that your brain is still on vacation, but today's a new day and I'd like to jump start it with a very important thought. Actually it's a thought about thought:

God has built into your soul the capacity to ponder ideas and concepts—and I'm not just talking about simple things that you can see or touch. You have the ability to contemplate things like love, truth, injustice, success... the most phenomenal issues of our existence having to do with purpose, meaning, direction, and vision for life.

In short, God has given us an amazing gift that no other creature has: the capacity to believe.

We are going to explore "belief" like you have never explored it before. Give me two minutes a day and we will share the adventure of discovering true belief—a journey that will take you to some of the farthest points on our globe and into some of the deepest corners of your soul. Let's start with one of Jesus' last commands:

> *Do not let your heart be troubled; believe in God, believe also in Me.*
> —John 14:1 (NASB)

The world has some "issues" right now. Only God knows what the future holds. **Our belief in Him and His truth is the key to entering the future with peace and power.**

Father, thank You for the gift of belief. Today, I give You my troubled heart. Replace my worries with a vibrant trust in You and Jesus. In the months ahead, shape my beliefs. Correct them. Develop them. Conform them to the truth You have revealed in Your Word. Amen.

Your Bible and Your Belief

I am not moved by what I see. I am not moved by what I feel. I am moved only by what I believe. —**Smith Wigglesworth**

What we believe matters. It matters every second of every day.

- A flood of negative circumstances rushes through your life. The existence of a good God begins to seem very questionable. Where do you turn?

- Two nicely dressed men knock on your door wanting to teach you about their religion. The things they are teaching don't seem completely accurate.

- You reach mid-life. Nothing you have been working for seems to be worth the sacrifices you make. There are choices ahead—choices that will determine the course of the rest of your life.

- After years of faithful prayer and worship, the "God experience" is drying up. You're emotionally sapped.

- Perhaps you are standing on the edge of a great compromise. There are major moral crossroads in front of you.

In critical times like these (and a million more you will face constantly), where can we turn to determine right from wrong? Where do we go to test our thoughts and our ideas to determine whether they are worthy of our belief? When all seems unstable, there is only one place to stand:

> *For the word of God is living and active. Sharper than any double-edged sword, it penetrates even to dividing soul and spirit, joints and marrow; it judges the thoughts and attitudes of the heart.* —Hebrews 4:12

My Lord, when my thoughts are muddled and my emotions are running amuck, pull my mind back into the truth of Your Word. This year, saturate my soul with Your living Word so that I might believe and live the truth. Amen.

Believing What Matters

What we play is life. —Louis Armstrong

Some beliefs matter more than others, of course. It's not a big deal if you believe it's going to be sunny today and it turns out to be cloudy. On the other hand, if you don't believe that you have cancer but you actually do, the consequences can be much more severe.

While many of our beliefs will have greater or lesser earthly consequences, none of them matter more than our beliefs in God. Throughout Scripture, belief in God is directly tied to the most valued aspects of our existence—to things like joy, peace, and purpose.

> *Abraham believed God, and it was credited to him as righteousness.*
> —Romans 4:3

It's interesting to note here that Abraham's righteousness did not come just from a belief in God. Abraham didn't just believe that God existed; he actually believed what God had told him. That's a subtle, but powerful, distinction that has led to big transformation in many people's lives. Yes, it's one thing to believe that God exists. The demons actually believe in Him, but this knowledge terrifies them. We, on the other hand, can embrace and believe what He says.

O God, I don't want to just believe that You exist. I want to believe what You have revealed through the Bible. Speak to me clearly through Your living Word so that I can know what is true about You, so that I can then know You more intimately on a real, personal level. Amen.

Do You Believe Belief Is Important?

What comes into our minds when we think about God is the most important thing about us. —A.W. Tozer

Belief is supernatural. If you think about it, there's really no reason on earth why a biological organism would ever evolve by natural processes to the point where it could contemplate and consider things outside of the natural physical world. No, the capacity to believe is a supernatural gift given to us by God:

- Belief determines our perceptions of reality.
- Belief shapes every thought, decision, and action.
- Belief defines the parameters of what is possible.
- Belief emerges from the soul—from that inner core of our being that defines who we are and what we do.
- Belief even alters the contour of eternity.

Why is belief so amazingly important? I think it's because belief is the bridge to a real relationship with God through Jesus Christ. Relationships can either be based on works and legalism or belief and grace. When Jesus was asked what works God requires in our relationship with Him, Jesus' answer must have stunned them.

> *Then they asked him, "What must we do to do the works God requires?"*
> *Jesus answered, "The work of God is this: to believe in the one he has sent."*
> —John 6:28-29

Jesus knows that life transformation does not come from your performance, but it comes from your belief in Him. Jesus knows that if you trust Him, your works will be a natural extension of the relationship you have with Him. That was a radical shift in thinking back then, and it still is today!

Jesus, am I really doing the work God requires when I believe in You? Transform my mind according to this truth, Lord! I don't want to be conformed to the ways of the world. I want the kind of belief that sets me free by setting You free to live through me. Give me that kind of belief according to the truth of Your Word! Amen.

Eternal Life Now

No government ever voluntarily reduces itself in size. Government programs, once launched, never disappear. Actually, a government bureau is the nearest thing to eternal life we'll ever see on this earth! —**Ronald Reagan**

Okay, so that's a clever quote, but it's not entirely true! Yes, government programs seem to never die; but, eternal life for us? We *can* see that on earth.

> *Believe in the Lord Jesus Christ, and you will be saved.* —Acts 16:31

> *Now this is eternal life: that they may know you, the only true God, and Jesus Christ, whom you have sent.* —John 17:3

On earth, our ability to know Him is clouded by our flesh, the world, and the devil. But that's not always going to be the case!

> *For we know in part and we prophesy in part, but when perfection comes, the imperfect disappears ... For now we see only a reflection as in a mirror; then we shall see face to face. Now I know in part; then I shall know fully, even as I am fully known.* —1 Corinthians 13:9-10, 12

Belief is the key that opens the door that starts the relationship—clouded as it may be while stuck in physical bodies on this earth. Your belief in Christ begins eternal life now, through a relationship with God, based on grace and love rather than fear and performance ... a relationship that will know perfection soon enough.

Jesus, I absolutely thank You and praise You, saved by my belief in You and what You have done for me on the cross. Thank You that my belief opens up the door to know You and experience You now. In the days and months ahead, open Your Word to me in new ways so that I might believe more clearly and know You more intimately. Amen.

Belief in the Trenches

Faith certainly tells us what the senses do not, but not the contrary of what they see; it is above, not against them. —**Blaise Pascal**

Sometimes, all this talk about belief starts to feel kind of fuzzy and "out there." Thankfully, Scripture has given us many, many flesh and blood examples of what belief can look like. In my opinion, Sarah and Abraham are great examples. Not because their belief in God was perfect, but because they are such a good example of the struggle to take God at His Word.

When we pick up their story in Genesis, they are way beyond a midlife crisis. Nice couple, but they're coming up on their hundredth birthdays and they don't have any children. (A major downer, particularly in their culture where status was directly linked to offspring). At this point, it's game over. But, then God makes a promise—a promise so unbelievable that it shook their belief to the core:

> *Abraham fell face down, and God said to him, "As for me, this is my covenant with you: you will be the father of many nations. No longer will you be called Abram; your name will be Abraham for I have made you a father of many nations. I will make you very fruitful; I will make nations of you, and kings will come from you."* —Genesis 17:3-6

That's a lot to dump on a man who is 99 years old! We will watch their belief unfold in the passages ahead, but what about you? This same God has given us a lot of promises through the prophets, the apostles, and His Son. How do you respond to promises that seem too impossible to be true? What are the boundaries of your belief?

God of Abraham, show me just one place where my beliefs do not line up with who You are. Show me a promise that I don't have the faith to claim. Then take me beyond those boundaries into a deeper walk with You. Amen.

Are You Wagering without Hesitation?

Belief is a wise wager. Granted that faith cannot be proved, what harm will come to you if you gamble on its truth and it proves false? If you gain, you gain all; if you lose, you lose nothing. Wager, then, without hesitation, that He exists.
—**Blaise Pascal**

Sarah and Abraham faced a crisis of belief when God promised them the impossible: though nearly 100 years old, God told Abraham that he would be the father of many nations. The apostle Paul was an offspring of one of those nations! In Romans 4, Paul gives commentary on Abraham and the details of his belief:

> *He [Abraham] is our father in the sight of God, in whom he believed—the God who gives life to the dead and calls into being things that were not.* (4:17)

Abraham and Sarah didn't have a lot of confidence, but their confidence was in the right place. That's the most important aspect of belief—that we believe *in God*.

Belief is confidence in a powerful person.

When you place your trust in Him to do what He promises to do for you, in you, and through you, then you find true peace and the freedom to obey. That's why it's so critical that you understand who God is and who He has revealed Himself to be. Because it's not just your belief that matters; it's your belief in *Him* that makes all the difference.

God, I am growing in my confidence that You are all-powerful. Where do You want me to "wager without hesitation" that You exist? Amen.

His Comfort in Your Pain

Faith is the refusal to panic. —David Martyn Lloyd-Jones

Life is difficult and life is painful. Contrary to popular belief, God never promised that life would be pain-free. *He does, however, promise to be present in the midst of the pain.* If we believe that, I mean really believe it, it gives comfort and hope.

Sarah and Abraham were unquestionably hurting over their childlessness—a heartache felt by many today, too. I'm sure that decade after decade, Abraham had hope, only to have his dreams crushed again and again. God does not promise offspring to all of us, but He did promise them to Abraham. Would Abraham be willing to risk the pain and hope again?

> *Against all hope, Abraham in hope believed and so became the father of many nations...* —Romans 4:18

I don't know what issues you are facing today. I don't know where you've been or what the future looks like from where you stand. But if you have opened your life to Jesus Christ, I do know that God is *with* you and *in* you right now. When you unleash that truth in your soul, true comfort can be found in the midst of any pain you are enduring. Because not only is belief a confidence in a powerful person, but...

Belief is comfort in the midst of pain.

Lord, You told us that we would have difficulty and pain in this life. I believe that. You also promised that You would bring comfort and peace in it. I believe that, too. Where I have lost hope, I ask that You would give me the faith to live according to Your promises. Amen.

Honesty in Your Belief

Few really believe. The most only believe that they believe...
—**John Lancaster Spalding**

I love learning about faith from people like Abraham and Sarah, because sometimes words like *belief* and *faith* imply that we're supposed to ignore the obvious and deny reality. Belief doesn't ignore the facts; it faces the facts and then applies faith.

Belief is candid about perplexing problems.

Abraham was very objective about his problem. He assessed the situation for what it was:

> *Without weakening in his faith, he faced the fact that his body was as good as dead—since he was about a hundred years old—and that Sarah's womb was also dead.* —Romans 4:19

As we go through life, our hopes and dreams are often shattered, like fine china falling against cold concrete. What a difference it makes when we face those bitter realities head-on. Instead of disintegrating under the stress, we can apply accurate biblical truth to the situation. God's Word gives us the perspective that we need to put the facts in their place so that we can respond in faith to what God says is true.

Holy Spirit, I don't want to just say I believe something when I really don't. And I don't want my belief to become some sort of blind faith where I lose connection with reality. But I do want my belief in what's true about You to be the most important factor in my life. Thank You for giving me that kind of faith! Amen.

Where You Are in Your Belief Today

We cannot exercise our faith beyond what we believe to be possible.
—John G. Lake

Sometimes "belief" is raised up as a measure of spiritual character and that can put a lot of pressure on a person. The super-elite spiritual people supposedly have a lot of it, and the rest of us losers just struggle to hang on to the little bit that we have. First of all, that totally doesn't fit what Jesus taught about faith and mustard seeds. Second, it doesn't reflect the fact that many of the main characters in the Bible rode roller coasters of belief most of their lives—and yet, God moved through many of them in mighty ways. And it doesn't fit with another observation Paul makes about Abraham and his belief:

> *Yet he did not waver through unbelief regarding the promise of God, but was strengthened in his faith...* —Romans 4:20

Faith is something that is strengthened over time. You don't get one shot that lasts your whole life. Do you know how long Sarah and Abraham waited for God to fulfill His promise? Almost *13 years*! Abe and Sarah weren't traveling to the best infertility clinics in Palestine all these years; they weren't getting their "readings" from the lab or trying various procedures. (At their age, it's doubtful they could do anything!)

No, they were just waiting, taking care of the flocks, keeping the tent dust free, cooking meals, cleaning dishes … and waiting. Thirteen years is a long time— plenty of time for Abraham's faith to be made stronger than it was at the time he received the promise. And remember, at the time of the promise, he had plenty of questions and doubts. What's to be learned from this?

Belief is consistent in its progress.

That encourages me. That means that where I am today in my belief is not where I will have to be tomorrow. I have a full lifetime to be strengthened in faith and to be bolstered in my belief. So do you!

God of Grace, thank You, thank You, thank You. Thank You that the little bit of faith I do have is enough because You are so perfectly faithful. Continue to strengthen my faith today so my belief can progress consistently! Amen.

Praising Him through the Fog

Faith is like radar that sees through the fog. —**Corrie Ten Boom**

I think the reason I like Sarah and Abraham's story so much is because of the timing of it all. It wouldn't have been so miraculous if Sarah had gotten pregnant earlier in life, even if it had been after prolonged barrenness. No, this account gets its punch because of the timing. At nearly 100 years of age, God's promise of a child came to them. But there's another important bit of timing that took place. Can you find it?

> *Without weakening in his faith, he faced the fact that his body was as good as dead—since he was about a hundred years old—and that Sarah's womb was also dead. Yet he did not waver through unbelief regarding the promise of God, but was strengthened in his faith and* **gave glory to God,** *being fully persuaded that God had power to do what he had promised.* —Romans 4:19-21

It's important to note the timing of Abraham's *praise.* **His son was not born yet, so his praise emerges in the midst of his pain.** He is still grappling with perplexing problems, but standing on the promise he received, he gives glory to God for things he cannot yet see and has not yet received.

Belief culminates in praise.

Abraham's heart, like our hearts, has the capacity to worship and give thanks based on who God is. Because the fulfillment of God's promise is certain, our praise of God need not waver, nor does it need to wait.

Eternal Lord, I believe in You. By the truth of Your Word and the power of the Spirit in me, I will not waver in faith in You. Fill my heart with thoughts of You today. Even when I can't see, I will not wait to praise You. Amen.

The Power Behind His Promises to You

Let God's promises shine on your problems. —Corrie Ten Boom

Quotes from someone like Corrie Ten Boom are so powerful. She let God's promises shine on her problems in the midst of the horrors and death of the Nazi concentration camps. That's because her belief was rooted in something more than the hope that God would cause her problems to go away. **She experienced the true promises of God *in the midst* of her problems.**

We find the same level of belief in Sarah and Abraham.

> *Yet he did not waver through unbelief regarding the promise of God, but was strengthened in his faith and gave glory to God, being fully persuaded that God had power to do what he had promised.* —Romans 4:20-21

Abraham and Sarah clearly knew what God was promising. **And like them, we, too, can be fully persuaded that God has the power to do what He promises.**

Do you know the promises of God? Do you believe them?

- Jesus promised that we would know trouble in this world, but urged us to take courage, because He had overcome the world. (John16)
- God promises that though we walk toward certain death, He will be with us every step of the way. (Psalm 23)
- Our Lord promises that when we are weak, He will be strong in us. (2 Corinthians 12)

So many of His promises seem contrary to our wishes (that we would not have trouble, that we would not get sick or die, that we would always feel strong, etc.). But the nature of God's promises are deeper than that, and we need to be willing to let the light of truth shine on our problems, too.

Dear God, fill my heart and mind with the incredible promises of Scripture! Tell me the truth. Reveal false expectations and give me a belief that is convinced of the pure, life-giving promises You have made. Amen.

Replacing the Next Lie

Faith and doubt are by no means mutually exclusive; doubt is rather the shadow which everywhere follows faith and trust. —**Wolfhart Pannenberg**

Doubt has been defined as "a status between belief and disbelief, involv(ing) uncertainty or distrust or lack of sureness of an alleged fact, an action, a motive, or a decision."

To a certain degree all of us live in this "status between belief and disbelief." Sometimes we doubt when we hear the truth about who we are in Christ or read the promises God has made about the future. It's natural for our flesh to doubt when we are first exposed to the Truth. Even the disciples wrestled with this.

> *Now Thomas (also known as Didymus), one of the Twelve, was not with the disciples when Jesus came. So the other disciples told him, "We have seen the Lord!" But he said to them, "Unless I see the nail marks in his hands and put my finger where the nails were, and put my hand into his side, I will not believe." A week later... he [Jesus] said to Thomas, "Put your finger here; see my hands. Reach out your hand and put it into my side. Stop doubting and believe." Thomas said to him, "My Lord and my God!" Then Jesus told him, "Because you have seen me, you have believed; blessed are those who have not seen and yet have believed."* —John 20:24-29

Don't feel pressured if you have doubts. You aren't being unfaithful or betraying God by questioning what you believe. **Belief is a courageous process.**

In fact, a sincere, growing faith *emerges* from doubt. **I think doubt, to a certain degree, will always be with us until that day when we can put our fingers into His nail-scared hand.**

God, I want to call You, "My Lord!" and live with You as "My God!" just like Thomas proclaimed. Thank You for understanding my doubts as I continually reject lies and replace them with Your truth. Show me the next lie that You want to replace! Amen.

Getting in God's Wheelbarrow

The problem with using quotes from the internet is verifying the authenticity of the source. —**Abraham Lincoln**

It's one of those stories that just gets better with time. Like most good stories it began with a certain amount of truth. Yes, there was once a French man named Charles Blondin, and yes, he used to walk a tightrope across Niagara Falls in 1859 doing all sorts of stuff like wearing a blindfold, carrying his manager on his back, and cooking himself an omelet (no joke). He even pushed a wheelbarrow once. But that's when "history" gets a little fuzzy.

For decades, preachers have been telling about the day that Blondin crossed The Falls with the wheelbarrow and yelled, "Do you believe?" "Yes!" the crowd cheered back. "Then get in the wheelbarrow!" The story goes that only one man was willing to volunteer and off they went. There is even a version of this story in a noted Christian book where a man (who had a wager that they would fall) cut one of the supporting cables, causing the wire to sway dangerously. The man in the wheelbarrow jumped into Blondin's arms who carried him the rest of the way as the wheelbarrow tumbled into the white water abyss.

Yes, a great story that just gets better. Too bad we can't find any record of it actually happening.

But you know what? Because this is such a great illustration of biblical truth, I'm going to go with it! (Just don't quote me on it. Tell people you saw it on the internet and they will believe you for sure.)

Here's the deal: We say we believe, but do we really? God will continue to ask us to get into the metaphorical wheelbarrow on a regular basis, risking our emotions, our reputations, our money, and even our very physical well-being. **Do we believe? Will we get in?**

Lord, I believe … to a certain extent at least. I, at least, believe that a great adventure awaits me if I place my trust in You. I know that the faith of a mustard seed can move a mountain. Give me an opportunity to "get in Your wheelbarrow" today. The little bit of faith that I have in You, I give to You. Amen.

When Your Road Darkens

Faithless is he that says farewell when the road darkens. —J.R.R. Tolkien

Through Sarah and Abraham we have learned a lot about biblical belief. Belief in God is:

- Confidence in a powerful person
- Comfort in the midst of pain
- Candid about my problems
- Consistent in progress
- Culminating in praise
- Convinced of God's promises
- Courageous in process

These things are the skeleton of belief. In the months ahead, we will be putting meat and muscle on that skeleton. Yes, we believe … but what exactly do we believe in? And do we really believe or is our belief tainted and incomplete? How do we do when the road darkens and all we can see are shadows and no light?

In Mark 9:24 we find one of most honest prayers in the whole Bible. A man has come to Jesus with a son who is possessed by a violent evil spirit. The man desperately asks if Jesus is able to help him. Jesus tells him, "All things are possible to him who believes." Perhaps our most honest responses to God at this point are the same words that the father of the demonized child exclaimed to Jesus:

Lord, I do believe. Help my unbelief. Amen.

Your Belief and God

Do you know why most of us miss the adventure? It's because we've never learned to plug our theology into our biography. —Tim Hansel

God.

That's a very simple word: *God.* Three letters, one syllable, very easy to say. We see this word on our money; we print it on our bumper stickers and plaster it on billboards. Preachers say it with such confidence—as if they have the meaning of this word all figured out—*God* squished in a box of fancy-sounding words and quotations by long-dead theologians. Too often, we hear this word thrown around casually and carelessly, like punctuation at the beginning or the end of a sentence. It's even common to hear someone use His name as an outcry of petty disgust!

What does *God* mean? Does belief in what stands behind that little word matter? **The answer is an unquestionable "yes."** Different beliefs about it have caused wars and have healed families. The word *God* has been used for great comfort and misused causing great pain. It causes some to feel peace and others to boil with anger.

> *The simple believe anything, but the prudent give thought to their steps.*
> —Proverbs 14:15

Polls tell us that 90-95% of Americans "believe in God." I'm assuming that if you're reading this devotional, you "believe in God," too. But do you know what you believe when you say that? What do you mean when you say, "God"? As more of God's nature is revealed through the Bible in the coming weeks, I hope and pray that your understanding of and belief in Him will be deepened and sweetened.

God, open my heart, mind, and soul to Your Word as we learn more about who You are. I already "believe in You," but I want to Believe in You! Reveal Yourself to me so I can live in You in new, truthful ways. Amen.

Three Big Questions You Must Answer

What comes into our minds when we think about God is the most important thing about us. —A. W. Tozer

The issue of "God" cannot be avoided. Immediately, when we consider our belief in God, three vitally important questions must be addressed:

- Do you know *about* Him?
- Do you *know* Him?
- Do you *make Him known*?

And do you see the need for all three?

- To know God, but to not know *about* Him … **is that possible?**
- To know about God, but to not *know* Him … **is that not tragic?**
- To know God, but to not *make Him known* … **is that conceivable?**

Since the dawn of creation, these three questions about God have been central to the plight in the history of all humanity. Consider Moses, one of the great leaders of the Old Testament:

> *Moses said to the LORD, "You have been telling me, 'Lead these people,' but you have not let me know whom you will send with me … If you are pleased with me, **teach me your ways so I may know you** and continue to find favor with you."* —Exodus 33:12-13

Teach me your ways so that I may know you … it's a humble but desperate request, isn't it? We must know about Him so that we can know Him, so that we can then make Him known. **What we believe about God is the most important thing about us.**

God, I know some about You, but I want it to go further than that. Help me to know You more so I can love You more, and, in turn, make You known to those around me! Amen.

Who's Your Daddy?

It doesn't matter who my father was; it matters who I remember he was.
—Anne Sexton

People will often build their views of God based on how they view their earthly fathers. **But are earthly fathers a good picture of your heavenly Father?**

It depends.

For some, "father" brings up feelings of comfort and security. Yet for others, just imagining the sound of your father's footsteps raises an instinct to try to hide. You might look back at your father and think, "If God's anything like my old man, I don't want to have anything to do with Him!"

So when we talk about "God the Father," our minds, not our emotions, must dominate. We need to let God's Word, not our feelings or earthly experiences, be our guide when we try to figure out what we mean by "God the Father."

Throughout the Bible we find the perfect picture of a perfect father. Moses' request in Exodus was a sincere one:

> *"If you are pleased with me, **teach me your ways so I may know you** and continue to find favor with you."* —Exodus 33:13

In the passages following this request, **God reveals no less than fourteen fatherly traits about Himself,** each of which is amplified in many other places throughout the Bible. These traits also make a decent model for those of us who are fathers on earth, but they aren't intended to be a guilt trip to try to make us perform better. Instead, they should encourage us all, as God's kids, with the wonderful news of our perfect parent who cherishes, values, and adores us.

Father, I pray that any misconceptions I have about You will be swept away by the truth of Your Word. I want to know You and want to learn about You in a rational way that is free from misleading emotions. Please help me clear my mind so Your Spirit can lead me to the truth. Amen.

The Present of Presence

My father? I never knew him. Never even seen a picture of him. —Eminem

The first fatherly trait in Exodus is one of the most important for any sort of relationship: *He's around.*

> *The LORD replied, "My Presence will go with you…"* —Exodus 33:14

When Moses asked who would go with him, God said, "I will go with you." We find this all throughout Scripture. **Wherever you go, God will be there.**

My dad traveled a lot when I was young. When we were living in England, Dad would sometimes be in the States for months at a time. We missed him terribly. One of the reasons we moved to Milwaukee in 1970 was so that my father could be more invested in our lives—so he could be "around" more. During the years of his absence, my mom pointed me to the "Fatherness of God." **She taught me that He is always around, no matter where I am or what I am doing.** While dad was gone, I was forced to seek God's Fatherness in my life … and His presence became a reality to me.

God is with you right now, even as you read these words, intricately involved in your individual life as a very present Father. No mountain is too high, no valley too low, no river too wide to keep Him away from you. You might even try to run away from God or turn your back on Him, but the moment you stop, you'll realize that He is still there with you. I mean, look what happened to Jonah!

Consider this:

> *The LORD your God is with you, the Mighty Warrior who saves. He will take great delight in you; in his love he will no longer rebuke you, but will rejoice over you with singing.* —Zephaniah 3:17

Not only is God with you, but He ENJOYS being with you! He desires to love you in every way possible.

God, thank You for Your constant presence. Thank You for loving me enough to never abandon me. Please help me remember that You are with me all the time. Amen.

The Ultimate Release

Thou hast made us for Thyself, O Lord; and our hearts are restless until they rest in Thee. —**Augustine**

Life's a struggle. Anybody will tell you that. No matter where we end up, we will wrestle with problems, be they financial, emotional, physical, or a host of other difficulties. As many as there are, so are there more tactics to deal with them. Fathers of earth will have millions of different solutions, be it to let them sort out themselves or to slam your nose to the grindstone until there's nothing left.

Unlike either of those stances, our heavenly Father tells us one thing that encompasses any problem we might face:

> *...and I will give you rest.* —Exodus 33:14

God will give us *rest*? Some of us had fathers who pushed and pushed us to the brink of mental and physical exhaustion. God the Father is different. ***He comforts us.*** Yes, He has things for you to do—and those things are very important—but Scripture makes it clear that those things are done by depending on *God's* strength working through us, rather than by us using *our* strength to try to do things for Him.

> *It was I [God] who taught Ephraim to walk, taking them by the arms; but they did not realize it was I who healed them. I led them with cords of human kindness, with ties of love. To them I was like one who lifts a little child to the cheek and I bent down to feed them.* —Hosea 11:3-4

In this passage from Hosea, we see that God not only takes our burdens, but He WANTS to take them because of His unending love for us! There is no limit to what He is able to handle, nor to what He will do for you. That brings up a pretty deep question:

What have you been struggling with in your own strength, rather than trusting it to the Father who loves you?

Father, take the burdens I've placed on myself. I can't tackle these things on my own. I release what I've been trying to do myself to You. I give up trying on my own. I trust in Your strength so I may constantly rest in Your comfort. Amen.

You Are Set Apart

Could we change our attitude, we should not only see life differently, but life itself would come to be different. —**Katherine Mansfield**

I did a chapel for the Milwaukee Brewers a number of years ago. That was a big deal. Where I used to live, the Brewers were the gods of bat, ball, and diamond. Every devout Wisconsinite watched them on TV. Those who could afford tickets would regularly make the pilgrimage to County Stadium to worship in person. But to enter into the locker room? That was the "holy of holies"—the inner sanctuary of the temple where no mere-mortal fan would ever think of gaining access.

But I had an "in": Paul Molitor. Paul was the captain of the team and because I knew him, I was welcome at the lockers—I was even allowed to speak to the players face to face. I shared with the whole group thoughts from the Bible and they listened ... all because of Paul. *He* elevated me to a different level in the eyes of these amazing athletes. They were willing to listen to me because of my relationship with him.

Here's a similar situation with God and the Israelites:

> *Then Moses said to him ... "How will anyone know that you are pleased with me and with your people unless you go with us?* **What else will distinguish me and your people from all the other people on the face of the earth?"**
> —Exodus 33:16

God the Father does the same thing for us. His presence in our lives separates us from others. *He distinguishes us.* Some may not recognize God as being the source of our uniqueness, but He is. When we become aware of our position as God's children, we start to project that in our behavior and attitude ... we become elevated, changed, unique in the world ... and many will be willing to listen to us as we make Him known as a natural extension of that relationship with the Father.

Father, I pray that You would elevate my lifestyle in such a way that I am obviously different from the world. Let me be an example of what life is like in You so that others may know Your awesomeness. Amen.

Your Perfect Provision, NOW

If God owns everything and knows everything, if he loves us and is perfect and holy in all he does, then everything he gives and everything he withholds can rightly be recognized as a good gift from him, even if we are unable to see it as such. —T. A. Hillard

Sometimes people put unreasonable expectations on God. They expect things He never promised and then get frustrated when they don't have them right now. But God doesn't give us everything that we want. He gives us what we *need*.

Moses was aware of the great need he and the Israelites had for God's presence. It wasn't just a desire; it was a necessity.

> *Then Moses said to him… "How will anyone know that you are pleased with me and with your people unless you go with us?* **What else will distinguish me and your people from all the other people on the face of the earth?***" And the LORD said to Moses, "I will do the very thing you have asked…."*
> —Exodus 33:16-17

God knew that Moses' request reflected a real need for their mission—His presence. So God said He would do it, and He provided for their need because He is a perfect provider.

- God owns everything. (Psalm 50:10-12)
- God is generous. (Acts 14:16-17)
- God is aware of our needs. (Matthew 6:31-32)

Therefore, we not only ask God for what we *hope* He will provide, but we can be confident *He's providing the very things we need right now!* If this is true, shouldn't our prayers be focused on aligning our desires with what God clearly says that we need?

Can you tell the difference between your desires and what a loving Father knows that you need? Do you believe God is providing for you *right now* everything that you truly need, just as He will provide for you in the *future*?

God, thank You that You're providing everything I need today. Make the difference between what I want and what I need very clear. Amen.

The God Paradox

My deepest awareness of myself is that I am deeply loved by Jesus Christ and I have done nothing to earn it or deserve it. —Brennan Manning, *The Ragamuffin Gospel*

Maybe it was through art, maybe through fiery, angry sermons. I don't know where, for sure, but somewhere along the line **many of us got the idea that God the Father is angry,** and He's sitting up in heaven on a cloud … keeping score … all the time. He has a list of laws and rules in one hand and a lightning bolt in the other. He's just waiting for you to screw up. And when you do? *Kapow!*

Is that accurate?

Not even close. Look at what God told Moses when he requested God's presence:

> *I will do the things you have asked because I am pleased with you…*
> —Exodus 33:17

God is pleased with us. God told Moses that He would be present among them because He was pleased with him. Now you might say, "Yeah, that's because it's Moses. I am no Moses." Moses is supposed to be this great godly leader, right? Well, he's supposed to be, but he's not. Do you know what happened right before this passage? Moses' followers built a huge, golden cow and worshiped it instead of God. If Moses was supposed to be some great leader, shouldn't his followers like, maybe, *follow*? But in reality, his people were a mess … just like we are, just like *you* are. **But still, God finds pleasure in us, in spite of poor performance.**

Lord, it's so hard to understand that even though humanity is broken, You still love us, even in the worst of times. Thank You for finding pleasure in me in Christ where the world only sees failure! Amen.

The God Who Hears You

Always respond to every impulse to pray. The impulse to pray may come when you are reading or when you are battling with a text. I would make an absolute law of this – always obey such an impulse. —Martyn Lloyd-Jones

How important would you feel if your father had 3 billion kids' phone numbers in his iPhone, and you were just one of them? How much attention could one man give that many children? Virtually none. But our heavenly Father has no limitations on His power, His knowledge, or His ability to be everywhere for everyone all at once! This was made clear in His talk with Moses when He said:

> *"I am pleased with you and I know you by name."* —Exodus 33:17

Years ago, I was sitting with thousands of college students at the Urbana conference at Illinois University. The arena was packed to the rafters. At one point in the program, they asked all 20,000 of us to pray ... out loud. I was overwhelmed not just by the noise or the cumulative effect, but by the simple fact that God was capable of hearing each prayer and answering it perfectly.

For God the Father, *every* prayer we pray is the *only* one He hears. **There's no such thing as background prayers.** Why?

Because He's interested.

> *"Are not five sparrows sold for two pennies? Yet not one of them is forgotten by God. Indeed, the very hairs of your head are all numbered. Don't be afraid; you are worth more than many sparrows."* —Luke 12:6-7

God knows your name, and it's always on His heart. If you have a thorn in your foot, He cares about it even though there may be floods and famine elsewhere on the planet. He can give you 100% of His attention and not have any less for anyone else. That's your significance in God's eyes!

Father, I'm thankful that You are listening to this prayer and can give Your 100% attention to me! Thank You for being interested in me, for caring for me, for loving me. Amen.

Your Compassionate Father

I choose kindness ... I will be kind to the poor, for they are alone. Kind to the rich, for they are afraid. And kind to the unkind, for such is how God has treated me. —Max Lucado

I love the passages that talk about God being compassionate.

> *... for the LORD your God is gracious and compassionate. He will not turn his face from you if you return to him.* —2 Chronicles 30:9
>
> *The Lord, the Lord, the compassionate ...* —Exodus 34:6

Verses like these make it clear that God the Father is full of compassion for us. He really cares and He feels that caring toward you and me.

That is a very radical thought, if you think about it. *Compassion* simply means "with passion"—but consider the implications of these three words: *God. Compassion. You.* Your heavenly Father is not mechanical in His love for you; **He feels it.**

I was in the Philippines with a mission team during college. In one village, we came across a boy with leprosy. He was shunned by all—an untouchable. But the gracious pastor of the tiny evangelical church reached out with his hands. He was the only one willing to embrace the grotesque face, the stumps for hands, and the disfigured legs.

But I'll never forget the morning I came around the corner and found this little boy sitting in the lap of one of my teammates, Randy. Randy had taught him how to play "Patty-cake." **As stumps hit palms, the distorted face burst into a twisted but pure smile, and I saw a visible picture of the compassion of God ... with one big twist: I'm the boy sitting in the lap of God.**

Father, sending Your Son to suffer for me was the ultimate form of compassion! Let me see myself as the leprous child on Your lap. Thank You for loving me with a passion only You could muster, for loving me to wholeness. Please help me to see the world through Your eyes so I may also show Your compassion to the world! Amen.

Grace Is Good

Don't judge me. I made a lot of money. —**Samantha Bee**

We are constantly bombarded and judged in the world because of our performance, our appearance, and our possessions. Although it's never really said outright, your earthly value is based on all of these things. Without them, you are nothing.

God deals with us in no such way. Because He is love, our acceptance is based on something entirely different:

> *Then the LORD came down in the cloud and stood there with him and proclaimed his name, the LORD. And he passed in front of Moses, proclaiming, 'The LORD, the LORD, the compassionate and gracious God, slow to anger, abounding in love and faithfulness, maintaining love to thousands, and forgiving wickedness, rebellion and sin.'* —Exodus 34:5-7

He is gracious.

That's the God we call "Father." His grace changes the rules on all things. He lavishes His best on us even though we have done nothing to deserve it.

> *For it is by grace you have been saved, through faith—and this not from yourselves, it is the gift of God—not by works, so that no one can boast.* —Ephesians 2:8-9

What can you say to that? How do we respond to such love?

God, thank You SO much for holding us to a different standard than the world. Releasing me from the constantly changing expectations that are unachievable is relieving. Help me to focus on Your gift, a salvation I cannot earn, and find worth in that above anything else! Amen.

God's Patience towards You

Lord, give me patience, and give it to me NOW! —**Unknown**

I mentioned a couple weeks ago that people often build their view of God based on what their earthly fathers are like. Whereas many of us have great, loving dads, some people have a father figure who is constantly mad at his family. Perhaps, he vents stress from other parts of his life onto the nearest and least resistant source. Or maybe he holds the people nearest to him to ridiculously high standards and reacts irrationally when they aren't met. Regardless of the source, angry dads can lead people to think that God the Father is like *their* father, angry at everybody and everything, lacking the want to, that's not only wrong, **but contradictory to what the Bible tells us!** God revealed Himself to Moses as the Father who is "*… slow to anger …*" (Exodus 34:6). David sang of the Father with words like these:

> *The LORD is compassionate and gracious, slow to anger, abounding in love …*
> *As a father has compassion on his children, so the LORD has compassion on*
> *those who fear him; for he knows how we are formed, he remembers that we*
> *are dust.* —Psalm 103:8, 13-14

God the Father is *patient.*

I'm learning this one the hard way. I've done some basketball coaching over the years. Back when my son Liam was just a little guy in elementary school, with years of learning ahead of him … I am embarrassed by how often I expected him to be where I was when I played in college! I would see what he was doing, expect something else, deal with him in "coach" lingo, and see his eyes well up with tears. Oh, how I sometimes wish it was God coaching that team and not me! I was impatient with him, expecting him to be what he will one day be, today.

God knows our weaknesses. He knows how we have been made, and He gives us slack when others might just cut us off. **Amazingly, He sees us as we are "in Christ," and knows full well who He is shaping us to become. He recognizes the process of development and growth and is thoroughly patient with us as we trudge along the path.** I don't know about you, but I am thoroughly happy we have a Father like that!

Father, Your patience is long, deep, and loving. I don't deserve such an act of caring, so thank You for caring enough to act like that towards me. I pray this patience would be shown in my life as I interact with others so they can see what You've done in me! Amen.

Giving Credit Where It's Due

'Knowing' in the Biblical sense is a very intimate thing. It implies to actual experience. It is not just head knowledge, cerebral assent, or muscular posing. John 8:32 says, 'You shall know the truth and the truth shall make you free.' You participate; you experience life and make it 'biographical.' So, your theology becomes your biography. —Tim Hansel, *Holy Sweat*

The past few weeks, we've been looking at several different aspects of who God the Father is, talking about what He wants to do in our lives, about how He wants us to act towards Him. These are definitely important things to have in your head …

But the buck doesn't stop there.

It's one thing to know all of these things in our head (to know this *about* God), but what a tragedy it would be if we never go further than this! God's revelation causes a response in the heart of those who are sensitive to His leading. When Moses received God's revelation, he saw himself in proportion to the God he now knew. And how did he respond?

> *"Moses bowed to the ground at once and worshiped."* —Exodus 34:8

He saw that ***God is praiseworthy.***

Moses praised God with his whole being. It wasn't just something he knew in his head. He was experiencing God in a radical way, getting to know Him personally. Not only does praise put us in our place and God in His, it also changes our hearts and deepens our experience of spiritual intimacy with the Creator.

After Moses praised Him, God began to make Himself known to others through Moses. God had revealed Himself as Father. Moses saw himself as a child. **And together they walked forward in truth to the glory of God.**

Father, whenever I get the chance to learn more about You, I pray that You take what I'm putting in my head and move it to my heart. Make this REAL in my life. I want to radically experience You every day. I love You, and You are worthy of ALL my praise!!! Amen.

Focused for You

Your love never fails, it never gives up, it never runs out on me.
—*One Thing Remains* by **Jesus Culture**

Fathers can be busy people. Oftentimes they have jobs that will require all their attention, energy, and time. Sometimes they will *make* time for hobbies, golf, and the weekend binge of TV football … leaving other parts of their life (like their kids) neglected and forgotten.

God has not only billions of people to interact with, but He also has the rest of the universe to play with. **Chances are that the inner workings of a solar system are way more interesting than anything we have to capture God's attention!** And yet, what does the Bible tell us about God's attitude toward us?

> *"The LORD, the LORD, the compassionate and gracious God, slow to anger, abounding in love and faithfulness, maintaining love to thousands, and forgiving wickedness, rebellion and sin."* —Exodus 34:6-7

Because God is God, He doesn't get sidetracked; He doesn't get distracted; He doesn't get bored. He has everything He needs right now. He won't leave you, give up on you, or go somewhere else.

He is faithful. Do you get that? Think about it, because no human being is like that.

My dad is a faithful man. In fact, I know what I'm going to say about him at his funeral: "He was faithful to his Savior, to his bride, and to his calling." We were fortunate to have that kind of human faithfulness in our family. But compared to God, Dad's faithfulness is miniscule. **God never changes, never flounders, never turns His back.**

When we believe in His faithfulness, peace and relief descend on our fearful souls. He's not going anywhere; He'll keep His promises; and He'll follow through with His pronouncements. This makes the faith walk possible *and* logical.

> *"And surely I am with you always, to the very end of the age."*
> —Matthew 28:20

Father, thank You for Your incredible faithfulness, and for being the constant in my life. Help me take to heart the promise of Your presence. Amen.

The Big Hitter

Alas! how difficult it is not to betray one's guilt by one's looks. —**Ovid**

Guilt is huge … and heavy. Like a lead anchor strapped to our feet, our sins both big and small from the past can submerge us in the ocean of shame. This has made some of us sincerely believe that our sins are unforgivable by man (which is probably true), and sometimes even by God (which isn't true!). We can end up with the notion that God doesn't *want* to forgive us, or worse yet, that He *won't* forgive because what we did was so shameful that we can't even bear to think about how we failed Him.

And yet, like so many times before, we know from the Bible that God is quite the opposite. … *and forgiving wickedness, rebellion and sin.* (Exodus 34:7)

God the Father forgives the one who truly believes in Him. He forgives everything, and does so completely.

He is forgiving.

You might need to let that soak in for a moment.

The Bible is a description of the forgiving character of God. The New Testament shows you the *person* that He has chosen: Jesus Christ. It also shows you the *method*: the crucifixion and resurrection. It's all because He is a forgiving Father.

God, I am not worthy of Your love, and much less of Your forgiveness because of my sin. Thank You SO much for having compassion, for being gracious, for being patient with me. You not only look past my sin, but save me from it! Thank You for Your forgiveness. I believe in it. Amen.

The Absolute Necessity of Justice

Everybody wants to see justice done, to somebody else. —Bruce Cockburn

In some families, fathers punish their children in ways that are not right or fair. Maybe he's too harsh on his child for a small mix-up in the house, or maybe he punishes them by denying something that gives them pleasure for no good reason.

Earthly fathers can misuse the power given to them. And if we apply these imperfections to our concept of God, we will question His authority, motives, and even His right to punish.

If anyone should have been inclined to think that God is unfair, it would've been Job. He lost everything he had, yet still kept his cool and stood by his innocence. His friend, Elihu, helped to make sense of it all by affirming God's fairness:

> *"He repays everyone for what they have done; he brings on them what their conduct deserves. It is unthinkable that God would do wrong, that the Almighty would pervert justice."* —Job 34:11-12

God loves His people, but that doesn't erase the fact that He is also fair. **He is perfect, so everything He does is right and good—meaning that He cannot overlook sin.**

He is just.

We can thank Him that justice was satisfied on the cross that horrid day when Jesus paid the price for our sins so we could be forgiven. That act of sacrifice allows God to be both loving and fair. **If we are *in* Christ, the punishment for our sin falls *on* Christ.**

But for those who refuse this gift, His punishment and judgment will be swift and just.

It's unpopular, but it's true. Without an awareness of God's holy justice, we would have complete mayhem in our world and total subjectivity in our relationship with Him.

Father, don't let earthly injustice taint my perspective of You. Give me eyes to see the cross as the historical place where Your power and justice and love came together perfectly for me. Amen.

Where to Find the Love You're Looking For

FEB
1

It is staggering that God should love sinners; yet it is true. God loves creatures who have become unlovely and (one would have thought) unlovable … love among men is awakened by something in the beloved, but the love of God is free, spontaneous, unevoked, uncaused. God loves men because He has chosen to love them. —J. I. Packer, *Knowing God*

God is enormous. There is more to God than we could ever hope to understand on this earth. Fortunately, out of His incredibly vast self, He chose to reveal the most important and most accessible parts about Himself to us. And there's one trait He's revealed that's the most incredible of them all.

… abounding in love … maintaining love to thousands … —Exodus 34:6-7

He is loving.

This attribute of God is at the core of all we seek—the answer to all the questions we ask about knowing about Him, knowing Him, and making Him known:

Dear friends, let us love one another, for love comes from God. Everyone who loves has been born of God and knows God. Whoever does not love does not know God, because God is love. This is how God showed his love among us: He sent his one and only Son into the world that we might live through him. This is love: not that we loved God, but that he loved us and sent his Son as an atoning sacrifice for our sins. —1 John 4:7-10

Deep inside each and every one of us is the desire to be loved. And while we might find love in limited measure from things the world offers us, the true love we seek can only be found in God, because He *is* the love that we seek.

O God, I can't possibly thank You enough for what You've done for me! Your love is endless and unconditional. Make that love apparent in my life as I interact with others. Before Your love, I was lost, but now I'm found! Live through me in such a way that Your love brings others to Yourself! Amen.

Turn His Facts into Your Faith

It ain't those parts of the Bible that I can't understand that bother me, it is the parts that I do understand. —**Mark Twain**

With revelation comes responsibility. With knowledge comes opportunity. That's certainly the case when it comes to God as our perfect Father. **We can learn all the basic facts about God the Father easily enough. But are we willing to allow the Holy Spirit to live through us in such a way that those facts become faith?**

The city of Jerusalem didn't make that transition from fact to faith. Though the prophets came time and time again, the people of Jerusalem still chose to live independently of God.

> *Woe to the city of oppressors, rebellious and defiled! She obeys no one, she accepts no correction. She does not trust in the LORD, she does not draw near to her God.* —Zephaniah 3:1-2

Ouch. What a waste! Knowing the truth about God is like a huge invitation to an incredible festival. Open that invitation and it says:

Hey you! Come feast with Me! Come rest in Me! Come as you are and just be with Me! RSVP ASAP, God.

Ask God, right now, to focus your heart on just one of His attributes—the one fact that He wants you to transfer into faith today:

- He's around
- He's comforting
- He elevates
- He provides
- He's pleased
- He's interested
- He's compassionate
- He's gracious
- He's patient
- He's praiseworthy
- He's faithful
- He's forgiving
- He's just
- He's loving

Father, take this one truth about who You are and conform my life to it. I rest in You now. I stop my own efforts. I ask that, in Jesus, You would redirect me, give me trust in You, and draw me into deeper intimacy with You because of this truth. Amen.

Trusting in the Father Who Never Fails

What this country needs is more free speech worth listening to.
—**Hansell B. Duckett**

For some reason, talking about God feels awkward … perhaps even stressful. I'm not sure why that is. Maybe we are afraid of rejection. Maybe there is a component of spiritual warfare that intimidates us. Either way, it doesn't really make sense, since 95% of Americans believe in "God" and most people love to share their thoughts and opinions.

How do we get the conversation rolling? **Talking about *earthly* fathers is an easy transition into talking about God as the *perfect* Father.** It's really natural to compare and contrast fathers and *the* Father in regular conversation. That's a simple way to acknowledge who God is and share what we believe and know about Him.

> *Let us acknowledge the LORD; let us press on to acknowledge him. As surely as the sun rises, he will appear; he will come to us like the winter rains, like the spring rains that water the earth.* —Hosea 6:3

God is our Father and we can let His Spirit live through us in a way that is a natural reflection of who Christ is in us. Our lives become aligned with His truth, and this truth naturally expresses itself outwardly to the world as we press on to know Him more deeply.

Think about a friend that you know well who doesn't believe in "God the Father." What do you know about their earthly father that could be a springboard for talking about some of the attributes of God?

Father, I joyfully acknowledge You in my life today! Would You bring Yourself up in conversation in some way with someone today? Glorify Yourself as the Perfect Father we all desire. Amen.

How You Can Hear God's Voice

We need to find God, and he cannot be found in noise and restlessness. God is the friend of silence. See how nature—trees, flowers, grass—grows in silence; see the stars, the moon and the sun, how they move in silence ... We need silence to be able to touch souls. —**Mother Teresa**

"God."

That's a very simple word: *God.* Three letters; one syllable; very easy to say.

How could such a small word ever describe the Almighty Father that we find in the Bible? It can't. No words can; and yet, in the Bible, God reveals Himself to be the One we can know about, and the One we can know personally—and then make known to others.

Learning about God is important. **But the time quickly comes when words must cease and we must be silent and let God speak to us.**

We have barely tasted a drop of water in the ocean of God's essence. Every moment of every day, it's as if we are standing on the shore with our toes barely wet. Are you ready to wade in deeper, or perhaps even jump headfirst into intimacy with God? That doesn't normally happen in the noise and chaos of modern life. It often comes in quiet, thoughtful moments where the truth of Scripture becomes alive.

> *The LORD is compassionate and gracious, slow to anger, abounding in love. He will not always accuse, nor will he harbor his anger forever; he does not treat us as our sins deserve or repay us according to our iniquities. For as high as the heavens are above the earth, so great is his love for those who fear him; as far as the east is from the west, so far has he removed our transgressions from us.*
>
> *As a father has compassion on his children, so the LORD has compassion on those who fear him; for he knows how we are formed, he remembers that we are dust.* —Psalm 103:8-14

Heavenly Father, I want to know You; really know You. I don't just want to know about You, and I don't want to know You like a casual acquaintance. You've revealed Yourself in the Word. Now, please reveal Yourself in my heart. Lead me toward a pure understanding of You as my perfect Father. Then let the reality of You in my life be a light of truth to those in the darkness around me! Amen.

See Your Knowledge through God's Perspective

Dear GOD, Are you really invisible or is that just a trick? —Lucy (8 years old)

Calvin Miller tells the story of a little girl who asked her father what God was like. Pulling her into his lap he said,

"Suppose you took all your sand in your sandbox and scooped it into a little mountain in the yard. Then suppose you went everywhere in the world and got all the sand in all the sandboxes of the world and added it to this mountain. Then, after you got all the sand in all the sandboxes, you went to all the beaches of the world and got all the sand from all those beaches and continued to add it to your mountain of sand. Then, at last suppose you went to all the deserts of the world and got all of that sand and added it to the mountain. Finally, you would have a terribly large mountain. Then, say you licked your index finger and went up and stuck it on the side of that huge mountain. When you drew your finger back, some grains would be stuck to your finger. But let us suppose that you took your other index finger and flicked away all of the grains that had stuck to your finger, except for one grain. That one grain of sand would represent what we know about God, and the mountain that is left would represent what we have yet to learn about him."

Calvin's word picture is not an exaggeration. Paul mentions this in his letter to the Roman church:

> *Oh, the depth of the riches of the wisdom and knowledge of God! How unsearchable his judgments, and his paths beyond tracing out! "Who has known the mind of the Lord? Or who has been his counselor?"*
> —Romans 11:33-34

It will no doubt take an eternity to understand Him!

Dear God, thank You for revealing Yourself in a way I can comprehend, and that matters to my life. Give me just one more little glimpse of who You really are today. Amen.

Seeing a Small Picture of God's Power

Dear GOD, I bet it is very hard for You to love all of everybody in the whole world. There are only four people in our family and I can never do it.
—**Nan** (age 7)

There are two sides to God's coin. On one side is the word *Father*. We can relate to the father thing because of our earthly fathers. But the other side of the coin says *Almighty*. There are definitely people on earth who have a lot of might, but none of them have *all* might. We have no comparisons when we talk about God being "Almighty," so we humans have concocted a variety of different words and metaphors to try to describe this aspect of God:

> sov.er.eign *n*. One that exercises supreme, permanent authority, especially in a nation or other governmental unit, as a king, queen, or other noble person who serves as chief of state; a ruler or monarch.

> tran.scend.ent *adj*. 1. Surpassing others; preeminent or supreme. 2. Lying beyond the ordinary range of perception. 3. Being beyond the limits of experience and hence unknowable. 4. Being above and independent of the material universe.

Words like this might help describe Him, but all words, no matter how descriptive, fall short of the fact that He is truly indescribable. We've discussed what it means to believe, what it means to have God as a perfect father, but what can we say when we discuss Him as all powerful?

Almighty God, I bow before You in awe. Can You give me a little picture of Your power? I ask You to keep me humble as I continue to learn about You. Even though it will be impossible to understand You completely, what we can know is incredible enough! As I learn even more about Your nature, give me the heart of worship and praise that You deserve. Amen.

How Great Is God's Glory?

Dear GOD, I think the stapler is one of your greatest inventions.
—**Ruth (6 years old)**

When we last left Moses, he had asked God to describe Himself so that he would know who it was that was "going with him" as they made the trek to the Promised Land. God had revealed at least 14 attributes about His character. But then Moses pushes a little bit further:

> *Then Moses said, "Now show me your glory."* —Exodus 33:18

God said "no" to this request—and for good reason. Moses was asking if he could step beyond the boundaries of human understanding and know God in ways that are truly unknowable. God held back. He knew that if His glory was fully exposed, it would blow Moses' mind into a million pieces. His soul would not be able to absorb it. His body would not be able to tolerate it. To see God in all His glory would kill him.

When we use the word *Almighty*, we're standing on holy ground, on the edge of the infinite, at the pinnacle of something that is not just wonderful and awesome, but even *dangerous*.

So, while we might be able to see God as a "father," we must also, in humility and wisdom, recognize that God is also "farther," He is *beyond* our comprehension. There are critical aspects of God that we have no ability to understand or embrace. Power, wisdom, and awesomeness echo from God being farther, much farther, than our ability to understand or experience.

Yes, we can know about God. We can even know Him in a personal way. But in other ways, He is completely unknowable … *infinitely beyond* our comprehension.

God, thank You for restraining Your awesome glory on this earth to a level that doesn't lethally overwhelm us! I can't wait to experience the entire glory of Your presence in heaven. Until then, show me everything You would have me know about You on this earth, so I can worship and trust You more. Amen!

How Much Does God Know about You?

Dear GOD, Maybe Cain and Abel would not kill each other so much if they had their own rooms. It works with my brother. —**Larry (9 years old)**

There are some really impressive theological terms that describe God's attributes and abilities. Several of them begin with the prefix *omni*, which means "all" or "total:"

- Omni*present*: God is everywhere. (Psalm 139:7-12)

- Omni*potent*: God has all power. (Jeremiah 32:17, 27)

- Omni*science*: God is all scientific … No, that's not it—at least not how the word science is used today. The root of the word *science* is actually "knowledge," so this simply means that God knows everything. (1 John 3:20)

In Luke 1:37 the angel Gabriel proclaimed, "For no word from God will ever fail." You've probably heard something like this before—but have you ever really thought about it? *Anything* that He chooses to do that is in accordance with His character, He *can* do.

> *"For my thoughts are not your thoughts, neither are your ways my ways,"* declares the LORD. *"As the heavens are higher than the earth, so are my ways higher than your ways and my thoughts than your thoughts."* —Isaiah 55:8-9

God also knows everything. The problem, of course, is that we can't grasp the expanse of His might or wisdom. He's just in a totally different league than we are! He is Father, but He is also *farther*—farther than our minds can reach.

Food for thought: Why might someone be uncomfortable with the truth that God the Almighty knows everything about him or her? What attributes of God the Father would ease their concerns?

Almighty Father, thank You that Your all-knowing power is mixed with Your complete love. Yes, there are things I try to hide, but You know it all … and still You love. Free me to be open with You about everything. I trust You with my "secrets." Amen.

How to Relate Knowledge with Love

Dear GOD, I went to this wedding and they kissed right in church. Is that okay?
—Neil (age 11)

Yeah, I love kids' innocent ignorance. Isn't it so much more refreshing than an adult know-it-all arrogance? In fact, Jesus even said that the young'uns have an edge:

> *Truly I tell you, anyone who will not receive the kingdom of God like a little child will never enter it.* —Mark 10:15

We really need to think about this. Yes, we might know more than a kid, but compared to what there is to know about God, we only know about 0.000000036% more than the children who wrote the quotes we smiled at this week—and we must be like *them* to experience His Kingdom.

> *We know that "We all possess knowledge." But knowledge puffs up while love builds up. Those who think they know something do not yet know as they ought to know. But whoever loves God is known by God.* —1 Corinthians 8:1-3

Belief in God isn't about how much we know about Him. The only thing we really need to know and understand is that He loves us to the point that He would die for us. That knowledge directly affects the most important part of our faith, the state of our heart—where our love for God originates.

Maybe kids are so quick to believe because they're just learning about the world and haven't been calloused like adults whose hearts are toughened by life's experiences. Regardless of the reason, kids see God in a simple, clean-cut way. Yeah, kids don't know everything in the world, but God is not of this world anyway!

O God, You tell us to come to You as a child does. Please make me childlike in my faith so I can believe in You more intimately than I do now. I will continue to increase my knowledge about You, but please, don't let that interfere with my relationship with You. I don't know much, but what I do know is that I love You, Lord. And it's great to be known by You, too! Amen.

Getting a Small Glimpse of the Divine

Our real idea of God may lie buried underneath the rubbish of conventional religious notions and may require an intelligent and vigorous search before it is finally unearthed and exposed for what it is. Only after an ordeal of painful self-probing are we likely to discover what we actually believe about God.
—A. W. Tozer

Don't we all wish God would reveal more of Himself? Moses did, too.

> *The LORD replied, "My Presence will go with you, and I will give you rest." Then Moses said, "Now show me your glory." —Exodus 33:14, 18*

Moses didn't know what he was asking. **When he asked God to see His glory, it was like asking God to pour the oceans through a thimble.** The thimble couldn't possibly handle it. Neither could we. We couldn't possibly handle God's infinite glory with the limited mind we possess. Thankfully, God reveals Himself *partially*.

> *And the LORD said, "I will cause all my goodness to pass in front of you, and I will proclaim my name, the LORD, in your presence. I will have mercy on whom I will have mercy, and I will have compassion on whom I will have compassion. But," he said, "you cannot see my face, for no one may see me and live." —Exodus 33:19-20*

This partial revelation is more than enough for us today! With the Word of God in our minds and the presence of His Spirit in our hearts, we can "see" more than we need to respond appropriately:

- We *respect* Him greatly.
- We *revere* Him continually.
- We *replace* Him with nothing.

Glorious God, thank You for Your merciful restraint in revealing Your glory. Thank You for showing me more than enough. Reveal my true beliefs, painful as that may be, and conform my beliefs about You to the Truth so that the Truth can set me free. Amen.

What Are Your Priorities?

Cure for an obsession: get another one. —**Mason Cooley**

Because we aren't able to fully comprehend God, it can be easy to turn our attentions to more finite things—things we can comprehend on a much more tangible level.

Moses got an intense glimpse of God's glory on Mount Sinai. He then descended the mountain with supernaturally carved tablets containing the law of the holy and powerful God. It might be safe to say that he was excited to go and tell his people what God had to say.

But what did he find? While he was gone, the Israelites made a large golden calf … and they were worshiping it as if their lives depended upon it!

> He said to Aaron, "What did these people do to you, that you led them into such great sin?" "Do not be angry, my lord," Aaron answered. "You know how prone these people are to evil. They said to me, 'Make us gods who will go before us….' So I told them, 'Whoever has any gold jewelry, take it off.' Then they gave me the gold, and I threw it into the fire, and out came this calf."
> —Exodus 32:21-24

"**Make us gods who will go before us.**" That is the essence of *idolatry*. Idolatry takes place *anytime* we allow *anything* to take the place of God as the central life-giving almighty force in our life. In the Western world, golden calves are pretty much out of vogue, but in their place, we have managed to create a huge list of other things that become our substitutes for God:

- Girlfriends/boyfriends
- Careers
- Money
- Reputation
- Cars, houses, clothes
- The body, physical pleasures
- Knowledge
- Comfort
- Security

The list goes on and on.

These things will stay with us and vie for our ultimate attention for the rest of our lives. However, it's our choice to give in to these things. Always choose God above all, because He is perfect and will never fail.

God, remind me to keep You where You belong in my priorities. Keep me faithful and joyful in what You've given me. Amen.

How You Can Find Total Fulfillment in Christ

Can you leave it all behind? I hope so, because you can't go back. —**Unknown**

We often make a distinction between people who believe in God and those who do not. If someone knows about God, we think that is better than them not knowing about God. But that is not the distinction the Bible makes. The Bible says that people either believe in the true God, or they believe in idols.

Knowledge of God doesn't change the state of your heart, and it's the heart that matters the most. It's in the heart where idols are created. We can touch and see and feel them. We imagine them filling our thirsty souls. They continually lure our passion and faith away from the true Almighty God. Idols can be *metal* or they can be *mental*, but there is a constant temptation to put trust in them rather than in God.

> *Is there any God besides me? No, there is no other Rock; I know not one. All who make idols are nothing, and the things they treasure are worthless. Those who would speak up for them are blind; they are ignorant, to their own shame. Who shapes a god and casts an idol, which can profit nothing?*
> —Isaiah 44:8-10

God and God *only* is Almighty. There is not a single idol on the face of the earth that we can fully depend on to meet our needs. They simply aren't *able* to do so … and so they eventually leave our hearts empty, our expectations broken, and our dreams shattered. Even the idols that appear to be able to sustain us will ultimately crumble at the moment of death, for they are completely unable to help us beyond the grave.

Father, I say that You are all I need in this life. But, in all honesty, I don't fully believe it. Speak to me now. Reveal the idols that I cling to. Show me what I am relying on to fulfill my needs and enable me to choose You for fulfillment instead. Amen.

Trusting in God's Ability to Save You

If you have not chosen the Kingdom of God first, it will in the end make no difference what you have chosen instead. For you have missed the purpose for which you were formed, and you will have forsaken the only thing that satisfies.
—**William Law**

God (merciful as He is) was unwilling to blow Moses out of the water by showing him His glory. But even so, God was willing to show him the *effects* of His glory. He allowed Moses to see His back, to see the results of His abilities.

God does that same thing today. Because He's almighty, there are certain things that He, and only He, is able to do. We may not be able to understand how or why He does these things—for His ways and His motives are far beyond our own—but as a consequence of the things that we cannot see, there are certain things that we can see that reveal God's glory to us.

> *Therefore he is able to save completely those who come to God through him, because he always lives to intercede for them.* —Hebrews 7:25

God is able to save us.

At the core of the Gospel is the truth that God is able to find someone who has been lost. He can find them and He can save them. He can do this physically, emotionally, and spiritually. Though we have rebelled and gone our own way, God is able to reverse the consequences of our arrogant, ignorant choices. He is able to save us from the wrath and judgment that we are due because He paid the penalty for those sins Himself when He came to earth as a man and died on the cross in our place.

Yes, He is able … but the choice to reach up and allow Him to do it is yours.

Savior, although I can't see You, I know You are real because of what You've done on this earth. Your mercy is awesome, and I can't get enough. With empty hands I reach up to receive Your salvation. Thank You for saving my lost soul. Amen.

In Whose Power Do You Trust?

God will never put you in a situation that you can't handle. —**Unknown**

I hear that saying all the time. Sometimes I automatically nod my head because it just sounds right, like a plaque on your mom's fridge. It is usually presented as a concise summary of God's care for us. The problem is, it isn't true …

We've all hit obstacles in our walks that aren't possible for us to pass. **In fact, I'd even say that God puts things in our lives that we can't take care of on purpose.** If we could handle everything on our own, there would be no need for us to rely on God, and that's how we were designed to live!

> *And God is able to bless you abundantly, so that in all things at all times, having all that you need, you will abound in every good work.*
> —2 Corinthians 9:8

He is able to empower us.

Because of God's grace, we are able to do things that we would be unable to do on our own. How does that work? I have no idea! I don't know how it is that He energizes our thoughts or the molecules in our bodies to allow us to accomplish things and choose things that we couldn't without His strength. But we know that He does. And when we obey Him and allow Him to work through us, we also experience it.

Father, it's tough to take on the challenges that I sometimes have to face. I don't want to try it on my own. I'm weak. You are strong. Be my strength. May others see what You're doing through me and be amazed by it. Let the world know through Your works in me that You are the source of this power! Amen.

Your Divine Protection

I believe in Christianity as I believe that the sun has risen: not only because I see it, but because by it I see everything else. —C. S. Lewis

When I was playing basketball in college, we had the opportunity to take a trip to Europe to play some international teams. Our travels took us to Amsterdam. I was completely ignorant to the reputation of the city and apparently my coach was too because he gave us a night off to "enjoy the city."

Walking the dark streets with some of my teammates, we happened across the red light district—a clean, legal, organized, and repulsive venue for soliciting prostitutes. I glanced into a large window pane and was mortified to see an almost naked young woman enticing me towards her. It was a recipe for disaster. But in that moment, something inside took control. My eyes reflexively glanced down at the cobblestone street and stayed there. I had memorized 1 Corinthians 10:13 as a child and the Holy Spirit instantly brought that verse to mind:

> *No temptation has overtaken you except what is common to man. And God is faithful; he will not let you be tempted beyond what you can bear. But when you are tempted, he will also provide a way out so that you can endure it.*
> —1 Corinthians 10:13

For the benefit of my equally terrified and tantalized teammates, I started to quote the verse. "Eyes down boys!" I shouted. "God will provide a way out." I looked up and saw a road leading to a quiet residential street. Recognizing it as our "way out," we sprinted for safety.

We are constantly bombarded with temptation in this world. **But God says that He will give us a way out when we need it, and because He is in us, will walk us through it.**

Dear Father, thank You for Your divine protection and the support that upholds us from the inside out. Give me the discernment to see temptation for what it is. Give me the wisdom and humility to allow You to move in me so that I'll take the way of escape You have provided. Amen.

God's Working Today through You

Absence sharpens love, presence strengthens it. —Thomas Fuller

Have you ever wondered why we don't see God's active handiwork and presence like we do in the Old Testament? God revealed Himself in some pretty radical ways back in the good ol' days: Disembodied hands writing on walls, pillars of fire leading the crowds, even having dinner with God on Mount Sinai with Moses and the 70 elders of Israel. (No joke! Check out Exodus 24:9-11.)

With such radical signs of God's hand in the world in Scripture, it's easy to look around and wonder if He even works like that anymore. I'm convinced that He has never stopped working supernaturally across the globe, but I'm not just astounded by what He is doing "out there." I'm astounded by something even more incredible: *God is able to work "in us."*

> *Now to him who is able to do immeasurably more than all we ask or imagine, according to his power that is at work within us, to him be glory in the church and in Christ Jesus throughout all generations, for ever and ever! Amen.*
> —Ephesians 3:20-21

This is definitely one of the great mysteries of the faith—and yet one of the most practical and profound. God works *through* those of us who know Him and trust Him to bring honor and glory to Himself. How does He do that in all believers all of the time? I have no idea. But I'm sure glad that He does. Without God living through us, it wouldn't just be difficult to live the Christian life; it would be *impossible.*

Holy Spirit, thank You for Your indwelling power that is at work within me. As I go about my day, use me to do Your amazing works in the world. I believe You are able to do more than I can ask or imagine. Live through me to bring glory to You in Christ today, in any way You choose. Amen.

Extreme Makeover: YOU Edition!

The atheist finds himself enslaved by the need to prove himself an unbeliever. In denying the existence of God he finds nothing greater than himself and other selves in the universe. His greatest creed centers in 'I believe in myself.'
—D. Bruce Lockerby

One of my good friends has a son named Ben. When Ben was little, he wasn't so different from your average five year old—his room was messy; he never ate his vegetables; and he painted the walls instead of paper … but never had his dad seen someone so young care so much about his appearance. He used to stand and yell for mom and dad to rush into the room. The emergency? Sleeves touching the wrists, or shoelaces with uneven loops!

It was an early sign of a future, larger struggle he would deal with—a struggle that we all wrestle with:

- Obsession with outward appearances
- Focus on earthly belongings
- Satisfaction from impressing others through looks and actions

That's the bad news. The good news is that *God is able to transform us.*

God is in the business of remodeling. He is able to transform our spirits and our minds, and one day He'll even transform our bodies. Sometimes the remodeling is painful and ugly. **He comes in and tears out the walls, the furnishings, and the old appliances that He knows must go if we are to reflect Jesus Christ outward through authentic lives.** And one day, He will even take our decaying bodies and transform them into something glorious, reflecting His glory.

> *But our citizenship is in heaven. And we eagerly await a Savior from there, the Lord Jesus Christ, who, by the power that enables him to bring everything under his control, will transform our lowly bodies so that they will be like his glorious body.* —Philippians 3:20-21

Almighty God, please break my obsession with earthly appearances and possessions. Get rid of the things that keep me in worldly bondage so I can be free in Christ to be all that You made me to be now and forever. Amen.

What Can Wash Away Your Sin?

When it snows, you have two choices: shovel or make snow angels. —**Unknown**

When Christ comes into our lives, He usually comes giving us a heightened awareness of sin. This can weigh heavy on our minds, but thankfully the purpose of this awareness is to teach us one of the great realities of Christian spirituality: **We are unable to purify ourselves from the stain of our sin; and only He can heal us of the shame of sins against us.**

Sin is a give-and-take ordeal. We do it; it is often done to us. Even if it wasn't your "fault," the sins done to you can leave you under a heavy weight of shame and filth. You wish you could wash yourself both from the outside and from the inside … but you can't. You're not able to. God Almighty, however, can. *He is able to purify us,* both from the sins we have committed and from the shame and pain left by sins that have been committed against us.

> *To him who is able to keep you from stumbling and to present you before his glorious presence without fault and with great joy—to the only God our Savior be glory, majesty, power and authority, through Jesus Christ our Lord, before all ages, now and forevermore! Amen.* —Jude 1:24-25

God is all-powerful. We might try to describe that with all sorts of theological-sounding words or with earthly analogies, but the fact is this: He is able to do far above and beyond anything that we can imagine or think. **He can even joyfully present us blameless before Himself because of who He has made us to be in Christ.** It truly is too incredible to fully understand. What can we do but kneel with our hearts and hands raised toward heaven in worship and thanks?

Father, Son, and Holy Spirit, today, I thank You for the amazing grace You have poured out on me. Thank You for cleansing me of my sin. Thank You for healing me from the sins committed against me. You and You alone are worthy of glory, majesty, authority, and worship. I give that to You now. Amen.

Reality Checkup for You

Our bodies are apt to be our autobiographies. —Frank Gillette Burgess

The human body.

This topic is of *immense* concern in our culture. Look at the diet ads on television after New Year's day, the plastic surgeons' advertisements in the yellow pages, the latest infomercial touting a machine that can make you look like a Greek god in less than two minutes a day.

Consider women's "body language." Women's conversations almost invariably end up focusing on their bodies: Clothes, makeup, hair … and the dreaded "F" word—*fat*.

But enough about what *we*, the books, and tabloids say about this … what does *God* say about the body?

> *I praise you because I am fearfully and wonderfully made; your works are wonderful, I know that full well.* —Psalm 139:14

Your body is wonderful.

Do you believe that? Could you praise God for *your* body? Do you?

That's not a simple question, is it? Many of us praise God *in spite* of how our bodies seem to be made. Some of us can't think of any reason to thank Him at all. As our bodies interact with the world, they often experience pain, disease, injury, and … eventually, death.

Sure, our bodies might be "wonderful," but not always in the "good" sense of the word. Is it possible that we have been made in a way that is "full of wonder" in the sense that we might have more questions than answers?

God wants you to praise Him for the way He has made you, and to thank Him, by faith, for your body. That might seem like a real stretch right now. But if that's what He wants for us, He stands ready to make it happen through us.

Dear Lord, thank You for Your many blessings and for shaping me to reflect Your perfect image. Help me to see my body as You see it. Please expose the lies that I have believed about how I am made. Open my eyes and mind so I can see the full wonder of the body You have given me. Amen.

You Are His Masterpiece

The human body is a machine which winds its own springs.
—Julien Offroy de la Mettrie

Modern technology has uncovered a phenomenal biological world inside the human body. Its complexity far exceeds anything that anyone ever imagined ... and in many ways, we haven't even begun to explore it.

Dr. Lang, a friend of mine who was once Head of Cardiology at Johns Hopkins in Baltimore, showed me just how incredible the human body is with these statistics:

There are 74 trillion cells in the human body. The white blood cells in the lymph tissue can form 10,000-100,000 different antibodies. They fight against foreign tissue and can make these anti-bodies at a rate of 2000 per second. A single white blood cell can kill as many as a hundred bacteria. Over the course of a lifetime, the heart will pump an average of 52,560,000 gallons of blood. That's enough to fill a New York skyscraper! I could go on, but you get the point:

Your body is incredible.

> *Then God said, "Let us make mankind in our image, in our likeness, so that they may rule over the fish in the sea and the birds in the sky, over the livestock and all the wild animals, and over all the creatures that move along the ground." —Genesis 1:26*

When God sculpted humanity in His image, an amazing amount of detail went into the works, resulting in an amazing, intricate masterpiece. **He created life the way He did to glorify Himself, but He took another step further with humanity in His love: He designed us to represent Himself!**

But best of all, God designed us to be inhabited by His Spirit, a personal relationship shared by no other living thing in existence. All of these things work together to create a complex, beautiful creature that cannot be replicated.

Father, I rejoice that You shaped me and You designed me to be in a relationship with You. Help me to remember how special I am; that because You made me, I am special, unique, and beautiful in Your eyes. Amen.

Your Essential Earth Suit

Take care of your body. It's the only place you have to live. —Jim Rohn

These days in Christian culture, we are often taught to look away from our earthly selves and focus on God. This appears most often in response to problems like physical temptations, obsession with personal image, or substance addiction. While it is certainly important that we do not become our own idols and serve our own fleeting wants, let's not forget our bodies are "fairly important" for the act of living on earth (sarcasm intentional). Let's be realistic, you can't live here without it!

Counselor Bill Gillham calls the human body an "earth suit." Just as a spacesuit keeps an astronaut alive, the body is essential for our earthly existence.

Your body is indispensable.

> *May your whole spirit, soul and body be kept blameless at the coming of our Lord Jesus Christ.* —1 Thessalonians 5:23

The Bible says human beings are made up of a spirit, soul, and body. In God's creation, we are confined to a limited existence so we can reach others and tend to the creation He entrusted to us. While it is really important to pay attention to the growth of your spirit and soul, the body is what sustains those things on this earth. We must treat it with healthy respect. **Each part of us sustains the other, so being negligent to one part is just as bad as paying too much attention to it. Paul told us to take care of our whole selves, and that includes our body.**

Father God, I need You to balance my life the way You meant it to be. I can't do that on my own. I want to care for this "earth suit," but I don't want to do that in my own wisdom or strength. I surrender them all to You. I submit to Your Spirit, in me, in every area. Show me how to care for them all, keeping my attentions in check when they become pointed or selfish. Amen.

Settling in for the Long Haul

I don't generally like running. I believe in training by rising gently up and down from the bench. —Satchel Paige

Life is like a marathon. It's a good long race that lasts a long time (Lord willing). But you don't decide on Saturday to run a marathon on Sunday. Marathons take preparation, vision, and training. The apostle Paul says that we're supposed to do the same thing in life. We are supposed to discipline and train our bodies as the race ahead of us is long.

> *They do it to get a crown that will not last; but we do it to get a crown that will last forever. Therefore I do not run like someone running aimlessly; I do not fight like a boxer beating the air. No, I strike a blow to my body and make it my slave ...* —1 Corinthians 9:25-27

Your body is trainable.

That's actually very exciting news because the Scriptures also say that offering our bodies is *worship*:

> *Therefore, I urge you, brothers, in view of God's mercy, to offer your bodies as living sacrifices, holy and pleasing to God—this is your spiritual act of worship.* —Romans 12:1

Training and disciplining the body is also *worthwhile*:

> *Do not offer any part of yourself to sin as an instrument of wickedness, but rather offer yourselves to God as those who have been brought from death to life; and offer every part of yourself to him as an instrument of righteousness.* —Romans 6:13

What a great perspective to have about your body: **It is a living sacrifice, an instrument of righteousness in the hands of God!** THAT is a good reason to be joyful if I've ever seen one!

O God, I am so glad that I can prepare myself to resist the world and better myself for You! Continue to give me strength as I settle in for the long haul. I worship You as I change and offer my whole self to Your will. Amen.

Looking Beyond the Physical

Health is not valued till sickness comes. —Dr. Thomas Fuller

After God created Adam and Eve's bodies, He said everything was "very good." But that was before sin; that was before Adam and Eve were kicked out of Eden. Sadly, we no longer live in the best place to take care of our bodies the way we want/need to. This is bad news because despite its complexity, despite its importance (or even arguably partly *because* of these), the human body is vulnerable to things it was never designed to withstand.

Your body is susceptible.

God intended for the human body to be used in a certain way. If it's used differently than He intended, there are going to be natural consequences. Too much alcohol, too much food, sex outside of a monogamous life-long union ... **if you don't follow Scripture, you can bring upon yourself obesity, heart disease, alcoholism, sexually-transmitted diseases, etc.** God has our best interest in mind when He commands things like this:

> *Do not join those who drink too much wine or gorge themselves on meat.*
> —Proverbs 23:20

Because we live in a world bombarded with the effects of the Fall and sin, **many things may come upon us through no fault of our own.** Allergies, Alzheimer's, cancer ... many ailments are not always caused by our actions or result from any sins we may commit, but that does not lessen their effects in the slightest.

Are you feeling the susceptibility of your physical body today? God's Word puts it in eternal perspective:

> *Therefore we do not lose heart. Though outwardly we are wasting away, yet inwardly we are being renewed day by day. For our light and momentary troubles are achieving for us an eternal glory that far outweighs them all. So we fix our eyes not on what is seen, but on what is unseen. For what is seen is temporary, but what is unseen is eternal.* —2 Corinthians 4:16-18

Eternal Father, give me the willingness and ability to look beyond the physical and the temporary today, that I might see what is unseen and find hope in the eternal. Amen.

Staying Strong When Your Body Weakens

He is no fool who gives what he cannot keep to gain what he cannot lose.
—Jim Elliot

Imagine you're sitting in the office of your family physician … but this isn't just any doctor, it's the office of the Great Physician. You thought it was just a routine visit to make sure everything is okay with your body, but with gentle and serious eyes, God asks you to sit down.

"I've got good news and bad news," He starts … and deep inside you know He isn't making a joke.

Might as well start with the bad news?

Your body will deteriorate.

> *Therefore we do not lose heart. Though outwardly we are wasting away, yet inwardly we are being renewed day by day.* —2 Corinthians 4:16

When I was in college, I set a life goal for myself: To be able to dunk a basketball on my 50th birthday. The week of my 30th birthday I got an excruciating pain in my lower back. Turns out I have three bad discs in the lower portion of my spine. It's tough to work out now—though eating still comes easily.

At the beginning of my 45th year, I decided to get serious about dunking that basketball again. With a fresh new year's resolution, I set out on a short run on January 1. "Pop!" By the middle of January, I was on the operating table repairing a torn meniscus.

I'm getting pretty close to the big 5-0, now, but I actually dunked for the first time in 13 years last week. I've been working hard towards it and I was pretty pumped. But I also know it's a temporary accomplishment.

Second Corinthians 4:16, indeed. **Yeah, there is plenty of bad news, but there is amazingly good news, too.** In the days ahead, may we get a clearer, Truthful diagnosis through God's Word!

Great Physician, thank You for our life-sustaining bodies. Use the reality of my deteriorating body to teach me about life. I don't want to lose heart. Renew my soul daily, Lord, as I look toward my future on earth and beyond. Amen.

Finding True Comfort in the Face of Death

Of all great wonders, none is greater than man. Only for death can he find no cure. —**Sophocles**

A pastor was on a plane filled with people who had just gotten off cruise ships in Miami. Everybody was still in the party mood, but then, reality caught up with them. One of the women in the front of the plane began having a hard time. **Then all at once, she slumped forward ... dead. Right there in the middle of the airborne party.** They landed in Dallas, removed the body, and resumed their journey to Los Angeles.

The pastor told the flight attendant, "Ma'am, I'm a pastor. If anyone would like to talk to me about what's happened, I'm in seat 12A." The flight attendant responded, "No problem, sir. We are going to give everyone free drinks for the rest of the flight." And she was right. Within an hour, everyone was back in the festive party mood.

Isn't that the way most of us try to deal with death? It's like were floating along on this big cruise ship called "life." Every once in a while, somebody around us falls out of the party. **It catches our attention for a moment; but rather than dealing with it, we grab on to anything we can to numb our feelings so the party can continue.** But if we're honest, we must face the fact that all of us will die physically.

Your body will die.

> *Why, you do not even know what will happen tomorrow. What is your life? You are a mist that appears for a little while and then vanishes.* —James 4:14

Aristotle said that death is the "most terrible" of all things. Epicurus said that death is "the most terrifying" of all things. But Jesus said the truth sets us free. **Is it possible that believing the truth about death could bring life into clearer, more purposeful focus?**

Eternal God, let the truth about the inevitable death of my body propel me into a more vibrant life today. Amen.

What Happens When You Die?

Our Lord has written the promise of resurrection, not in books alone, but in every leaf in springtime. —**Martin Luther**

Okay, here's one truth that no one likes to think about too much, particularly after watching the latest zombie flick: *Your body will decompose.*

Yuck. No need to talk about this one much. Whether your body is cremated, put in a casket, or donated to medical science ... the result will be the same:

> *All go to the same place; all come from dust, and to dust all return.*
> —Ecclesiastes 3:20

What happens after that? There are several very popular theories out there (but none of them can be backed up with the Bible):

- *Soul sleep.* This is the "eternal nap" theory. The soul still exists, but in death it goes into an unconscious snooze forever.

- *Nihilism.* I call this the "poof" theory. After death, the soul and spirit just kind of evaporate and cease to exist altogether.

- *Reincarnation.* This is the "repeat" theory. When any living thing dies, its soul goes into other living things—actually becoming something else over and over again in a never-ending cycle of life and death.

None of that sounds like a great option, in my opinion. However, there is definitely a flip side of the coin of death—*if* you know Jesus Christ personally:

Your spirit will dwell.

> *For we live by faith, not by sight. We are confident, I say, and would prefer to be away from the body and at home with the Lord.* —2 Corinthians 5:7-8

When the body dies, our spirit is freed from tangible flesh and we can be with the Lord at home—*home*, where we will be alive and aware, *home* with the Father experiencing His love without distraction, *home* where we belong.

Father, release my grip on physical life, which I cannot keep, so I can live freely in light of eternity. Amen.

The Hope You Have in the Resurrection

A lawyer's dream of heaven: every man reclaimed his property at the resurrection, and each tried to recover it from all his forefathers.
—Samuel Butler

Have you ever seen a chrysanthemum seed? They look like little brownish shriveled up things. *But,* if you take that seed and you bury it in the dirt, what happens? You get this amazing flower—totally unlike the seed that was planted.

> *But someone may ask, "How are the dead raised? With what kind of body will they come?" How foolish! What you sow does not come to life unless it dies. When you sow, you do not plant the body that will be, but just a seed, perhaps of wheat or of something else. But God gives it a body as he has determined, and to each kind of seed he gives its own body.* —1 Corinthians 15:36-38

Do you see what Paul is getting at here? If our body (usually little brownish shriveled up things) dies, how will God raise us and what will we look like when that happens? **We are foolish to even ask the question, because the difference between what dies and what is resurrected is as different as the chrysanthemum seed is from its flower.**

I think it's fair to let our imaginations run with this for a little while, because I believe that our new bodies will be *beyond* anything that we can imagine.

Holy Spirit, open my mind, please, to be able to imagine—even just a little bit—what life will be like with You once I shed this body of flesh. Amen.

How to Focus on Eternity

Death is no more than passing from one room into another. But there's a difference for me, you know. Because in that other room I shall be able to see.
—Helen Keller

Imagine, again, that you are back in the office of the Great Physician. God's diagnosis of death and decay has left you stunned; your soul is reeling with that reality. But now He's leaning towards you. He's taking you by the hand and He's lifting your chin and looking you in the eyes—He has something to say:

"My child, the death, the pain, the decay … it is all temporary—an immeasurably small moment in light of the eternity that awaits you. What lies beyond is incomparable. The asthma, the cancer, the bruises, scabs, and scars … these will not last. Trust Me. Look to the future and see with the eyes of faith a heavenly, timeless, and painless existence—an existence of an entirely different kind, a body of an entirely different kind. Be patient, My child; have faith. For with a flash of light you will be changed."

I'm not making this up. God has written it down for us in His Word:

> *The sun has one kind of splendor, the moon another and the stars another; and star differs from star in splendor. So will it be with the resurrection of the dead. The body that is sown is perishable, it is raised imperishable; it is sown in dishonor, it is raised in glory; it is sown in weakness, it is raised in power; it is sown a natural body, it is raised a spiritual body… in a flash, in the twinkling of an eye, at the last trumpet. For the trumpet will sound, the dead will be raised imperishable, and we will be changed.* —1 Corinthians 15:41-44, 52

Yes, our physical bodies will decay, die, and decompose, but we will be resurrected, and our spiritual bodies will have an imperishable glory and power. **Your body will be *different.*** Not just healed and not just better … it will be *radically* different.

The Great Physician is finished talking for the moment. God pushes back and gives you a moment to let this soak in. Are you thinking about it, I mean *really* thinking about it? Do you see the big picture now?

God, I know that this day will be filled with decay and death, but focus my heart on the full diagnosis! Make this future reality a practical truth today. Amen.

Making Your One Shot a Good One

Arise O Sluggard! In the grave there will be sleeping enough.
—Benjamin Franklin

A number of years ago the legendary professor Howard Hendricks was speaking at Dallas Theological Seminary, an all-male school at the time. He stood up and said, "Gentlemen, some of you are so hopelessly out of shape that I'm not going to invest my time in you. I would rather invest my time on someone who's going to live for a long time. So get in shape or get out of school!"

Harsh? Absolutely. But the point he was making was deathly serious: **You get one "earth suit." There are no returns and there's no warranty. When it's done, it's done.**

You must care for your body. Give it exercise; fuel it with good food. Give it enough sleep; optimize its efficiency with vitamins and nutritional supplements. **And what about your weaknesses?** Remember that the body is susceptible. Alcohol? Tobacco? Junk food? Paul said:

> *Do you not know that your bodies are temples of the Holy Spirit, who is in you, whom you have received from God? You are not your own; you were bought at a price. Therefore honor God with your bodies.*
> —1 Corinthians 6:19-20

Figure out your weak spot and allow Christ to be your strength; trust in Him moment by moment to deliver you because your body is an instrument of worship and righteousness. Dr. Hendricks spoke with authority on the issue because he had been similarly challenged as a young "out-of-shape" man. He made lifelong, lifestyle adjustments that enabled him to serve at the seminary for nearly 55 years!

But remember: You are destined to failure when you try to change your flesh in the strength of your flesh. **Any lasting success is the result of trusting the Lord to do these things through you, rather than trying to do them on your own.**

Loving Father, keep me from choosing things that will wear me down. Give me strength to choose the things that will build me up in such a way that I can be the person You made me to be! Amen.

Living in Light of the Eternal

Even though I walk through the valley of the shadow of death, Your perfect love is casting out fear. —Oh, Lord You Never Let Go **by Matt Redman**

God's Word makes it really clear that **our bodies are temporary.** If you believe the prognosis given to you by the Great Physician, it will not only change your perspective on physical death and the fact that it is unavoidable, it will change your life now. There is a very tangible sense of peace that comes with aligning your beliefs with what is true about the death and resurrection of your body.

Why not live fearlessly? Why not live with focus? Why not live with fervor?

If you only have one earthly life to live, why not take calculated risks? Why not push the envelope of your comfort zone and allow Christ to live through you and lead you into worthwhile and demanding new endeavors? We can be sure that God will be with us and support us:

> *Even though I walk through the valley of the shadow of death, I fear no evil, for You are with me....* —Psalm 23:4 (NASB)

Benjamin Franklin lived without fear and he lived boldly for the things in which he believed. He was a great writer, but few words of his (or anyone else's, for that matter) are as powerful as the words that he wrote for his tombstone. Knowing these would be his last words left for the world to read long after he was gone, he wrote:

The body of Benjamin Franklin, its innards torn out and stripped of its lettering and gilding like the cover of an old book, lies here. Yet the work itself shall not be lost. But it will, as he believed, appear once more in a new and more beautiful edition corrected and amended by the Author.

Mr. Franklin is a prime example of *living in the shadow of* death. *"What's the worst that can happen to you? You will die. What's the best that can happen to you? You will die!"*

What do you want written on your tombstone?

Loving Father, I want to use the short time I have to do what You plan for me! As I start to look outward for ways for You to live through me, give me Your eyes so I can see where I'm meant to be. Overcome my fear and author my story in radical ways. Amen.

Your Body and the Eternal Word

"Remember man, as you walk by, As you are now, so once was I, As I am now, so shall you be, Remember this and follow me." —Words engraved in a tombstone in England. To which someone replied by writing these words beneath: *"To follow you I'll not consent, until I know which way you went."*

Our bodies are temporary. Yeah, yeah, we all know that … in our heads at least, but *contemplating* that absolute fact puts the rest of life in vivid *perspective*. God told the prophet Isaiah to proclaim this in a big way, but Isaiah wasn't sure what to say! This is how he recorded his conversation with God in Isaiah 40:

> *"For the mouth of the Lord has spoken." A voice says, "Cry out." And I said, "What shall I cry?" "All people are like grass, and all their faithfulness is like the flowers of the field. The grass withers and the flowers fall, because the breath of the Lord blows on them. Surely the people are grass. The grass withers and the flowers fall, but the word of our God endures forever."* (v. 5-8)

I love the contrast in Isaiah's message. **Our bodies WILL wither like the grass, BUT God's words last forever. See the perspective change here? It's a paradigm shift that should cause us to reconsider our earthly priorities.** Yes, I believe that our bodies are a temporary gift which need to be cared for, but they are given for a purpose—to live and proclaim the eternal life-giving Truth of God's words. Notice how Isaiah follows up with a charge:

> *You who bring good news to Zion, go up on a high mountain. You who bring good news to Jerusalem, lift up your voice with a shout, lift it up, do not be afraid; say to the towns of Judah, "Here is your God!"* (v. 9)

Not only do we have the words of God available to us in written form, but we have Jesus, the living Word, in our hearts—and both are ready to be spoken and lived through us today!

Lord, I completely surrender myself to You today. I collapse in Your arms. Without You, I can do nothing eternal. I will listen for Your voice today. Speak to me through Your eternal word and through Your Spirit in me. I ask that You will show me specific ways that You want to live through me so that others will see You and say, "Here is your God!"

Waiting for Your Ultimate Victory

A good character is the best tombstone. Those who loved you and were helped by you will remember you when forget-me-nots have withered. Carve your name on hearts, not on marble. —Charles Spurgeon

Here lies an Atheist. All dressed up and no place to go. —Tombstone in the Thurmont, Maryland cemetery

When Paul wrote his first letter to the Corinthians, he spent a good amount of time talking about the human body. He called it the "natural body" and referred to it as "flesh and blood." He also said that it can't "inherit the kingdom of God," and then he talked about the mystery of death and **the transformation that will take place when we are resurrected with spiritual bodies. In our struggle against the flesh and death, it will be the final home run, slam-dunk, Hail-Mary touchdown pass into the end zone.**

> *When the perishable has been clothed with the imperishable, and the mortal with immortality, then the saying that is written will come true: "Death has been swallowed up in victory. Where, O death, is your victory? Where, O death, is your sting?" The sting of death is sin, and the power of sin is the law.*
> —1 Corinthians 15:54–56

Yeah, that's what the future holds for the bodies of Christians: the perishable gets exchanged for the imperishable, the mortal with the immortal. That's not just a wish, that's the truth. We can look forward to that with certainty and boldness. **But we're not there, quite yet.**

> *But thanks be to God! He gives us the victory through our Lord Jesus Christ. Therefore, my dear brothers, stand firm. Let nothing move you. Always give yourselves fully to the work of the Lord, because you know that your labor in the Lord is not in vain.* —1 Corinthians 15:57–58

Take one last look at your body. No, it's not going to last, and yes, it will be changed. **But for now, it is a tool waiting to be used by God to bring glory to His name.**

Dear Jesus, I give myself fully to Your work knowing that's what really matters in the end. I look forward to the new body You will give me, and I ask that You would use the one You have given me today for Your glory. I believe I've been crucified with You and that You now live in me. Live through me today, moment by moment. Amen.

What's the Story of Your Life?

Live so that when the final summons comes you will leave something more behind you than an epitaph on a tombstone or an obituary in a newspaper.
—**Billy Sunday**

My dad hadn't been back to his father's grave in England for ages. The stone etched with the name "Stanley Briscoe" had fallen; the weeds had grown over the withered stone and my father's face reflected a pensive disappointment. We huffed and heaved as we righted the slab and pulled weeds out of the sacred ground.

The graves of those who have gone before us conjure up a strange mixture of emotions and thoughts. They wash over us—like tsunamis crashing down on the soul. And the blatant reality eventually hits us: One day, it'll be us. *Our bodies will die. Our lives will end.*

I wish I had known my grandfather. The day we stood beside the grave my dad filled in some of the gaps with tales of the man:

- Keeping the family grocery store open through the War and the Depression.

- A man of his word ... a man of the Word.

- A lay preacher who spoke what he knew each weekend in a corrugated metal building they called "The Tin Church."

Nothing fancy here. Just a simple faith that knew the value of community, honesty, truth, and the value of investing life in something worth dying for.

Between birth and the casket, there are an unknown number of days God gives us to live for His purposes in our physical body. Some day it will be changed into a perfect body, but for now it is wearing out. Yet, it continually waits to be used for eternal purposes.

Soon enough the dust of my body, of your body, will mix with the soil beneath a tilting headstone. Will the cemetery be kept up? Will weeds grow there too? Does it matter? Perhaps it is best to let the gravestone lay.

"Show me, Lord, my life's end and the number of my days; let me know how fleeting my life is. You have made my days a mere handbreadth; the span of my years is as nothing before you. Everyone is but a breath, even those who seem secure." —Psalm 39:4-5

The Christian Faith Is a Mystery

Mysterion: noun. Greek.

    1. A mystery. Something unexplainable by normal means.

    2. What theologians call something when they don't have a clue about what is going on.

If you are like me, you like to have everything figured out. Most Christians in the Western world feel the same way. We have systematic theology, four spiritual laws, diagrams and charts to describe the Trinity, constitutions and bylaws to spell out what church is, etc. That's all well and good … but it's not enough. I mean, it's *really* not enough.

Authentic Christianity doesn't come from just facts and figures; it comes out of a mystery. Sure, *religion* is based on formulas and to-do lists, but a *relationship* with Jesus Christ takes place in a completely different realm: The realm of the *mysterious.* The apostle Paul spoke about this in Colossians 1:25-26:

> *I have become its* (the church's) *servant by the commission God gave me to present to you the word of God in its fullness—the mystery that has been kept hidden for ages and generations, but is now disclosed to the Lord's people.*

What is a mystery? According to Scripture, a mystery is something formerly hidden in God from all human eyes, but now revealed through Christ, and made understandable to His people by the Holy Spirit.

In other words, "There ain't no way we can figure this out on our own." We can read about it, listen to sermons about it, and study it all we want, but unless God brings it to life in us, we aren't going to get it. This is particularly true when it comes to our self-identity.

Second only to our concept of God, our concept of "self" is the most important thing about us—and in a world that is bombarding us with lies, we desperately need to know the mysterious Truth about who we are.

Lord Jesus, You have taught us that if we want to experience "the mystery," then we've got to surrender to the Holy Spirit. I'm doing that right now. I want to know the Truth. Reveal the mystery to me. Make Your Word come alive in my heart. Take the blinders off my eyes, unveil it. I want to know the Truth about who I am so that the Truth can set me free. Amen.

Christ in You, the Hope of Glory

Who are you? Who, who? Who, who? —The Who

The 1960s were pretty confusing times for everyone. Some have said, "Anyone who says they remember the 60s must not have been there." It seemed like everyone was asking the hard questions, but no one had the answers. Case in point, the rock band "The Who." The repeated question from their hit song still echoes across the airways. **But does anyone have an answer to this most important question? Who are you?** The apostle Paul did:

> *To them* (believers in Christ) *God has chosen to make known among the Gentiles the glorious riches of this mystery, which is Christ in you, the hope of glory.* —Colossians 1:27

In this passage, Paul identifies the mystery of the mystery. He answers the question of our identity at its deepest level: **What really matters is not who you are, but Who is in you.** The answer to that question should never cease to stun us, because it is our hope of glory, it is our glorious riches … and it is the great mystery: "Christ in you."

Lord Jesus, by faith and by the truth of Your Word, I ask that You would lead me into this mystery—this powerful profound truth about who I am in You. I want to know this in my soul, and experience it in my life. By Your grace, I want to understand this mystery that goes far beyond my understanding. Reveal to me, my Lord, this Truth that You are in me, and I am in You. Amen.

You Are the Truest You When You're in Christ

I always wished I would grow up to be somebody. Maybe I should have been a little more specific. —Lily Tomlin

Everybody wants to be somebody, but how do we know who that somebody is? That's another question that is often asked. In this situation, however, the influencers in our world are happy to give you their answer … and then sell you what you need to make it happen. There is no mystery here. **In the modern Western world, your identity is almost always determined by four different things: 1) What you look like, 2) What you do, 3) What you have, and 4) Who you know.**

Every time we buy into this value system, our life becomes consumed with "I must have," "I ought to," and "how do I get people to like me so I can get what I need?" It's a vicious, never-ending cycle that only gives temporary results. It's tragic, when you think about it—and usually very expensive.

Christ offers an option to this cycle. **Rather than basing our identity on possessions, performance, or people, He calls us to enter into the mystery of the ages—to experience the profound realization that our true identity is found in Him, not in ourselves.** Remember Paul's description of this powerful mystery:

> *To them* (believers in Christ) *God has chosen to make known among the Gentiles the glorious riches of this mystery, which is Christ in you, the hope of glory.* —Colossians 1:27

If your life today is consumed with finding your identity in the things of the world, freedom and peace are at hand. **By discovering who you are in Christ and who He is in you, rest and peace can be yours.**

Heavenly Father, show me the ways that I have bought into the world system of possessions, performance, and people to determine my self-worth and my identity. Set me free from the clear demands of this world around me. Lead me into the mystery and the peace and the rest that come through understanding who I am in You and the fact that You are in me. Lord, this is a huge mystery. It is so much easier to buy into the rules that the world gives me. But I'm tired. I want the real thing. Show me who I am in You. I want to be that somebody. Amen.

We Need the Spirit's Help to Comprehend God

The Word became flesh and dwelt among us. Then, through the theologians, they turned Him back into words again. —**Karl Barth**

We usually come at God intellectually. It's one of the great mantras of Evangelicalism. You know the emphasis: "Love the Lord your God with all your heart, soul, mind, and strength." We say that if you learn it, then you will live it!

Please hear me: I love to think! But experiencing "Christ in you" is not learned that way! **Experiencing Christ in you is learned through God's power, by His Spirit, as opposed to human wisdom.** Consider Paul's words:

> *When I came to you, I did not come with eloquence or human wisdom as I proclaimed to you the testimony about God... No, we declare God's wisdom, a mystery that has been hidden and that God destined for our glory before time began.* —1 Corinthians 2:1, 7

One commentator said, "This mystery is too profound for human ingenuity." Another said, "It is wisdom that has been hidden and that God destined for our glory before time began." God wants us to fully enjoy a mystery previously hidden, long prepared, and unfortunately, missed by most.

> *"None of the rulers of this age understood it, for if they had, they would not have crucified the Lord of glory. However, as it is written: 'No eye has seen, no ear has heard, no mind has conceived what God has prepared for those who love him'—but God has revealed it to us by his Spirit."* —1 Corinthians 2:8

In other words, you can't hear it, you can't see it, and you can't think it. I don't care how smart you are, none of you can figure out on your own what God has prepared for those who love Him. The Apostle Paul could not be clearer: If you want to experience the mystery, you will not be able to do it coming at it from an intellectual position. It doesn't work that way.

Dear Father, I need more than teachers and doctrine. I need You. I want to experience the reality of being in You, and You in me. Take me deeper, by faith, into the mystery of Your Son, Jesus Christ. Amen.

Living Your 'Now' with the Next World in Mind

If I find in myself desires which nothing in this world can satisfy, the only logical explanation is that I was made for another world. —C.S. Lewis

Believers in Jesus live on two planes of existence simultaneously. Don't worry, I'm not about to go science fiction on you. (Actually, this is even *crazier* than sci-fi!) The truth is that we live in Christ ... and we also live in Dallas/Phoenix/London, or wherever. We are *in* Christ spiritually, and yet we are in our physical location, living our lives with work, family, and other commitments.

Yeah, it sounds nuts, but the New Testament is full of this dual reality. Consider Paul's salutation in Colossians 1:1-2:

> *Paul, an apostle of Christ Jesus by the will of God, and Timothy our brother, to the holy and faithful brothers in Christ at Colossae.*

Notice the four words at the end of this verse. IN Christ AT Colossae. **He is saying that they are in Christ, but that they are also in Colossae.** How can someone be in both places? Think about what Paul wrote in another letter, 2 Corinthians 4:18:

> *So we fix our eyes not on what is seen, but on what is unseen. For what is seen is temporary, but what is unseen is eternal.*

The words *temporary* and *eternal* are key here. The world we live in can be seen; it's physical and visible, and we interact with it continuously. It's also temporary. It's here for a while, but then it will go.

Then there is the invisible world. It is Christ and all that comes with Him. He is our purpose for being, the reason we go about things in the physical world.

We like to compartmentalize and sort things. That's why label makers and organizing software sell well. **But we can't compartmentalize the eternal and the temporary. The two are interchangeable for believers. We live in both right now! And if we're paying attention to the eternal, our temporary life will show it.**

Jesus, thank You for putting eternity into my heart. Thank You for the timeless perspective You give me. Help me live in such a way that my temporary life points to Your eternal work! Amen.

Take Regular Time to Marvel at God's Greatness

What we do in life echoes in eternity. —Maximus, Gladiator

I often think of the galaxies in outer space as being symbolic of God's eternal vastness. No doubt, it's hugeness beyond our comprehension. Light from some of the closest stars takes 2,000 years to reach earth. Beam me up! But that's just the physical world.

Eternity is *infinitely* bigger than that! It's changeless, timeless, and it's the realm of spirituality and God's mighty attributes. It's the realm of ultimate reality of completeness and wholeness, where things are finished and settled. It's the realm of *right now.*

When God called Moses at the burning bush, He told Moses to tell the people that "I AM" sent him. (That's terrible English grammar, but perfect theological grammar, so I suppose theology wins out over English!)

I AM is the way God wanted Moses and the people to think about Him. I AM is eternity past, right now, and always in the future—all at the same time. Yep, it's pretty baffling. **That's the point!** *God is so infinite and vast that to describe Him is an exercise in futility.*

Is God that infinitely large in your prayers and worship?

Lord Jesus, how awesome is Your eternal vastness. Praise Your mighty name. Keep eternity fixed in my heart. Keep my mind set on things above. I need to be reminded all the time of Your greatness. Do whatever it takes, Holy Spirit, to keep You first in my heart, as the Lord beyond measure in all ways. Amen.

Prioritizing the Eternal Over the Temporary

Happiness is neither without us nor within us. It is in God, both without us and within us. —Blaise Pascal

Kids and Christmas morning—that's the temporary world in the extreme. The holiday season now officially starts shortly after Valentine's Day, followed by months of hype that fuel the hopes and the dreams of children (and retailers) everywhere. When the big day arrives, it's over in approximately 47.29 seconds.

It's a rush, to be sure. And who doesn't like getting nice presents, even as an adult? But don't you also notice how fast it's all over and the kids just move to the next thing?

So it goes with *everything* in the temporary realm. It has a timeline, a beginning and an end. It's a realm of activity, of processes, and of physical needs. It's the realm where we see both good and evil. There is birth, growth, and death. With all our senses, we can experience God's gift of creation in mountain ranges and valleys full of wildflowers. With our hands and our minds we can joyfully receive all the great stuff He has given us in the temporary realm.

But this is actually the danger of the temporary realm: It *does* have a lot of great stuff. **And it's really easy to love stuff—to love stuff more than the One who made it.** (That's like telling God, "I like You, but what I really love is Your *stuff,* as long as You give it to me.")

Ouch.

What parent yearns for *that* reaction from their kids? **When we lust after the temporary pleasures of this temporary realm, we trade the best for the stuff that's not even going to last a moment in eternity.**

Father, I want more than just Your stuff. I want Your heart, not just Your hand. Thank You for the temporary realm that You have created and the joy that it brings, but I want to live for what is above it. I want my life to be a pursuit of the eternal. Transform my heart; enable the eyes of my heart to see the things above that will last forever. Give me the humble wisdom to allow You to live through me in a way that makes my temporary pursuits be a reflection of all that is eternal. Amen.

Prioritizing Your Relationship with Christ

Reality is the leading cause of stress amongst those in touch with it.
—Jane Wagner

When I was twenty-two years old, you could say my life was characterized by ESPN and the Golden Arches. I watched sports when I got home and ate McDonald's while I did. If that would have been the rest of my life, I'd probably have been pretty cool with that.

Then one day, I was standing in the church lobby and I noticed this beautiful blond named Libby. I'd known her since I was seven, but I'd never noticed her before.

The rest is history. After the knot was tied, we basked in euphoria and bliss as newlyweds … for a while. Several years into our marriage we started pastoring and the kids started coming. We spent less and less time together, until one day we had to sit down and say, "We need to change some things. We're growing apart."

Do you remember those early days when you came to Christ? How it felt like you couldn't soar any higher in your spirit? Then life took over, and you still loved Jesus, but the blinding excitement of it eventually faded.

On earth, there is constant tension between the temporary and the eternal. It's natural and normal to feel this tension. We ought to feel the pangs of yearning for the eternal. At the same time, we need to seek joy in Christ as we go about the normalcy of today.

In the same way that Libby and I sat down and made it a priority to talk about our relationship, you need to do that regarding your relationship with Christ.

Overcome the tension and cut through the clutter of the temporary. Sit down, be still, and listen to the Holy Spirit as you read the Word.

Jesus, I feel tension. Sometimes I have great days, and sometimes I have terrible ones. Teach me and grow me. Give me an awareness of Your presence in me and around me right now. Quiet my soul, that I can be still and know that You are my God, still. Amen.

Set Your Heart on Things Eternal

Cause I'd rather feel pain than nothing at all. —Pain, Three Days Grace

Ask most young people about why they like the latest popular music hit and chances are they will say, "It sounds real." **There is a strong desire in the human heart for anything that is real.** Even depressing, dark, or painful things are better than the numbness that comes when a temporary high wears off—and that's all the temporary world has to offer—fast thrills and numbness.

To find out how to live for joy, we need to look to Jesus. How did He survive when He was living on earth, caught up in the tension between the temporary and the eternal?

Jesus kept His heart and mind set on things eternal. Just read the Gospels and see how often He talks to the Father. It's constant. At every step in His journey on earth, Jesus was *totally* dependent on the Father. Look at how He cries out to the Father in His greatest hour of need, just before the crucifixion:

> *"Father, if you are willing, take this cup from me; yet not my will, but yours be done."* —Luke 22:42

Those are the words of our Lord focused on things above, on things eternal and not temporary. *Temporarily,* He was about to undergo a lot of pain and suffering. *Eternally,* He kept His eye on the glory to come.

May we do the same. May we understand that spiritual growth is about experiencing eternal truths while living in a temporary world. **We are being made new through the grace of Jesus. The Holy Spirit lives in us. The Father's love never fails us. Desperate dependence on Christ, the Spirit, and the Father is what we are after.** We cannot do a single thing of value for the eternal realm without His power.

With Christ comes the fullness of joy—*apart* from Christ, temporary and cheap thrills.

Jesus, You are the Great King. This world seeks cheap thrills and tawdry pursuits. I don't want that, and I don't want it for those around me. Teach and shape me. I want to live for eternity while on earth. Show me how much joy You have, Father, when I submit to You. Amen.

Don't Pass Over Passover

A man can eat his dinner without understanding exactly how food nourishes him. A man can accept what Christ has done without knowing how it works: indeed, he certainly would not know how it works until he has accepted it.
—**C. S. Lewis**

My guess is that you, like me, have had some awkward moments at meals. You know, spilling red Jell-O on your white shirt in front of the curly-haired boy/girl in elementary school. Or prom (awkwardness defined for hundreds of dollars) or "meet the parents" moments with your fiancé's family (let's not go there!).

I want to take you back to that fateful Passover night. Jesus was going to celebrate the Last Supper with His disciples. I'm sure that some of the disciples had some wonderful, high expectations. It was the Passover. Jesus had just come into Jerusalem, with all the crowds adoring Him, and this was like *energy*; there was *electricity in the air.* So now they were going to celebrate Passover with the most popular guy in Jerusalem … so it seemed. But, do you know what? Everything went wrong during that meal. There were plenty of awkward moments described for us in John's Gospel:

> *It was just before the Passover Festival. Jesus knew that the hour had come for him to leave this world and go to the Father. Having loved his own who were in the world, he loved them to the end.*
>
> *The evening meal was in progress, and the devil had already prompted Judas, the son of Simon Iscariot, to betray Jesus. Jesus knew that the Father had put all things under his power, and that he had come from God and was returning to God.* —John 13:1-3

In this picture of the last meal, as the disciples shared with Christ, we see realistic images of what it means to be *in* Christ. **Snapshots of life with this Jesus.** It's a meal full of moments of misunderstanding, selfishness, and betrayal. Yes, AWKWARD (to say the least)!

Lord Jesus, as I look at the awkward meal that You shared with Your closest followers, open my eyes anew to the realities of being with You, being in You, and You living through me. Reveal to me new aspects of my identity as Your child. Amen.

Allowing Jesus to Serve You

In the Kingdom of God, service is not a stepping-stone to nobility: it is nobility, the only kind of nobility that is recognized. —T. W. Mason

The last meal that Christ shared with His disciples was filled with awkward moments—lots of them. The first one happened when they arrived. The preparations for the meal were definitely last minute. When Jesus and the guys got there and sat down, the servant who was probably supposed to wash their feet didn't show up for work—didn't get the memo or was out of range at the camel races or something.

Anyway, with no designated servant around, the disciples were left looking at each other. *Who is the foot-washing guy? Peter, is that your job? And they're all kind of pointing their fingers. Well, who is the low man on the totem pole? Who's going to do it? Who is going to take the role of the servant?* No one does.

Jesus gets up, takes off His cloak, wraps it around His waist, and starts washing their feet. Oh, what an awkward moment. I mean, the Master is *not* supposed to do that. He gets to Pete (my namesake, coincidentally?) and, of course …

> *"No," said Peter, "you shall never wash my feet." Jesus answered, "Unless I wash you, you have no part with me."* —John 13:8

Was there awkward silence in the room, maybe? Absolutely. An awkward snapshot of a pervasive new principle that is revealed throughout the New Testament:

The Christian life begins with, and is sustained by, Jesus' service to us … not by our supposed service to Him.

Pride and arrogance in our flesh will protest, but the bottom line is that our identity in Christ is dependent only on what He does and has done for us … not on what we do for Him.

In what ways do you need to allow Jesus to serve you and sustain you today?

Jesus, this seems so backward, yet I ask You to humble me. Show me my need for You today. Break through my pride and make me willing to let You serve me today, enabling me, filling me, strengthening me so that I can experience who I truly am in You. Amen!

Letting Jesus Serve through You

Quit being so selfish and give it to ME! —4-year-old to a sibling

Jesus was letting them have it all. During the last meal He shared with His disciples, He was simultaneously putting them in their place and communicating who they would shortly become in Him after Pentecost. No doubt, the boys were a little confused and conflicted at that moment. He had just told Peter that unless he let Him serve him by washing his feet, he had no place with Him. *"You do not realize now what I am doing, but later you will understand"* (John 13:7). **Jesus had just reversed the roles, then He changed the rules, and then He threw a major curve ball:**

> When he had finished washing their feet, he put on his clothes and returned to his place. "Do you understand what I have done for you?" he asked them. "You call me 'Teacher' and 'Lord,' and rightly so, for that is what I am. Now that I, your Lord and Teacher, have washed your feet, you also should wash one another's feet. I have set you an example that you should do as I have done for you. Very truly I tell you, no servant is greater than his master, nor is a messenger greater than the one who sent him. Now that you know these things, you will be blessed if you do them." —John 13:12-17

Do verses like these feel like a burden to you? They shouldn't, *if* you consider the full "example" that Jesus set for us. He was fully dependent on the Father every step of the way. God moved Him so that He could serve us … and now He calls us to the same. **This very Jesus, the servant Jesus, lives in us. As we live in Him, it will be the most natural thing in the world for us to serve others.**

Where has God placed you today so that He can serve others through you?

Lord, make me a servant! No, more than that, would You serve through me today? I am fully dependent on You to love and serve those around me—particularly the difficult ones! I stand aside, surrendering my self-effort. I give in to Your Spirit in me … give me some feet to wash. Amen!

What to Do When You Feel Like Judas

The greatest happiness of life is the conviction that we are loved—loved for ourselves, or rather, loved in spite of ourselves. —Victor Hugo

By the time they shared their last supper alone together, Jesus and His disciples had been living day in and day out together for three years. They knew each other very well … or so they thought. One of them was about to betray Jesus, and the moment must have been intensely awkward:

> *"I am telling you now before it happens, so that when it does happen you will believe that I am who I am." … Jesus was troubled in spirit and testified, "Very truly I tell you, one of you is going to betray me." So Jesus told him [Judas], "What you are about to do, do quickly." But no one at the meal understood why Jesus said this to him … As soon as Judas had taken the bread, he went out. And it was night.* —John 13:19, 21, 27-28, 30

Our flesh and mind are still vulnerable to temptation. This can lead to "betrayals" of many kinds. Sometimes, you might even feel like Judas … a haunting awkwardness followed by the feeling that you have left Jesus and gone out into the night by yourself. Yeah, you might *feel* that way, but the cool thing is that Jesus hasn't left you at all! If you have given your life to Christ and asked Him to come in, He has done just that! His Spirit now lives in your spirit. **You can rest in His promise that He will never forsake you and never reject you** (Hebrews 13:5).

Jesus, I praise You for Your unconditional love that is infinitely greater than my betrayals. Though I feel distant from You when I sin, I thank You for Your promise that You will be with me always (Matthew 28:20). Use my sin as a graphic reminder of Your forgiveness, mercy, and grace so that I will rest and depend on You to live through me. Amen!

Resting in His Strength

Pride is to character, like the attic to the house—the highest part, and generally the most empty. —**Sydney Howard Gay**

Peter was "the man." Even his name means "rock." The first to speak, the first to take up the sword—yeah, that guy. As Jesus continues the Passover meal with the disciples, bold Peter provides the next moment of awkwardness—a turn of events that no one was anticipating. They start to have conversation again. Jesus actually does a little Q and A time. (Now the favorite teaching method of unprepared Sunday school leaders worldwide.)

Peter asked a question; Philip asked a question; Jesus answers those questions and in the course of this conversation, Jesus talks about the fact that He's heading to death. Peter opens his mouth and prepares to insert his foot:

> *"Lord, why can't I follow you now? I will lay down my life for you." Then Jesus answered, "Will you really lay down your life for me? Very truly I tell you, before the rooster crows, you will disown me three times!"* —John 13:37-38

Ouch. That must have stung. Or not. My guess is that Peter didn't believe it (even though it came from the lips of his Lord.) **Peter's good intentions, vocal professions, and public declarations of allegiance were not enough—and this bold confidence was likely the source of his demise**—he believed himself to be strong, but before the rooster crowed, his denials were complete.

> *So, if you think you are standing firm, be careful that you don't fall!*
> —1 Corinthians 10:12

Oh Jesus, I am weak, but You are strong! You are the way, the truth and the life; by myself, I can be like Peter or even Judas. Without You, I am nothing and can do nothing. Though I share Peter's intentions, professions, and declarations, left to myself, I can betray You like Judas. I recognize and confess that I cannot live as I should in my own strength. I rest in You and trust in You to live Your life through me today. Amen!

Are You Listening?

I am about to—or I am going to—die: either expression is correct. —*Last words of Dominique Bouhours,* **famous French grammarian**

You've probably been in churches when the pastor is there for his last Sunday. He's retiring or resigning, or being retired or resigned, and so it's his last opportunity to preach. If you've ever heard one of those sermons, boy, a lot of times, you'd say, "Well, if he had preached this way all the time, we would have kept him!" Pastors let it all out on those last Sundays. All the things that they've always wanted to say, always felt led to say, but were afraid to say, they finally say but they've lost their job, it doesn't matter, and off they go.

Last words are powerful and often become famous. Jesus' last words to His disciples during the Last Supper are what many theologians call "The Farewell Discourse." Jesus holds nothing back (not that He was ever in the practice of doing so!). He makes it very clear what He wants His disciples to know and to remember. Those words transcend time and distance to speak to us today: love, obedience, truth, fear, being alone—all important issues we wrestle with as we discover who we are in Christ. Jesus speaks clearly about these things. Are we listening?

> *I am the way, the truth and the life.* —Jesus

Lord God, as the noise and pressure of earthly life presses in on my soul, give me the willingness and the ability to be still and know that You are my God, that You are my counselor and my comforter. I want to engage with Your living Word—even some of those dusty verses I heard so long ago. May Your words be the meditation of my heart as I live as one who is free. Amen.

Letting Jesus' Love Flow through You

Why not? After all, it belongs to him. —Last words of comedian Charlie Chaplin, in response to a priest who was reading him his last rites and said, *"May the Lord have mercy on your soul."*

As Jesus reclined with His disciples during the Passover, His last words to them were pointed and clear:

> *A new commandment I give you: Love one another. As I have loved you, so you must love one another. By this everyone will know that you are my disciples.* —John 13:34-35

A new command only hours before His death? Yes, Christ is just about to usher in the "New Covenant"—a fulfillment of all the law and the prophets, yet a 180-degree shift in the direction of human spirituality. Man-made religion and legalism would soon be nullified by the sacrificial death of Jesus "because God so loved the world …" Love is the new standard. But this new command, is it just a new thing we must do? A new burden to carry? Not if you look at the context and Jesus' prayer that follows:

> *I have made you known to them, and will continue to make you known in order that the love you have for me may be in them and that I myself may be in them.* —John 17:26

At the very end of the discourse, **Jesus says that it will be *His* love in us that will distinguish us as His disciples!** He is in you, it is *His* love that will fulfill this new command to love others.

God of Love, the Son showed me the Father's love on the cross. By the Spirit, stir up the genuine love for You that You created within me. I do love You! Your love is real and you have placed it in me. Let it flow, Jesus! This is beyond me, yet I ask that You make it real in my heart and mind today. Amen.

The Holy Spirit Lives in You

Pardon me, sir. I did not do it on purpose. —Last words of French Queen Marie Antoinette. She had accidentally stepped on the foot of her executioner on her way to the guillotine.

Before the Passover Festival, Jesus knew that His time was up. In a few short hours, He would leave the world and go to His Father. No question about His love for the men He was sharing His last meal with. The next day, He would prove His love for the whole world. They had moved beyond the awkwardness from earlier in the meal, but for those closest to Him, the words of His pending departure caused confusion and concern. As part of His "Farewell Discourse," Jesus offered them words of comfort:

> *And I will ask the Father, and he will give you another advocate to help you and be with you forever—the Spirit of truth. The world cannot accept him, because it neither sees him nor knows him. But you know him, for he lives with you and will be in you.* —John 14:16-17

Help was on the way: An Advocate, a Counselor, the Spirit of Truth. The prepositions Christ used are revealing. This Spirit had been *with* them. Soon, He would be *in* them. This is no small distinction! Not for them, not for us. The Holy Spirit of God is not just *around* us, not just *among* us. He is IN us—in YOU (if you have opened the door of your life to Christ and allowed Him to come in). The movement of the Farewell Discourse is profound: From "with us" to "in us."

Of all the "famous last words" spoken, are not these, perhaps, the most important we could hear? His final words telling us who we are because of Who is in us.

Holy Spirit, let me never, never get over the wonder and awe of who I am in Christ and who You are in me. Give me the peace to ponder this, the passion to envision it, the faith to live out the truth that You indwell me. Amen.

When Things Go from Bad to Worse

I can't sleep. —J. M. Barrie, author of Peter Pan

He could see it in their eyes. They were starting to get scared. This was not some sort of parable or illustration ... this was for real. Jesus was telling them of His impending death and departure, and Judas had already left the group, destined to set in motion the events that would climax in His innocent blood being shed.

> *Do not let your hearts be troubled. You believe in God; believe also in me. My Father's house has many rooms; if that were not so, would I have told you that I am going there to prepare a place for you? And if I go and prepare a place for you, I will come back and take you to be with me that you also may be where I am.* —John 14:1-3

Jesus knew that over the next hours, days, months, and years His disciples would have to learn how to trust and believe Him. He knew that in centuries to come, we would need to learn the same. In His final discourse to the disciples, and His future encouragement to us, His teachings were twofold: The Spirit will be in you on earth, and I will come back for you one day. Trust Me—I have it all figured out.

Jesus, what can I do but praise You for Your provision? You have given me everything and the only thing I truly need on earth: Your Spirit in me. I trust and believe in You. Even when circumstances on earth go from bad to worse, I trust and believe in You. And on the other side? I trust and believe that You will be coming back to take me to a place prepared for me. I trust and believe. Amen.

Identifying with Christ

We cannot close our eyes to the reality of suffering, for it is the reality chosen by the one we name Lord and Christ. And the path he walks here is the one he bids us to follow. —Theodore W. Jennings, Jr.

If you're like me, you sometimes dream of a God who gallops into the scene on His white stallion, shoots up all the bad guys, and then rides off into the eternal sunset with everybody in town saying, "Wow, who was that mysterious God?" And then (in my dream) everybody is knocking down my door begging me to share the Gospel with them so that they can have this God on their team, too!

It doesn't appear to work that way. "Bad guys" come in many forms today, and bad guys bring suffering of many kinds. It might be physical, emotional, or even spiritual. And no, Jesus doesn't scare them all away. Suffering was *His* reality; suffering is *our* reality.

> *Therefore, since we have a great high priest who has gone through the heavens, Jesus the Son of God, let us hold firmly to the faith we profess. For we do not have a high priest who is unable to sympathize with our weaknesses ... Let us then approach the throne of grace with confidence, so that we may receive mercy and find grace to help us in our time of need.* —Hebrews 4:14-16

I think God may even allow suffering to gently move us toward Jesus so that we can identify with Him. That's a deep thought, and it's definitely worth thinking about as we celebrate Easter. Our suffering is a shared experience with Jesus— something that can bring deeper intimacy in our relationship with Him. He may not rescue us the way that we wish, but in His goodness, I believe He offers some things far more valuable. He invites us to "approach the throne of grace" and "receive mercy." He's really offering Himself to us, welcoming us into intimacy through shared suffering.

Dear Jesus, I ask You to open my heart and my mind. Use my suffering to help me more closely identify with Your suffering, so that we can share these experiences in unity. I do need Your mercy and grace in my time of need. I thank You for becoming a human so that You can sympathize with my struggles. Thank You that I can enter into Your presence with confidence because of what You have done for me on the cross. Amen.

His Pain, Your Gain

We have so theologized the passion and death of this sacred man that we no longer see the slow unraveling of his tissue, the spread of gangrene, his raging thirst. —Brennan Manning, *The Ragamuffin Gospel*

The images in the movie "The Passion of Christ" stunned us all. After decades of dissecting the meaning of the cross, some of us had become desensitized to the fact that the crucifixion was all too real that day in Jerusalem: Real whips, real nails, scarlet blood, steaming sweat, bitter tears—real suffering.

> *Surely he took up our pain and bore our suffering, yet we considered him punished by God, stricken by him, and afflicted. But he was pierced for our transgressions, he was crushed for our iniquities; the punishment that brought us peace was on him, and by his wounds we are healed.* —Isaiah 53:4-5

The writers of the Gospels don't go into the gory details of the cross. They described His mode of torture and execution as quite a matter of fact. (Historians and Hollywood have willingly filled in the graphic descriptions.) Prior to the cross, Jesus knew the normal demands and limitations of the human body. We don't have an indication that He got sick, but He may have. We do see plenty of hunger, thirst, and being physically tired. **He definitely understands physical suffering; He certainly sympathizes with our physical suffering.**

The important thing is that Jesus is here and Jesus cares. And did something about it. Because of the suffering that He endured through His death on the cross, we can know a peace that surpasses all comprehension, a joy in spite of our circumstances, and an intimacy with Him through that shared experience.

Lord Jesus, Isaiah predicted that You would carry my sorrows and take up my infirmities. So I leave them with You now. Thank You for the peace that was bought through Your punishment and the healing that I can know through Your wounds. I claim that now through faith in You! Amen.

Beyond Symbolism

*To the abandoned child wailing in the city street, the mother weeping over her stillborn infant, the man moaning in the torture cell, the parent with no food or medicine to give a dying child, the Indian hunted down by ranchers' dogs, the one betrayed by a friend–to all the wounded and suffering, despised and dishonored, the Gospel points to Jesus and says, 'Behold your suffering, behold your God!' —*Theodore W. Jennings

Just before the Last Supper, the night before His death, Jesus needed to make a point to His disciples: *You need to be sacrificial servants.* So He took out the cloth and the wash basin and washed the grimy feet of His followers. It was powerfully symbolic. A real attention getter: The "haymaker" that made His lecture a knockout. Washing feet? Yes, it was the perfect conclusion to the message that He was communicating to His somewhat remedial disciples.

> *Now that I, your Lord and Teacher, have washed your feet, you also should wash one another's feet. I have set you an example that you should do as I have done for you. I tell you the truth, no servant is greater than his master, nor is a messenger greater than the one who sent him. Now that you know these things, you will be blessed if you do them.* —John 13:14-17

They got the message. The sermon was over. Or was it?

What if the foot washing wasn't just a "lesson illustration?" **What if Christ's actions weren't just symbolic? What if the foot washing was authentic—an extension of who Jesus really is?**

I worry sometimes that Christian "faith" has become too theoretical and not enough actual; *practical* Christianity has been put in a *symbolic* box—particularly the things that require sacrifice and suffering. But again, Christ's suffering and our suffering are a shared experience. His sacrificial service to us cost Him His life. Our sacrificial service to each other and the world is also costly. But it's the real deal! And suffering as servants brings about a freedom because it's actually an extension of who we really are in Him.

Dear Jesus, I don't want to live in the theoretical. Lord, I believe that I am in You and that You are in me. Live through me today as a sacrificial servant in a practical way. May this be another experience that we can share together that will add unity to our relationship as we love the world together. Amen.

Your True Source of Acceptance

Yet while none of its suffering can be exaggerated, the fact remains that the cross' greatest cause of anguish may not have been the nails impaling the hands and feet. The greater cause may have been its shame. —D. Bruce Lockerbie

Jesus Christ was a human being with emotion. The Bible says He suffered from loneliness (Matthew 26:40), frustration (Mark 8:21), anger (Mark 3:5), and He experienced the feeling of abandonment (Mark 15:34).

However, when He was on the cross, He shared in the most painful of all human emotions: Rejection.

- He was *rejected for who He was* by the authorities who scoffed at His claim to be the Son of God. (Matthew 26:63-66)

- He was *rejected by those who loved Him* when the disciples abandoned Him in His time of need—when Peter denied Him *three* times. (Matthew 26:73-74)

- He was *regarded worthless* by those in charge. At the insistence of the crowds, Pilate released a notorious prisoner, Barabbas. For the sake of political convenience he gave into the crowd's demands to "Crucify Him!" (Matthew 27:15-22)

In the end, only a few women and John stayed by Him. When He was finally recognized and received for who He was, it was too late.

Are you experiencing the agony of rejection? Rejection is yet another aspect of suffering that can draw you into deeper intimacy and unity with Christ. Christ *can* sympathize with you and this shared suffering can be a major point of contact between the two of you, because not only has He been there, but He promises to always be here, with you, and never ever leave you or forsake you.

So yes, when it comes to rejection, Jesus "gets it." He understands big-time. And He's with you and in you right now, ready to walk through it together.

Jesus, honestly, I really desire that the people around me would fully accept me and unconditionally love me. But that's never going to be reality, is it? I thank You for using this desire to draw me into a more intimate relationship with You, who will never reject me, and never leave me! Thanks for using the suffering of rejection to lead me to You, the true source of love and acceptance. Amen.

Where Christ Is in Your Suffering

As the sacrifice of Jesus Christ reached its climax, as the sins of the world were being paid for by His suffering and death, there was a moment where God the Father Almighty turned His back on Jesus Christ, His Son. On a spiritual level, Jesus Christ realized that His Father (with whom He has been intimately bound since eternity past) had turned away.

> *From noon until three in the afternoon darkness came over all the land. About three in the afternoon Jesus cried out in a loud voice, "Eli, Eli, lama sabachthani?" (which means, "My God, my God, why have you forsaken me?").* —Matthew 27:45-46

This suffering, the most spiritually acute of any suffering that one could imagine, was fully felt; but it did not last. When the sacrifice was complete and all that had been prophesied was fulfilled, "Jesus called out with a loud voice, 'Father, into your hands I commit my spirit.' When he had said this, he breathed his last" (Luke 23:46) and His inseparable union with the Father was reestablished.

Jesus really did suffer in every way humankind does. By being separated from the Father, there is no doubt that Jesus suffered spiritually.

We suffer a "cloudy" spiritual existence today as well. We see God only "dimly." When we finally leave these fleshly bodies behind, we will finally relate to Him "face to face" (1 Corinthians 13:12). When Jesus ascended to the Father, He made the promise, "I will be with you always, even to the end of the age." (Matthew 28:20)

Will we experience suffering? Yes. Spiritual dimness? Yes. Spiritual separation? Never again!

Jesus, I believe that You died, completely paying the price for my sins. Thank You that this opens the way for continued spiritual intimacy with You! Would You show me what that means for today? In the hours ahead, lead me into a deeper experience of Your ongoing presence in me. Thank You, Lord. Thank You for the cross. Amen.

The Power of Christ's Resurrection

Our Lord has written the promise of resurrection, not in books alone, but in every leaf in springtime. —Martin Luther

Sunday morning the disciples were still locked away in hiding. The body of Jesus was still sealed securely in the tomb … or so they thought.

God had performed a miracle. Molecule by molecule He defied the natural laws. He restructured cell walls, purged toxins, replaced decayed biochemicals, expelled the microscopic scavengers … until the body was ready once again.

And with a breath, the soul and Spirit of Christ came to earth again. Supernatural? By all means it was. God's business is *supernatural*—reversing decay and giving new life. God's business is *resurrection*, and those who are in Christ are part of it, right here, right now:

> *We were therefore buried with him through baptism into death in order that, just as Christ was raised from the dead through the glory of the Father, we too may live a new life. If we have been united with him like this in his death, we will certainly also be united with him in his resurrection.* —Romans 6:4-5

This is all part of the incredible mystery of life "in Christ." It's a mystery, but when we see it in action, it's undeniable. A couple of years ago, right after Easter, this email said it all:

> *Dear Pete,*
>
> *It was 7 years ago Easter weekend that I was at the end of my downhill spiral. I had just spent the weekend choosing drugs over life, and the custody of my first son, and felt as though I had nothing left to live for. I cannot describe the overwhelming peace and joy that I experience today! I was allowed to serve at two services and attended the third. It's like there is no other place I belong on Easter morning…*

This precious woman met the *risen* Christ. Today she walks with Him in forgiveness and grace and shameless worship. If you really want to see the resurrected Jesus, just look at people like her, because she, somehow, was resurrected with Him, too.

Jesus, You are God, able to do far more than I could ever comprehend. By faith, Lord, I accept that my old self was crucified and that I have been raised with You for new life in You. Make this mystery a reality in my life today! Amen.

Having Faith in the Resurrection

And I tell you that the evidence for the life, the death, and the resurrection of Christ is better authenticated than most of the facts of ancient history...
—**E.M. Blaiklock, Professor of Classics at Auckland University**

Christians, in general, seem to have a pretty good handle on the theology of the cross. I mean, that's how we got into a relationship with God in the first place. Jesus died for us so that we could be forgiven, so that we can relate to God on an intimate personal level.

But what about our theology of the resurrection? What if Christ was not raised from the dead? Let's let the apostle Paul answer that:

> *And if Christ has not been raised, our preaching is useless and so is your faith. More than that, we are then found to be false witnesses about God, for we have testified about God that he raised Christ from the dead. But he did not raise him if in fact the dead are not raised. For if the dead are not raised, then Christ has not been raised either. And if Christ has not been raised, your faith is futile; you are still in your sins. Then those also who have fallen asleep in Christ are lost. If only for this life we have hope in Christ, we are of all people most to be pitied.* —1 Corinthians 15:14-19

If His body is still in the grave, faith is useless, we are still in our sins, none of us will be raised, and we are (basically) idiots to be pitied more than everybody else. But the list of objective evidence regarding the resurrection is substantial.

- Jesus' body was dead.
- The stone was rolled away.
- The tomb was empty.
- The Roman guards were AWOL.
- The grave clothes were present.
- Hundreds of witnesses reported what they saw.

Books and books written on this topic make for great inspirational reading. If Jesus *wasn't* raised, it's game over. But if He was—and if we believe it—then the game has just begun.

Living God, through the Truth of your Word and the power of the Holy Spirit, give me genuine faith. Allow me to move beyond superficial belief and begin to experience the mystery of the resurrection and all of its implications. Amen.

The Transforming Power of the Resurrection

What gives special authority to the list (of witnesses) as historical evidence is the reference to most of the five hundred brethren still being alive. St. Paul says in effect, 'If you don't believe me, you can ask them.' —**Dr. Edwin Yamauchi, Professor Emeritus of History at Miami University**

There is no question that the Romans were successful in crucifying Christ. The apostle John personally confirmed His death when he saw Him jabbed in the side with a spear causing water and blood to flow from His heart (John 19:33-35). Many others saw His body wrapped and placed in the tomb.

But Sunday revealed a stone that had been rolled away, guards who had fled for their lives, and an empty tomb. People started seeing Him alive. The apostle Paul recorded that the living Christ appeared to Peter, the disciples, and more than 500 other people (1 Corinthians 15:3-8).

Many of these witnesses were hostile towards Christ before they encountered Him. The most notable of all these was the apostle Paul himself who encountered the resurrected Christ long after the fact. In his words:

> *Then he [Jesus] appeared to James, then to all the apostles, and last of all he appeared to me also, as to one abnormally born. For I am the least of the apostles and do not even deserve to be called an apostle, because I persecuted the church of God. But by the grace of God I am what I am, and his grace to me was not without effect.* —1 Corinthians 15:7-10

This encounter with Jesus impacted Paul personally—transforming him from an arrogant religious leader into a humble, faithful servant … a man transformed by the grace of God.

May it be the same for each of us!

Dear Jesus, what a tragedy it would be if the proof of Your resurrection became an object of my pride, rather than fuel for my faith. I am truly nothing without You. It is only by Your grace that I am what I am. I praise You, Lord. Glory to Your name! Amen.

The Hope Found in an Empty Tomb

It's Friday, but Sunday is coming! —Tony Campolo

I love Peter. Not only is he my namesake, but I can appreciate the way he was prone to live on the extremes: He was bold and boisterous when he was with Christ, but when he was separated from Christ, Peter was a pansy. He caved under the pressure, even cowering to the questions of little girls, denying that he had ever even known Jesus at all. (See Mark 66-72).

We might look at the cross today as symbolic of some sort of victory, but it was devastating in the moment. The significance of Christ's death was the shedding of innocent blood—the perfect and final sacrifice for human sin. But what is the significance for us if He *was* raised? I can't answer that any better than Peter:

> *Praise be to the God and Father of our Lord Jesus Christ! In his great mercy he has given us new birth into a living hope through the resurrection of Jesus Christ from the dead, and into an inheritance that can never perish, spoil or fade—kept in heaven for you, who through faith are shielded by God's power until the coming of the salvation that is ready to be revealed in the last time. In this you greatly rejoice, though now for a little while you may have had to suffer grief in all kinds of trials. These have come so that your faith—of greater worth than gold, which perishes even though refined by fire—may be proved genuine and may result in praise, glory and honor when Jesus Christ is revealed.* —1 Peter 1:3-7*

What a contrast! Yes, Jesus had to die and we had to be crucified with Him to get to this point. But what a difference the resurrection made to Peter and what an astounding difference it makes to us. **In the mercy of the Father, through the resurrection of Jesus, God has given us two crucial things: New birth and a living hope.**

Where would we be without either of those?!

Jesus, touch me with the Truth today. Quiet my heart that I may ponder what You did on the cross. Ignite my heart that I may celebrate what You did through the resurrection. Amen.

Being Forever Changed by the Living Jesus

The resurrection gives my life meaning and direction and the opportunity to start over no matter what my circumstances. —**Robert Flatt**

Information alone rarely changes lives. But when someone experiences the truth, their future is often changed for good. This is certainly the case of the disciples, who went from frightened to fearless very quickly. So what happened?

> *On the evening of that first day of the week, when the disciples were together, with the doors locked for fear of the Jews, Jesus came and stood among them and said, "Peace be with you!" After he said this, he showed them his hands and side. The disciples were overjoyed when they saw the Lord.*
> —John 20:19-20

This encounter with the living Christ transformed them from men who hid behind "doors locked for fear of the Jews" into an unstoppable team. History and tradition show us that the disciples were tortured, exiled, and killed for their faith:

James of Zebedee	Beheaded, A.D. 44
Philip	Scourged and crucified in Phrygia
Matthew	Martyred in Ethiopia, A.D. 60
James	Stoned and clubbed, A.D. 94
Matthias (Judas' replacement)	Stoned, beheaded in Jerusalem
Andrew	Crucified in Edessa
Peter	Crucified
Bartholomew	Beaten and crucified in India
Thomas	Thrust with a spear
Simon the Zealot	Crucified, A.D. 74
Judas of James	Crucified in Edessa, A.D. 72
John	Exiled to Patmos

Billions of people can testify to the change that the resurrected Christ has made in their lives! Information is important. But it can't just be head knowledge!

How would your life be changed if you had a fuller awareness of the resurrected Jesus?

Risen Christ, I want more than just the facts that show You rose from the dead. I am open to experiencing You today, on a personal level, in any way that You choose! Amen.

No Longer Sinners, We Are Holy Sons and Daughters

God creates out of nothing. Wonderful, you say. Yes, to be sure, but He does what is still more wonderful: He makes saints out of sinners. —Soren Kierkegaard

You are not a sinner saved by grace.

Let me explain. At one time you were a sinner, but now that you are saved, your sin-driven past is behind you. **You are now a saint who sometimes sins.** The difference is in how God looks at you. Look at how Paul describes who you are in Christ:

> *Paul, an apostle of Christ Jesus by the will of God, and Timothy our brother, to the holy and faithful brothers in Christ at Colosse: Grace and peace to you from God our Father.* —Colossians 1:1-2

The term "holy" is the same word used for "saint." If you continue to say that you are "just a sinner saved by grace," you're saying your identity is still that of a sinner.

Not true! **At the very moment you trusted Christ, you stopped being a sinner and started being a saint.** You were saved by grace from your sin, but your identity as a sinner is gone. You are now a child of God (John 1:12-13).

If we walk around constantly identifying ourselves as sinners saved by grace, we are communicating to ourselves and to others that we are defined by our previous identity. It's tricky, isn't it? We want to fully acknowledge to the Father and those around us that we continue to sin, but the Father does not want His children to identify themselves as sinners.

Am I just playing with words here? Absolutely not! **The distinction between seeing yourself as a sinner or seeing yourself as a saint makes a huge difference in the way we live our lives.** *Because no human being can act contrary to the way they believe themselves to be.* Think about that one for just a little bit! This week we're going to explore the importance of that in more detail.

Lord Jesus, I am not defined as being a sinner any longer. I am a saint who sometimes sins. Give me the strength and courage to recognize this and to begin to live in the victory that it proclaims! Amen.

Managing Your Sin Never Really Works

O to grace how great a debtor daily I'm constrained to be! Let Thy goodness, like a fetter, bind my wandering heart to Thee. Prone to wander, Lord, I feel it, prone to leave the God I love; Here's my heart, O take and seal it, seal it for Thy courts above. —Come Thou Fount of Every Blessing

Someone who believes they are a "sinner saved by grace" tends to focus on sin management more than pursuing intimacy with God. Managing sin keeps us looking down in the dumps. We're never quite able to see beyond the next mistake.

What a tiring way to live! Now, no one is saying that the saint in Christ is going to live a sinless life. (Actually, some people do say that, but that goes contrary to Scripture, too). What this means is that our *identity* is not that of a sinner.

Paul had an interesting take on the believer's relationship with sin:

> *Here is a trustworthy saying that deserves full acceptance: Christ Jesus came into the world to save sinners—of whom I am the worst.* —1 Timothy 1:15

Here, Paul is affirming the sinfulness of his actions, never denying that it's God's grace and not his behavior that saved him. In passages like Philippians 3, Paul tells people to imitate him. (He wouldn't tell them that if he was still the worst of sinners!) **He's acknowledging the reality of sin, but wants his readers to understand that it's rooted in their *old* self, residue from their past life and the flesh.**

We are indeed prone to wander, like the old hymn says. Instead of seeing the Christian life as merely a struggle to manage sin, we can embrace the thrill of being a believer in spite of our sin.

Lord, by the power of Your spirit in me, focus my heart and my thoughts on Your perfection, rather than on my imperfections. Consume my heart with Your purity and Your presence so that the reality of my sin would be drowned out by Your blazing light. Amen.

Hoping in Christ Helps Free You from Sin

Joy is the serious business of Heaven. —C.S. Lewis

In 2009, the world was enraptured with the harrowing rescue of 33 men trapped in a mine in Chile. The drama played on some of the greatest human fears: Darkness, suffocation, isolation, you name it. But thanks to a small burrowed hole, the men were able to receive goods from the surface. Interestingly, despite their dire predicament, the men later admitted that things were occasionally tense, although overall they were never that terrified.

That seems odd, doesn't it? Turns out that a team of psychological experts recommended that the rescue commanders on the scene come up with projects and activities for the men to do while the rescue tunnel was drilled. *These tasks did not technically assist them in their rescue, but it did something just as important. It kept hope alive.* They overcame tremendous hardship because they had tremendous hope.

Because of who we are in Christ, we can latch on to a similar, tangible hope of rescue from sin.

> *Praise be to the God and Father of our Lord Jesus Christ! In his great mercy he has given us new birth into a living hope through the resurrection of Jesus Christ from the dead.* —1 Peter 1:3

You can almost hear Peter shouting this encouragement. He's bursting with infectious enthusiasm. He's desperate for the people to see that the Father has done something so wonderful that their entire lives need to become consumed with it.

Go back to when you first came to know Christ. Why was it so exhilarating? A big part of it was probably because you felt something like Peter was describing in that verse: *Living hope.* For perhaps the first time, you truly felt purpose. You had a sense of lasting joy and fulfilled life. You shed your old self for new beginnings.

Knowing who we are in Christ, understanding the unconditional love of a perfect father—it's like that mineshaft of hope that brings light into our darkness. And yes, that hope is our way of escape. There is no longer a need to feel trapped in an inescapable hole of sin and darkness. Hope has come!

Lord, I have no hope apart from You. Thank You for breathing life into my soul, for transferring me from the kingdom of darkness into the Kingdom of light. Amen.

Live for Christ with All You've Got

Part of the fun of sports is debating who is "the greatest." There's no way to subjectively measure such a concept, but in sheer influence and success, many would agree that John Wooden was the greatest coach of any sport, *ever*. He won ten NCAA basketball national championships, including a span of seven consecutive titles. That's the all-time record—and with the revolving door of collegiate athletic sports (where entire teams are replaced every few years), it was an astounding feat.

A Christian, Wooden always rightly gave thanks to the Lord for his success. But make no mistake; he was a fervent believer in the power of hard work and discipline. He drilled his players hard. He demanded their very best. Many of his principles have been studied the world over and applied to businesses and countless other career fields.

> *Do you not know that in a race all the runners run, but only one gets the prize? Run in such a way as to get the prize.* —1 Corinthians 9:24

A saint runs to win. Why? Because that's part of our identity. We give Christ everything, naturally, when we understand who we are in Christ because we know that everything belongs to Him anyway. Without Him we can do nothing. Through Christ all things are possible. **The key is this: Stop trying to become something you already are.** You were made a saint by the loving sacrifice of Christ, and the reality of His Holy Spirit in you. If you think you are a sinner, you will need to try to establish your own righteousness. That leads to legalism, despair, and failure, because it simply can't be done; it's not the way we were designed. **The design of the Christian life, beginning in the upper room of Acts chapter 2, is an intimate passionate walk in the Holy Spirit, where we rest in who we are in Christ and allow Him to live His life through us. That's how the race is won in the Christian faith.**

Heavenly Father, I have been called by Your name, and You call me a saint. I desire to be one of Your champions. Yet, I openly confess my failures and my shortcomings—both the things that I have done and the things that I have not done. Show me how to run this race! Remind me continually of my inability to live the Christian life. I now stand aside from my own efforts and ask that the power of Your Spirit in me would live the life that You intend for me to live. You and You alone are "the greatest." I surrender my will and my strength to You. I ask that You would use me, shape me, in any way that You desire. In the name of Your precious and gracious Son, Amen.

Let the Holy Spirit Take Control

I recently had my annual physical examination, which I get once every seven years, and when the nurse weighed me, I was shocked to discover how much stronger the Earth's gravitational pull has become since 1990. —Dave Barry

We all have a physical representation of who we are in this physical world. That's a fancy theological way of saying that we have a body.

The human body is miraculous in its complexity. The greatest minds since the beginning of time have studied it, and continue to study it to this day, and we still aren't even close to knowing everything there is to know.

Scripture has a lot to say about our bodies:

> *Do not offer the parts of your body to sin, as instruments of wickedness, but rather offer yourselves to God, as those who have been brought from death to life; and offer the parts of your body to him as instruments of righteousness.*
> —Romans 6:13

The physical body is neutral. It isn't good or evil any more than a gun is good or evil. It's a gun; it can be used for good or evil.

It's what happens *inside* the body that determines whether evil or good occurs *outside* the body. Today, are you allowing the Holy Spirit, who is inside of you, to have His way with you and your body? Or are you trying to control things yourself? The answer to those questions can make all the difference in the world for you today!

Jesus, I thank You for my body. Thank You for giving me this temporary vessel to live in on this earth. Today, I offer myself to You. All of me. Take my body and make it an instrument of Your righteousness. I surrender and ask that You would take control of it. Use it for Your glory as an instrument of worship, prayer, and loving service to those around me. Amen.

Jesus Will Take Care of Your Soul

He disliked emotion, not because he felt lightly, but because he felt deeply.
—John Buchan

Sometimes people refer to really great music as having a lot of *soul*. There's a reason for that. **No other word really communicates the depth of humanity as much as the word "soul."** When music or any other form of art taps something deep within us, it's tapping something very soul-ish: the part of us that can't be seen.

The Greek word for *soul* is "psuche," from which we get the word *psychology*. The study of psychology is the study of our soul, and "psyche" is used a lot of different ways in Scripture, but it can be summarized this way: It is the combination of our mind, our emotions, and our will. It's our total personality. So when we make a decision, it is our mind and emotions informing our will. **Our mind is the *processor* of information. Our emotions are the *feelers*. The will is the *decision maker*.**

Your soul is going to be constantly tired because of the regular trials of life. Everything will tug at you. Some days it will be your mind harassing you, on others your emotions will rage out of control. Your will is tossed and turned like a ship in a storm. Jesus calls to us out of that storm offering a different way to live:

> *Take my yoke upon you and learn from me, for I am gentle and humble in heart, and you will find rest for your souls.* —Matthew 11:29

Jesus wants you to rest your soul. He's got it. **Only Jesus understands and tenderly loves your soul, so give it to Him today. He will take care of it!**

Jesus, I want rest for my soul. I want to take Your yoke and toss off the one I now carry. You promise that Yours is light and easy to carry, and it seems like my soul is always exhausted. Thank You for Your promises. Amen.

What It Means to Be Genuinely Spiritual

When you examine the lives of the most influential people who have ever walked among us, you discover one thread that winds through them all. They have been aligned first with their spiritual nature and only then with their physical selves.
—**Albert Einstein**

Being "spiritual" is really trendy right now. Just look at Hollywood. Undoubtedly, some hybrid of Judaism/Hinduism/Buddhism is the latest rage in Beverly Hills. Atheism isn't popular at all, so everyone at least claims to be "spiritual" even if they don't adhere to any orthodox beliefs.

That's all ultimately silly because what are they clinging to? It's certainly not anything real that will address what is wrong with them. **Until Christ becomes Lord, spirituality is just another empty, cheap trick.**

So what does it mean to be genuinely spiritual?

Dwelling deep inside your being, in your "core" (to use the latest workout-craze term), is your spirit. The spirit is distinct from the soul and the body, but they are not separate. They work and function together:

The Greek word for *spirit* is "pneuma" and it's found everywhere in the Bible. Your spirit is where your identity is truly found. **Everything that is born again and made holy by Christ is in your spirit.**

Your spirit is finished and complete. It's what is perfect about you, and why you aren't identified as a "sinner" anymore. God can look at us and say that we are without blemish because He is looking directly at our spirit, cleansed by the blood of Christ!

> *May God himself, the God of peace, sanctify you through and through. May your whole spirit, soul and body be kept blameless at the coming of our Lord Jesus Christ.* —1 Thessalonians 5:23

Lord Jesus, thank You for giving me a new spirit. Because of Your work on the cross, I will no longer be a slave to sin. It's not who I am anymore. May my spirit be a pleasant aroma to You, and give me what I need today to live in Your Spirit. Amen.

The Purity of Your Heart

The heart has reasons that reason does not understand.
—Jacques Benigne Bossuel

When someone demonstrates a special amount of courage or bravery, we say that they have "a lot of heart." Somehow everyone knows what is meant by that phrase, and it's not that cardiologists are in awe of the size of the blood-pumping organ behind the breastbone.

"Heart" describes all of the stuff about us that we can't see. It's a great catch-all word. Scripture uses the concept of "heart" in a very broad range of contexts. Body, spirit, and soul are specific enough that you can grasp them pretty clearly. **Where the spirit and the soul mingle is where you have the heart. It's the summation of all that is the invisible attributes of who we are.** That's why you can see one verse that tells you that your heart is pure...

> *Blessed are the pure in heart, for they will see God.* —Matthew 5:8

..and another verse that seems to indicate that having a pure heart is impossible:

> *The heart is deceitful above all things and beyond cure. Who can understand it?* —Jeremiah 17:9

While your spirit is perfect and pure, made so by Christ, you have emotions and a mind that are most assuredly not perfect and pure. Toss in your body and its lusts, and you have a toxic brew called "flesh." So the Lord can easily look at us and say, "Your heart is wicked," because He would be accurately describing our flesh, and yet He'd also be able to say, "Your heart is pure," because He is looking at our perfect spirit.

As we battle the flesh for control of our hearts, we depend on the Spirit to remind us that we have been made new in Christ. Believers want to have a pure heart before the Father. We want Him to see our complete trust and dependence on the Spirit for every need.

Lord, give me a pure heart. Give me clean hands. I am fearfully and wonderfully made from the inside out, and I want to worship You with my whole heart. Let every corner of my heart cry out to You. Holy Spirit, take control of my flesh that I may be about Your business with all of my heart. Amen.

The Power of Being Crucified with Christ

Seeing someone really sold out for a cause is inspiring. Other times it's silly. Like those guys at football games in the middle of winter at an outdoor stadium who paint their shirtless bodies with team colors, wear goofy wigs, and scream for their team at the top of their lungs. You know that during every play of that game, their entire being, body and heart, is consumed with cheering their team on.

The whole of us is created to worship God in that same way. When we feel intense exhilaration for something temporary, we're seeing a reflection of that idea. In the best case scenario, we cry out to God in worship with our minds, bodies, and souls. **Every nook and cranny of us is eager to praise the Name from every rooftop. Euphoria is too light a word.**

But our bodies or our mood can become foul quickly. Not every synapse fires at the same time, unfortunately.

> *I do not understand what I do. For what I want to do I do not do, but what I hate I do.* —Romans 7:15

Kind of feels like your day, right? We want to please God so much. We try so hard in so many areas and can reach incredible heights, but it seems like we're always just splashing to earth and finding ourselves in need of rescue by the Coast Guard.

There is amazing grace for us, friends. Christ does not expect your whole life to be lived blamelessly. The greatest saints of all time opened the door into their noses on countless occasions. Only one man was ever perfect, and He was God in human form. Amazingly, Scripture says that that man, Christ, now lives in you. You were crucified with Him and your life has been replaced with His! Being "sold out" has little to do with your own effort. **Christ lives in you today! He knows how to worship, He knows how to serve, He knows how to live His life through you to bring you joy and to bring God great glory.**

Lord, I give You all I have. By the power of Your spirit within me, I choose to love You with my whole being: My body, soul, spirit, and heart embrace Your mercy and grace, Jesus. I want it in unlimited amounts. Thank You, thank You for giving me all that I need. Amen.

The Joy and Mystery of Pursuing Jesus Christ

Nobody knows anything. —William Goldman

My favorite word in the Bible is *but*. (Well, maybe it's actually *Jesus*, but I'm trying to make a point here, okay?) The reason I love *but* is because it's a sad news/good news word. Before the word occurs in a verse, there's almost always sad news ... BUT, *after* the sad news comes the word *but*, and then we get the good news we need. Consider 1 Corinthians 2:8-10:

> *None of the rulers of this age understood it, for if they had, they would not have crucified the Lord of glory. However, as it is written: "No eye has seen, no ear has heard, and no mind has conceived what God has prepared for those who love him"—but God has revealed it to us by His Spirit.*

Normally, it is contradictory to have bad news and good news in the same sentence. BUT what we see here is God allowing a glimpse behind the veil of the mystery of who He is and who you are in Him.

The verse says that we can't even fathom the wonders God has in store for us. If it ended there, it'd be a little frustrating because our first reaction would be, "Bummer. That's sounds terrific, but why tell me WHAT I have in store without showing me HOW to get it?"

Thankfully, we have the *but! ... but God has revealed it to us by His Spirit*. It's not that we are simply given power to understand—we will *never* fully understand. It's not something we can wrap our minds around. BUT God reveals it by His Spirit.

It's not supposed to be easy to figure God out with our minds. If it was, they'd have an iPhone app for it by now. To be sure, there's no way to ever fully figure out God or the amazing things He has prepared for us. BUT the process of allowing Him to reveal Himself and His ways in His time peels away the layers of the mystery ... and is one of the most fulfilling parts of pursuing Him.

Lord Jesus, bless Your name for shrouding Yourself in mystery. It makes You holy and unapproachable in my own strength. And yet, I thank You for giving me the hope that I can approach You in the power of Your Spirit, and that I can spend my life pursuing You, understanding more and more of what You have in store for me as I do. Amen.

Why You Shouldn't Rush God's Timing

These are the things God has revealed to us by his Spirit. The Spirit searches all things, even the deep things of God. —1 Corinthians 2:10

Ever wonder why God kept the mystery of the good news of Christ hidden for so long? Generations went by before this most profound truth in the universe was finally unveiled. When Adam and Eve were booted out of the garden, why didn't He stand at the gate and shout, "Hey! Hey, guys! Don't worry! I just want you to know that I have good news! This is what is going to happen ..."

For centuries, the mystery of Christ was stored away in the Old Testament prophecies. Old Testament figures like Abraham and David knew that God was merciful, but even they would not have understood it if God had simply drawn it out on the conference room whiteboard.

Three things historically had to take place before it would be even remotely possible for humans to grasp the mystery.

> Jesus had to die.
> Jesus had to rise again.
> Jesus had to ascend and send His Spirit to live with us.

The death, burial, and resurrection of God's Son had to physically take place. The Gospel doesn't work in *theory*. It's too contradictory by its nature that a holy, just, and righteous God would make such a profound sacrifice and essentially define the whole concept of grace. BUT, as soon as Jesus died, rose again, ascended, and sent His Spirit, He whispered down to Paul and said, "Okay Paul, here it is—reveal this!" Suddenly, it all made sense *in reality*.

Never rush the Lord's timing. He reveals His will in His own perfect time. Someday, we will understand.

Precious Jesus, thank You for allowing Yourself to die, be buried, and then resurrect Yourself in Your own infinite power for my benefit. Thank You for Your timing. It's always perfect, even when I don't see it myself. By the power of Your Spirit in my spirit, give me the faith to live and dance in the mystery of Your unconditional, sacrificial love for me. Amen.

Everything You Need to Live Your Abundant Life

The Spirit searches all things, even the deep things of God. For who knows a person's thoughts except their own spirit within them? In the same way no one knows the thoughts of God except the Spirit of God. What we have received is not the spirit of the world, but the Spirit who is from God, so that we may understand what God has freely given us. —1 Corinthians 2:10-12

I'm fascinated by the way animals camouflage themselves in the wild. There is a fish in the Pacific called the Merlet's Scorpionfish. (Neat name for sure!) Scorpionfish blend perfectly into one particular type of coral. You can be staring at this coral and thinking to yourself, "My, oh my, that's unique and beautiful," and you would have no idea you were looking at a fish.

There's an old phrase that my wife loves to use: "It's hidden in plain sight." This refers, of course, to something that is apparently obvious but that people still miss. If you know there is a fish in the photograph of the coral, you're better able to spot it. It's still tricky, but, eventually, you'll see it—because you've been tipped off that the fish is there.

The apostle Paul is saying in this verse that the same is true with God. No one knows what's really going on inside God's mind unless He tips us off and reveals it through His Word and/or His Spirit. How does He go about doing that?

> *What we have received is not the spirit of the world, but the Spirit who is from God, so that we may understand what God has freely given us.*
> —1 Corinthians 2:12

What we need has already been given to us: The Spirit.

Everything you need to live your abundant life you already have. He's already given it to you. It may be "hidden in plain sight," but you know it's there. The Holy Spirit is the Teacher who wants to show it to you.

Father, teach me to find You. You are in plain sight, and yet I seem to always miss You. Give me the wisdom and discernment by Your Spirit that I need to understand and apply Your purpose for me. I can't do this on my own. I trust in You to reveal the mystery in Your time. Amen.

Do You Really Know Him?

The only questions that really matter are the ones you ask yourself.
—Ursula K. LeGuin

There is an anomaly that we need to tackle in church culture. It's the Christian who *in principle* is focused on Christ but *in practice* is still focused on themselves. In principle, they say all the right things, they look the right way, they carry the right Bible, they go to the right Bible studies, etc. In principle, they're focused on Christ, but in practice, it's still about themselves. Sure, it all *looks* Christian, but it's not focused on Christ; it's focused on activity, religion, and self-effort.

Sad.

So the question must be asked: Do you really know Jesus? Some of you have heard over the years that Christ lives in you. You know *about* that, but have you experienced it? Do you know what it looks like? Have you ever truly asked Him into your heart? Thanked Him for going to the cross for you? Praised Him because of His mercy and grace?

I want to particularly aim these questions at those of you who might feel like you know a lot about God, Jesus, the Spirit, and His Word. If you think you have a lot of religious knowledge, you actually might not know anything! (1 Corinthians 3:19). The core reason for this is that true Christianity is not adherence to doctrine and devotion. It's a mystery that can only be known in the context of relationship.

If you have the Holy Spirit in your spirit and God's Word in your hand, all things pertaining to the mystery and all things pertaining to salvation and life in Christ are available to you. You can understand them as the Holy Spirit reveals them to you. As you submit to the Holy Spirit and ask Him to do that, He will be faithful to do it.

Do you really know Him?

Let us know; let us press on to know the LORD. His going forth is as certain as the dawn; And He will come to us like the rain, like the spring rain watering the earth.
—Hosea 6:3

Father, I want to go beyond knowing You in principle and instead, know You personally, in close relationship, submitting to the guidance of the Holy Spirit. I want to know what it means to be truly free. Amen.

Living Up to What You Have Already Attained

God is waiting for a settlement of all of our controversies with Him.
—Watchman Nee

The thought of being anything other than British is repulsive to ... well, to the British. I can say this from experience, because I was born in England. So, not too long ago when I became an American citizen, it was likely met with a few raised eyebrows by some of my fellow Brits. During the citizenship ceremony, I had to raise my right hand and say (paraphrasing), "I renounce all allegiances to any foreign sovereigns and powers." So basically, they were asking me to renounce my homeland. That was hard for me! I had to promise to do that because the United States does not accept dual citizenship.

That's how it is for all of us in Christ: We now have complete allegiance to Him. When I raised my hand and renounced my allegiance to Britain, I became dead to Britain. When I came to Christ, I became dead to my old self. Significantly, this death is something that has already happened in Christ—it is a mystery, for certain, but it is done.

> *Only let us live up to what we have already attained.* —Philippians 3:16

We don't have to work for this. Everything we are was attained by Christ. We're "living up to what we have already attained." Britain is still alive and well across the pond. My renunciation of my allegiance did not cause the Queen to step down and dissolve Parliament. My flesh still hangs around, too. **I belong to Christ but my flesh still beckons.** (I'm not saying that Britain is the equivalent of sinful flesh–please don't run with that analogy!)

But there is no dual citizenship. We are all members of His kingdom first and foremost.

Father, I praise You for calling me Your child and an heir. Thank You for letting me be a citizen of Your kingdom, with no higher allegiance. Holy Spirit, teach me how to live up to what I have already attained by Your death for me, through the power and presence of Your Spirit in me, according to the truths you have recorded and revealed in Scripture. I renounce any allegiance to my fleshly desires. I pledge allegiance to You and You only! Amen.

Offering Yourself to Christ Alone

Cricket to us was more than play; it was a worship in the summer sun.
—Edmund Blunden

Sports bring out the "crazy" in people. Nowhere else can you have a stadium full of ordinarily rational human beings go from euphoria (We scored!) to soul-crushing heartache (They scored!) in a matter of seconds. Sports are a funny manifestation of a deep truth: **We absolutely crave something to worship.**

To properly worship the Lord, we must make an "offering" of ourselves. It doesn't happen instantly (which really rubs us raw in this age of fast food and instant messaging). We demand things *right now*. If it's not quick and easy, we convince ourselves it must not be worth our effort.

This type of thinking makes it unusually hard to discipline our minds and bodies. But that is what God calls us to: Disciplined minds and bodies offered up to Him in the service of worship.

We *will* worship something or someone. It's how we are designed, as creatures of worship. It's why we cheer at sports events passionately—and also scream in anguish at a loss.

> *For we know that our old self was crucified with him so that the body of sin might be done away with, that we should no longer be slaves to sin—because anyone who has died has been set free from sin.* —Romans 6:6

When we become a believer, our spirit becomes alive to God and dead to indwelling sin, so indwelling sin is no longer master over us. **You discover this in your mind. As the Holy Spirit enlightens your mind and illuminates Scripture as you study it, you discover truths about who you are—a creature of worship designed to bring glory to God.**

Knowing this, I mean *really* knowing it, is what helps us make the decision to offer ourselves as instruments of worship to Christ and not to sin.

Lord Jesus, my desire is to become an offering to You and nothing else. Reveal to me the plan You have for me today. I praise You and thank You for freeing me from sin when I was crucified with You. By the power of Your spirit, I choose to worship You! Illuminate Your Word as I read it, and give me the patterns of thought and action that naturally reflect who You are in me and who I am in You. Amen.

You Have Freedom Over Your Emotions

Emotions were designed by God to follow and not to lead. —Pete Briscoe

We were once on a family horseback ride at a family friend's ranch in East Texas. My son Liam was riding a horse named Easy Money, and while we were trotting happily along, Easy Money decided he was done and made a beeline back for the stables. Poor Liam was holding on for dear life! But at that moment our guide shouted, "Liam, pull back on the reins!" So Liam yanked hard, and that two-thousand-pound animal stopped on a dime. The horse responded just as our emotions ought to respond.

> *But the fruit of the Spirit is love, joy, peace, patience, kindness, goodness, faithfulness, gentleness and self-control. Against such things there is no law.* —Galatians 5:22-23

In this passage, Paul communicates what a person acts like when they have their emotions under the authority of the Spirit. The emotions might feel like a runaway horse, but we control the reins when **we don't allow our emotions to dictate our decisions.** You could feel incredibly infatuated with someone in a moment, ready to marry them just on sight. But do you sign a contract with someone you met one hour before because you feel like it? Of course, not. You do your due diligence before you sign it. **Emotions can enhance our lives when properly channeled, but when they are out of control, they can be very harmful.**

Believe in your mind what God has promised you in His Word and don't let your emotions run rampant like Easy Money. When those emotions try to take off in their own direction, grab the reins of God's truth.

You are what God *says* about you, not what you *feel* about you. There's a big difference.

- You are forgiven!
- The Spirit of Christ lives in you!
- The Spirit of Christ empowers you to do God's will!
- You are significant and of supreme value to God and His purposes!

Holy Spirit, I claim the power You give me over my emotions. I am what You say about me, not what I feel about myself. I renounce the lies that feel true, and by Your power in me, choose to act according to who I am in You. Thank You, my Lord, for the forgiveness You have given me and the freedom I have over my emotions in Your name. Amen.

Giving God Permission to Live through You

Life is pain, your highness. Anyone who says differently is selling you something.
—**Wesley, The Princess Bride**

I once read through a magazine that was profiling "The 50 Most Influential Christians in the World" or something like that. George W. Bush was on the cover. I was curious and flipped through it to see if my parents made the list. I got all the way to number 50 and instead of seeing my father or mother, I saw ... *Dr. Phil!*

I was incensed at the injustice of it all! I even went to lunch with a pastor friend and complained about how Dr. Phil was all flesh-based in his advice, etc. My friend quietly informed me that his dad led Dr. Phil to the Lord almost thirty years ago.

Bam! At that moment, I pretty much heard the Spirit say to me, "Look at the poison coming out of your mouth. Pete, that's not who you are."

> *Do not conform to the pattern of this world, but be transformed by the renewing of your mind. Then you will be able to test and approve what God's will is—his good, pleasing and perfect will.* —Romans 12:2

Our minds and bodies need renewing. Lots of renewing. So much, in fact, that it takes us our entire lives. No one gets to the point of total perfection while here on earth, and anyone telling you otherwise is selling you something.

And yet, that needn't be discouraging. What a wonderful thought, that Christ loves us enough to give us the Holy Spirit to teach and lead us as we grow! **We are already saints, perfect and holy in our spirit before God. Now we need to simply allow God to live up to what we have already attained in Christ in our souls and bodies!** I know that sounds crazy, but it's true. God is ready to live through you in a way that is a natural extension of who He has made you to be in Christ. **Will you give Him permission to do so?**

Lord God of my strength and salvation, I know what my true identity is. I am a saint, a holy one called out by You for Your purposes and my ultimate joy. I stand aside now and ask only that You will make that truth come alive in all areas of life. I accept the fact that this is a lifelong journey full of moment-by-moment decisions to renew my mind. I bow before You as someone totally dependent on You to make it happen. Thank You for promising that You will. Amen.

Saying "Yes" to God

As I look back over fifty years of ministry, I recall innumerable tests, trials and times of crushing pain. But through it all, the Lord has proven faithful, loving, and totally true to all his promises. —David Wilkerson, author of *The Cross and the Switchblade*

Once in a while, I will think about the fact that my father will pass on to be with Jesus. There will be a memorial service, and I already dread that because of the likelihood that I will be asked to say something. I'm a blubbering idiot in most scenarios anyway, so I can't imagine what will come out of my mouth. Hopefully, it will sound something like, "My dad was faithful to his wife, and faithful to his calling." Then I will sit down as fast as I can, because there really isn't much more you can say about a person that is better than that. The word "faithful" in that context means that you kept your promises and followed through with what you said you were going to do.

But that's not the only use of the word "faithful" we need to understand.

> *Paul, an apostle of Christ Jesus by the will of God, and Timothy our brother, to God's people in Colosse, the faithful brothers and sisters in Christ: Grace and peace to you from God our Father.* —Colossians 1:1

The simplicity here is wonderful. Paul uses his introduction to give them the most encouraging compliment one can give: Calling them faithful. **How are they faithful? Because they simply believed and trusted in God.**

We don't always get it perfectly right. But **the pattern of our lives should show evidence of saying "yes" to God more often than not.** We believe in Him, trust in Him, and put all our hopes in Him. At the end of our own lives, no other eulogy would be necessary than being remembered for putting our hope in Christ. The Bible is so clear about this. We can be faithful because Christ in us is faithful:

> *May God himself, the God of peace, sanctify you through and through. May your whole spirit, soul and body be kept blameless at the coming of our Lord Jesus Christ. The one who calls you is faithful, and he will do it.*
> —1 Thessalonians 5:23-24

Lord, I want to be Your faithful servant. I want to be known as devoted to You above all. You are faithful. Empower me to be faithful to You, for it is my heart's desire. Amen.

What Is Your Faith Rooted In?

Faith is the art of holding on to things your reason has once accepted in spite of your changing mood. —C.S. Lewis

It's fashionable to have "faith," and pretty much noncontroversial. I have faith in my office chair when I sit down in it. People have faith that things are going to get better. They have faith in higher powers, themselves, the economy, and—depending on the results of the last election—faith in government. The concept of faith is warm and cozy, and daytime talk shows ooze happiness when discussing it. "Having a hard time? Just have faith!" Yeah, faith is back in vogue. You are cool if you have it.

The sticky part of faith is this: What is your faith rooted in?

> *So then, just as you received Christ Jesus as Lord, continue to live in him, rooted and built up in him, strengthened in the faith as you were taught, and overflowing with thankfulness.* —Colossians 2:6-7

Faith has to be grounded in something. It's just goofy when we have this vague concept of faith and fuzzy feelings that have no basis in reality. Scripture teaches us that we are "built up" in Christ Jesus, the firm foundation. We have faith in Him because He is worthy of it. We are not to have faith in humanity (that goes poorly). We have faith in Christ.

Faith in Christ allows us to live in Him and be empowered for the mission by Him. He gives us that kind of faith when we ask it of Him.

Jesus, You are the only one worthy of faith. I don't want to put my faith in false promises of man or temporary highs. I want You and the refuge You offer. Amen.

What Is Faith?

Faith is not trying to believe something regardless of the evidence; faith is daring something regardless of the consequences. —Sherwood Eddy

It may help us understand what faith is by occasionally "breaking down" who we are. This will help us avoid being taken captive through deception, as Paul warns.

Our spiritual anatomy, you may recall, consists of a body, a soul, and a spirit. In the soul, we have our minds, our emotions, and our will. In our spirit, which is our true inner being, we have our life in Christ.

So we receive life in the spirit, we experience life in the soul, and we express life in the body. Unfortunately, we also have flesh—the desire to do things in our own strength, ingenuity, and skill. Indwelling sin dwells in us, too, and encourages us to make poor choices.

What, then, is faith? It's a decision of the will to act on what the mind believes is true. The mind reads something in Scripture, and in our spirit the Holy Spirit says, "Yes, that's true," and we say, "Yes, that's true," and then in our will we make a choice to step out in that truth. That step is faith. **There is no power in faith itself. The power is found in the object of faith: Jesus Christ.**

> *See to it that no one takes you captive through hollow and deceptive philosophy, which depends on human tradition and the elemental spiritual forces of this world rather than on Christ.* —Colossians 2:8

Father, thank You for forming me and forging me into a special creation by Your mighty hand. You have given me the capacity to have faith, and I want to have faith in the proper way: In Your son Jesus Christ. Teach my will to act on what is true, as revealed by the Holy Spirit in the Scriptures. Amen.

Realigning the Direction of Your Faith

I may not have gone where I intended to go, but I think I have ended up where I intended to be. —**Douglas Adams**

If you were to say that we can continue to live by swallowing, I would say that's pretty much true. If we swallow food and water, we can sustain life, so swallowing is a conduit by which we live.

But it's also a mechanism for death. Swallowing poison will go badly for you. So it's not really swallowing that lets us live; it's *what* we swallow that gives us life.

> *For in Christ all the fullness of the Deity lives in bodily form, and in Christ you have been brought to fullness. He is the head over every power and authority.* —*Colossians 2:9-10*

We have been given "fullness" in Christ. **He is sufficient for us.** In the same way that we don't exist by swallowing, we don't have faith in mere faith. Faith needs to be directed at Christ. He has all authority on heaven and earth. It is much more reassuring to trust in Christ than it is to trust myself. I know just how incompetent I really am, and if you're honest, you probably feel the same way. **Better to direct the focus away from ourselves to where it properly belongs.**

What are you swallowing today? What is the food and water that you are feeding your soul? Where is your faith directed? Are you trusting in people? Things? Are you hoping that your faith in faith will get you through?

Father, You are the great king. Heaven is Your throne and the earth is Your footstool. My faith is in You and not in myself or anything else. Amen.

Why Faith in Yourself Is Deadly

Faith is deliberate confidence in the character of God whose ways you may not understand at the time. —**Oswald Chambers**

Everyone is a person of faith. The reason I know this is because, around the world, people use chairs. (Stay with me a bit, this will make sense).

If you were to sit down in a chair and it crumbled beneath you into a thousand pieces, I would not run up to you and say, "Ha! You don't have enough faith!" What I would say instead is that the object of your faith was inadequate and you need to choose better next time.

A lot of TV preachers will tell you that it's okay to have faith in faith, but the apostle Paul would tell you to have faith in Jesus for salvation, and faith in Jesus for sanctification. **In the same way you were saved by faith, *live* in faith.**

> *Whoever claims to live in him must live as Jesus did.* —1 John 2:6

There's proof as to whether or not we live by faith, and it's demonstrated by how we are walking with Christ. I, for one, know I cannot walk as Jesus did on my own. I must have faith in Him to empower me to do so. Faith in myself is cute for the self-help section of the bookstore, but it will ultimately be my destruction.

Praise His name that we have a firm foundation to put our faith in.

Lord Jesus, give me clarity when it comes to what I put my faith in. May it only be You and nothing else. Help me tune out the false wisdom that surrounds me and hear the truth from Your Spirit. Amen.

Depending on a Completely Dependable God

I think Superman should go on the Larry King show and announce that he would come back to life if people in all 50 states wanted him to.
—**Random quote by Dave Barry**

The definitive comic book character is Superman. He has all of the amazing powers, but what makes him so intriguing to me is his disguise as Clark Kent. He would behave as Clark Kent as he went about normal human living, but when the need arose, he'd tear off the suit and fly off in his blue spandex to save the day.

We tend to think of Jesus in the same way. I mean, He walked around in His little human suit, and whenever He had to do human things, like some carpentry, He was human Jesus, but then when the supernatural was necessary, the buttons of His human suit popped off revealing the big "G" (for God) on His chest. The Super Jesus God would do all this amazing stuff and then when that was all taken care of, He went back into His carpenter clothes—just like Superman putting on his tie and suit to become Clark Kent again.

But that's not what we get from Scripture:

> *So Jesus said, "When you have lifted up the Son of Man, then you will know that I am he and that I do nothing on my own but speak just what the Father has taught me."* —John 8:28

Jesus is fully God, yet He chose to live a life of complete dependency on the Father. He could have chosen to assume His God powers at any time, but He chose instead to remain wholly dependent on the Father.

He was modeling complete faith dependence on God. *We are not called to live super-human lives through our own hidden powers.* We are designed to live in dependence on God. When we are weak, He is strong. When we are foolish, He is wise. When we don't know what to say, He gives us the words. We are the students and He is the teacher, telling us—if we are willing to listen—which way to go.

Lord Jesus, thank You for showing me what it looks like to completely depend on the power of God. Reveal to me the ways that I try to be independent of You. Lead me into a more intimate and dependent relationship. I want to have a heart like Yours was while You were on earth, one that is completely dependent on a completely dependable Father. Amen.

Why Christ's Miracles Are More Than Cool

A Christian is a perpetual miracle. —Charles Spurgeon

Miracles are, without question, cool. But the fact that Jesus performed miracles was not reason enough to believe that He was God. Elijah performed many miracles, but he never once laid claim to his own deity. **Christ Himself was adamant that His miracles were not just evidence of His deity, but of His dependence on the Father:**

> *But if I do them, even though you do not believe me, believe the works, that you may know and understand that the Father is in me, and I in the Father.* —John 10:38

He never downplayed the miracles He performed. He just wanted to make sure the people understood *how* and *why* He was doing them. **Miracles *do* point to the fact that the Father was in Him, He was in the Father, and He was dependent on the Father.** Jesus didn't need to come to earth as a man just to do things in His own divine power. God had already been dealing with man in that matter. (Things like giant pillars of fire and floods covering the earth come to mind!)

Jesus is fully God, but on earth He wanted to demonstrate physically to the people what it was like to so totally depend on the Father for everything that all else would fade.

Lord Jesus, the miracles You performed were amazing. I believe. I know that they weren't just cheap magic tricks to dupe me into believing in You, but instead tangible manifestations of Your power when we depend on You completely. Strip away my independence, Lord. Thank You for showing me Your might and what life can look like in dependence on the Father. Amen.

It's Time to Give Up

I have to admit that I'm one of those people that thinks the dishwasher is a miracle. —Clarence Thomas

There are two ways to split logs for a fire. One is the "character building" way (as countless fathers have told their sons), which is swinging an ax over your head until your arms fall off, slowly accumulating a small pile. It's exhausting and back-breaking. The other is by using a motorized log splitter. You can do it four or five times faster and save yourself a lot of effort.

We forget that we have access to an amazing power in Christ through the Holy Spirit. It is miraculous, I daresay ... easily the difference between an ax and a log splitter:

> *Very truly I tell you, whoever believes in me will do the works I have been doing, and they will do even greater things than these, because I am going to the Father.* —John 14:12

Think about this! This is not the time to try to explain away the clear meaning of His words. **Jesus promises us that, through the power of the Holy Spirit, we will be able to do anything and everything that the Father wants to accomplish through us.** It's not up to us to gird our loins and "git 'er done." The key is to allow the power of the Spirit to do it through us.

If you are tired of swinging an ax *for* God, working your hardest *for* Him (and if you think you've already built enough character this way!), it's time to give up. Quite frankly, He doesn't need your help anyway. God's design is a walk of faith, not works. **Faith in Jesus opens up a new way of living, where we are empowered *by* His Spirit *in* us, as we allow Him to work *through* us.**

Lord Jesus, I believe that I have access to amazing power through Your Spirit within me. I'm tired of trying to do this in my own strength for You. I want to be used for Your glory, but I want to do so in Your strength through me alone. Thanks.

If Christ Was Dependent on God, Why Shouldn't We Be?

Let your religion be less of a theory and more of a love affair.
—Gilbert K. Chesterton

When my kids were little, they were totally dependent on me for everything: Food, shelter, love, all of it. They could do nothing without my provision. When we think of dependent people, Jesus probably isn't even on the list. But He was. Big time.

The granddaddy of all the passages that teach that Jesus was dependent on the Father during His time on earth is John 14. It's a beautiful picture of the dependence of a son on his father … of *the* Son on *the* Father, showing the intimacy Jesus and the Father share—an intimacy He invites us into. In verse six, we get a glimpse of something deeper:

> *Jesus answered, "I am the way and the truth and the life. No one comes to the Father except through me. If you really know me, you will know my Father as well. From now on, you do know him and have seen him."* —John 14:6

Christ is our only access to the Father. By knowing Christ, we get to know the Father. Jesus was teaching His disciples that they shouldn't just look to Him to get stuff, because there is no other way, no other path, to the presence of God.

It's easy to lose track of why we worship. We tend to want to worship Jesus because of the stuff we think He'll give us in return. It doesn't work that way. **He offers us not only salvation, but the Father.** It's that simple, and it's enough.

God, I praise You that You offer so much more than simple provision. You offer us access to You through humble dependence. That is enough, Father. You are enough for me. Amen.

A New Way to Live

You can safely assume that you've created God in your own image when it turns out that God hates all the same people you do. —Anne Lamott

Remember back in school how there was always one kid who asked the question that everyone was thinking, but everyone was too scared to ask because it sounded dumb? And remember how grateful you were for that person?

Well, the disciples were no different, and Philip was that kid. Jesus had just told the disciples something truly amazing in John 14:6: *"I am the way, the truth, and the life. No one comes to the Father except through me."* It was a stunning truth, a paradigm shift in all of their brains.

But Philip pipes up and says, *"Lord, show us the Father and that will be enough for us"* (v. 8). You can almost hear the frustration in Jesus' voice in His response:

> *Jesus answered: "Don't you know me, Philip, even after I have been among you such a long time? Anyone who has seen me has seen the Father. How can you say, 'Show us the Father'? Don't you believe that I am in the Father, and that the Father is in me? The words I say to you I do not speak on my own authority. Rather, it is the Father, living in me, who is doing his work."* —John 14:9-10

We similarly miss the message once in a while. We see Christ do amazing things in lives all around us, and yet, we still tend to "miss the point" or fail to see the implications of this mystery. Jesus is the revelation of the Father to us. When we see the Son, we see the Father, too—a supernatural unity with Jesus in the Father and the Father in Jesus.

The point is that we have become sons and daughters of the Father, too. When we get to know Jesus, we get to know the Father as well. We have been adopted into the family, where we share in the intimacy and fellowship of the Father, Son, and Holy Spirit. It's not just theology. Jesus modeled a dependency on the Father over and over, showing us a new way to live today.

Dear God, stun me with the reality of Your truth. Touch my soul with the spiritual reality that the Son is in the Father, the Father is in Son, and that through Jesus only, I can come to the Father in the same way. I praise You and thank You for what You have done. I bow in awe and worship. Amen.

Turning Your Affections Toward God

The hunger for love is much more difficult to remove than the hunger for bread.
—**Mother Teresa**

Major Ian Thomas wrote about something he called "The Threefold Interlock." Sure, it sounds like a wrestling move, but what he was describing is how we live a life of faith:

1. We love God.
2. That love for God leads to dependency on God.
3. Dependency on God results in obedience to God.

That's good stuff, but it's not the whole story. Love doesn't start with us. Our love for God could never originate from our own hearts. And unlike a lot of love we experience on earth, God doesn't love us because we love Him first ... that's actually backwards. We love God for a very specific reason:

> *We love him, because he first loved us.* —1 John 4:19

Our love for Christ comes in response to His amazing love for us. I don't think we can actually wrap our minds around how much He loves us. He *died on the cross* for us. He knows about all of our wicked sin, and yet He still loves us and accepts us. When you truly recognize that kind of love for what it is, and the Spirit shows it to you, you will find yourself enraptured with love for Him—it's not something that you have to manufacture on your own. Just give it some thought. Pray it through. Ask God to make you willing to see, feel, taste, hear His love with all your senses. Close your eyes; vividly imagine you are in the crowd that day the Son of God bled and died.

Lord Jesus, Your love for me is deep and powerful, and I really can't comprehend it. I just embrace it. Help me to see it, Spirit, and turn my affections toward You. Amen.

How You Get Power to 'Do All Things'

A journey is like marriage. The certain way to be wrong is to think you control it. —John Steinbeck

When I first began a relationship with my wife, I wasn't dependent on her. We fell deeper in love, we got married, we made a commitment to become dependent on one another, and over time it became more and more natural to become dependent on one another.

Love is the motive we have for not only getting married, but also becoming dependent on Christ. True love is like that; it draws us together in a way that makes separation and independence seem impossible. **Through our love for Him, we become dependent on Him.** As we immerse ourselves in His unconditional love, allowing Him to accept us just the way we are, a new strength is found within:

> *I know what it is to be in need, and I know what it is to have plenty. I have learned the secret of being content in any and every situation, whether well fed or hungry, whether living in plenty or in want. I can do all this through him who gives me strength.* —Philippians 4:12-13

Being dependent on Christ is how we get power to "do all things." We are equipped for His service by being attached to Him, relying on Him for everything. What a relief! It's not up to us!

Lord Jesus, thank You for being my Source. May Your love become so real that it just naturally overflows, moving me to do "all things" through You who gives me strength. Thank You for empowering me through Your love for my tasks to the glory of Your name. Amen.

The Key to Joyful Obedience

A boy can learn a lot from a dog: obedience, loyalty, and the importance of turning around three times before lying down. —Robert Benchley

Being loved and empowered by God leads us into obedience to whatever He asks of us. We don't just begrudgingly submit to His commands like He is some far-off tyrant. We don't have to obey to earn His favor or acceptance, or be fearful or tentative when our efforts fall short. That's not the way He designed it to work. It's actually joyful!

> *And this is love: that we walk in obedience to his commands. As you have heard from the beginning, his command is that you walk in love.*
> —2 John 1:6

In our human terms, we don't normally equate love with obedience. But that's just how God set it up. Since He loves us so much, we are hardwired to return that love by joyfully obeying Him. We know where *true* joy is—not in quick-fix earthly stuff, but in a steady relationship with Christ. If we have experienced His unconditional love, we will love Him back, and if we love Him, we will naturally follow His lead.

Father, I yearn to walk in obedience, but it gets tough when I look at You as some sort of killjoy. I resist when I feel like I have to perform to earn Your love. Shower me with an experience of Your unconditional true love. May that love empower me to serve in heartfelt joy! Amen.

Letting God's Love Move You

It is for each of us freely to choose whom we shall serve, and find in that obedience our freedom. —Mary Richards

As eager as we can be to obey God, leaping in too quickly is also a problem. In modern evangelism, we can occasionally skip over love and empowerment—the necessary first two steps—and dive right into action. **Without the motive of love or the power of dependence on Christ, we blast away and cause damage.**

> *Because of the service by which you have proved yourselves, others will praise God for the obedience that accompanies your confession of the gospel of Christ, and for your generosity in sharing with them and with everyone else.*
> —2 Corinthians 9:13

So you can see what obedience done right looks like: Others will see it and praise God. Apart from a heart that is truly learning to love God, we will have no motivation for obedience other than the abject fear of punishment. A lack of understanding of love and dependency always leads to legalism.

Is obedience important? Yes! Do we produce it out of the flesh? No! **Our love for Him, yielded to Him as He lives within us, is where we should find ourselves walking in obedience.**

Holy Spirit, give me the proper perspective on being obedient to You. I don't want to jump in too quickly, nor do I want to miss it if You are nudging me. Teach me and guide me. Break me, if needed, to strengthen my dependence. I stand ready to let Your love move me today. Amen.

How NOT to Serve God

God's commands are designed to guide you to life's very best. You will not obey Him, if you do not believe Him and trust Him. You cannot believe Him if you do not love Him. You cannot love Him unless you know Him.
—**Henry Blackaby**

Do you tend to serve because you are afraid God will reject you if you don't? Do you serve because a preacher stands at a pulpit and makes you feel inferior if you don't? I hope not, because that will end badly.

Service by guilt is decidedly not the best way to go. Guilt-induced obedience, tradition-based ritual … it's all just an empty shadow of how we have been designed to live in Christ. It's just generally a bad idea to serve for any other reason than being filled with love.

> *For I desire mercy, not sacrifice, and acknowledgment of God rather than burnt offerings.* —Hosea 6:6

I'd suggest you take a little inventory here. What is your *true* motivation? Pleasing people, insecurity, fear, guilt, tradition, obligation … within all our hearts lurk false and destructive motives. Ask God to reveal them to you.

> *Search me, God, and know my heart; test me and know my anxious thoughts. See if there is any offensive way in me, and lead me in the way everlasting.* —Psalm 139:23-24

One motive is pure. One motive will keep you from burning out when the task is huge. One motive will keep you from condemnation when you fail. One motive will keep you from self-righteousness when you succeed. That pure motive is the love of God itself—the source of all true worship and service. That launches "The Threefold Interlock" life of faith:

1. We love God.
2. That love for God leads to dependency on God.
3. Dependency on God results in obedience to God.

Lord, I want to serve You with my whole heart, a heart full of Your love. Free me from false, destructive motives. Fill me with love and affection for You. Empower me to become ever more dependent on You. May Your love be the power behind every move I make for Your glory. Amen.

Which Road Are You On?

Christians are notorious for only asking questions that they already have answers to. —Tony Campolo

I think there are only a few answers to the vast majority of the questions that people are asking today. The problem is this: **Many times we are asking the wrong questions, or we have become dulled to the answers that really make a difference.**

Asking the right question can lead us to some astounding conclusions. It can also be terribly disconcerting. I ran into one of those questions while reading Bruce McNicol's book, *TrueFaced.* I'm going to share it with you so that you can be disconcerted, too. (I don't want to be disconcerted all by myself! Kind of lonely being perplexed all alone!) Bruce poses the question like this:

"I want you to imagine you're walking through the woods on a quite narrow path, and you go on that path for quite some time, and all of a sudden it comes to a Y, and there's a path going off to the right, and there's a path going off to the left, and there's a sign right down the middle … **The marker leading to the left, says simply, PLEASING GOD! The one leading to the right, reads TRUSTING GOD!** It's hard to choose one over the other because both roads have a good feel to them. We discover there's no third road, and it becomes obvious that we need to choose one … We are not able to jump back and forth, only one, and the one we choose will indelibly mark the way we live."

> *Give careful thought to the paths of your feet and be steadfast in all your ways.*
> —Proverbs 4:26

Which way is the right way? Before we start to search out the answers, I only ask that you would pause and pray and ponder the question. **Which road are you on? Which one will you choose for the future? Are you trying to live a life that is** *pleasing God?* **Are you choosing to** *trust Him?*

Holy Spirit, You are my counselor. By the truth of Your living Word, and the reality of Your presence inside of me, I ask that You would lead me this week. Lord, I stand aside and ask for You to work in my heart and in my mind. Give me the willingness to allow You to search my heart and reveal my thoughts so You can answer my questions correctly. Amen.

Are You Pleasing God or Trusting God?

You are doomed to make choices. This is life's greatest paradox. —Wayne Dyer

The problem with questions is that sometimes they lead to more questions. That's where I found myself while reading Bruce McNicol's book, *TrueFaced*. I do a lot of reading, but his questions stopped me in my tracks:

Am I trying to please God, or am I trusting God?

Quite frankly, I didn't like the idea of having to choose between these two. So I connected with my friend, Dr. Ramesh Richard from Dallas Seminary. "Ramesh, have you read through *TrueFaced*? (Of course, he'd read it; he's read everything.) I asked him what he thought. He said, "You know I really like the concept. I would probably word it a little differently, but I think Bruce's wording is completely clear and accurate." Rats. I was still on the hook to figure this thing out. The question seemed to be boiling down to this:

1. I can choose to trust in myself, and in my own efforts in order to earn God's pleasure.

2. I can choose to trust in Christ, allowing Him to live His life through me, to enable me to live a life that is pleasing to God.

At first, it seemed like a very subtle difference. *Maybe this was all just a little word game?* **But the more I thought about it, the more the significance of this choice impacted me.**

- The question revealed what I believed about my own abilities outside of Christ.

- The question revealed my true beliefs about God's grace and mercy.

- The question revealed a lot about the natural tendency all humans have towards self-righteousness.

- The question revealed what I believed about God, and how I thought He saw me in Christ.

How would I answer the question? How would *you* answer the question?

Search me, O God, and know my heart; Test me and know my anxious thoughts.
See if there is any offensive way in me, and lead me in the way everlasting.
—Psalm 139:23-24

The Road Most Traveled

As a child my family's menu consisted of two choices: take it or leave it.
—Buddy Hackett

Christianity offers us two choices: Please God or Trust God. —Bruce McNicol

Religion is all about "pleasing God." If we have to choose between that and "trusting God," "pleasing God" seems to be the logical choice. Simply trusting Him just seems too passive. **Striving to live a life that is "pleasing to God" shows our sincerity, our commitment, and our appreciation for what God did for us. Right?**

"Pleasing God" seems to be the priority of serious believers. Right? If you head down that road, you see that the path is very well traveled. But where does it lead? In Bruce McNicol's words, it soon leads to a door with a sign on it that reads:

> *Striving to be all God wants me to be!*

And there's a label on the doorknob with the word, *EFFORT!* On the other side of the door is a vast hall filled with people who are sincerely determined to live God-pleasing lives. In public they ooze well-groomed devotion—though it comes across rather … um, "plastic." They display dedication and continual smiles—but sometimes that smile seems rather … um, "uncertain." Still, their hearts seem noble and their quest is clear:

> *Strive to be free from sin and work to achieve an intimate relationship with God.*

Yes, it sounds and looks sort of right, but almost imperceptibly the road of "pleasing God" turns into a rut of "What *I* must do to keep God pleased with me."

Does this resonate with you? Has the road you have chosen lead to good intentions where you are trying to flesh out a life that pleases God?

Holy Spirit, reveal to me which road I am on, and the implications of that choice. Amen.

Your Identity Option

MAY
7

It is our choices... that show what we truly are, far more than our abilities.
—J. K. Rowling

If you are striving to "please God," there are a bunch of voices in your head telling you things like this: *I should be more sold out for God. I should care more. I need to get on fire. I must buck up, shape up, and tighten up.* Yes, it sounds like the mantra of good intentions and spiritual humility. But …

> *There is a way that appears to be right, but in the end it leads to death.*
> —Proverbs 16:25

Thankfully, God has provided another route. **But we must back up to the intersection where we made the choice to go with the religious crowd in an attempt to please God by our own self effort.** At this intersection, another sign points down a different road. It says, "Trusting God."

This road is definitely less worn than the other one, and it seems illogical. If you are uncomfortable with trusting God rather than pleasing God, a bunch of other voices in your head are saying things like this: *When do I get to do something for God? Where's the part where I get to prove my sincerity? Where are my guidelines? Where do I get to give God my best?*

If you overcome those voices and walk this path, you come to another door which says, "Living Out Who God says I Am." The doorknob reads, "Humility." It's a room full of people who are obviously imperfect, full of compromise and struggle—**yet they are authentic—and underneath any expression is a genuine joy.**

It's not nearly as orderly as the room filled with those who are trying in their own effort to "please God." But there is a peace that surpasses all comprehension around them. This group knows who they are in Christ, and they are resting in what He has done for them.

As Bruce McNichol says, "Welcome to the room of Grace!"

Abba Father, I cry out to You as Your adopted child. Show me the path I am on. Give me eyes to see the consequences of the choices I have made. Lead me in the way that leads to Life. Lead me in the everlasting way. Lead me to the room of Grace. Amen.

The Road Less Traveled

Two roads diverged in a wood and I took the one less traveled by, and that has made all the difference. —Robert Frost

Bruce McNicol's book, *TrueFaced*, brought me face to face with a paradoxical, perplexing dilemma—a question that all of us must answer: Am I trying to live a life that is pleasing God, or am I trusting God?

It really came down to trust, faith, and whom I was placing my trust in.

1. I can choose to trust myself and my own efforts to earn God's pleasure.
2. I can choose to trust in Christ, living His life through me, to enable me to live a life that is pleasing to God.

Trusting God means a life of faith. It is a life of deepening intimacy and moment-by-moment surrender and dependency. **Amazingly and paradoxically, this road of trusting God is the one that actually leads to pleasing God!**

Consider Hebrews 11:5-6:

> *By faith Enoch was taken from this life, so that he did not experience death: "He could not be found, because God had taken him away." For before he was taken, he was commended as one who pleased God. **And without faith it is impossible to please God**, because anyone who comes to him must believe that he exists and that he rewards those who earnestly seek him.*

That's the twist that brings it all together. "Pleasing God" and "trusting God" are not mutually exclusive after all!

Do I choose to "please God" or will I "trust God?" The choice is yours, of course. Moment by moment, day by day until this one life is over, you must choose your path. Just know this: **The road of trust leads to** *both*. **The road of attempting to please God leads to** *neither*. Choose wisely.

God of Grace, by the power of Your Spirit in me and the Truth of Your Living Word, I choose the road of trust. I trust in You—and You alone—to live through me in a way that is pleasing to You. Amen.

Trusting God with the Small Stuff

Few delights can equal the presence of one whom we trust utterly.
—George MacDonald

Life is filled with little burdens. Lots of them. You know, the details of life like bills and carpools and in-laws (not *my* in-laws, of course). The flesh tells me that God is pleased when I carry the load, that He will help me when I help myself—particularly on the trivial, little stuff.

Sure, I know I can trust God to carry the burden on the things that are beyond my ability—like getting me to Heaven or curing a child's cancer ... or getting me out of a speeding ticket (ahem). *But why should I bother Him with the small stuff when He has all these wars and earthquakes to deal with when I can deal with it myself?* Another good question. Why exercise faith and trust Him in the little things?

Because God evaluates "success" differently than we do. We measure "success" based on what the flesh can produce, whereas God measures success based on the degree of trust we show.

Choosing to do things myself is called *independence*—the exact opposite of moment-by-moment *dependence* that brings intimacy with God through trusting Him.

> *Trust in the LORD with all your heart and lean not on your own understanding; in all your ways submit to him, and he will make your paths straight.* —Proverbs 3:5-6

Walking in the Spirit is how we have been designed to live as followers of Christ—every day, every moment, through every burden, large or small. This intimate dependency is part of our new identity in Christ!

Lord Jesus, change the method I use to define "success." I want to place my trust in You, even in the little stuff. Live Your life through me in such a way that brings intimacy between You and me, no matter what the result. I'm all Yours. You are in me. Make my life today a natural expression of trust in that fact. Amen.

Gambling on God

Faith is the strength by which a shattered world shall emerge into the light.
—Helen Keller

In these times, God's people must trust Him for rest of body and soul.
—David Wilkerson

When we chose to *trust* God (rather than try to *please* God), we enter into the realm of faith, believing in what cannot be seen; yet acting as if we can see it. It's a gamble!

> *Now faith is confidence in what we hope for and assurance about what we do not see. This is what the ancients were commended for.* —Hebrews 11:1-2

Our identity and position in Christ is "unseen" in the physical world. In fact, the world screams out the exact opposite, telling us that we are failures, guilty, and inadequate. **It takes real faith to act on God's proclamation that we are accepted, forgiven, and complete in Christ.** It's putting our lives in His hands, even though we can't see Him.

> *By faith we understand that the universe was formed at God's command, so that what is seen was not made out of what was visible.* —Hebrews 11:3

The physical evidence for God's creation is conclusive, yet it still takes faith for us to believe that God created the universe because we weren't there to see it happen— **but I think it also takes faith to believe that God has made us new creatures in Christ!**

> *... anyone who comes to him must believe that he exists and that he rewards those who earnestly seek him.* —Hebrews 11:6

Blaise Pascal, the famous French philosopher, physicist, and mathematician put it this way:

> "Belief is a wise wager. Granted that faith cannot be proved, what harm will come to you if you gamble on its truth and it proves false? If you gain, you gain all; if you lose, you lose nothing. Wager, then, without hesitation, that He exists."

Dear God, I believe that You exist. I believe that by trusting You, I am pleasing You. This day, by the promise of Your Holy Spirit, my Counselor, I choose to believe what You say is true about me. I am loved, adopted, acceptable, and cherished by You in Christ!

Skipping the Middle Part

Learning to trust is one of life's most difficult tasks. —Isaac Watts

Jesus loves the Father and lived His entire earthly life fully dependent on the Spirit who dwelt within Him—and He calls us to do the same. Our love for God should lead to dependency on God. That dependency leads naturally to obedience.

Our love for Him ▶ dependency on Him ▶ obedience to Him.

But we tend to skip that second part. We tend to say, "I love God, thus *I* must obey!" "*I* want to please God, so *I* will obey Him." We skip the middle part—the dependency, the faith, the trust—and try to do it in our own strength in order to please God rather than by faith in God.

Check out Noah in Hebrews 11:7:

> *By faith Noah, when warned about things not yet seen, in holy fear built an ark to save his family. By his faith he condemned the world and became heir of the righteousness that is in keeping with faith.*

How do we know this guy had faith? We see Noah's faith because he built a boat. Likewise, our faith leads to action as Christ lives His life through us. **The Christian life is not lived on the couch flicking through the channels with a spiritual remote.** Christian faith leads to action in the power of Christ through us as we trust in Him.

James put it to us this way:

> *But someone will say, "You have faith, I have deeds." Show me your faith without deeds, and I will show you my faith by my deeds* (2:18).

The bottom line is this: **Our identity in Christ is *not determined* by our deeds. Our identity in Christ is *displayed* by our deeds.**

True faith *will* display itself!

Dear God, I love You! Break the independent desires of my flesh. Give me the wisdom and faith to depend on You with increasing trust. Then, God, I ask that You would enable me to follow You in joyful obedience into any work that You have prepared for me to do. Amen.

Are You Able or Abel?

Never be afraid to trust an unknown future to a known God.
—**Corrie Ten Boom**

If your kids are driving each other nuts, you can find some comfort in Cain and Abel. They were the first brothers on the planet and waged the first sibling rivalry in the universe. And they were *really* good at it.

Cain was a farmer. He offered God a sacrifice of fruit and grains. Abel was a shepherd and he gave a sacrifice of blood and fat from the firstborn of his flock. But God rejected Cain's offering. Why? The Genesis passage doesn't say why, so Christians have debated this for centuries—almost as long as they have been arguing about the virtues of pews versus chairs.

- Philo said that Abel's offering was living and Cain's was lifeless.

- Josephus said that God is more pleased with things that grow spontaneously than things that you have to work to produce.

The debate could have been shortened if they had just looked at the book of Hebrews. (Come to think of it, this devotional could have been shortened if I had just done that too. Oh well!)

> *By faith Abel brought God a better offering than Cain did. By faith he was commended as righteous, when God spoke well of his offerings. And by faith Abel still speaks, even though he is dead.* —Hebrews 11:4

Cain and Abel each must have made critical choices in how they related to God. Abel must have said, "I'm going to trust God; because *He* is able." Cain must have said, "I'm able to impress God on my own, because *I* am able." Abel chose to trust in God with faith. Cain chose to try to please God because he thought he was able.

So today, are you walking in faith like Abel or are you acting as if you are able?!

Holy God, thank You for forgiving me when I try to live independently of You. I want to bring You a sacrifice of faith. You are able; I am not. I rest in You and trust in You to make my life a living sacrifice of praise to You! Amen.

The Walk of Trust

Love all, trust a few, do wrong to none. —William Shakespeare

Trust everybody, but cut the cards. —Finley Peter Dunne

It was a "rug-rat" conversion. I see them all the time. Young adults tend to walk their own way for a season or two, walking independent of God. Then bambino numero uno comes along and the new parents decide it's time to get their spiritual household together for the sake of the little rug-rat ankle-biter. So be it! Whatever it takes!

Rug-rat conversions have been going on for a long time, certainly as far back as Enoch in Genesis 5:21-22:

> *When Enoch had lived 65 years, he became the father of Methuselah. After he became the father of Methuselah, Enoch walked faithfully with God …*

In Jude 1:14-15 we see that God used Enoch to reveal a horrific revelation of a future flood. Enoch now had a choice. **With doom somewhere over the horizon, he could be overwhelmed by a potent fear of the future OR he could chose to step out and trust God moment by moment.** Enoch took the first step of faith. Then he took another. Then he took another …

> *Enoch walked faithfully with God 300 hundred years and had other sons and daughters. Altogether, Enoch lived 365 years. Enoch walked faithfully with God; then he was no more, because God took him away.* —Genesis 5:22-24

We can draw many life lessons in this historical account. One is the way Enoch "walked with God" in the face of destruction, step by step until the end.

> *By faith Enoch was taken from this life, so that he did not experience death: "He could not be found, because God had taken him away." For before he was taken, he was commended as one who pleased God.* —Hebrews 11:5

But don't let the simplicity of the situation slip by, because **"By faith … he was commended as one who pleased God."**

Heavenly Father, You are worthy of my trust. By Your Spirit—my Comforter—in my spirit, move in such a way that I take the next step of faith, and then another, until I have walked with You the rest of my life as one who has pleased You. Amen.

A Strange Battle You Face Every Day

I do not feel obliged to believe that the same God who has endowed us with sense, reason, and intellect has intended us to forgo their use. —Galileo

Living out who we are in Christ, and experiencing who Christ is in us, is a challenge. There are reasons this does not come easily! **Every step requires faith, and that faith has some powerful enemies.** We battle three things that keep us from trusting God:

- Christian philosophy
- Paralyzing fear
- Personal flesh

Behind each of these "foes of faith" are thoughts and ideas that war with our minds.

> *The weapons we fight with are not the weapons of the world. On the contrary, they have divine power to demolish strongholds. We demolish arguments and every pretension that sets itself up against the knowledge of God, and we take captive every thought to make it obedient to Christ.* —2 Corinthians 10:4-5

If your desire is to please God, the way you accomplish that is by trusting Him. It is through faith that we bring pleasure to Him. If we wake up today and say, "I'm going to trust Him today, I'm going to trust Him moment by moment," we can end up in quite a fight! **But thank God that we do not fight this battle for the mind alone. Just as He was *with* the Israelites, He is *in* you:**

> *The LORD your God is with you, the Mighty Warrior who saves. He will take great delight in you, in his love he will no longer rebuke you, but will rejoice over you with singing.* —Zephaniah 3:17

Mighty Warrior, I praise You for Your presence in me and around me. I proclaim Your victory. In the days ahead, reveal the philosophical, fearful, fleshly enemies that attack my faith, and quiet my heart in Your love. I trust in You to fight this battle. Amen.

Moving Beyond Christian Philosophy

The devil is a better theologian than any of us and is a devil still. —A.W. Tozer

Our theology must become our biography. —Tim Hansel

Learning about who we are in Christ is important stuff. Remembering our true identity as forgiven, adopted, children of the King of Kings is essential to experiencing Life as God intended it. A.W. Tozer was big on theology (the study of God) and is famous for saying, "What we think about God is the most important thing about us."

The problem is that many of us (really *all* of us), to one degree or another, have reduced our theology into a Christian philosophy rather than letting it grow into the kind of faith that pleases God. Christian philosophy is something that we believe in our minds but it doesn't make any difference in the way we live. It's just a theory, it's a philosophy, it's a faith-based system, and nothing ever changes.

> *Faith is the heroic effort of your life. You fling yourself in reckless confidence on God. God has ventured all in Jesus Christ to save us. Now He wants us to venture our all in abandoned confidence in Him … step out of the crowd and bank your faith on the character of God.* —Oswald Chambers

How is God specifically leading you to venture your all "in abandoned confidence in Him" today?

Father of my Faith, I trust You to search my mind. Show me where I have let my faith be reduced to philosophy. I want a faith that becomes "heroic effort" of my life, flinging myself "in reckless confidence" on You because of who You are, and who You are in me. Amen.

The Fear Foe

It's wonderful to climb the liquid mountains of the sky. Behind me and before me is God and I have no fears. —Helen Keller

I was listening to Neal Anderson recently. He gave a fabulous example of what fear is really all about—the kind of fear that robs us of faith:

"In order for fear to happen, there needs to be something that we're afraid of that is both present and potent."

Present. It has to be here, now.

Potent. It has to be a strong threat to something important.

Fear causes us to shrink our faith back into philosophy. It's the primary reason we choose to not trust God:

- We're afraid of what God might ask us to do.
- We're afraid of actually doing it.
- We're afraid of what people might think if we do it.
- We're afraid of letting go of the things that we know we're going to have to let go to do it.
- We're just afraid, so we choose not to trust Him fully.

Listen to this: The Omnipotent One, the Omnipresent One, the Omniscient One … The Omni-*Everything* One says, "What are you afraid of? I'm more *potent* than anything that's come in front of you, and I am always *present* in you and around you. Besides that, I *know* about everything and I *love* you more than you can imagine or understand. TRUST IN ME!"

Lord, my heart's desire as an individual, as a saint, as a child of God is to walk in moment by moment dependence as You live Your life through me. Jesus, enable me to do just that—enable me to trust You. Even faith is a gift from You, Jesus. Please give me that gift, too! So I offer myself to You that I might experience Life in who I really am in union with Christ, the Son of God, and the King of Kings. I pray these things in Jesus' precious name. Amen!

Fighting Your Flesh

All generalizations are false, including this one. —Mark Twain

Of the three enemies of faith (Christian philosophy, Paralyzing fear, Personal flesh), my personal weak spot is the flesh. *That* is not a false generalization! **Flesh says, "I can take care of this!" Flesh says, "I don't need God; I can do it myself." Flesh says, "Independence from God!"** Flesh preaches the antithesis of dependence; it promotes the opposite of the faith that pleases God.

I tend to try to do things on my own. In ministry I know how over my head I am, so I tend to stay pretty dependent. However, my flesh shows up in areas where I think I have some capabilities—like coaching my children's basketball teams— where the drive to win unleashes my flesh to run wild in all its demented glory. Romans 8:8 says:

> *Those who are in the realm of the flesh cannot please God.*

So even when I "win" in the flesh, I lose. But God isn't asking, *What did you win for Me today?* He's asking, *Did you trust Me or not?*

Did you hear me? **If your goal is to please God, and you're trying to do it in the flesh, you can't please Him no matter what you accomplish, no matter what you win.** You are not going to reach your goal of pleasing God unless you are doing it out of trust in Him and His presence in you. Bill Gillham says Jesus tells it to us this way:

> *Your job is to do the very best you can, trust that I'm doing it through you, and leave the results to Me. If it turns out well, praise Me. If it doesn't, praise Me anyway, and let Me handle any problems that are created as a result. Your job is to concentrate on your method which is 'dependency!'*

God of Peace, I surrender to You again. You are my Lord, my strength, my wisdom, my very life. Thank You for Your grace, mercy, and promise that You will never leave me or forsake me—no matter how many times I find myself in the flesh again. I send up the white flag, laying down my fleshly impulses of independence, pride, and self-glorification. What can I do but bow before You and ask You to have Your way in me and through me? Amen.

The Kiss of the Family of God

Any man who can drive safely while kissing a pretty girl is simply not giving the kiss the attention it deserves. —Albert Einstein

If a picture is worth a thousand words, I'd say a kiss is worth at least ten thousand. But even then, can words do it justice? In his book *Your God is Too Safe*, Mark Buchanan attempts an objective description of the kiss:

"Two people press their moist, creased, facial orifices together; cinch tight the sphincter muscles that draw the flesh around the orifice together into a bulbous mound, and exchange saliva and breath."

Hmmm. That doesn't describe the smooches I exchange with my wife in the kitchen (usually followed by my kids' calls to "get a room!!!"). **The fact is, sometimes you have to experience something to understand it. This is true with kisses … and it's also true with the family of God.**

An important element of our identity in Christ is our integration into the family of God, as Paul assumes in Colossians 1:1-2:

> *Paul, an apostle of Christ Jesus by the will of God, and Timothy our brother,*
> *To God's holy people in Colossae, the faithful brothers and sisters in Christ:*
> *Grace and peace to you from God our Father.*

"Brothers and sisters" is translated from the Greek word *adelphos* (which literally means "a male sibling with at least one parent in common"). In context, it clearly means "God's holy people"—those of us who have become brothers and sisters *in Christ,* and as they say, "You can pick your friends, but you can't pick your family." **Whether intimate or estranged, unified or conflicted, we are brothers and sisters in Christ, siblings in the family of God.**

Dear Father—Father of us all—define in my mind what You have planned for me as a member of Your family. More importantly, my heart longs to experience it! Show me what it means to be in Christ Jesus in Your family. Please, Father, my heart is open to You in this. Amen.

Seeing Others as God Does

Families are like fudge – mostly sweet with a few nuts. —Author Unknown

If you don't believe in ghosts, you've never been to a family reunion.
—Ashleigh Brilliant

Leave it to brothers and sisters to bring on plenty of embarrassment. When our daughter Annika was in middle school, her older brother would yell out of the van, shortly after she was dropped off at school, "I love you Annika, and Jesus does too!" He was trying to embarrass her, and, each morning, it worked.

God's family is no different—partly because we are all so different, partly because we really pull some swift ones sometimes … legit mess-ups that give plenty of reason to hang our heads and walk away in shame. Yeah, families can be embarrassing, but only if we look at each other from an earthly perspective. **When we see ourselves and each other from God's perspective, it's totally different.**

> *In bringing many sons and daughters to glory, it was fitting that God, for whom and through whom everything exists, should make the pioneer of their salvation perfect through what he suffered. Both the one who makes people holy and those who are made holy are of the same family. So Jesus is not ashamed to call them brothers and sisters.* —Hebrews 2:10-11

Jesus calls us brothers and sisters, and never for an instant is He embarrassed by us. Is that an act of God's grace or what? No doubt about it: **Every family has its share of nuts and its share of ghosts. God's family is no different**—and God never hid that fact throughout Scripture. **The requirement for belonging has never been our performance.** We have been perfected through His suffering; we are holy because of who we are in Him.

O God, check my heart on this one. Am I embarrassed by my brothers and sisters? Have I done things to embarrass them? Lord, by Your grace and the power of Your Spirit in my spirit, give me the willingness and ability to boldly embrace my siblings in Christ, calling them "brothers and sisters" (no matter how many ghosts they have). And thanks for forgiving me of those times when I'm the "nut" who does the embarrassing stuff around my family. Amen.

How You Can Live Differently

You don't choose your family. They are God's gift to you, as you are to them.
—Desmond Tutu

Our church supports a missionary family in India, a family that displays perfectly the family of God—not because they are perfect (Ha!) but because **they aren't perfect, yet they have been assembled perfectly, just as God has assembled us.**

It all started one day when they came out of their home and found a naked, one-day-old girl lying on their front step. Alone, abandoned, dying. They picked her up, bundled her up warmly and held her to their chests. She lived, and they kept her as their own. They began to hear about others who had been thrown out like trash (literally) on the side of the road. One by one these newborn girls have been brought into the missionary's home. At last count, there are more than twenty of them who are growing in Christ in this crazy family. It's messy and loud, but it's real. Really real. **When the mother was asked what she was going to do with all these girls, she replied "I'm going to give them my name!"** And in a sea of nameless orphans, that's a huge, life-changing gift. With a name, they belong.

Another picture of what God has done for each of us—and a challenge to live differently in the family of those who are saved.

The Church takes orphans, the Church takes deserted people, the Church takes abandoned people and pulls them in, and He gives them His Name, and He gives them a family.

> *See what great love the Father has lavished on us, that we should be called children of God! And that is what we are!* —1 John 3:1

- Are you willing to allow Jesus to live out this reality through your own life?
- Do you see yourself as an orphan saved into a new family?
- Are you willing to be used by Him to expand His family in this way?

Father, by Your love and strength, may it be so. Amen.

Your Role in God's Family

The family. We were a strange little band of characters trudging through life sharing diseases and toothpaste, coveting one another's desserts, hiding shampoo, borrowing money, locking each other out of our rooms, inflicting pain and kissing to heal it in the same instant, loving, laughing, defending, and trying to figure out the common thread that bound us all together. —Erma Bombeck

That kind of sums up the family of God, too, doesn't it? "Sharing … hiding … locking each other out … inflicting," etc. As brothers and sisters in Christ, the same longings and desires drive us toward what we could be; meanwhile, experiencing what we are and aren't: **"A strange little band of characters trudging through life … trying to figure out the common thread that bound us all together."**

The "common thread" is there, however, written clearly in the lines of the Bible— it's something deeper than the random victories and defeats we experience together, something stronger than the "good times" when we seem to meet each other's needs as we stand shoulder to shoulder for a common cause:

> *In love he predestined us for adoption to sonship through Jesus Christ, in accordance with his pleasure and will … In him we were also chosen, having been predestined according to the plan of him who works out everything in conformity with the purpose of his will, in order that we, who were the first to put our hope in Christ, might be for the praise of his glory.*
> —Ephesians 1:4-5,11-12

God has a plan for His family; we are that plan. Destined and adopted, we are living in harmony with His pleasure, His will, to His glory.

Father, give me eyes that can see through the mess of life in Your family. Flawed as we are, give me a heart of faith that can accept myself and my brothers and sisters around me as part of Your perfect plan. I surrender in "conformity to Your will," that my life might be lived "for the praise of Your glory." Amen.

No Favorites, ALL Favorites

Be not angry that you cannot make others as you wish them to be, since you cannot make yourself as you wish to be. —Thomas Kempis

About the only time I complain about "favoritism" is when I'm not the favored one. **In the world, it's all about favorites, actually.** We reward those who behave as we wish, act as we wish, look as we wish. That's the way it works in the flesh, but God has a different standard in His family:

> *So in Christ Jesus you are all children of God through faith, for all of you who were baptized into Christ have clothed yourselves with Christ. There is neither Jew nor Gentile, neither slave nor free, nor is there male and female, for you are all one in Christ Jesus. If you belong to Christ, then you are Abraham's seed, and heirs according to the promise.* —Galatians 3:26-29

Knowing who you are as an individual in Christ can transform your individual life. In the same way, a corporate understanding of who we all are in Christ can transform the Church. God's truth trumps temporary social distinctions every time. **Earthly ethnicity, gender, or social standing do not define us in God's eyes.** If we are in Christ, we are brothers and sisters. The Church of Jesus Christ is the one place where ethnicity, gender, and social standing should not matter.

- Is it possible that we must learn to walk in the Spirit as a family just as we must learn to walk this way as individuals?

Father, You show no favorites. In Your infinite love, You love all your children with individual, eternal equality ... and that's the way You love me! I praise You that I am—that we all are—Your favorite. Thank you for forgiving me—for forgiving us—for the favoritism we show every day in Your family. By the power of your Spirit in me, free me to see all others as "one in Christ" ... and give me the willingness to let You love all equally through me. Amen.

Why He Is Closer Than a Brother to You

Insanity runs in my family. It practically gallops. —Cary Grant

On a hill deep in the dusty Jordan country, Jesus taught the most famous of all sermons: The Sermon on the Mount. Powerful words, stunning words … words that defied conventional wisdom. Two of these words are as life-changing as any words ever spoken:

> *Our Father …* —Matthew 6:9

Jesus was showing us a way to pray. For thousands of years since, this "Our Father …" salutation has been, perhaps, the most common (and, unfortunately, probably the most brainlessly repeated) prayer introduction ever. Let's fix that.

"Our." Jesus', prayer started with the plural-possessive pronoun. **That means that whatever is to follow is something that is shared by us.** In this case, that "something" is amazingly important: **"Father."**

> *The Spirit you received does not make you slaves, so that you live in fear again; rather, the Spirit you received brought about your adoption to sonship. And by him we cry, "Abba, Father."* —Romans 8:15

"Abba" is Aramaic for "Daddy." It's the word little kids used in Jesus' neighborhood. And this is the name that Jesus used to call on the heavenly Father. He got in a lot of trouble with the religious leaders for it. It was so informal, familiar, so un-religious … and it's the word, "Daddy," that we're encouraged to use too, when we pray, when we talk with Him.

Our Father, I want to know You more, to see You as You are so that I can see who I am in You—who WE are in You. You are my DADDY, You are OUR Daddy. We are family. Brothers and sisters with Jesus, in Jesus, dependent on You. By Your Word and the counsel of Your Holy Spirit within me, show me the Truth, and set me free. Thanks, Dad.

God as Your Father

I will be a Father to you, and you will be my sons and daughters, says the Lord Almighty. —2 Corinthians 6:18

I love my dad. My dad loves me. That's important. For one thing, it makes it a lot easier to believe that our heavenly Dad loves me, too. **Psychologists and counselors tend to agree that our view of our earthly father really shapes our concept of our Father in heaven—both good and bad.**

On the down side, my dad was gone a lot when we were kids. Mom was always there to fill in the gaps, but Dad's ministry often left an empty chair at the dinner table and an empty seat in the bleachers. During those formative years of faith, it wouldn't have been difficult for me to view God the Father in the same way.

- What good attributes of your earthly father coincide with the truth about our heavenly Father? (Forgiving, generous, stable, intimate, understanding, etc.)

- What negative attributes of your early father have infiltrated your thoughts about our heavenly Father? (Distant, critical, abusive, condemning, unsatisfied, absent, etc.)

The truth is that our Abba Father is our *perfect* Daddy, the One who is all, knows all, and works all things for our good—even when our earthly fathers drop the ball ... or worse.

Our Father, we need You, desperately, to show us where our fathers have influenced our perceptions of You. We need You, desperately, to empower us to forgive where we have been neglected and abused. We need You to replace lies with truth about who You are, so that we can be free to be all You have created us to be in Christ. Thank You, Daddy, for doing this. Amen.

God Always Has Time for You

I just received the following wire from my generous Daddy – "Dear Jack, Don't buy a single vote more than is necessary. I'll be *&$% if I'm going to pay for a landslide." —John F. Kennedy

It's one of the most famous photos in America: A picture of a little boy playing under his father's desk while the father goes about his work. Sure, it's "cute," but "cute" doesn't make a picture famous—yet this photo has endured (and endeared) for more than four decades. Why? Because of *who* the father is and where the child is. It's JFK Jr. in the Oval Office.

Complete access to the most important people in our lives is one of the most important things. My dad continues to travel the world and I'm one of the few with his personal cell phone number. He will pick up any time he can. No, I've never called him in the White House, but I always have access to him.

The same goes with our Abba Father.

As brothers and sisters in Christ, our Father has left open the door of the Oval Office of the universe, allowing us unhindered access, because we are in Christ. The heavy veil that symbolically separated sinful humanity from the holy presence of God was torn the day Jesus died:

> *Sacrifice for sin is no longer necessary. Therefore, brothers and sisters, since we have confidence to enter the Most Holy Place by the blood of Jesus, by a new and living way opened for us through the curtain, that is, his body ...*
> —Hebrews 10:18-20

The Son promised that He would be *with* us always (Matthew 28:20). He promised the Holy Spirit would always be *in* us (John 14:17). With His life, He gave us complete access to the office of the Father. That's a pretty good family to be a part of, I'd say.

Our Father, I praise You and thank You that You have given us uninhibited, 24/7 access to You through Christ. I praise You that You are never too busy for us, that You are never distracted by other things, that we can experience Your intimate attention and full affection any time and all the time. Amazing. Amen.

Being a Part of God's Family

As I have discovered by examining my past, I started out as a child. Coincidentally, so did my brother. My mother did not put all her eggs in one basket, so to speak: she gave me a younger brother named Russell, who taught me what was meant by 'survival of the fittest.' —Bill Cosby

It was Sunday morning, and all hell had cut loose that weekend. Literally. The one they called Jesus had been beaten, bloodied, and hung in the Middle Eastern sun to die humiliated. And with Him died the dreams of the masses who had followed Him as their Lord. That morning, Mary Magdalene discovered through her tears that even His body had been stolen. When all hope was lost, a man who Mary thought was the gardener, turned and said to her,

> *"Mary." She turned toward him and cried out in Aramaic, "Rabboni!" (which means "Teacher"). Jesus said, "Do not hold on to me, for I have not yet ascended to the Father. Go instead to my brothers and tell them, 'I am ascending to my Father and your Father, to my God and your God.'"* —John 20:16-17

The nuances of His words were lost, I am sure, in the light of what had just been revealed. "... my brothers ... my Father and your Father ... to my God and your God ..." It was a power-packed morning, with enough blatant impact to last an eternity. But in between the lines, **Jesus also affirmed what He had been displaying His whole earthy life: That He was a son, dependent on the Father, and that the ragtag collection of men and women who followed Him were sons and daughters of the Father, too ... making them (and us) siblings of the firstborn Son of God.**

> *For those God foreknew he also predestined to be conformed to the image of his Son, that he might be the firstborn among many brothers and sisters.* —Romans 8:29

God's purpose in redemption is to give Jesus brothers and sisters. How cool is that? God wants a big family! He wants you and me to be in it, children of the perfect Father, siblings of the ultimate big Brother.

Our Father, Your Word says that if we receive Christ, You give us "the right to be called children of God." Lord, I want to live as Your child; I want to be a sibling of Your Son. I want to learn dependence on You as I learn to live by grace with my other brothers and sisters in Christ. Thank You for Your mercy. Thank You for Your love. Amen.

Your Place in the Family of God

A father is someone who carries pictures in his wallet where his money used to be. —**Unknown**

There is just something about this adoption thing. Something about the way a child is chosen and accepted by choice, not by reluctant obligation, but out of pure joy—often at great expense. **If God carried a wallet, your picture would be in it, and you would know that it cost Him everything to put it there**—an eternal love that paid the ultimate price so we might become one with Him and His family. That's a special kind of love—a love that goes in search of someone to receive, and then chooses to do so.

> *For he chose us in him before the creation of the world to be holy and blameless in his sight. In love he predestined us for adoption to sonship through Jesus Christ, in accordance with his pleasure and will.* —Ephesians 1:4-5

Yes, our adoption is by the Father's choice and desire. Pulling us into a family where Christ calls us brothers and sisters. But like all families, dynamics change. For a time, Jesus walked with our siblings in physical person, but He knew that things were going to change, and so He prayed a most remarkable prayer to our Father. May our prayers echo His prayer:

> *My prayer is not for them alone. I pray also for those who will believe in me through their message, that all of them may be one, Father, just as you are in me and I am in you. May they also be in us so that the world may believe that you have sent me. I have given them the glory that you gave me, that they may be one as we are one— I in them and you in me—so that they may be brought to complete unity. Then the world will know that you sent me and have loved them even as you have loved me.* —John 17:20-23

An Amazing Aspect of Who You Are in Christ

The Word became flesh, and then, through the theologians, He became words again. —Karl Barth

I love theology. I also love theologians. But sometimes they can use unnecessary verbiage that obfuscates simple prepositional assumptions. The same thing can happen when we use religious terms to describe simple truths. Yeah, it really sounds spiritual, but **do we really understand the simplicity and the power of the message?** And sometimes even if we do get the message, we can shrug it off because it seems so far from our experience.

Today, no shrugging allowed. Check out the simple straightforward meaning of these two passages:

> *The Son is the radiance of God's glory and the exact representation of his being,* *sustaining all things by his powerful word. After he had provided purification for sins, he sat down at the right hand of the Majesty in heaven.* —Hebrews 1:3

> *For those God foreknew he also predestined to be conformed to the image of his Son,* *that he might be the firstborn among many brothers and sisters. And those he predestined, he also called; those he called, he also justified; those he justified, he also glorified.* —Romans 8:29

God is at work this very moment, conforming you to the image of Jesus, who is the radiance of God's glory and the exact representation of His being!

That's not just good theology, that's an amazing aspect of who you are in Christ.

Abba Father, Your Word says that Jesus is the firstborn of many brothers and sisters. I am one of those brothers and sisters! By faith, I believe that You are now my life and that You live in me. I believe that You are conforming me into the image of Your Son—the One who brings radiant glory to Your name and an earthly representation of Your being. I believe, Lord. Help my unbelief! Amen.

Being Truly Alive

Unbeing dead isn't being alive. —E. E. Cummings

I'm sure you've already realized that this whole "identity thing" is really important to me. Knowing who we are in Christ is … well, I think it's one of the most important concepts in authentic Christian spirituality. Living it is the difference between "unbeing dead" and being truly alive.

> *For those who are led by the Spirit of God are the children of God. The Spirit you received does not make you slaves, so that you live in fear again; rather, the Spirit you received brought about your adoption to sonship. And by him we cry, "Abba, Father." The Spirit himself testifies with our spirit that we are God's children. Now if we are children, then we are heirs—heirs of God and co-heirs with Christ ….* —Romans 8:14-17

I grew up in the 1960s, and I've heard it said, "Anyone who says they remember the 60s clearly wasn't there." It's kind of like that with this passage. "Anyone who says they know what Romans 8 means clearly hasn't read it." Now, I'm not talking about the simple meaning of the *words*. **I'm talking about what these words mean for *us*. It's profound stuff. It's mystical and full of wonder. And it's powerfully practical.** Read it again.

Imagine that you are living out the meaning of these words … because you can. **This is who you are in Jesus Christ.**

- Led by the Spirit.
- Adopted as a child.
- Crying out to God as your "Abba" Dad.
- An heir of the Father with a full inheritance shared with Jesus and other brothers and sisters.

Abba, Daddy, my mind can only take me so far. Conform my beliefs to the truth of Your Word. Then, Lord, would You make these truths come alive in my heart? I want to follow You, Father, for who You are as my Dad, for who I am as a fully adopted child. I stand aside and submit to the leading of Your Spirit! Amen.

Your Full Inheritance as God's Child

I beg your pardon, I never promised you a rose garden. I could sing you a tune or promise you the moon, But if that's what it takes to hold you, I'd just as soon let you go. —Lynn Anderson *(and maybe the Father too?)*

Normally, when we hear the word *inheritance*, we immediately think of money, cars, houses, and businesses passed on to us by a relative. Cool! It's free stuff given because we just happen to be part of the family. **Scripture says we are co-heirs with Christ in God's Kingdom. That's just nothing but awesome, too … right? Well, yes and no.**

> *The Spirit himself testifies with our spirit that we are God's children. Now if we are children, then we are heirs—heirs of God and co-heirs with Christ, if indeed we share in his sufferings in order that we may also share in his glory. I consider that our present sufferings are not worth comparing with the glory that will be revealed in us.* —Romans 8:16-18

Somewhere along the line, Christianity was injected with the idea that if we give our lives to Jesus, "everything is going to turn up roses." Yes, the blessings of being one of God's children are beyond our comprehension. But no, those blessings don't always come as we want them to. **He never promised us a rose garden, and if that's what it takes to hold us, I think He would just as soon let us go. As brothers and sisters of Christ, we don't just share the "good" stuff with Christ; we share** *all of it.*

Jesus, You promised me that I would have trouble in this world (John 16:33). Give me the faith to embrace my sufferings on this Earth as part of the full inheritance of the Father just as You did. Give me just a glimpse of the glory that will be revealed in me so that my suffering can be accepted from an eternal perspective. Amen.

Being Fully Free in Christ

Freely you have received, freely give. —Jesus, *Matthew 10:8*

Back in Paul's day, the Macedonians were dirt poor. In a devastated drought-stricken land, many of them would have been sleeping in the gutters, except that they didn't have any gutters. Yeah, it was the kind of "poor" that many of us rarely, if ever, see—let alone experience. Those Macedonians have something to teach us today about the family of God:

> *And now, brothers and sisters, we want you to know about the grace that God has given the Macedonian churches. In the midst of a very severe trial, their overflowing joy and their extreme poverty welled up in rich generosity. For I testify that they gave as much as they were able, and even beyond their ability. Entirely on their own, they urgently pleaded with us for the privilege of sharing in this service to the Lord's people.* —2 Corinthians 8:1-4

Sharing resources is part of what it means to be a family. It's a huge blessing, and not just for those who freely receive, but also for those who freely give. **What a strange mixture of words shows up in this passage! "Very severe trial … Overflowing joy … Extreme poverty … Rich generosity …"** As Paul helps define our identity as brothers and sisters, isn't it possible that he's teaching us an even deeper lesson about what it means to be truly free in Christ? Consider these words from J. G. Whittier:

> *Nothing before, nothing behind: The steps of faith fall on this seeming void, and find the rock beneath.*

Jehovah Jira, Heavenly Father, even Your Old Testament name declares that You are "God my Provider." You are the Father, and I am Your child. As You have freely given to me, I ask that You would freely give through me. Strengthen my faith that I might discover You as "The Rock beneath" so that I can be free indeed. Amen.

Making Boredom a Thing of the Past

To live is so startling it leaves little time for anything else. —**Emily Dickenson**

If your household is like my household, things start to go really, really badly when there's nothing to do. It usually starts with kids wandering aimlessly around the house with a blank stare. Bickering shortly follows. "You're in my room!" "It's my turn!" These statements are usually precursors to infighting, insurrection, geothermal and nuclear war, and the end of civilization as we know it.

All these things could be avoided and peace on earth could be restored if we recognized one of the earliest warning signs of such looming global catastrophe. I'm sure you've heard this warning before. It sounds like this: "I am soooooooooooo bored!" (and it's proclaimed as the ultimate injustice as if you were tearing off their toenails with a pair of pliers or something).

Boredom, yeah, it's a problem with children in nearly every household—including children in the household of God. (And it can lead to adult behavior in the church that is equally pathetic!) **We were designed to live with purpose—purpose in something that matters.** Consider Paul's description of one of the brothers in the early church:

> *But I think it is necessary to send back to you Epaphroditus, my brother, co-worker and fellow soldier, who is also your messenger, whom you sent to take care of my needs. For he longs for all of you and is distressed because you heard he was ill. Indeed he was ill, and almost died … he almost died for the work of Christ. He risked his life to make up for the help you yourselves could not give me.* —Philippians 2:25-30

It's a little hard to imagine Epaphroditus whining about not getting his turn on the Xbox. Is it possible that God is calling us, as brothers and sisters of Christ, to live so focused on Christ and what He wants to do through us that boredom and its insidious consequences become a thing of our past?

Father, thank You for forgiving me when I become bored and lose focus on the cause. I repent of the petty bickering and infighting that I fall into. I surrender myself to You, to be enlisted as a "fellow soldier." Make me so un-bored that I will be willing to risk my life for the cause that You wish to live through me. Amen.

The Mystery of Your Faith

Now comes the mystery. —Last words of evangelist Henry Ward Beecher, *March 8, 1887*

If we are to be sincere, if we are to be honest, if we are willing to be real about our faith and our beliefs, we must regularly return to the realization that much of what we embrace is a mystery. As the hour of Jesus' death loomed closer and closer, He was sharing with His disciples final words that were simple to understand yet so full of mystery that they could not comprehend. Jesus held nothing back. He made it very clear what He wanted His disciples to know and to remember. His words transcend time and distance to speak to us today: Love, obedience, truth, fear … and being left alone. Listen as Jesus speaks into that concern:

> *I will not leave you as orphans; I will come to you. Before long the world will not see me any more, but you will see me. Because I live, you also will live. On that day you will realize that I am in my Father, and you are in me, and I am in you.* —John 14:18-20

Is this not the great mystery again? Jesus is in the Father; we are in Jesus; Jesus is in us. Someday, the mystery will become our full experience. Beecher's last words reflect that he understood that death was his passage into full reality of God. "Now comes the mystery," he knew.

For now, though, on this side of the grave, we live it by faith.

O, Jesus thank You for being real and honest with me. Thank You for speaking into my fears with truth. Thanks for holding nothing back in the final words You spoke to the disciples—the words that You speak to me today. You have not left me. You have come. You live and I will live because I am in You! Amen.

Who Jesus Is in You

The word 'Christian' means different things to different people ... if we get our information from the biblical material, there is no doubt that the Christian life is a dancing, leaping, daring life. —**Eugene Peterson**

Grapes and grapevines were important back in Jesus' day—very important. They were a vital source of nourishment and nutrients. Symbolically, grapes and grapevines also represented provision, abundance, and life itself.

One day Jesus and His disciples were walking past the Jewish temple, a magnificent structure which was decorated with grapes and vines. As they gazed up at that incredible building, He made an amazing claim:

> *I am the true vine.* —John 15:1

Anyone else who overheard this claim would have been shocked by His apparent arrogance. *Who does this guy think He is?!* Thankfully, Jesus didn't leave them all hanging in the confusion. Like a school teacher to her children, He carefully explained it all by painting a picture of our identity as believers:

- Jesus is the vine.
- The Father is the gardener.
- We are the branches, the connection between the vine and the fruit that brings the Father glory.

Could this word picture help us enter the "dancing, leaping, daring life" we find in Scripture? Is it possible that He is showing us a fresh, empowering, new paradigm for life as believers as we learn to live out our identity in Him?

"I am the true vine." At least one thing is perfectly clear from these five words: Jesus is claiming to be something that is essential, irreplaceable, and life-giving. He uses the grapevine as a powerful metaphor to describe who He is ... "the way, the truth, and the life."

Are you experiencing Christ in that way today?

Holy Spirit, I want to see Jesus for who He is—the true vine. Let this truth make its way to my heart, that I might feel its full emotional, spiritual, and personal impact. Let my life be a clear reflection of who I am in Jesus, and who Jesus is in me. Amen!

Finding Your False Vines

All men seek happiness. This is without exception. Whatever different means they employ, they all tend to this end. The cause of some going to war, and of others avoiding it, is the same desire in both, attended with different views. The will never takes the least step but to this object. This is the motive of every action of every man, even of those who hang themselves. —Blaise Pascal

Pascal was brilliant. The French mathematician and physicist was way ahead of his time. He created the first adding machine, pioneered incredible advancements in science and even designed the first mass transit system … all in the 1600s. But he was aware of the futility of all that stuff, too. Later in life he penned his most enduring words:

> *There is a God shaped vacuum in the heart of every man which cannot be filled by any created thing, but only by God, the Creator, made known through Jesus.*

Created things cannot provide the happiness and fulfillment that we crave. Our possessions, our appearances, our abilities … none of them make the grade in the end; none of them fill the vacuum.

When Jesus said, "I am the *true* vine" (John 15:1), He claimed to be the way to *true* fulfillment. He also implied that there are plenty of *false* vines out there—things that promise to give us happiness and purpose but never fulfill in the end:

- Money
- Power
- Recognition
- Physical pleasure
- Possessions
- Respect

The list goes on and on. Each item offers the illusion of fulfillment, but the results are temporary at best.

Yes, we all seek happiness. "This is without exception." The only question is *where* do we seek it?

Dear Jesus, I believe You are the true vine. Reveal to me today the false vines that I am trusting in to give me life, purpose, and meaning. Then lead me in the everlasting way. I want to experience the true life that only comes from You. Amen.

Finding Your Place

It's not what I don't understand about the Bible that bothers me; it's what I do understand that bothers me. —Mark Twain

The disciples were born in the Old Covenant and they died in the New Covenant, which means that they lived in a completely unique time in history. Their relationship with Jesus was not exactly equivalent to our relationship with Him either. They walked with Him in person, before He was crucified and resurrected. Then they experienced Him afterwards as He was zipping through walls and showing up at random places wherever He wanted. Finally, after Pentecost, they experienced Him as we do through His Spirit that comes into every believer.

Those must have been amazing days, probably confusing, too. We have a definite advantage looking back at it all through the Bible. It's a lot easier to understand it now—but just because we can understand it doesn't mean it isn't going to bother us!

You see, the Bible teaches us that there is an irreversible, supernatural transformation that takes place the moment that we put our trust in Christ. We are radically changed for all of eternity and that radical, irreversible transformation can never be lost. We are now children of God, we are in Christ, and we are in union with Him.

> *I am the vine; you are the branches. If you remain in me and I in you, you will bear much fruit; apart from me you can do nothing.* —John 15:5

But that also means that our days of self-centered, independent living are over! Jesus is the vine. We are the branches that grow off of that vine. We can produce true fruit *only* if we stay connected with Him in an intimate, dependent relationship.

I have to admit, that bothers me sometimes. My pride and self-righteousness don't care for it one bit! How about you? Are you okay with the fact that apart from Jesus "you can do nothing?"

Jesus, there are plenty of times that I wish I could bear fruit for You by myself. It just seems like it would be so much easier ... and then I could take credit for it! But it's far better to remain in You through intimate dependency so that You can bear true fruit through me. So I give it all up to You. You are the vine. I am the branch. Live through me as You wish, because on my own, I know that I can do nothing that really counts. Amen.

Trusting the Master Gardener

Men do not reject the Bible because it contradicts itself, but because it contradicts them. —E. Paul Harvey

The branches of a grapevine must be trimmed back if the whole plant is going to grow properly. Without a good pruning, the thing goes crazy and ends up in an overgrown tangled mess. **If Jesus is the vine and we are the branches, then somebody has to keep those branches in check. That's the job of the Father.**

> *I am the true vine, and my Father is the gardener. He cuts off every branch in me that bears no fruit, while every branch that does bear fruit he prunes so that it will be even more fruitful.* —John 15:1-2

Some of us might think that if God is producing fruit through us, we should be exempt from the cutting. Not so. The fruit-bearing branches still need to be trimmed and pruned. It's not a very pleasant thing, it hurts, it might even be embarrassing. We will probably even protest big time. *Hey! What's the deal!? I'm growing fruit over here! Why are You working on me?*

Well, for starters, He can certainly do whatever He chooses (one of the privileges of being God!). Second, if we accept what Jesus taught about the vine, branches, and fruit, we can't claim that *we* are the ones producing the fruit (and so we can't claim that we should be exempt from pruning because of the fruit!). **But most importantly, why would God cut away at our lives when we are bearing fruit? Because it's for our good and to His glory ... even when it's really hard.**

O Father, I am a branch; You are the Master Gardener ... and I trust You. By faith I even thank You for pruning me. Thanks for cutting me back down to size when need be. Thanks for trimming off the extra baggage that weighs me down. I want to live in harmony with You and Your Word. Do whatever it takes for me to be set free to be all You have created me to be! Amen!

Finding Rest in the Vine

The Lord Jesus has done everything for us, and our need now is to rest confidently in Him. He is seated on the throne, so we are carried through in His strength. It cannot be too strongly emphasized that all true spiritual experience begins from rest. —Watchman Nee

Howard Hendricks once said, "I have never met a Christian who sat down and planned to live a mediocre life." I believe that's true. Shortly after entering into a personal relationship with Jesus Christ, our hearts and minds are filled with wonder, awe, and the expectation that we will be able to do great things for God.

Sometimes this lasts for a little while. Some people manage to keep it up for years. But sooner or later, we hit the wall. It might come through long slow burnout or our lives might seem to explode in a catastrophic ball of flames. The problem? *We* were never designed to do great things for God, and though *we* may try and try again, the result is usually the same: Discouragement, despair, even depression.

No, *we* were not designed to do it ... not alone, that is. God's gracious design is revealed throughout the New Testament and Jesus gives us a powerful word picture for the design in John 15:

- Jesus is the true vine.
- The Father is the gardener.
- We are simply the branch between the vine and the fruit.

> *Remain in me, as I also remain in you. No branch can bear fruit by itself; it must remain in the vine. Neither can you bear fruit unless you remain in me. I am the vine, you are the branches. If you remain in me and I in you, you will bear much fruit.* —John 15:4-5

In a world that is driven by expectations, high standards, and the constant pressure to "do it ourselves," these words are like a splash of cool water to a thirsty and tired soul. The vine shows us that true fruit comes *through* us, not *from* us, by resting, connecting, remaining, and responding in Jesus!

Dear Jesus, show me how to live a fruitful life in You! What a relief it is to be able to release the burden of trying and trying to live the Christian life on my own. I can see it now; I can rest in You today. In every situation I face, in each particular situation that comes my way, I trust in You to bear fruit through me. Amen.

Bearing the Fruit of Joy

Joy is the flag flown high from the castle of my heart for the King is in residence there. —Source unknown

I once figured out that I worked a week on Sunday. Let me explain. I tried to get into the office a little before 6:00 a.m. to finish up my sermon and get ready for the day. At 9:00 a.m., I preached the first sermon. According to researchers, the energy exerted in a sermon is roughly equivalent to the energy exerted at a desk job in an eight-hour day. (I've done both; I think it's pretty close.) I used to preach four services each Sunday so that's thirty-two hours right there plus the three-hour warm-up in the morning, plus a couple of hours of informal meetings afterwards and "Presto!" I've worked at least a forty-hour day before the sun even sets.

Okay, so the math isn't all that solid, but this is all to say that when I plop down on the couch on a Sunday evening, I start to get that it's-the-end-of-finals-week feeling that only comes after that last exam in college. It's that same sensation that comes from taking your ski boots off after a great day on the slopes. And as I put my feet up, I think "Oh, *that* is the biblical concept of JOY!" Why? **Because JOY in Scripture is the exuberance of a completed act!** Let's connect that type of experience with Jesus' teaching about the vine from John 15:

> *If you keep my commands, you will remain in my love, just as I have kept my Father's commands and remain in his love. I have told you this so that my joy may be in you and that your joy may be complete.* —John 15:10-11

There are at least five kinds of "fruit" that we bear when we rest and remain in a loving relationship with Jesus. The first is a completed joy. **People are looking for joy all over the place, but what this text teaches us is that complete joy presupposes complete and unqualified obedience!** No one is more miserable that the Christian who hedges on his or her obedience. (I know this too well, and you do, too.) If you want to experience complete joy, that's found at the end of obedience as we walk in the Spirit.

Where are you seeking joy today? In an intimate relationship with Christ? Or are you looking somewhere else?

Lord Jesus, make my heart sensitive to Your commands today. Give me the desire and the ability to hear Your Spirit guiding me each step of the way. You are the vine, I am the branch. Only You can bring about this fruit of obedient joy. Thank You for doing it! Amen.

Bearing the Fruit of Sacrificial Love

The Bible tells us to love our neighbors, and also to love our enemies; probably because they are generally the same people. —G.K. Chesterton

At the very beginning of Jesus' farewell discourse, He said, *"Hey, a new commandment I give to you, love each other as I have loved you. This is how they'll know you're My disciples."* **He was telling them to love the way *He* loved. Is that possible? NO!** So, why did He tell us to do it? Because He was assuming we would be abiding in Him; that we would remain in Him, so that Jesus would be doing the love through us.

> As the Father has loved me, so have I loved you. Now remain in my love. If you keep my commands, you will remain in my love, just as I have kept my Father's commands and remain in his love. I have told you this so that my joy may be in you and that your joy may be complete. My command is this: Love each other as I have loved you. Greater love has no one than this: to lay down one's life for one's friends. —John 15:10-13

"Remaining in Christ," just as a branch must remain in the vine, bears supernatural fruit: Obedient, joy-saturated acts that can only be attributed to Jesus. Sacrificial love is one of those fruit. It is not an option, but rather a natural outpouring of Christ's love for others when we allow Him to live through us … and this speaks louder to the world than any words. **We are described and we are defined as His disciples by this love moving through us**—and note that this is all spoken to *us as a group*. It's not one big vine, with one little branch (you) on it. It's a vine *covered* with branches (all of us!), and these branches, as we abide in Christ, produce fruit of many kinds … and one of the fruit we produce is love, true Christ-like, sacrificial, grace-laden love.

Has God placed a neighbor or an enemy in your path today?

O Jesus, You love me just like the Father loves You. I want to remain in that love, I want that joy, I want the obedience that springs forth from being a branch on Your vine. Well, I sort of want that! In all honesty, my flesh wants to judge and condemn and punish! But I choose to give in to Your love instead. I shout out that I no longer live, but You live in me! Love others through me just as You love me—I need You to do this through me—that I would joyfully lay down my life for others. Amen.

Marching Orders

I know, I know. We are Your chosen people. But, once in a while, can't You choose someone else? —Tevye to God in Fiddler on the Roof

In most situations, I like being chosen. I love the fact that Libby, my wife, chose me over all the guys that were chasing her at the time. I loved that feeling in elementary school when we were picking teams and one of the best players would take a chance on me. "Briscoe! Over here!"

Yeah, being chosen is a pretty cool thing. It is a privileged position, and sometimes we can start to get a little full of ourselves, particularly as Christians. It's a short distance between realizing that *we* are branches in Jesus' vine and looking down on others because they might not be. As Jesus continued His teaching about the vine and the branches, He gave the disciples a little attitude check right then and there:

> *You did not choose me, but I chose you and appointed you so that you might go and bear fruit—fruit that will last.* —John 15:16

Remaining "in Christ" gives us the privilege of bearing the fruit of joy, sacrificial love, and inside information. It also comes with the responsibility of marching orders.

He appointed us, He chose us for a reason, and He appointed you to go and bear fruit—fruit that will last. We were set aside and we were sent forth. Christ will use us as conduits of His love to reach others with His grace. So, it's not okay for us just to say, "You know what? I'm just going to abide in Jesus! I don't need anybody else and nobody else needs me." We abide in Jesus in the context of community.

It's also not okay for us as the Church to ever say, "Well, we're just going to abide in Jesus together." NO, **we are commissioned to bear the fruit of love and joy so that we can make a difference in our community to people who don't have that yet.** Yes, we have insider info, but Jesus wants us to live and share that info with the world. As we go out to them on the mission that He has given to us, we will see people coming to know Christ as a result of Christ living His life through us … a fruit that will last *forever*.

Lord of the Harvest, search my heart and show me if there are any hurtful ways in me. Reveal any sense of pride and arrogance that I have let creep in. I humbly lay myself before You as a tool to be used in Your hands to reach this world as You see fit. To Your name be the glory! Amen.

The Prayers of a Branch

As long as there are tests, there will be prayer in schools. —**Author unknown**

Prayer. Seems like it should be a simple enough topic. But just take a little sample of what people say about it:

- "God punishes us mildly by ignoring our prayers and severely by answering them."—Richard J. Needham

- "Prayer does not change God, but it changes him who prays." —Søren Kierkegaard

- "Practical prayer is harder on the soles of your shoes than on the knees of your trousers." —Austin O'Malley

- "I prayed for twenty years but received no answer until I prayed with my legs." —Frederick Douglass, escaped slave

- "Give a man a fish, and you'll feed him for a day. Give him a religion, and he'll starve to death while praying for a fish." —Author unknown

- "When we talk to God, we're praying. When God talks to us, we're schizophrenic." —Jane Wagner

Jesus had a lot to say about prayer, too. In John 15, as He finishes explaining the vine and the branches, He offers us another important facet of prayer to consider:

> *If you remain in me and my words remain in you, ask whatever you wish, and it will be done for you. This is to my Father's glory, that you bear much fruit, showing yourselves to be my disciples.* —John 15:7-8

This passage is so much more than some sort of formula to get what we want. Note the preconditions to answered prayer: "If you remain in me … if my words remain in you…." **Jesus is talking about an intimacy so real that our will becomes conformed to His—so that anything we ask will be a reflection of who we are in Him and who He is in us.** Isn't this the vine-and-branch relationship at its simplest, most profound level? If you are living in the context of His love, there *will* be joy, sacrifice, and obedience … and **whatever you pray, consider it YES, because you will be praying the right things!**

True Vine, align my desires with Your will! I want my mind to be renewed and my life to be transformed so deeply that my prayers will be a natural reflection of Your will. I understand that this will require many things to be pruned from my life as You lead me and empower me for obedience to the Father's glory. Amen.

Looking at Life through the Lens of Christ's Love

For when I know the love God has for me, then my mental confusion disperses like fog on a summer's morning. —**Malcolm Smith**

Life can be plenty confusing and overwhelming. Sometimes, a lot of religious talk only seems to make things more confusing. H. L. Mencken said, "A philosopher is a blind man in a dark room looking for a black cat that isn't there. A theologian is the man who finds it." Gee, that helps clarify!

Thankfully, when Christ used the analogy of the vine and the branches, He gave us a simple word picture we can conceptualize. What's it all about? **He invites us to remain in Him, just as a branch remains in the vine, with this being the only way for it to produce true fruit.** Then He gives us another sentence to think about:

> *As the Father has loved me, so have I loved you. Now remain in my love.* —John 15:9

What does it mean to "remain in Christ," or "abide in Christ?" The meaning is obviously closely linked to "love."

- It means to continue to dwell and to celebrate and to live in His love, experiencing it fully day by day, moment by moment.

- It means to rejoice in the reality of God and in His unconditional acceptance.

- It means to engage in what delights the Lover by letting His passion become ours.

- It doesn't just mean to believe in Jesus; it means to *live in union* with Him.

In the end, it means we have the opportunity to trust in Him even when everything else seems to be falling apart around us in a heap of confusion. Tough times at work? Family difficulties? Financial struggles? **When we abide in Christ and remain in His love, knowing that God is real and that His love is real—and that we can actually dwell in that love—our problems don't magically disappear, but the confusion in our heart can.**

Dear Jesus, I want to remain in Your love in a way that puts everything else in perspective. I take the challenges that I am facing this week, and I ask You to help me see them through Your lenses. Amen!

Choosing Your Vine

We move about the earth with unprecedented speed, but we do not know, and have not thought, where we are going, or whether we shall find any happiness there for our harassed souls. —William Durant, 1929

When we come to Jesus and find our rest in Him, our burdened souls are lifted. I think the real challenge is getting *to* that point. It's so easy to place our hope in so many other things. We can tell we are abiding in other things when those things fail us. In those moments of personal revelation, **we have a choice: Will we choose to abide in Christ? Or will we become angry and embittered by the failure of things that were never designed to meet those core needs in the first place?**

When our spouse doesn't love us the way we thought our spouse was going to love us and we are disappointed in the lack of love we find there, what do we do? We leave it to Jesus Christ, we abide and we rest in His love! We find our needs met there, regardless of what our spouse does. When our teenagers start to go off the wall, running in every direction except the one we're pointing them toward, what do we do? We trust in Jesus' love, we rest there. When we're teenagers and our parents are turning up the screws and they just don't get it, what do we do? We rest in Jesus' love! We abide there, moment by moment, day by day.

The list could go on and on. **Because it's not just people that fail us, it's money, entertainment, our health, etc. etc. etc. But the pattern remains the same.** Anytime we face difficulty we have the choice to either become embittered or to embrace our relationship with Christ and remain in Him and His love to bring peace to our souls.

Jesus, You are the true vine. Give me the wisdom to quickly see when I am trusting in anything other than You. Give me the willingness to readjust my focus quickly away from the things that are doomed to fail me. By faith and the truth of Your Word, draw me into an intimate personal relationship with You so I can find rest and peace for my soul. Amen.

How to Give Up Doing Anything on Your Own

There are three ways to get something done: do it yourself, hire someone, or forbid your kids to do it. —**Unknown**

When Jesus said, *"Apart from me you can do nothing,"* He clearly didn't mean that we can't do *anything.* Obviously there are things we can do. We can drive a car, we can go to work, we can pay our mortgage—we *can* do things. What He is saying is, "If you're going to do something of eternal significance—if you want to make a difference in people's lives, if you want to bear real spiritual fruit that matters eternally—apart from Me you can't do any of that. You cannot create true fruit in the power of the flesh."

If we choose not to remain in His love, if we choose not to abide in Him, not to allow His power to work through us, we're just like a branch that's not even connected. There's no difference. **Why would we even want to live that way?** (Well, *pride* for starters, but let's just pretend that was a rhetorical question.)

The point is this. We were designed to "remain" in Christ and in His love for us, dependent on Him to live His life through us.

> *This is to my Father's glory, that you bear much fruit, showing yourselves to be my disciples.*

What happens when we bear fruit? Two things:

1. **We show ourselves to be disciples.** The true fruit of the Spirit makes it obvious that we really are disciples—because only He can bear this kind of fruit. If it's borne, then it's obvious He did it through us, and we're disciples.

2. **The Father gets the glory.** And there is something that is just so right about that. It's like everything falls into its proper place when people look past us and praise God from whom anything good flows.

Jesus, I know there are a whole lot of things that I can do outside of You. But I can't do anything that's going to matter in eternity unless I rest in You. I surrender it all to You right now. Teach me to become more and more dependent on You. Thanks!

A Reality Check for You

The unexamined life is not worth living. —Socrates

Everyone knows that things aren't always what they appear to be. But I'm pretty sure the original disciples were pretty shocked by the betrayal of Judas, even though there is no place where you see him bearing any fruit at all. When he does come to the forefront of the action, he's complaining about spending too much money on perfume for Jesus, etc. But even those who lived with him for years were stunned when he walked away from the Last Supper to commit treason against Jesus. **This means you can hang around with disciples for a long time, and not truly be one yourself.** In Matthew 7:20-23, Jesus gives very clear warning about this:

> *By their fruit you will recognize them. "Not everyone who says to me 'Lord, Lord,' will enter the kingdom of heaven, but only the one who does the will of my Father who is in heaven. Many will say to me on that day, 'Lord, Lord, did we not prophesy in your name, and in your name drive out demons and perform many miracles?' Then I will tell them plainly, 'I never knew you. Away from me, you evildoers!'"*

What He is pointing out is that there are some people who kind of look like they're in Him, but they're not really! They look like a disciple, they're going through the motions, they're doing all the things that disciples do, but they don't really know Him and aren't producing the true fruit that comes from remaining in the true vine. And the eternal consequence? *"He cuts off every branch in me that bears no fruit."*

Sobering.

If the life of Christ is in a believer, fruit and growth are inevitable—that naturally happens. The *lack* of true fruit is one possible indicator of the *lack* of the life of Jesus. But just because there appears to be fruit in our lives doesn't mean that it's true fruit either. **The only true test is a self-test, where we look deep into our own hearts and ask the questions: Have I really become a branch on the true vine? Am I resting in Him? Does His love abide in me?**

Father, thank You for forgiving me of all my shortcomings and the things that I do and think that are wrong. Thanks for taking the punishment for these things to the cross. I sense You calling me into an intimate, abiding, "remaining" relationship with You. Only You can do this. Please come in and create that kind of relationship between us. With eternal thanks, Your child.

Are You Clouding the Issue?

We must try to speak of his love. All Christians have tried, but none has ever done it very well. I can no more do justice to that awesome and wonder-filled theme than a child can grasp a star. Still… as I stretch my heart toward the high, shining love of God, someone who has not before known about it may be encouraged to look up and have hope. —A. W. Tozer

Disobedience tends to cloud the experience of His love for us. I've seen this many times.

My wife was talking with a friend who was living in disobedience. The friend was complaining that she hadn't sensed God's love lately. Libby looked her in the eye and spoke truth, "The problem is you're living as though you're separate." **The fact was that she was a believer in Jesus Christ, she** *was* **in union with Christ,** *but she was living as though she wasn't.* She was living as though He didn't matter (even though He always does). She was living as though she was separate, but she wasn't (God's presence in her and around her never changed). So as a result, there was all this discord in her soul. She couldn't sense the love of Christ. Ponder Jesus' words again from John 15:9-10:

> *As the Father has loved me, so I have loved you. Now remain in my love. If you obey my commands, you will remain in my love, just as I have obeyed my Father's commands and remain in His love.*

This is important stuff—not just in what it does say, but in what it doesn't say. Jesus is *not* saying that obedience is necessary to earn God's love, OR to retain it. That is contra-biblical. What He is saying here is this: **As the Son, I experience the Father's love in its fullness as I walk in natural obedience. As you walk in obedience, you too will experience My love in its fullness.**

Because, you see, disobedience tends to cloud the experience of His love for us.

Lord, I would really like to experience Your love more and more. Show me the disobedience that might be clouding that experience. I surrender that disobedience to You and claim full dependence on You to motivate and empower me today. In Your strength, Amen.

Getting the Full Picture of God's Grace

If you do not raise your eyes, you will think you are the highest point.
—Antonio Porchia

I was taking a walk with my daughter at a camp some years ago—through the woods, down into the river, and up the cliffs—great father-daughter moments. But as we were heading back towards the camp, we came to a fork in the trail with a sign pointing in different directions. One was the "easy" way back to camp. The other pointed to "Classmen Falls." By the looks of the trail, it was clearly the "road less traveled." We took it.

We were pushing brush away when all a sudden I could hear the falls in the distance, and then it hit me; we were not headed for the lake at the bottom of the falls (as we had the day before). We were headed for the top of the falls. What a spectacular view it was from up there—completely different from down on the bottom. We looked down into the crystal clear water. We could see large fish swimming in the blue water. We could see people wading and wandering. We could take in the expanse of the cliffs all around. Everything looked different in the camp below … in fact, I would never see that camp quite the same again.

Perspective matters. From up top, we got the "full picture" and it made all the difference in the experience.

Same goes for our walk with Christ.

In order to get the full picture of God's grace and what it means to be "in Christ," we need to get above and take a look down from God's perspective, from the top of the waterfall.

Jesus, take me on the path less traveled! Give me the full picture and the full story of what it means to be in You. Lord, I know that my perspective is limited and narrow. Broaden that perspective so that I might have a deeper understanding and appreciation for who I am, who You are, and the unity that we have in You. Amen.

Your Role in the Great Story

God created man because He loves good stories. —Elie Wiesel

Good stories. We love them. We watch them. We read about them. And we are *living* them. Almost all good stories follow a pattern.

- First, everything starts out **ideal** and happy.

- Second, a **crisis** emerges or explodes—something terrible that destroys the ideal with serious consequences.

- Then, the **hero** arrives and sacrificially intervenes to fix the problem and clean up the mess.

- Finally, the story ends with some form of **restoration**. Though the world might never be the same, and consequences remain, good stories generally end well—some sort of "happily ever after."

By understanding the pattern of a good story, we can easily see that we are living in the midst of something epic—the *Great* Story—the story of Eden and Satan and Jesus and us and Heaven. **As you read through the Bible, you will see that outline laid out for you—and we are still right in the middle of it—one big story being lived out in a thousand little stories day by day.**

> *For it is God who works in you to will and to act in order to fulfill his good purpose.* —Philippians 2:13

- What roles are you playing in this Great Story?

- If you had a clearer, big-picture perspective of the Great Story, would that affect the roles you play?

Holy Spirit, I want to live out my role in the Great Story! I believe that You live in me. I believe You are at work in me according to God's good purposes. Quiet my mind so that I can sense Your leading as You direct me and empower me to live out the roles that You have prepared for me today. Amen.

Getting a Glimpse of God's Holiness

Greedily she engorged without restraint, And knew not eating death.
—John Milton, *Paradise Lost*

You have to admit, the Bible starts out pretty darn sweet. In a flash, God creates everything from nothing. It's so good that He calls it, well, "good." After He creates a man and a woman to live in it, He actually calls it "very good." In short, there was God, His perfect world, and a man and woman walking together with Him in perfect unity.

This was Eden.

It lasted for a good three pages.

When the man and woman chose to doubt what God said and chose instead to believe the deception of the serpent, this perfect world was thrown into complete crisis. Adam and Eve were cast out of the garden. One of their sons murdered their other son. Insurance rates went way up. The stock market crashed. The consequences were all over the place—and all of these consequences emerged from one central, fundamental problem:

> *Surely the arm of the Lord is not too short to save, nor his ear too dull to hear. But your iniquities have separated you from your God; your sins have hidden his face from you, so that he will not hear. For your hands are stained with blood, your fingers with guilt. Your lips have spoken lies, and your tongue mutters wicked things.* —Isaiah 59:1-3

This, indeed, is the central crisis of the Great Story: **A perfect and holy Creator is separated from the creatures He loves because of their choice to live independently of Him, because of the barrier of sin between them.**

Have you recently pondered the full consequences of sin separating humans from our holy God?

Jesus, by the power of Your Spirit and the description of Your Holy Word, allow me to imagine the great gulf that existed between You and me before my redemption. Give me a glimpse of Your staggering holiness. Give me this bigger picture so that I can more fully celebrate the incredible things that You accomplished on the cross. Amen!

Don't Miss the Big Picture

Only he who knows the greatness of wrath will be mastered by the greatness of mercy. —Gustav Stahlin

Without the big picture view of human history, we can lose perspective on some of the most important elements of the Great Story. If you've ever walked into the middle of a movie, you know what I mean. It's hard to make sense of the middle and end of the story if you don't know how it began.

It's like that with our Christian faith as well. If we don't understand what life was like before Christ and before the cross, we don't get the full picture of God's character and don't get an appreciation of who we are in Christ.

The problem is, of course, that we don't view sin the way God does. In fact, some of us, if we were really honest, would say, "I'm not even sure that God is a 'wrathful' God. I think He is a God of love, I think He will be nice to everyone in the end." **Many of us don't really believe in God's righteous wrath and only see Him as our "buddy pal."**

The Old Testament prophets knew better.

The prophet Isaiah was blown away when he was given a vision of the glory of God. How did he respond?

> *"Woe to me!" I cried. "I am ruined! For I am a man of unclean lips, and I live among a people of unclean lips, and my eyes have seen the King, the Lord Almighty."* —Isaiah 6:5

We lose that perspective if we don't look at sin the way God does. A biblical view of depravity gives us a much greater appreciation for the love of God and the cleansing forgiveness that we have in Christ. (By the way, it's well worth it to read *all* of Isaiah 6 to get more of that perspective.) **Can God be fully loving and fully wrathful at the same time? Absolutely. But if we lose perspective on either of these aspects of His character, we miss the big picture of the Great Story.**

Holy Father, apart from what You did through Christ on the cross, I would still be a person of unclean lips, ruined, living among unclean people. Thank You, thank You that I am now in Christ—forgiven, cleansed by His blood, accepted by You as an heir and a child! What can I do except raise my voice in praise to You for what You have done for me? Amen.

Who You Are and Would Have Been

It is partly because sin does not provoke our own wrath that we do not believe that sin provokes the wrath of God. —R. W. Dale

The Bible and life are filled with stunning contrasts. We need those contrasts to put things in perspective. What's one of the most important contrasts? It's the contrast between what life looks like when we are "in Christ" and what life looks like for someone who is "out of Christ." (I just made that phrase up. Don't go looking for it in your concordance!)

Without that contrast we lose the "full picture"—we lose perspective on the Great Story of the Gospel we are living in. When that happens, **we lose the reference point for our true identity in Christ as we forget who we would have been apart from Him:**

> *There is no one righteous, not even one, there is no one who understands, no one who seeks God. All have turned away, they have together become worthless; there is no one who does good, not even one. Their throats are open graves; their tongues practice deceit. The poison of vipers is on their lips. Their mouths are full of cursing and bitterness. Their feet are swift to shed blood; ruin and misery mark their ways, and the way of peace they don't know. There is no fear of God before their eyes.* —Romans 3:10-18

Let's be clear about this: Someone who is "out of Christ" is also out of luck. It's **the crisis:** There is simply no way that a holy and just God could have fellowship with someone like that. Be eternally thankful that the story doesn't end there!

> *But because of his great love for us, God, who is rich in mercy, made us alive with Christ even when we were dead in transgressions—it is by grace you have been saved.* —Ephesians 2:4-5

Righteous Father, may the contrast between these two passages soak deep into my soul ... and then may the truth of who I am in Christ leak out into my life. Amen.

Do You See the Crisis?

I tell you, brethren, if mercies and if judgments do not convert you, God has no other arrows in His quiver. —Robert Murray M'Cheyne

God has put us in the middle of an amazing story—the Great Story of His mercy and wrath unfolding in history. **But do we "get it?" I mean, do we really see the intensity of the drama and the true implications of the crisis between our sin and His holiness?** The more clearly we see the crisis, the more accurately we will see ourselves without Christ and in Christ.

The Old Testament prophet Ezekiel was given a glimpse of his sin in the light of God … and it blew him away. God gave him a vision full of windstorms and lightning and even a fire that looked like it was full of glowing metal. He did not even see the Lord. He did not even see the glory of the Lord. He did not even see the likeness of the glory of the Lord. **He just saw "the *appearance* of the *likeness* of the *glory* of the Lord" (Ezekiel 1:28). How did he respond? Bam! He fell flat on his face.**

The same thing happened to Daniel. God gave him a vision and …

> *I had no strength left, my face turned deathly pale and I was helpless … my face to the ground … A hand touched me and set me trembling on my hands and knees.* —Daniel 10:8-10

I think this part of the story gets left out way too much. And that's tragic. **You will never run to mercy until you really come to grips with the wrath of God and His fierce opposition to sin.**

Wrathful and Gracious, Just and Forgiving God, thank You for Your perfect justice. In a world devoid of it, it is so comforting to know You have Your eye on the cruelty and injustice in our world. Thank You also for Your mercy, granted freely to us in Christ, so we might escape the ultimate consequence of our sin and rest in You! Amen!

Closing the Distance Between You and God

Such is the mercy of God that he will hold his children in the consuming fire of his distance until they pay the utmost farthing, until they drop the purse of selfishness with all the dross that is in it, and rush home to the Father and to the Son and the brethren—rush inside the life-giving Fire whose outer circle burns.
—George MacDonald

Sin separates. The cross closes the gap.

The separation caused by sin is *haunting*, actually. We were created for the very purpose of being in intimate union with God. Yet over and over again, *distance* was used as a symbol of God's transcendence for those who were not in Christ. God was not only high above us, our sin kept us away from Him.

> *I saw the Lord, high and exalted, seated on a throne; and the train of his robe filled the temple.* —Isaiah 6:1

> *Keep a distance of about two thousand cubits between you and the ark; do not go near it.* —Joshua 3:4

> *Put limits for the people around the mountain and tell them, "Be careful that you do not approach the mountain or touch the foot of it. Whoever touches the mountain is to be put to death."* —Exodus 19:12

That seems really harsh. **It was actually merciful. God kept a distance because He knew anything that is unholy that comes in contact with Him is obliterated instantly.** His wrath is indiscriminate. If there is sin, it is destroyed. Period.

Praise God that for those who are "in Christ," the distance is closed by the cross!

> *For by one sacrifice he has made perfect forever those who are being made holy. … **let us draw near to God with a sincere heart and with the full assurance that faith brings,** having our hearts sprinkled to cleanse us from a guilty conscience and having our bodies washed with pure water. Let us hold unswervingly to the hope we profess, for he who promised is faithful.*
> —Hebrews 10:14, 22-23

O Lord, help me to measure the full distance of sin's separation, that I might be astounded by the fact that I have "drawn near" to You and You have pulled me so close to You—so close that Your Spirit actually lives in me! Amen.

Can You Face the Light?

The vague and tenuous hope that God is too kind to punish the ungodly has become a deadly opiate for the consciences of millions. —A. W. Tozer

It happens every year at camp. At the evening campfire, there is some little girl who has the newest, brightest turbo-charged flashlight. It's got like a car battery on the back of it, a big huge bulb, and a beam that rivals the Star Wars Death Star. The problem is that she thinks it's funny to shine that thing in your eyes. BA-ZAAAP! It actually *hurts;* melting your corneas and cooking your retinas—just like 1 Timothy 6:15-16 (seriously!):

> *God, the blessed and only Ruler, the King of kings and Lord of lords, who alone is immortal and who lives in unapproachable light, whom no one has seen or can see. To him be the honor and might forever.*

God is Light, but there are places in Scripture where it tells us that He is a *blinding* light. That's the image here in 1 Timothy. God is holy and, before we knew Him, we were not! Some people hope that God is *only* kind, and will not punish. **But the fact is *you couldn't approach Him because of sin*.** When the light comes on, BA-ZAAAP! You *must* turn away …

… unless you are "in Christ."

This critical aspect of your new identity makes *all* the difference.

> *Let us then **approach God's throne of grace with confidence,** so that we may receive mercy and find grace to help us in our time of need.* —Hebrews 4:16

We can approach a perfectly holy God with confidence?! Yes. In Christ we can embrace the Light!

Holy Father, I thank You from the depths of my heart for what You did through Christ so that we can approach You with confidence. I fully recognize that it is only through Your amazing grace (and not by anything I have done), that this is possible. I praise You! Amen.

Can You Take the Heat?

The quality of mercy is not strain'd, it droppeth as the gentle rain from heaven upon the place beneath. It is twice blest: it blesseth him that gives and him that takes. —William Shakespeare

Back at camp, we were cooking some s'mores around the campfire. We had the graham crackers, the chocolate all ready to go and the marshmallows on the stick. Just one problem: The fire was too hot. The little girls tried to roast their marshmallows, but had to turn away before they could get close enough. So it was the dads' chance to prove their masculinity. As the fire got bigger and bigger, the hair on our arms and eyelids got shorter and shorter. We all just kept backing farther and farther away, unable to stand near the fire's presence, risking getting consumed if we got too close.

> *Therefore, since we are receiving a kingdom that cannot be shaken, let us be thankful, and so worship God acceptably with reverence and awe, for our "God is a consuming fire."* —Hebrews 12:28-29

God's wrath makes His grace and mercy all the more stunning. **Knowing that God is both wrathful and loving empowers our worship with reverence and awe.** Then we can look into the growing flames with praise and thanksgiving for Christ and who we are in Him.

Consuming Fire, I praise You that "there is no condemnation for those who are in Christ Jesus" (Romans 8:1). I thank You that "Christ ... suffered once for sins, the righteous for the unrighteous" (1 Peter 3:18) so that He could bring me to You without getting burned! Amen.

Your Identity and His Wrath

Wrath: God's personal, divine, repulsion to evil, and His personal vigorous opposition to it. —Leon Morris

With enough negativity bombarding us every day, **why talk about God's wrath when talking about our identity in Christ?**

- Because it gives us the fuller picture from God's higher perspective.

- Because it gives us a more authentic appreciation for what He did on the cross.

- Because the Great Story of God's unconditional love and forgiveness really doesn't make any sense without it!

- Because we need to feel that wrath in some way in order to grasp the extreme reconciliation we have in Christ.

The righteous wrath of God is not a "downer." It's the perspective that makes the mercy and grace and love and forgiveness have vivid, real-life meaning! **Understanding the wrath we have been spared because of Christ makes the gift of forgiveness all the sweeter!**

It's the view from the top of the waterfall. It gives us the full, beautiful context of the Great Story we are a part of.

God of Grace, thank You for Your Word. Thank You for the full picture it gives. Give me the fuller view of Your wrath so that I can more fully celebrate Your graciousness. Thank You for making me a part of the Great Story of Life! Amen.

Enter the Hero

It's just another war, just another family torn … My voice will be heard today … It's just another war … The countdown begins to destroy ourselves, I need a hero to save me now —Skillet

Every story needs a hero. Just when everything seems lost and there is nothing left to do about it, hope and help comes from the hero just at the right time. The story of humanity began in the ideal of Eden, dissolving into the cataclysmic consequences of sin—the great crisis that sent shockwaves through our world and through our personal lives every day. **And since we are living in the Great Story, we need a Great Hero.** We need a hero to save us now.

Who is the hero? JESUS! He is the only one with the qualifications to pull it off. Fully, absolutely, categorically God! Fully, absolutely, categorically man. He lived on this earth, a perfect sinless life, and He came for a reason:

> *You see, at just the right time, when we were still powerless, Christ died for the ungodly. Very rarely will anyone die for a righteous person, though for a good person someone might possibly dare to die. But God demonstrates his own love for us in this: While we were still sinners, Christ died for us.* —Romans 5:6-8

Make no mistake! This is the absolute climax of the story of humanity. **At "just the right time," Christ made the ultimate sacrifice for the powerless sinner.** The reason He came was to deal with the crisis, to fix it! But not just to fix it in a general theological way, or a political way … He came to fix it in a *personal* way. God in the flesh, personally putting it all on the line for you and for me.

That's the climax of the Great Story.

Are you in it?

Father, some of us have heard this story for as long as we can remember. For some of us it is brand new. I pray that You will make the story come alive to me today in all its power and all its glory. By the power of Your Spirit, open the eyes of my heart so that I can vividly see what You did for me—what You are still doing for me—so that I can embrace You as my full-on hero! Amen.

Your Crisis, His Solutions

God will not overcome evil by crushing it under-foot—any god of man's idea could do that—but by conquest of heart over heart, of life over life, of life over death, of love over all. —George MacDonald

Heroes respond to needs. They see the crisis and take action. Jesus took radical action! He spanned the gap of eternity to enter our world and then gave it all. Why? There are at least three good reasons, all wrapped up in the crisis called "sin."

1. **Because of God's justice, our sins required forgiveness.** He couldn't just say, "Well, never mind! I love you, so I won't worry about your sins." He is just! He is perfectly just so He can't do that! We couldn't forgive ourselves, so He had to come up with a way to forgive us!

2. **Because we were dead in sin, we needed Jesus to provide life for us.** We could not provide life for ourselves because, well, we were dead.

3. **Because of our rebellion, our relationship with God the Father required restoration.** We couldn't restore it, because we were dead in our sins, but Jesus could, and He came to bring us back together.

The most heroic act in history took place one day on a cross in Jerusalem. There Jesus voluntarily submitted Himself and substituted Himself for us.

> *For Christ also suffered once for sins, the righteous for the unrighteous, to bring you to God.* —1 Peter 3:18

That's worth pondering for a moment, isn't it? This is the new view from above. **The wrath of God has been satisfied by the sacrifice of God so that we can experience the intimacy of God.**

Dear Jesus, thank You for responding to my deepest needs! You have given me forgiveness, Life, and relationship with the Father. Let those truths be my rest. Amen.

Your Personal Hero

Christ is the Son of God. He died to atone for men's sin, and after three days rose again. This is the most important fact in the universe. I die believing in Christ.
—**Watchman Nee** *(note found under his pillow, in prison, at his death)*

War stories are filled with heroes—men and women who put themselves on the line for the good of others, sometimes using their own bodies to protect someone else. That's what Jesus did for you.

When coming to our rescue in the depths of humanity's greatest crisis, **Jesus "took the hit" for us. Separated from God by sin, He paid the ultimate price to purchase a restored intimacy with the Father.**

> *This is love: not that we loved God, but that he loved us and sent his Son as an atoning sacrifice for our sins.* —1 John 4:10

When Jesus was hanging on the cross—perfect and sinless—at a certain moment in time, God poured the sins of every single person who ever lived—past, present, future—all of our sins, into Christ. Not only did He receive all of our sins, but God's wrath, because of those sins, was poured out on Christ, too. So, we can understand why Jesus, hanging there, said,

> *"Eli, Eli, lema sabachthani?" (which means "My God, my God, why have you forsaken me?").* —Matthew 27:46

In that moment, Jesus experienced the consequences of sin for all humanity. **The separation caused by our sin—by your sin—came between Jesus and the Father. Your personal Hero intervened.** He took your sins to the cross, and He received the wrath that you deserved. Thus, you don't have to carry your sin anymore, and you have escaped the wrath that you deserve.

Jesus, I only ask today that You would somehow take the cross and all You accomplished there and make it real in my heart and in my mind. It makes sense in theory. Help me to envision it as true so that I experience it as my reality. Amen.

Giving Credit Where Credit Is Undue

Learn to know Christ and him crucified. Learn to sing to him, and say, 'Lord Jesus, you are my righteousness, I am your sin. You have taken upon yourself what is mine and given me what is yours. You have become what you were not so that I might become what I was not.' —Martin Luther

The sacrifice of Jesus Christ on the cross gave us things that are, truly, too great to fully understand. **Throughout the Great Story of human history, some very important things were "imputed"**—that is, they were credited and passed on to someone else. Yes, hard to understand; yet by the counsel of the Holy Spirit, we can understand these things through faith:

1. When Adam sinned in the garden, his sins were credited to you and me, because we are Adam's seed. So we wake up as a baby in this world "in Adam," and his sin is on our record, and then we add to it profusely.

2. When our sins were placed on Jesus on the cross, they are credited to Him and He died with them there.

3. When we put our trust in Jesus Christ, our sins are not only erased from the record forever, but we become "in Christ," and His righteousness is credited to us.

Simply put, God is offering you a deal through Christ:

- **He gets your sin.**
- **You get His righteousness.**

> *God made him who had no sin to be sin for us, so that in him we might become the righteousness of God.* —2 Corinthians 5:21

That, my friends, is the best deal that could ever be offered! I would encourage you to seize this immediately if you have yet to do so, because you will never hear a better one.

Dearest Jesus, I have done nothing to deserve what You are crediting to me. You take my sin. I am taking Your righteousness—I have become the righteousness of God. Enable me to begin living the Truth of this great mystery! Amen.

The Hero Inside You

The legacy of heroes is the memory of a great name and the inheritance of a great example. Nurture your mind with great thoughts; to believe in the heroic makes heroes. —Benjamin Disraeli, British Prime Minister and Novelist (1804-1881)

Not only does each of us need a hero, but let's be honest, each of us wants to be a hero. Deep down inside there's that desire to be looked up to, to be appreciated, and to give our lives for something that truly matters.

If you search for quotes about being a "hero," you'll find tons of stuff, including this by Will Rodgers: *"Being a hero is about the shortest-lived profession on earth."*

And then there is this chorus to the song *Hero*, sung by Mariah Carey:

There's a hero
If you look inside your heart
You don't have to be afraid
Of what you are.

Okay, I have no idea where Mariah is coming from with this. But if, by chance, she's talking about being "in Christ," then this song nails it! (On the other hand, if someone tries to be a hero *outside* of Christ, then they *should* be afraid!). The foundational verse about our identity simply cannot be overemphasized:

> *I have been crucified with Christ and I no longer live, but Christ lives in me.* —Galatians 2:20

This is certainly one of the powerful mysteries of the faith, but it's so practical. In some supernatural way, we were crucified, dead and buried in Christ, and then raised to new life in Him. In Romans 6 and 7, Paul expounds on this: **Not only did Jesus take our sins to the cross, He also crucified our "old man" (our old, sinful nature).**

Then Romans 8 tells us that the risen Christ indwells us by the Spirit and changes us from the inside out. **He is waiting to live heroic deeds through you in a world that needs Him.** Study His life well. What kind of hero was He? What are the possibilities?

Jesus, I am no hero, but I believe that You, the True and Great Hero, live in me. Give me ears to hear and eyes to see what heroic deeds You want to accomplish through me today. I can't do it. You can. Do it, Lord. Amen.

Your Internal Renewal

I saw that the kingdom must be interior before it can be exterior, that it is a kingdom of ideas, and not one of brute force; that His rule is over hearts, not over places; that His victories must be inward before they can be outward; that He seeks to control spirits rather than bodies; that no triumph could satisfy Him but a triumph that gains the heart; that in short, where God really reigns, the surrender must be the interior surrender of the convicted free men, and not merely the outward surrender of the conquered slave. —Hannah Whitall Smith

We are living in a very interesting chapter of the "Great Story" of human history. **Eden** is in the past. The great **crisis** emerged because sin separated humanity from a righteous and Holy God. Then came the **climax** of the cross were Jesus Christ heroically sacrificed Himself so that we might have unity and intimacy with our Creator one more time.

Is that the end of it? Not at all. Christ will return again and human history, as we know it on Earth, will end as the full-blown Kingdom of God is reestablished throughout the universe 100%.

But we are not there yet. We are living in the "already, but not yet," a finite season where the Spirit of God is renewing the spirits of men and women who draw near to Him in faith—from the inside out—setting the stage for His physical return. Story writers call it the **restoration**.

> *Therefore we do not lose heart. Though outwardly we are wasting away, yet inwardly we are being renewed day by day. For our light and momentary troubles are achieving for us an eternal glory that far outweighs them all. So we fix our eyes not on what is seen, but on what is unseen. For what is seen is temporary, but what is unseen is eternal.* —2 Corinthians 4:16-18

How is your heart today? Are you worried about exterior concerns or are you experiencing the peace of inner renewal?

Heavenly Father, give me eyes to see the unseen, so that I might walk by faith in a decaying body through a world that is going from bad to worse. Open up Your Word to my mind that I might be able to embrace this season of in-betweenness and celebrate what You have done in me through Christ. Amen.

Realizing Your Union with Christ

Union with Christ is really the central truth of the whole doctrine of salvation not only in its application but also in its once-for-all accomplishment in the finished work of Christ. —John Murray

In Revelation 1:17, when the apostle John was ushered into Heaven in the vision, he found himself in the presence of the Almighty One, and fell at His feet as though dead! All great people, when they came in contact with the Holy God, fell on their face—the holiness of God blew them away. They knew that *in and of themselves,* they were toast because of their sin.

But get this: **At the moment in time, when you said, "Jesus, I trust in You for salvation," God instantly began to see you in a completely different way.** Now, when God the Father looks at you, He sees the cross in front of you. It doesn't matter what you did today, either good or bad. What He sees is Christ and His righteousness in you.

> *We have been made holy through the sacrifice of the body of Jesus Christ once for all.* —Hebrews 10:10

> *Therefore, there is now no condemnation for those who are in Christ Jesus.* —Romans 8:1

Please, believe this, because God means what He says! You have been made holy. You are not condemned. This is the key to experiencing Life in this season of "already, but not yet" and renewal. You will not be condemned by God for anything that you do because all your sins are covered. When He looks at you, He sees Christ!

Do you see yourself that way too?

Jesus, renew my mind. By the counsel of Your Spirit in me, conform my thoughts to the truth of who I am in You because of the cross. I deeply desire to live as a restored, renewed child of Yours in unity. Give me the willingness and ability to believe! Amen.

Your Sins Are Yesterday's News in Christ

It is not thy hold on Christ that saves thee; it is Christ. It is not thy joy in Christ that saves thee; it is Christ. It is not even thy faith in Christ, though that be the instrument; it is Christ's blood and merit. —Charles Haddon Spurgeon

In the ancient days, there was a table in the town square. On the table they would put a very thin layer of wax—and this was their newspaper! The sun would rise in the morning, heating the wax until it become soft. Then, someone who had good handwriting would write the news of the day in the wax, and when the sun went behind the buildings and the shade came, the wax would harden and everyone would walk by and read the news of the day. The next morning the sun would rise again, and the wax would heat up again. Then, the writer would take something like a flat spreader, smooth out the news of yesterday, and it would disappear in the wax.

That motion of smoothing out yesterday's news is the same word that David uses in Psalm 32 and can be translated "covered." Paul expounds on that passage in Romans 4:5-8:

> *However, to the man who does not work but trusts God who justifies the wicked, his faith is credited as righteousness. David says the same thing when he speaks of the blessedness of the man to whom God credits righteousness apart from works:*
>
> *Blessed are those whose transgressions are forgiven, whose sins are covered. Blessed is the one whose sin the Lord will never count against them.*

"Blessed is he whose yesterday's news is wiped away." Paul says, "The same thing I'm saying here, David said centuries ago." **Can you see that as God sees it? Imagine, truly imagine, your sins written in that wax, smoothed over like yesterday's news by the nail-pierced hand of Christ.**

Jesus, You and You alone have restored me and are renewing me daily. Open the eyes of my heart so that I can see it—see the truth of what You have done and who I am in You. Amen.

You Are Double-Justified

Christ is at once the spotless descent of God into men and the sinless ascent of man into God, and the Holy Spirit is the Agent by whom this is accomplished.
—John G. Lake

The writers of Scripture used some pretty impressive words to describe powerful theological truths. One of those words is *justified*. I'm afraid the word has lost some of its punch over the years since it was first translated into English. Certainly, it has a lot more to do than whether your margins are smooth on the right or the left hand side of your page!

What does it mean to be *justified*?

A legal declaration that we are completely forgiven and no longer liable for punishment.

> *If, in fact, Abraham was justified by works, he had something to boast about—but not before God. What does the Scripture say? "Abraham believed God, and it was credited to him as righteousness." Now to the one who works, wages are not credited as a gift, but as an obligation. However, to the one who does not work but trusts God who justifies the ungodly, their faith is credited as righteousness.* —Romans 4:2-5

Wow, what a contrast with our experiences in the world, where we *rarely* experience any sort of affirmation outside of our fleshly efforts. But in Christ, God declares us righteous through our faith in what Jesus did, not because of our works. That is a huge, huge distinction. Do you see the *practical* difference for us?

We always have to keep our guard up and be on our best behavior in the world. But we can truly rest in Christ.

In your mind, do you make a clear distinction between how the world accepts you and how God justifies you?!

O Father, may I never seek forgiveness from You by my works. May I never try to be righteous through my own efforts. You have forgiven me fully and made me completely righteous in Christ! I stand aside and ask that You would naturally demonstrate that through me today. Amen.

Are You Writing a Better Story?

You can call it God or a conscience ... but there is a knowing I feel that guides me toward better stories, toward being a better character. I believe there is a writer outside ourselves, plotting a better story for us, interacting with us, even, and whispering a better story into our consciousness. —**Don Miller**

I've read a lot. Every once in a while, I come across a book that says something in such a way that I want to give it to my child and say "Wow, do you get this?!" These rare books change the angle from which I'm able to look at the Great Story of God and humanity through history. Don Miller's, *A Million Miles in a Thousand Years*, was one of those books—like standing on the top of a waterfall looking down—and yes, I gave it to my son.

Don proposes that not only is there a Great Story going on, but that we are living stories within that Story, and if we choose, we can write better stories—stories that shatter boredom, stories that matter, stories that will give us something to talk about with God in eternity. Paul would agree:

> *You yourselves are our letter, written on our hearts, known and read by everyone. You show that you are a letter from Christ, the result of our ministry, written not with ink but with the Spirit of the living God, not on tablets of stone but on tablets of human hearts. Such confidence we have through Christ before God. Not that we are competent in ourselves to claim anything for ourselves, but our competence comes from God.* —2 Corinthians 3:2-5

What kind of letter are you sending to the world? What kind of story are you writing?

Master Writer, during this chapter of renewal and restoration in the Great Story of Life, I surrender the story of my life to You. Make me a "letter from Christ ... written with the Spirit ... on the tablet of human hearts." I claim confidence and competence through Christ. Write what You wish; live it through me. Amen.

Nicodemus and You

I do not know what I may appear to the world, but to myself I seem to have been only like a boy playing on the seashore, and diverting myself in now and then finding a smoother pebble or a prettier shell than ordinary, whilst the great ocean of truth lay all undiscovered before me. —Isaac Newton

He came seeking truth. And he came at night. A member of the Jewish-ruling council—the Sanhedrin—an exclusive council that ruled the religious life in Jerusalem. He was in the "Who's Who" of the religious group in Jerusalem. Yet, there he was walking through the darkness seeking something from the homeless Galilean preacher known as a "friend of sinners":

> *Rabbi, we know that you are a teacher who has come from God. For no one could perform the signs you are doing if God were not with him.* —John 3:2

Jesus had just turned a whole bunch of water into wine at a marriage feast in Canaan and the news had gotten out. Nicodemus had come to Him for something—we never really find out what it was—perhaps a question? But leave it to Jesus to dispense with the pleasantries and get right to the answer:

> *Very truly I tell you, no one can see the kingdom of God unless they are born again.* —John 3:3

Interesting. I've read this passage many times, and preached it to people who are far, far from God, as well as people who have no interest in God. But Jesus wasn't speaking to one of those; **He was speaking to a "mature" religious person.** (Perhaps someone like *you*? Or maybe *me*?) And still he came to Jesus seeking truth—and Jesus told him, "You must be born again." He says the same to any of us who come seeking.

Because, if you want to be in His Kingdom, you've got to start over.

Jesus, I pray simply that Your Spirit will speak boldly and clearly. You said that I must be born again to see Your Kingdom. Use Your Word as a double-edged sword in the power of the Spirit to allow me to explore the great ocean of truth beneath these words. Amen.

Beyond Born-Again Babble

I gave in, and admitted that God was God, and knelt and prayed: perhaps, that night, the most dejected and reluctant convert in all England. —C.S. Lewis

In our culture today, the words "born again" are definitely a loaded phrase. Those two words have been politicized and socialized so much that to the outsider they are little more than a misunderstood cliché—a convenient label to categorize conservative Christians. If you can laugh at yourself a little, you might appreciate the irony and humor in these quotes:

> *The trouble with born again Christians is that they are an even bigger pain the second time around.* —Herb Caen

> *Why do born-again people so often make you wish they'd never been born the first time?* —Katherine Whitehorn

> *Making fun of born-again Christians is like hunting dairy cows with a high powered rifle and scope.* —P. J. O'Rourke

> *Born again?! No, I'm not. Excuse me for getting it right the first time.* —Dennis Miller

How about you? Are you embarrassed by the label? Is it just an adjective with fuzzy meaning? A cliché? Just remember that no matter what it means to those around us, Jesus said,

> *You **must** be born again.* —John 3:7

The fact is that this "born again" thing is not an option. It wasn't an option for C.S. Lewis who came "dejected and reluctant." It wasn't an option for the elite religious seekers in Jesus' day. It's not an option for the church-goer (or anyone) today. **It's a prerequisite for entering and seeing the Kingdom of God.**

Jesus, search my heart and show me my ways. Show me what I think and believe when I hear the words "born again." Don't let these words be a catch phrase, punch line, or cliché. Transform me by the renewing of my mind through the mystery and majesty of what this truly means! Amen.

Is It About Your Behavior or Your Being?

Hypocrisy desires to seem good rather than to be so; honesty desires to be good rather than seem so. —**Arthur Warwick**

When Jesus said that we must be "born again," He wasn't talking about a behavior change, or change of our political affiliation, or even believing in a certain creed or Statement of Faith. Human religion can be hypocrisy as people try to behave in ways that seem good. A lot of pretending going on. But Jesus certainly wasn't talking about any sort of behavior change that would make us "seem good." No, He was talking about something much deeper than that … something so deep, in fact, that it would transform the core of our entire *being*. It is a brand new beginning, a complete rebirth, the exchange of something new and alive for something old and dead.

Because of the sin of our ancestors, **when we are physically born the first time, we are born in sin**—spiritually dead and separated from God. "Flesh gives birth to flesh," Jesus said, BUT:

> *the Spirit gives birth to spirit. You should not be surprised at my saying, 'You must be born again.'* —John 3:6-7

Being born the second time is a supernatural, spiritual event. An internal, instantaneous, radical life transformation takes place in the inner core of who we are. The *pretending* ends. The *being* begins.

When you think of being born again, do you think about "behavior" or "being?"

Holy Spirit, slow my thoughts. Still my heart. Let this soak in. Only You can give birth and insight to my spirit, only You can illuminate the truth about my core being having been born again. I sincerely, humbly ask that You would do that now. I am listening. Amen.

Do You Take It Literally?

God's greatness flows around our incompleteness; Round our restlessness, his rest.
—Elizabeth Barrett Browning

The little phrase "born again" became really popular in the seventies. Jimmy Carter was our President, and he said, "I am born again." *Time* magazine published an article, "What Does it Mean to be Born Again?" People started getting "born again" all over the place, which I'm all for. I think it's great!

But then the term started to show up other places, and **it started to get watered down.** A movie star in Hollywood came out of drug rehab and they said his career was "born again." The people in Dallas started talking about the Mavericks being "born again!" (They were "dead" after losing their first two games at home, then they went down to Houston, and they won the next two.)

So after that, the phrase kind of lost its oomph. Now, it means all sorts of things. But remember, Nicodemus had never heard this phrase before. To him it was completely new, out-of-the-blue fresh! Naturally, he thought Jesus was talking about the physical, and so he asked the obvious question:

> *How can someone be born when they are old? … Surely they cannot enter a second time into their mother's womb to be born! Jesus answered, "Very truly, I tell you, no one can enter the kingdom of God unless they are born of water and the Spirit."* —John 3:4-5

But just because it's a spiritual birth doesn't mean it's any less real than a natural birth. Don't let the meaning of this get watered down! It's *super*natural—an event that will certainly prove to be real.

Even more importantly for today, believing in this transforming spiritual birth gives meaning to what it means to be "in Christ." Jesus wasn't talking about an actor's career or basketball team's record. He was talking about you and the actual spiritual birth that happened when the Spirit came into your spirit!

Lord, I don't want my belief in You to be symbolic or metaphorical. Open the eyes of my heart so that I can see the supernatural, super-real spiritual birth that took place when I was born again. Amen.

For Real

What the caterpillar calls the end, the rest of the world calls a butterfly.
—Lao Tzu

Dottie liked her drinks and she was at the end. Like so many others, she looked for the relief from life's problems at the bottom of an empty bottle. Of course, relief was always temporary. Drink after drink, the problems only intensified until the addiction could not be controlled. Her marriage was on the skids and life was coming apart at the seams. She had three beautiful children yet thought, *You know what? Maybe if we had another kid, our marriage will get better.* So they had a fourth child, a daughter. Bad idea. Their marriage got worse and worse. When the baby girl was about eight months old, they decided to separate and divorce.

For years Dottie tried to find truth. In college she studied all the great religions of the world. **Nothing resonated.** Shortly before the divorce was final, she was sitting on the porch of her empty house one quiet night. She turned on her old black-and-white TV and adjusted the bent coat-hanger antenna as she turned the channels. Click, click, click … She stopped when she heard the voice of a young man with a soft southern drawl speaking of new life, the "good news" that she could be "born again." **It resonated.**

That night, Dottie bowed her knee to Jesus Christ. That was more than forty years ago, but if you were to run into her today, you would swear she met Jesus yesterday. A life transformed from the inside out, she is a beautiful example to me of what it means to be "in Christ."

Are stories like this for real? All I can say is that this one sure is for me. Dottie became a new person in Christ and today she is one of my closest, most respected friends. Her marriage was given new life as well.

And their eight-month-old daughter? She grew and became my wife.

Jesus, I thank You that I am in You. Your Word says that if I am in You, I am a new creature, born again through the birth of my spirit through Your Spirit. I bend the knee to You now, surrendering all to You, releasing all to You, resting in You. I thank You for Your complete forgiveness and permanent presence. Live through me today to do what only You can do. Amen.

The Ultimate Do-Over

If you ever get a second chance in life for something, you've got to go all the way.
—Lance Armstrong

Remember when you were young and you were playing four-square or something like that? Someone hit the ball, you couldn't tell whether it was in or out, and you argued about it, and finally someone would say, "**Let's just do a do-over!**" It is as though the thing you just did never happened, and you get to do it all over again.

If we are born again, we are part of the ultimate "do-over" because we have been "regenerated." Yeah, I know that sounds really theological and deep, but it's really simple. The etymology of the word is this: The prefix *re-* means "to do something again;" *generate* means "to bring into existence." So put them together and "Presto!" You get a second beginning, new existence, an opportunity to do it over.

And that's a good thing, because the first go-around was a real mess:

> *At one time we too were foolish, disobedient, deceived and enslaved by all kinds of passions and pleasures. We lived in malice and envy, being hated and hating one another.* —Titus 3:3

Yeah, I would say we needed the "*ultimate* do-over!"

> *But when the kindness of God our Savior and His love for mankind appeared, He saved us, not on the basis of deeds which we have done in righteousness, but according to His mercy, by the washing of regeneration and renewing by the Holy Spirit, whom He poured out upon us richly through Jesus Christ our Savior, so that being justified by His grace we would be made heirs according to the hope of eternal life.* —Titus 3:4-7 (NASB)

Is there anything better than a second chance?

Jesus, thank You for a second chance. By the power of Your Spirit, by the truth of Your Word, I want to make the most of the regeneration I have been given through You. Let me live in the truth of this regeneration. Let me live as a new creation in You! Amen!

How Would You Answer?

Before I refuse to take your questions, I have an opening statement.
—**Ronald Reagan**

Life is filled with perplexing questions—heartrending unknowns that follow us through the day and keep us awake at night:

- Why do we drive on a parkway and park on a driveway?
- Why do they have braille numbers on *drive-through* ATMs?

And for the more theological types:

- What is the difference between "justification" and "regeneration?"

Regeneration is the Siamese twin of justification, and these particular Siamese twins are the kind you cannot separate. Both are inseparable aspects of salvation; neither can take place without the other.

- **Justification is God declaring us righteous and just.**
- **Regeneration is God making us righteous and just.**

Justification happens outside of us; regeneration happens inside of us. They are inexplicably bound together. God can justify us only because He regenerated us:

> *God made him who had no sin to be sin for us, so that in him we might become the righteousness of God.* —2 Corinthians 5:21

> *He saved us, not because of righteous things we had done, but because of his mercy. He saved us through the washing of rebirth and renewal by the Holy Spirit.* —Titus 3:5

Regeneration is the core of being born again. **We give to Christ who we are (spiritually dead, guilty sinners) and He gives us everything that He is (righteousness, eternity, Life).** What an incredible trade!

God, thank You for regenerating me and justifying me. I know that I don't comprehend the magnitude of this merciful gift. But I do ask that You would take this theology and make it my reality, that I would somehow be able to experience it today so that my worship would be a reflection of these truths. Amen.

Your Heart-Level Regeneration

Our Lord ... warned people to 'count the cost' before becoming Christians. 'Make no mistake,' He says, 'if you let Me, I will make you perfect. The moment you put yourself in My hands, that is what you are in for. Nothing less, or other than that. —C.S. Lewis

A doctor on television was comparing two actual sets of hearts and lungs. One set was full of disease from smoking and too much alcohol. Dark and hardened, you could see the disease and decay ... a striking contrast to the soft, pink healthy one next to it. The Bible pulls no punches when it speaks of the dark disease of the heart born in sin:

> *The heart is deceitful above all things and beyond cure. Who can understand it?* —Jeremiah 17:9

When we talk about "regeneration," we are talking about a new birth of our spiritual hearts that is even more radical than the contrast between these two physical hearts. We're not talking about heart surgery here—we're not talking about self-improvement. We are talking about a complete transplant of our innermost being. Hundreds of years before Jesus came to the earth, Ezekiel predicted it when he said:

> *I will give you a new heart and put a new spirit in you; I will remove from you your heart of stone and give you a heart of flesh.* —Ezekiel 36:26

He's not just fixing your heart or making it a little better. He's taking your hard heart *out*, and He's putting a completely new heart *in*. One author said it this way, "You will never have a changed life until you experience the ex-changed life." Regeneration causes a radical resurrection from the dead; a dead spirit coming alive for the first time.

Sure, we have other "issues" we battle (the world, our flesh, and Satan) but inside, where it really matters, God's regeneration by the Spirit through Jesus has given you a perfect, pure, healthy pink heart!

Great Physician, I have stuff that I need to let go of—external things that are not of You and pull me down. Give me the willingness to surrender those things to You. Give me the wisdom to let You live Your life through me from the inside out—from the new heart You have given me through regeneration. Amen!

The New You

If you have eternal life at all, it simply means that you have the Son, Jesus Christ now! ... Eternal life is not a peculiar feeling inside! It is not your ultimate destination, to which you will go when you are dead. If you are born again, eternal life is that quality of life that you possess right now, at this very moment, in your own physical body, with your own two feet on the ground, and in the world TODAY. And where does this life come from? Of Him! He is that life! So if you have eternal life, it means that you have Somebody, Jesus Christ, and the life that you possess is of Him. —**Major Ian Thomas**

Ian Thomas had a big influence in my dad's life, and my dad had (and has!) a huge influence on mine. By challenging common Christian misunderstandings about life as a believer, they have been used to show many a new and different way to live: By letting the life of Christ live through them NOW.

When you were physically born, it was a one-time event—a birth date that you celebrate every year. **The same is true of your spiritual birthday—the day when the Spirit of God gave birth to your spirit (John 3:6). There's only one. It happens once, instantaneously, internally, supernaturally, and dramatically.** You can celebrate it the rest of your life, but it only happens once! At the beginning of this new life is what we call "regeneration," the mercy of God making you righteous and just through the sacrifice of Jesus.

> *Therefore, if anyone is in Christ, the new creation has come: The old has gone, the new is here!* —2 Corinthians 5:17

You may not always feel like it, you may not even act like it, but it's true TODAY, NOW!

Eternal Father, I believe, but help my unbelief today. My feelings and my actions don't always reflect what is true about who I am in Your Son. Please begin to live Your eternal life through me right now. No way I can do this on my own. I quit and ask that You would do it. Make the one-time birth of spiritual regeneration impact ongoing reality. Amen.

Your Do-Over Is a Done Deal

JULY 16

If at the outset we try to do anything, we get nothing; if we seek to attain something, we miss everything. For Christianity begins not with a big DO, but with a big DONE. —Watchman Nee

No one was responsible for their own physical birth. It wasn't your idea and you didn't birth yourself. Your mother did that, and if you give her half a moment, she'll no doubt remind you of it! It's called "labor" for a good reason. She worked hard to bring you into this world—but you didn't do any of it. It was *her* work, not yours—it *happened* to you!

Regeneration is *God's* work on our behalf! When you see the verbs that are used in Scripture to describe new life in Christ, the aorist tense is almost always used. The aorist tense is a punctiliar tense, which means "a point in time;" something that happens once. And those verbs are almost always in the passive voice. That means we didn't do it (that's the active voice) but that was done to us (the passive voice). All the key verbs in Titus 3:4-5 are in the aorist, punctiliar, passive voice.

> *But when the kindness and love of God our Savior appeared, he saved us, not because of righteous things we had done, but because of his mercy. He saved us through the washing of rebirth and renewal by the Holy Spirit.*

Regeneration is *God's* work. It's the ultimate second chance, one time, heart transplant by God that makes us righteous and just so He can declare us righteous and just.

So if you feel like you are under religious pressure or feel obligation to do good things to make yourself righteous and just, take the weekend off, will ya? Just focus on the amazing things that God did when He regenerated your spirit by His Spirit through Christ. And rest assured, **He will do whatever He wishes through you when you quit trying to do it yourself.**

Never forget: The "ultimate do-over" is a done deal!

O God, would You take away the nagging sense of religious obligation I feel to make myself righteous and just? I praise You that You have DONE this. Because You regenerated me, there is nothing left for me to do! I worship You for this incredible, mysterious truth. Amen.

The Chicken or the Egg? (Christian Style)

It may be hard for an egg to turn into a bird: it would be a jolly sight harder for it to learn to fly while remaining an egg. We are like eggs at present. And you cannot go on indefinitely being just an ordinary, decent egg. We must be hatched or go bad. —C. S. Lewis

Christians love to debate the craziest stuff. Here's a favorite: **What comes first: Faith (our assured belief in something unseen) or regeneration (God making us righteous and just)?** A group called "Calvinists" insist that regeneration comes first. They look at passages like Ephesians 2 and ask, "You know, if we *really* are dead in our spirit, how can we have faith? We have to be regenerated by God first *before* we can have saving faith and live in Christ." Hmmm. Good point. Another group called Arminians say, "No, no, no, no. Look at John 3:16. You have to believe first and *then* you get eternal life." Makes sense.

Frankly, this argument has been going on for at least a thousand years. I have thoughts about it. **But I'm far more concerned that the "which comes first" question causes division and could hamper people from entering the Kingdom.** Even Nicodemus, the well-educated Pharisee that came to Jesus in the night, got tripped up on the timeless, supernatural aspect of being born again:

> *"How can this be?" Nicodemus asked. "You are Israel's teacher," said Jesus, "and do you not understand these things? Very truly I tell you, we speak of what we know, and we testify to what we have seen, but still you people do not accept our testimony. I have spoken to you of earthly things and you do not believe; how then will you believe if I speak of heavenly things?"*
> —John 3:9-12

If you ask me "which comes first?", I tend to answer, "Yes!" There must be faith. There must be regeneration. Once again, this is God's work; we can't manipulate it. It's a gift given in God's timing and in God's way.

How about you? Do you get caught up in the "chicken or the egg" debates? It can scramble your mind if you aren't careful. I'm not yolking about that (sorry). **OR, are you blown away by the testimony of Christ that says you've actually been hatched into a new life in Him?!**

Jesus, don't let me get tripped up with things that my mind cannot comprehend. Rather, free my soul to experience being "born again." May the reality of my spiritual rebirth be the Truth that propels my life today in all I think, say, and do. Amen.

How to Know You're on the Right Track

A life without a purpose is a languid, drifting thing. Every day we ought to renew our purpose, saying to ourselves: This day let us make a sound beginning, for what we have hitherto done is nought. —Thomas à Kempis

Okay, so I'm not the best at navigating through new territory (hear my wife snicker). And yeah, I'm a guy; and there's just something about guys asking directions … we don't! (Don't ask me; I don't understand why. Blame it on Adam, Satan, or politicians on the opposite end of your spectrum.)

But anyway, as a guy, it's always nice to see signs that tell me I'm headed in the right direction. Same goes with being a new creature in Christ. **How can we know we are on the right track? God has graciously given us some "born-again signposts."**

The apostle John had a special relationship with Christ. He wrote one of the Gospels and then he wrote three encouraging letters to early believers who were navigating through new territory as Christians. The first letter is a "signpost" letting them know they are on the right track.

> *As for you, see that what you have heard from the beginning remains in you. If it does, you also will remain in the Son and in the Father. And this is what he promised us—eternal life …. If you know that he is righteous, you know that everyone who does what is right has been born of him.* —1 John 2:24-25, 29

According to John, one of the ways that you can tell if you're born again is that you are living "right." Does that mean "perfect?" No, it means that you have a perfect Spirit, and IF you choose to be led by the Spirit of Jesus in your spirit, the rest of your life will be catching up to that. (Fancy word for that is "sanctification.") Yes, you still live in a fallen world and there will be days when you make poor choices and walk in the flesh rather than in the Spirit. **But if you are born again, and you are trusting Christ to live His life through you, His righteousness will characterize your life!** That kind of "living right" becomes your heartbeat, and with it comes a humble assurance that, yes, you have been born again and Someone is at work in you and through you to God's good pleasure.

Holy Spirit, today, I lay aside my impulses to think and act on my own. I want to walk in Your Spirit. Live through me in a way that confirms I am on the right track—a little outward evidence that You are in me. Amen.

R U Lost?

Question: Why does it take millions of sperm to fertilize one egg?
Answer: They won't stop to ask for directions. —Old joke of unknown origin

Okay so that's pretty funny—maybe a tinge off-color, but you have to admit, funny. This enduring joke gets a chuckle because it feeds off the cultural belief that male members of our species really don't like to admit when they are physically lost. **But to the defense of my gender, males AND females of our species don't like to admit when they are spiritually lost.**

So God used John to put up some "born again signposts" along the road to help us know when we are on the right track and when we are on the wrong path. 1 John 3:7-9 is one of those signs. But be warned, this one is more like a billboard with blazing neon lights shouting out a desperate warning:

> *Dear children, do not let anyone lead you astray. The one who does what is right is righteous, just as he is righteous. The one who does what is sinful is of the devil, because the devil has been sinning from the beginning. The reason the Son of God appeared was to destroy the devil's work. No one who is born of God will continue to sin, because God's seed remains in them; they cannot go on sinning, because they have been born of God.*

The verb tenses in this passage are important. It doesn't mean that we won't sin from time to time (when we choose to walk in the fleshly independence rather than in dependence on the Spirit). The warning is this: If you "continue" and "go on sinning" without remorse, without repentance, and without a willingness to surrender this area of life over to Christ, then you may not be born again at all.

I can't sugarcoat this one. That's what the "sign" says. **If you aren't sure which way you are going, you might want to stop and ask for some directions.**

Holy Spirit, speak clearly to me through this passage of the Word. I'm depending on You to do this. I don't want any false assurance that I'm born again if I'm not. I don't need unnecessary guilt over sins that are already covered by the cross. Show me, Lord: Are my sins resulting from choices to walk in the flesh? Or are they a warning that I am continuing in sin because I'm not born again at all? Amen.

Join the Unburdened Overcomers

I sometimes just say, 'Lord Jesus, lovely Lord Jesus'" over and over and over slowly, there is nothing better or more healing … There hath not failed one word of all His good promises. All the promises of God are 'yea' and 'amen,' and that's enough right there to go on. —**Dottie, my mother-in-law**

Life on this planet can be tough. Jesus never promised otherwise:

> *I have told you these things, so that in me you may have peace. In this world you will have trouble. But take heart! I have overcome the world.*
> —John 16:33

John recorded that in his Gospel, but he doesn't leave it there. In his first letter, John puts it in perspective for those who are born again:

> *In fact, this is love for God: to keep his commands. And his commands are not burdensome, for everyone born of God overcomes the world. This is the victory that has overcome the world, even our faith. Who is it that overcomes the world? Only the one who believes that Jesus is the Son of God.* —1 John 5:3-5

The commandments to *love*, to *trust*, to *live in Him*, and to *rest in Him* give us victory. John says it's one of the "signs" that we are born of God. Personally, I know of no one whose life speaks as loudly to this as my mother-in-law. When my wife was born, Dottie's life was a complete mess, ravaged by brokenness. Now some forty-odd years later, her body is starting to break down. Yet listen to some of the words she wrote in a letter to us:

- "It all about Him, I take care of His business, HE takes care of my business."
- "LORD, it's your body, if this is what you want for it, be my guest!"
- "Every word that comes out of the mouth of God matters."
- "He is alive and real in me. Mercifully, He and I are inseparable."

Yes, MY mother-in-law (and NO, you can't have her) is an "unburdened overcomer" of the world—one of the true signs we've been born again.

Jesus, be the only true reality in my life. I release my worldly burdens to You. I take on Your commands which are not burdensome at all when I allow You to live them through me in Your strength. Amen

And *YOU* Will Know...

We are one in the Spirit, we are one in the Lord. We are one in the Spirit, we are one in the Lord. And we pray that all unity may one day be restored. And they'll know we are Christians by our love, by our love. They will know we are Christians by our love. —**Lyrics by Pete Scholtes**

John's first letter is loaded with encouragement to those in doubt. It's an awesome message, really. (Not too long either; you can read it in a short sitting.) He writes so that we might be *certain* that we are born of God. He is offering *assurance* to those who are born again. That certainty, however, comes only through an honest introspection that reveals the inner presence of the Holy Spirit overflowing through us. **Through Christ, are we living right? Defying sin? Overcoming the world?** John gives one more "born again signpost" to ponder:

> *Dear friends, let us love one another, for love comes from God. Everyone who loves has been born of God and knows God. Whoever does not love does not know God, because God is love. This is how God showed his love among us: He sent his one and only Son into the world that we might live through him. This is love: not that we loved God, but that he loved us and sent his Son as an atoning sacrifice for our sins. Dear friends, since God so loved us, we also ought to love one another.* —1 John 4:7-11

The old song says that the world will know we are Christians by our love. But do you know what? *You* **will know** *you* **are a Christian by** *your* **love, too!**

Agape God, I praise You for Your unconditional love and I believe that You ARE love. I desire You, Lord. I ask that, in Christ, Your love would be in me and then flow through me. May Your love flowing through me be a "born again signpost" to the world and a supernatural confirmation to me that I am Your child. Amen.

What's the Nature of Your Nature?

When we really understand who we are, we can walk away from this lonesome, needless fight that so many men and women battle, and rest in who God fashioned us to be. —Bill Ewing, Rest Assured

Life "in Christ" is a journey of exploration and discovery from beginning to end. "Christ in us" is the "great mystery," as Paul put it. And anyone who thinks they *fully* understand this mystery doesn't get it at all. This is incredible stuff!

When we began life in Christ, we began to experience all sorts of new things (regeneration, justification, sanctification, propitiation, and a whole slew of other neat sounding words that end in "-ation"). But all this *new* stuff brings up an interesting question: What about the *old* stuff? The question usually comes to me like this: **"Okay, Pete, after I get born again, do I now have two natures? At the core of my being, where it really matters, am I half good and half bad now?"**

Maybe you've never really thought about it. Maybe you are one of those who loves to debate this sort of thing at coffee shops while smoking a pipe. (Coffee shops are required for this type of discussion, but I suppose the pipe smoking is optional, particularly if you are female.) Either way, how you answer this question is *hugely* important. It's a perplexing question, full of emotion and experiences that pull us back and forth. **But here's the answer:**

"No."

Yeah, that's it. One little syllable; two little letters. But again, this is *huge*. If you are in Christ, you don't have two "natures"—you have one nature, and your nature is in Christ, too.

> *Therefore, if anyone is in Christ, the new creation has come: The old has gone, the new is here!* —2 Corinthians 5:17

Being born again first requires a death—a death deeper and more profound than anything we can fully fathom. Exploring that death brings fresh light to our journey of discovering Life.

Father, as I open Your Word, I anticipate that You want to teach me something—maybe something new; maybe a reminder of something I have long-forgotten. I know that by Your Spirit You want to do a work within me. So in the days ahead, I offer myself to You and Your teaching, so that I can experience more of who I am in Your Son. Amen.

WANTED: Dead and Alive

The old man has been put to death just as decisively as Christ died upon the accursed tree. —John Murray

Baptisms are one of the great things about being a pastor. When I get to dunk someone and then pull them out of the water—man, it's just like the best of the best. Water baptism is an outward expression of the inner transformation of Christ, and when someone makes that public expression, it just invigorates me from head to toe.

The word *baptize* means "to place into" or to "identify with." Sometimes that means into *water,* but sometimes it means something else:

> *Or don't you know that all of us who were baptized into Christ Jesus were baptized into his death?* —Romans 6:3

This is not a verse about water baptism. **It says we have been placed *into Christ* … and we have been placed *into His death*.** This is a God mystery, but it's true. The phrase is repeated again:

> *We were therefore buried with him through baptism into death in order that, just as Christ was raised from the dead through the glory of the Father, we too may live a new life.* —Romans 6:4

Whoa! What happened to the *old you*? **You were placed into Christ Jesus, *you* were placed into His death on the cross, and *you* were also placed into the tomb with Him when He was buried.** This is not theological trivia. This is how it happened— this is how it *had* to happen—in order that you too may live a resurrected life in Christ (because He can't dwell in something sinful). This is spiritual reality, the truth about your identity in Christ—something that only God can do and has done outside of the natural realm.

Father, I ask that You would give me a moment to pause, right now, to contemplate what You say is true about my nature—that I am both dead to sin, and alive in Christ. This is too deep, too profound for me. I need You to lead me into the Truth so that I can be free to live according to my new nature as the Spirit leads and empowers me. Amen.

Do You Know?

Our unity with Christ ... is terribly important and perhaps the most critical doctrine of salvation in Paul's writing. —James Montgomery Boice

In his letter to the Romans, Paul makes an assumption about his readers. It's such a foundational truth that he whips it out there before he gets to the guts of what he really wants to say—a fundamental principle that every one of us needs to know before we can apply what he has to say next:

> *For we know* that our old self was crucified with Him .... —Romans 6:6

Underline those words in your Bible and in your heart.

Our old, unregenerate personhood, the sinner with a heart of a rebel that we were before we knew Jesus, the person who was under bondage to sin, is dead. Please note that the verse is in the past tense. The old self *was* crucified. The person we used to be before we trusted Christ was put to death and buried. It's done! In fact, read Romans 6 and 7 and you will see that Paul goes out of his way to make sure we understand this truth!

Paul wanted his readers to know this to such a depth that it would change their lives in very practical ways. (We will get to some of those in the days ahead. It's awesome stuff, I promise). Sure, there are many questions that this foundational principle brings up, such as, "If my sinful nature is dead, why do I still sometimes sin?" (We will get to that, too). But before the answers make any sense, we must accept what is clearly taught in this passage: Your old self was crucified with Christ!

Do you *really* know it?!

God, this seems like something that I can "know" without really knowing it on a practical level! I accept it in theory; now move in my heart in such a way that I can accept it in reality! I want to live this truth, but I can't unless You live it through me. Renew my mind, transform my life according to Your Word, Lord. Amen.

Your Life, His Story

The subject of spiritual union is the most important, most profound and yet the most blessed of any that is set forth in the sacred Scriptures; and yet, sad to say, there is hardly any which is now more generally neglected. —Arthur Pink

When I think of the word *union*, nice things come to mind. I think of a marriage union, or a family reunion. And of course, almost everyone says they want to be in union with Christ. It's a coming together as one, a sharing of an experience, a unified existence … and it's nice, usually.

Paul speaks of being united with Christ on a level few of us have really thought about:

> *For if we have been united with him in a death like his, we will certainly also be united with him in a resurrection like his.* —Romans 6:5

The key word in this verse is obviously *united*. It connotes an intimate union with Christ. At some point, in some way, by God's grace, those of us who are in Christ were placed into Christ like one sheet of paper being slid into the pages of a book. Our story becomes meshed with His story as one. We are sealed in Him, and we become one with Him somehow—one plus one equals one. It's divine mathematics. (I got in trouble with that kind of math; God gets away with it.) In this unity, everything that happens to the Book happens to us.

We were united with Him in His death and His burial; so we can be born again and reunited in Him in His resurrection. Death to the old. Life through the new—that's how the Christian life began, and that is how it is lived out today.

Holy Spirit, make this passage real to me in a deeper way today. By faith, I accept what the Word says is true. I proclaim that my old nature was crucified and buried with Christ! Thank you that my old, sinful self is in the grave of Christ, so that I can be united with Him only today. Amen.

The Deception of Separation

Union with Christ is really the central truth of the whole doctrine of salvation...
—John Murray

The discussion about whether we have one or two natures—whether we are half good and half bad—really *does* matter. What we believe about our nature determines what we believe about our relationship with God. Scripture is so clear that our old, sinful self died with Christ and that He now lives in us (2 Corinthians 5:17). **Our belief doesn't change that reality; but it changes how we experience that reality.** Consider this:

> *But whoever is united with the Lord is one with him in spirit.*
> —1 Corinthians 6:17

The original Greek sentence doesn't have the phrase "with Him." It literally says:

> *He that is joined to the Lord, one spirit is.*

If you are in Christ, one spirit with Him you are. But until we understand that this union with Christ is tied to the fact that our old self is dead, we will constantly be confronted with the deception of separation. I use that word very carefully, *deception.* **I'm convinced it is a deception of the evil one to convince you, as a believer in Jesus Christ, that you are separated from God, that He is out there somewhere and you are down here.**

Now, if you're a non-believer, you *are* separated from God by your sin. But once you trust in Christ, you're *in* Christ. Your old self died and your new self lives:

- You are never separated from Him again ... ever.
- You are in perfect union with Christ in your spirit forevermore.
- You don't have to figure out how to get closer to God.
- You're already as close as you can get.
- You don't have to come up with a plan to get more intimate.

It just doesn't get any more intimate than complete union with Him. You can't get closer than "in!"

God of Truth, expose the "deception of separation" that keeps me from experiencing the unity of spirit between us. I reject the lie that my old sinful self is alive and separated from You. I rejoice that because my old self died, I am living in Him now and forever! Amen.

A Question of the Heart

There are two kinds of people in the world—only two kinds. Not black or white, rich or poor, but those either dead in sin or dead to sin. —Leonard Ravenhill

Sometimes a question is a window into the heart, showing us the struggle inside. That's the case with a question that I get asked from time to time. **"Pete, after I get born again, can I go on sinning?"** The only one true answer to that question is absolutely, categorically, unquestionably, and clearly, **"Yes" and "No."**

> *What shall we say, then? Shall we go on sinning so that grace may increase? By no means! We are those who have died to sin; how can we live in it any longer?* —Romans 6:1-2

This passage comes on the heels of five chapters of Paul's teaching on justification and grace—the fact that salvation is a gift of unmerited favor. **God accepts you by His grace! There's nothing you can do to make God love you more; there's nothing you can do to make God love you less.** Now Paul helps us breathe that oxygen.

When someone asks if they can "continue to sin," I usually find one of two things going on in the heart of the one asking:

1. If you are asking, "Is it **possible** for me to sin now that I have Christ living in me?", the answer is "Yes, it is possible" and "Yes, you will." People who ask if it's **possible** to sin tend to be **struggling** with a particular sin that they **can't** seem to shake, and they feel horrible about it.

2. However, the question can also be asking for **permission** to continue on sinning in conscious disobedience. The answer to that question is flat out "No." Grace does not give you **permission** to sin. People who ask for permission to sin tend to be **engaged** in a particular sin that they don't **want** to shake, and they are hoping they can continue without messing up anything else.

How about you? Do you ever ask if you will "continue to sin?" If so, does it reveal anything going on at a deeper level?!

Jesus, Your Word says that because I am in You, I "have died to sin." Show me what that means. Show me how I can apply this truth to my desire to not sin and my struggles. Let me see myself as You declare me. Amen

A Little Latin for You

The Bible will keep you from sin, or sin will keep you from the Bible.
—Dwight L. Moody

Several hundred years ago Augustine came up with three Latin phrases that describe the interaction of sin in nonbelievers and Christians.

- *Passé pacare* means "able to sin." It describes Adam before the fall, before sin entered the world. He had the *capacity* to sin, even though he had not sinned yet. Then, because he was able to, he chose to, and he walked into sin.

- *Non passé non pacare* means "not possible not to sin." Anyone who was born after Adam (and that's just about everyone!) starts with a sin nature that is dead to God but alive to sin. As a result, it's *impossible* for them to live without sinning.

- *Passé non pacare* means "able not to sin." God forgives our sins, and He comes to live inside us. By the power of the Spirit in us, it is *possible* not to sin. It is possible for you to have regular victory in that area you've been trying to overcome by yourself. It's even possible for you to change your mind about the things that you don't want to stop!

  We are those who have died to sin; how can we live in it any longer?
  —Romans 6:2

Think about that for a moment. **Paul says that since we have died to sin, it shouldn't dominate our lives anymore. Is that possible?** It may not seem like it, but take God at His Word!

  For no word from God will ever fail. … What is impossible with men is possible with God. —Luke 1:37, 18:27

Have hope! The truth can set you free! You ARE *passé non pacare. In Christ,* new things are possible if you are willing to surrender to the Spirit in you!

Holy Spirit, I give up trying to fight sin in my own strength. I even give up trying to want to fight sin. Your Word says all is possible in Christ. Counsel me through these biblical truths! You say I am "dead to sin." I embrace that truth. Live through me in a way that reflects that truth. Amen.

How to Count Yourself Dead to Sin

I would go so far as to say that Romans 6:2 is the most important verse in the Bible for believers in the evangelical churches to understand today.
—James Montgomery Boice

SIN: The three letter word with "I" right in the middle. I think the fact that we find ourselves right in the middle of sin is what makes it all so difficult. If we are in Christ, sin just doesn't "fit" in our life anymore. One writer calls sin a moment of "temporary insanity" in the life of a believer. Deep inside, the Spirit convicts us that sin is not consistent with who we are in Jesus … and it's uncomfortable.

> *We are those who have died to sin; how can we live in it any longer?*
> —Romans 6:2

Is it possible that if we truly believe that we are "dead to sin," we can break free from it? Paul's writings in Romans 6 sure point in that direction! This is the fundamental premise of the entire chapter:

> *Now if we died with Christ, we believe that we will also live with him… The death he died, he died to sin once for all; but the life he lives, he lives to God. In the same way, count yourselves dead to sin but alive to God in Christ Jesus.*
> —Romans 6:8, 10-11

This is incredible stuff! How many of us try to fight with something that is already dead?! Doesn't work very well, does it? But if we count ourselves "dead to sin," we embrace the truth that our old, sinful self was crucified with Jesus, that we are born again, regenerated, and made alive in the Spirit of Christ. We are no longer in bondage to the control of indwelling sin in our lives. **You can choose to walk in intimate dependency with Jesus moment by moment, because He is in you! If you think you have no choice, you've been deceived by the evil one into thinking that.**

My prayer is that you wouldn't just hear, but you would actually own that truth! Consider a specific area of sin you might be struggling with right now, then offer this prayer declaring your freedom:

Holy Spirit, I need You now, to take this truth from my head to my heart. Because I was crucified and buried with Christ, I proclaim that I am dead to this sin. Because You live in my spirit, I proclaim that I am alive to God in Jesus. I bow before You now. In my flesh, I am powerless. By abiding in You, I can do all things. I trust in You now to give me the willingness and the strength to follow You. Thank You. Thank You. Amen.

Check the Fine Print

He that falls into sin is a man; that grieves at it, is a saint; that boasteth of it, is a devil. —Thomas Fuller

To someone who struggles with habitual sin, all the talk about being "dead to sin" might sound too good to be true—kind of like the late night TV infomercial that promises to clean your dog *and* restore worn out leather *and* take inches off your thighs with one application and no effort if you buy by midnight on Friday. Yeah, right! Maybe it's time to read a little of the fine print.

This is really important—don't skip this paragraph! Being "dead to sin" doesn't mean that sin is dead, or that we are *immune* to sin. In Romans 1-5 *sin* is generally a verb, actions we do. Starting in Romans 6, *sin* is a noun, an entity. *Indwelling sin*, that internal voice that tempts us, is still alive and active in our lives even after we trust Christ. It is in us, but it is not who we are (like a sliver in my finger, it is in me, annoying, painful, but it is not "me.")

The "voice" of indwelling sin is very real and because it comes from inside us, it leads many to believe we still have a sin nature. Our flesh (our desire to do things in our own strength, independent of God) is still responsive to sin. So even though we are in Christ and have His Spirit in our spirit, when the world, Satan, the flesh, and indwelling sin team up on us, the allure of sin is still a powerful force! Anytime we don't choose to walk in the Spirit, BAMMO!—sin will follow. So yes, it's going to happen, but this is the cool part:

> *For sin shall no longer be your master, because you are not under law, but under grace.* —Romans 6:14

There is a huge difference between being vulnerable to sin and being mastered by it!

Jesus, thank You for forgiving all my past, present, and future sins. I realize that indwelling sin is still a powerful force in my life, but it is not who I am! So I praise You all the more that sin is not my master. I always have the choice to walk by Your Spirit! Make that choice a habit! Amen.

Living in the Past Tense

The greatest miracle that God can do today is to take an unholy man out of an unholy world and make him holy, then put him back into that unholy world and keep him holy in it. —Leonard Ravenhill

Sometimes I ask people, "How are you doing in your spiritual walk?" (You can usually see it in their discouraged and desperate eyes when it's not going so well.) They often respond, "Well, you know, I'm trying really hard to die to sin." They look at me like I'm Pastor-Gone-Off-The-Deep-End when I then ask, "Why are you trying to do that?!" When I see their crinkled forehead and raised eyebrow, I know they are ready to hear something vitally important: **Being "dead to sin" does not mean that you should continue to try to die to sin when it happens.**

> *In the same way, count yourselves dead to sin but alive to God in Christ Jesus. Therefore do not let sin reign in your mortal body so that you obey its evil desires.* —Romans 6:11-12

The word *died* is in aorist tense, which means "a single action which occurred in the past." It is not in the present tense as in, "We *are* dying to sin." And it's not in a future tense as, "One day we *will* die to sin." It says, "In the past at some point, we *died* to sin." **It's done.** This is a *present* reality and can become your immediate experience. The key is to see yourself already dead to sin, with the capacity to choose to act on that truth when temptation comes your way. Let me say that again, just a little differently: **The old master is still alive (sin), but the old slave has been crucified (your old self), so your old master is no longer your master because you are a new person with a new master, Jesus! The key is not to try to die to sin, but to believe your old, sinful self is already dead. When we take that one biblical truth to heart, then our choices and our behavior will be natural extensions of that truth!** Meditate on this powerful and extremely practical command:

> *Do not offer any part of yourself to sin as an instrument of wickedness, but rather **offer yourselves to God as those who have been brought from death to life; and offer every part of yourself to him as an instrument of righteousness.*** —Romans 6:13

To whom are you offering your body today?!

Lord God, I offer myself to You! You have brought me from death to life. I surrender to this truth. I quit trying and I offer my body to You to be used as an instrument of righteousness in Your hand today. Amen and Amen.

It's Your Choice

Understand that the old man is not there. The only way to stop living as if he were still there is to realize that he is not there. —D. Martyn Lloyd-Jones

Sometimes there really is a black and white. In trying to be sensitive to others' beliefs and trying to be open-minded about all ideas, sometimes we forget that. In many ways, Christianity is an "either/or faith." It doesn't leave much in the gray; a lot of questions are answered true or false. Remember Eden? God said, "You can *either* eat from this tree *or* this tree. You eat from that tree, you lose this tree and you lose the garden, so don't eat from that tree. Eat from this tree." It was one or the other. **Jesus was stunningly gracious and accepting, but He drew clear lines between black and white on critical issues,** such as:

> *No one can serve two masters. Either you will hate the one and love the other, or you will be devoted to one and despise the other.* —Matthew 6:24

He was talking about money there, but substitute anything for money and what He is saying is, "You either love God or forget it. **Either/or.**" And when it comes to your spirit, Scripture teaches categorically that it's either dead in sin or alive in Christ. Why am I spending so much time talking about this? **Because I'm convinced that most believers *think* that in their essence, in their spirit, in their nature, they are both good and bad.** They *think* they are both righteous and sinful … and as they *think* in their heart, so they are! (Proverbs 23:7). **This whole issue about being "in Christ" is not some sort of theological gobblety-goop! It's the real deal. What we think on a heart level determines how we choose to act and respond in a fallen world.**

Father, draw some lines in my mind! Using Your Word as my guide, I want the deep-down thoughts of my heart to be true, so I can live in the truth of who I am in Christ, Your Son. Amen!

Raised to New Life

If you are a Christian, it's a serious misunderstanding to think of yourself as having both an old and new nature. We do not have a dual personality! Assuming the dual nature of the believer could easily lead one to excuse all kinds of sins by blaming them on the old nature. The popular theological concept of the old man and the new man fighting each other is not biblically accurate.
—John MacArthur

Personally, I think there is plenty of bad news in the world. And though I'm not sure why, Christians seem to be wired for it. **Yeah, bad news sells, I guess. But the good news is that you don't have to buy it, particularly when it comes to who you are in Christ.**

A lot of bad news about our identity comes from a good dog/ bad dog analogy. It goes like this: Your nature is like two dogs, a bad dog and a good dog. In every tempting situation, the dogs get in a fight to see who is going to win. You just hope the good dog wins so you don't make a bad choice … and to be on the safe side, it's best to avoid any tempting situation at all, lest you risk feeding the bad dog … you'll set yourself up to fail at least half the time. You'll never find victory over sin. The truth is that the bad dog is a dead dog. He's in the past, freeing us for transformation today, and promising an incredible future:

> *Like the rest, we were by nature deserving of wrath. But because of his great love for us, God, who is rich in mercy, made us alive with Christ even when we were dead in transgressions—it is by grace you have been saved. And God raised us up with Christ and seated us with him in the heavenly realms in Christ Jesus, in order that in the coming ages he might show the incomparable riches of his grace, expressed in his kindness to us in Christ Jesus.*
> —Ephesians 2:3-7

The choice is yours. How do you see it? **When temptation comes, will you see two dogs fighting to an uncertain conclusion? Or do you see yourself alive with Christ, seated with Him in the heavens?!**

Stop, think, meditate, and then rest in it. I'm telling you, it makes a huge difference.

Holy Spirit, I am so thankful that You live in me—not a couple of dogs. I rest in Your promised presence. I surrender to Your strength and Your peace when temptation comes my way. Thanks for this good news! Amen.

Where's Your Focus?

The greatest truth we can ever be told is that our old self has gone. I can deal with the body of sin only as I realize that my old self has gone, and I have a new self. This is the most striking and amazing truth. —D. Martyn Lloyd-Jones

Yin and Yang, good dogs and bad dogs, the force and its dark side. I'm telling you, the Christianized version of Taoism isn't just wrong; it sets our minds on the wrong thing. **Think about it: If we are constantly worried about some sort of battle going on inside of us, we're constantly focusing on ourselves, right?** Our thoughts sound like this:

- *I* can't give in!
- *I* have to win this war that rages within me.
- *I* have to get my act together.
- *I* have to suppress the bad part of me so that the good part of me can show Jesus.
- Jesus, help *me*!

Sure, this looks pretty pious on the outside, but in reality, we have been tricked into a self-centered struggle to try to do what's right, rather than a Christ-centered celebration of what He has already accomplished on the cross.

> *Since, then, you have been raised with Christ, set your hearts on things above, where Christ is, seated at the right hand of God. Set your minds on things above, not on earthly things. For you died, and your life is now hidden with Christ in God.* —Colossians 3:1-3

Interesting, isn't it? The death of our old sinful self *can* change the focus of everything! Where is your heart set today?

Christ, I praise You for the death of my sinful nature with You on the cross. Shift my focus away from who I once was but am no longer. Set my heart on You, reigning in grace and righteousness with the Father! Amen.

It All Starts with What You Think

Before the believer came to Christ in saving faith, the old man in Adam, under the total dominion of sin's power was who we really were. After we came to Christ, the new man, the new woman, the new creation in him, having been set free from sin's reign is now who we have truly become. —Dick Flatten

Learning to live "in Christ" is not a matter of trying—it's really a matter of thinking, then trusting. **According to the New Testament, our problem is that we do not truly realize who we *are* in Christ, but we still go on thinking we are who we *were*.** Did you get that? The apostle Paul brings up the problem in different ways in his writings:

> *Do not lie to one another, since you have taken off the old self with its practices and have put on the new self, which is being renewed in knowledge in the image of its Creator.* —Colossians 3:9-10

Please note that the "new self" is being "renewed in knowledge." The more we understand this and act on it, the more we facilitate the new experience of our new self in Christ. No, we are not a hybrid of old and new, sinful and holy. We are new and holy in Christ.

> *His divine power has given us everything we need for a godly life through our knowledge of him who called us by His own glory and goodness. Through these he has given us his very great and precious promises, so that through them you may participate in the divine nature.* —2 Peter 1:3-4

Notice again that we are given everything we need "through our knowledge of Him." **Are you being transformed by the renewing of your mind about your true nature in Christ? It all starts with your thinking!**

Father, I don't want to be conformed to the Taoist thinking of the world. Renew my mind, transform me according to what is true about my true identity and my new self. Amen.

Another Good Question

A prudent question is one-half of wisdom. —Francis Bacon

Quite frequently I'll hear the question, "Why does my Bible tell me not to live by the sinful nature if the sinful nature is dead?" In Galatians 5:16-17 of the 1978 New International Version, for example, the apostle Paul says:

> *So, I say live by the spirit and you will not gratify the desires of the sinful nature. For the sinful nature desires what is contrary to the spirit and the spirit what is contrary to the sinful nature. They are in conflict with each other so that you do not do what you want.*

That sounds like the sinful nature is alive and well, doesn't it? The problem is that the original translators of the NIV made some decisions in their translation that have led to a misunderstanding. The old version of the New International Version translates the Greek word *sarx* into English as "sinful nature" 23 times. So when you see "sinful nature" in the old NIV, it's the word *sarx,* without exception. **But the word sarx means "flesh!"** If Paul had wanted to say "sinful nature," he would have said that. He didn't.

The Bible doesn't tell you not to live by the sinful nature. The Bible tells you not to live according to the flesh—which is a completely different thing! And thankfully, the most recent version of the NIV corrects this:

> *So I say, walk by the Spirit, and you will not gratify the desires of the flesh. For the flesh desires what is contrary to the Spirit, and the Spirit what is contrary to the flesh. They are in conflict with each other, so that you are not to do whatever you want. But if you are led by the Spirit, you are not under the law.*

What is "flesh?" It is living life out of our own resources (our mind, will, emotions, experience, heritage, etc.) instead of relying on the Holy Spirit. It is living independently instead of dependently. Relying on the patterns we have perfected over the years that protect us and provide comfort, outside of Christ. In other words, living by the flesh is living merely out of our natural, physical abilities rather than in Christ. That's the battle. Do we live in our own strength or out of Christ's strength in us?

Jesus, give me the wisdom to recognize my flesh as my foe! By the power of Your Word and the counsel of Your Holy Spirit, teach me more about this physical opponent in which I live, so that I can be led by Your Spirit and live free from the oppression of the law! Amen.

Figuring Out the Flesh You Battle

Know thyself. —Plato

Everyone one of us battles with the flesh. But what is it anyway? It's been defined in many ways. A literal interpretation would say that it is anything and everything physical about us including hormones, brain, etc. On a practical level, living in the flesh means living as we did before we had the Spirit. It means to live out of our own human resources independently of God—and it can look really, really different from person to person.

Bill Gillham painted a memorable picture of three different flavors of "flesh" among Christians:

- USDA Choice Flesh
- Homemade Vanilla Flesh
- Yuck Flesh

USDA Choice flesh usually comes with extraordinarily capable people. As a result, they live out of their own capabilities most of the time. It usually looks like it's working, but as far as God's concerned, it's nothing. The apostle Paul, when he was Saul of Tarsus, had USDA Choice flesh. I mean, he had a résumé a mile long of his accomplishments in the flesh, didn't he? In Philippians 3:4-6 he said:

> *If someone else thinks they have reasons to put confidence in the flesh, I have more: circumcised on the eighth day, of the people of Israel, of the tribe of Benjamin, a Hebrew of Hebrews; in regard to the law, a Pharisee; as for zeal, persecuting the church; as for righteousness based on the law, faultless.*

If you have this kind of flesh, it's a very dangerous place to be because you can go long periods of time without walking in the Spirit because you're so capable in the flesh. When Paul looked back at his USDA Choice days, in retrospect he said:

> *But whatever were gains to me I now consider loss for the sake of Christ. What is more, I consider everything a loss because of the surpassing worth of knowing Christ Jesus my Lord, for whose sake I have lost all things. I consider them garbage, that I may gain Christ.* —Philippians 3:7-8

Is this your flavor of flesh?

Father, teach me to recognize my flesh flavor and patterns, so that I can reject them, and live in intimate dependency on Your Son. Amen.

Figuring Out the Flesh You Battle — Part 2

There is no way to win the war by fighting the wrong battles. —**Unknown**

Yesterday we looked at the first kind of flesh that Billy Gillham identified. The second kind of flesh Billy Gillham identifies is Homemade Vanilla flesh. It looks pretty generic because so many of us live with it. The Bible says:

> *The acts of the flesh are obvious: sexual immorality, impurity and debauchery; idolatry and witchcraft; hatred, discord, jealousy, fits of rage, selfish ambition, dissensions, factions and envy; drunkenness, orgies, and the like.*
> —Galatians 5:19-21

Homemade Vanilla flesh tries really hard to cut out these acts. They win some; they lose some. I think it could actually be called "octopus-flavored flesh," but who is going to admit to being that?! The octopus has this big head and all these arms going out. For the sake of analogy, let's say that the arms represent the sins in that list. Everyone is struggling with one or two of them, right? So what do you do? You chop, and you hack, and you saw away at that arm, but just when one arm seems severed and you start to focus on hacking off another, "Bip!"—the other arm grows back.

> *Are you so foolish? After beginning by means of the Spirit, are you now trying to finish by means of the flesh?* —Galatians 3:3

It's interesting to note that the words *human effort* in that verse are translated from the Greek word "sarx." Paul is again talking about the flesh!

Listen to me, brothers and sisters. You don't kill an octopus one tentacle at a time. You kill it by chopping off its head. The head of the octopus is your flesh. That's where sin, the "acts of the flesh," come from. The way you overcome those sin-struggles is to stop doing things in your own strength. You walk in the Spirit, trusting Christ to live through you in all areas.

You say, "It sounds so simple." You know, at the end of the day it kind of is.

Spirit, vanilla-flavored flesh is so common, it almost seems right! But take me out of that losing battle. I quit trying to hack off one aspect of my sin in my own strength. I rest in You today. I cease trying on my own. I choose to let You live through me instead. Amen.

Figuring Out the Flesh You Battle – Part 3

One of the mysteries of the gospel tradition is this strange attraction of Jesus for the unattractive, this strange desire for the undesirable, this strange love for unlovely. —Brennan Manning

The last flavor of flesh identified by Gillham is Yuck flesh. Yuck flesh is failure flesh—those who feel they are out after the first three pitches; those who compare their performance to others and always come up short. Sometimes they have blown it so badly that they are pretty sure they are forever a lost cause. If they were asked to evaluate their impact for Christ, they would give themselves really low marks or even a big fat zero. Sometimes people with Yuck flesh constantly try to be a better Christian but no matter how hard they try, it never seems to work. Most of the time they give up altogether. Yeah, put a big Christian "L" on their forehead.

"Losers."

Sound like your flavor of flesh? If so, I have just two things to say to you:

> First, *Therefore, there is now no condemnation for those who are in Christ Jesus, because through Christ Jesus the law of the Spirit who gives life has set you free from the law of sin and death. For what the law was powerless to do because it was weakened by the flesh, God did by sending his own Son in the likeness of sinful flesh to be a sin offering. And so he condemned sin in the flesh, in order that the righteous requirement of the law might be fully met in us, who do not live according to the flesh but according to the Spirit.* —Romans 8:1-4

Secondly, *all* flesh is yuck. You're just fortunate enough to be able to see it for what it is.

O Jesus, thank You for coming. Thank You for receiving me just the way I am. Thank You for giving me another option to the flesh. Thank You for showing the way to live according to the Spirit ... thank You. Amen.

Flesh in Perspective

Thou hast made us for Thyself, and our hearts are restless until they find their rest in Thee. —St. **Augustine**

It doesn't matter what flavor of flesh you favor (USDA Choice, Homemade Vanilla, or Yuck), living by the flesh just doesn't work. Those with USDA Choice flesh end up self-righteous. Those with Homemade Vanilla flesh end up in a never-ending fight with sin. And Yuck flesh ends in guilt, failure, and despair. It just ends badly no matter what.

Yeah, that's all *bad* enough from a personal perspective ... but it's *tragic* from a divine perspective.

> *Those who live according to the flesh have their minds set on what the flesh desires; but those who live in accordance with the Spirit have their minds set on what the Spirit desires. The mind governed by the flesh is death, but the mind governed by the Spirit is life and peace. The mind governed by the flesh is hostile to God; it does not submit to God's law, nor can it do so. Those who are in the realm of the flesh cannot please God.* —Romans 8:5-8

Would you read that passage a couple of times and really let it soak in? I'm serious. Read it again.

Those words speak for themselves. There is nothing selfless or noble about trying to live life in your own strength. It's just wrong. It sets your mind on yourself, not the Spirit. Living according to the flesh is selfish, self-centered, "death" and "hostile to God." Period.

> *You, however, are not in the realm of the flesh but are in the realm of the Spirit, if indeed the Spirit of God lives in you.* —Romans 8:9

Listen, Augustine was right about this. God created us for Himself. He is the "realm" in which we are to live. He is to be the focus of our hearts and minds.

Dear God, I praise You that I am designed to live "in the realm of the Spirit" and that my restless heart can find its rest in You there. Indeed, Your Spirit lives in me. I reject the flesh today so that You can live through me in Your strength. Amen.

Leaping into Your New Existence

Question: There were five frogs on a log. Three decide to jump off. How many are left? Answer: Five. They decided, but never really jumped.

We've been digging deep into our identity in Christ, focusing on the Christ-like nature that we have since our old, sinful self was crucified. But how do you jump into this new life? **The question is this: Since we've been made holy, how do we walk in that holiness?** The apostle Paul openly wrestled with this issue. Throughout the book of Romans he talks about the tension with the law and sin.

> *We know that the law is spiritual; but I am unspiritual ... So I find this law at work: Although I want to do good, evil is right there with me. For in my inner being I delight in God's law; but I see another law at work in me, waging war against the law of my mind and making me a prisoner of the law of sin at work within me.* —Romans 7:14, 21-23

Paul freely admits that outside of Christ he is "unspiritual" (literally "fleshly"). He then describes what it looks like for a Christian who's attempting to live in his own strength:

- "I am ... sold as a slave to sin."
- "I do not understand what I do."
- "I know that nothing good lives in me—that is in my flesh."
- "For what I do is not the good I want to do. The evil I do not want to do, this I keep on doing."

Does this sound familiar? How do we jump off that log of despair and swim in holiness?

> *What a wretched man I am! Who will rescue me from this body that is subject to death? Thanks be to God, who delivers me through Jesus Christ our Lord!* —Romans 7:24-25

Jesus is the one who rescues us from this. As you function in Christ by His Spirit, Jesus overcomes the sliver of indwelling sin, the temptation to live in the flesh, and the oppressive burden of living by the law. But first, you do have to decide to jump.

O Jesus, I'm choosing today to leave the way I used to live. I place my faith in You, and not in my own strength. I trust You alone to live the Christian life through me. Amen.

Summoning Forth the Awesome Beauty of Christ in You

Now, more than ever, he [God] is summoning forth the awesome beauty and capacity that he has deposited among his people worldwide. —George Miley

I, for one, am really glad that God never gave us the "what to do" without also giving us the "how to do it." When God calls us into holy living, the call comes with the emerging conviction that our lives are supposed to be different. **But if we try to do it the way we used to, failure awaits us at every attempt.** We *are* called to be the amazing holy representatives of Him on this planet. But how do we do it?

> *Now if we died with Christ, we **believe** that we will also live with him … In the same way, **count** yourselves dead to sin but alive to God in Christ Jesus. … **offer** yourselves to God as those who have been brought from death to life; and offer every part of yourself to him as an instrument of righteousness.*
> —Romans 6:8,11,13

Believe. Count. Offer. These three keywords show us *how* we are to live in holiness in Christ. First, we must believe. Even if it's just a sliver of faith, even if it is simply a willful recognition of what Scripture says is true. Stepping out with belief, by faith, in what the Bible says is the first step toward the experience of walking in holiness in Christ. But if you're like me, your prayers might sound like the words of the man who confessed to Jesus, "I believe. Help my unbelief!" That's okay. I think Jesus likes honest prayers like that.

Lord Jesus, I put my faith and trust in You and in Your Word. I believe the Word. I believe that because I died with You I will also live with You. I trust that I am in You and You are in me today. And I rest in the fact that I can trust You to live a life of holiness through my spirit using this body. Glory to Christ! Summon forth the beauty and capacity that You have placed in me! Amen.

Stepping Beyond Your Belief

Unless there is a still center in the middle of the storm, unless a person in the midst of all their activities preserves the secret room in their heart where they stand alone before God, unless we do this we will lose all sense of spiritual direction and be torn to pieces. —**Anonymous fourth century desert monk**

Belief doesn't automatically cause life-change. That's probably one of the biggest hiccups in evangelicalism today: We think that if we *know* something in our heads, we're automatically going to *act* on it. Not the case. That's why there are so many believers stuck on the log of fleshly living. We have to step beyond belief in the brain only. We need to be willing to take a faith step by counting on it in our souls.

> *Now if we died with Christ, we believe that we will also live with him ... In the same way, count yourselves dead to sin but alive to God in Christ Jesus. ... offer yourselves to God, as those who have been brought from death to life; and offer the parts of your body to him as instruments of righteousness.*
> —Romans 6:8, 11, 13

The word *count* means to "mark it down," to "reckon it as right," to "make an account of it." It is what an accountant does when he is keeping his books. Writing it down doesn't make it true; it *is* true, so he writes it down. It is true that we are dead to sin but alive to Christ, count it! This is the great bridge between belief and application—it's where we begin to personally own truth and begin to count on it as we face battles in the real world.

- Are you a minister trying to flesh out a life of service and sacrifice for your congregation?
- Are you a single adult constantly desiring and constantly being pressured sexually?
- Are you a teenager trying to "just say no" to drugs and alcohol?
- Are you a parent desperately trying to control your tongue with your kids?

Take a little advice from the desert monk: Find a quiet space in the midst of your storm, right now, where you can stand alone with God and embrace the truth of His Spirit in you. Then, count on Him to make that truth a reality.

Holy God, I am counting on the truth that, in Christ, I am dead to sin and alive to You. I lay before You the temptations that I am facing today. Because I am alive in You, I count on the fact that I am dead to these things! I freely turn away from them now. By the power of Your Spirit in my spirit, lead me in the holy, everlasting way! Amen.

Living as an Offering

A vision of the possibilities ... should never overshadow the clear biblical principle that when we are weak then we really are strong because God's power is allowed full expression in our weakness. —David Bryant

We've been investigating the question, "How do I live in holiness?" That's a heavy-sounding question, and it seems like the answer is going to be loaded with a bunch of religious do-it-yourself pressure. But the answer that Paul gives has none of that:

> Now if we died with Christ, we **believe** that we will also live with him ... In the same way, **count** yourselves dead to sin but alive to God in Christ Jesus. ... **offer** yourselves to God, as those who have been brought from death to life; and **offer the parts of your body to him as instruments of righteousness.**
> —Romans 6:8,11,13

That's pretty straightforward! If we want to live holy lives, we actually step into what Christ has already done and then lay ourselves before Him to be used in any way that He sees fit.

- Believe that you live with Him.
- Count yourself dead to sin.
- Offer yourself to God as His instrument of righteousness.

What is your struggle today? What tasks are you facing? What temptations are clawing at you? Where do you feel inadequate for the challenges in front of you? Surrender and offer your body to Him!

Dear God, I don't want to function in my own strength. I lay myself in Your hands to be used as an instrument of righteousness. I give You my mind, that I might think Your thoughts. I give You my heart, that I might love as You love. I give You my hands, that I might serve as You serve. I give You my lips and my tongue, that my words might give grace to all who hear. I offer it all to You, Lord! Do with me what You wish! Amen.

Tapping into the Power of a Habit

Habit is habit and not to be flung out of the window by any man, but coaxed downstairs a step at a time. —Mark Twain

A long time ago, in a house far, far away, my kids learned to walk. First, a "scootch" became a crawl. Then, a crawl became a stand. Then, a stand became a step … followed immediately by a fall. Then another step, followed by another fall. Then, one day, two steps in a row! Then three! Soon enough, the stumbles became the exception. By the time they were taking 25 to 30 steps in a row, we knew they had it down.

They had learned to walk, just like we are learning to walk in holiness.

You see where I'm going here, don't you? Meditate on the words of Paul again:

> *Now if we died with Christ, we **believe** that we will also live with him … In the same way, **count** yourselves dead to sin but alive to God in Christ Jesus. … **offer** yourselves to God, as those who have been brought from death to life; and **offer** the parts of your body to him as instruments of righteousness.*
> —Romans 6:8, 11, 13

Most experts say it takes 25 to 30 days to create a new habit. After that, things become more automatic. By tapping into the power of a habit, one step at a time, the rest of your life can be changed.

- Believe that you live with Him.
- Count yourself dead to sin.
- Offer yourself to God as His instrument of righteousness.

Believe, count, offer. Believe, count, offer … It's the God-given pattern that draws you into dependent intimacy with Him moment by moment, and makes walking in holiness a natural habit.

Want to stay on the floor or are you ready to take some steps (and some stumbles) to learn the walk? For the next 30 days, write these words in your journal, or place them on a card by your mirror, or on your dashboard. Remind yourself of this great truth and ask the Lord to make "Believe, count, offer" your way of life.

Holy Spirit, I want to walk in Your holiness as naturally as I've learned to walk on the ground. I am willing to make the jump, but I am fully dependent on You to make it happen. I trust in You to take my body and use it as Your instrument of righteousness. Amen.

Mirror, Mirror on the Wall

Let us be grateful to the mirror for revealing to us our appearance only.
—**Samuel Butler**

There are days where I don't look, feel, or even smell righteous. I am the one who looks in the mirror and sees the wrinkles, the extra pounds, and the thousand other areas that need improving. I know my areas of temptation, my anger, and my tendency to be self-centered. Because of what I *see* and because of what I *feel* about me sometimes, **I have trouble believing I'm "in Christ"… not because I don't know *Him*, but because I know *me*.**

Thankfully, my identity is not based on appearances, feelings, or behavior. Neither is yours! It is all about what God says about you. His Word is the true mirror that shows you who you are in Him. Just a few reflections:

- I am very loved: John 15:9, Romans 8:38-39
- I am adequate in Christ: 2 Corinthians 3:5-6
- I have the Spirit's power: Acts 1:8, Ephesians 1:19, 3:16
- God rejoices over me: Zephaniah 3:17, Isaiah 62:5

The *Word* knows us from the inside out. The *world*, of course, teaches us to look at the external. For example, when the Jews were in need of a king, Samuel went looking and he found some impressive specimens. But God knew better:

> But the Lord said to Samuel, *"Do not consider his appearance or his height, for I have rejected him. The Lord does not look at the things man looks at. Man looks at the outward appearance, but the Lord looks at the heart."*
> —1 Samuel 16:7

Sure, your old heart was wicked and dead. **But now, when the Lord looks at your heart, He sees the new heart given in Christ, a heart that has been made pure and alive.** That's why the mirror of the Word, and not the mirror on the wall, tells you who you are.

Jesus, I embrace Your mirror of truth today! In faith, I hold on to the truth about who I am in You, regardless of appearances and feelings. Bring specific truths to my mind today that I might be a living reflection of You to the world. Amen.

The Devil Made You Do It?

It's later than it's ever been. —Flip Wilson

In the 70s a popular comedian, Flip Wilson, came up with a great tag line. He would do something wrong, get caught, and emphatically use this excuse: "The devil made me do it!" Before we knew about our identity in Christ, it would have been easy to use the same excuse. *When we mess up, just blame Satan, the world, and that old sinful nature in us!* Right? Nope!

This old way of thinking is obsolete and irrelevant. Being "in Christ" opens the door to a whole different mode of existence. Living a life of obedience to Him is just being true to who you are in Him. Your identity was settled at the cross. The life you live now is not your own; it belongs to Christ. You are His child, and you have become His righteousness! You still can sin, but the power of sin to control you is now gone. The battle between good and evil has already been won—that was done on the cross.

Hey, Satan is still alive and well on planet earth; I don't doubt that for a moment. He has an IQ of about a billion and an army of fallen angels carrying out his schemes. Before we were in Christ—and before we understood who we *are* in Christ—Satan kept our heads spinning with his lies. No more.

> *You, dear children, are from God and have overcome them, because the one who is in you is greater than the one who is in the world.* —1 John 4:4

Now that we have been set free with Truth, he can't *make* us do anything. On the other hand, when we rest in Christ and trust in His presence in us, the righteousness of God becomes our experience.

> *I can do all this through him who gives me strength.* —Philippians 4:13

Now, when you walk in righteousness, you can rightfully proclaim, "Christ made me do it!"

Jesus, I praise You that You are in me and that You are greater than Satan who is in this world. I rest in that truth. I lay all of the choices I will make today at Your feet. As I make them one by one, I trust that You will move through me to make my actions and my words a reflection of the righteousness of God that is in me because You are in me. Amen.

Your Nature or Your Nurture?

Love among men is awakened by something in the beloved. But the love of God is free, spontaneous, unevoked, uncaused. God loves men because he has chosen to love them. —J. I. Packer

Believe it or not, there is a controversy going on that is even older than whether we should sing more hymns or more choruses in church. It's the "nature vs. nurture" debate. There's a lot of discussion in our culture about why people do the things they do, especially *bad* things. (For some reason, they don't seem to be too concerned when humans actually do good things.)

Some say it's the way we were *nurtured*: parents, people, and environment determine how we turn out. Others say it's our *nature*: our genetic, physical, mental makeup determines whether we will be naughty or nice this Christmas season. Trust me, it's one of the oldest debates on the planet and if you dwell on it too long, your head is bound to explode.

I say, "Time out! Let it go! What difference does it make if it's nature or nurture?" Once we become Christians and are placed in Christ, we get that new heart—the new nature. **But that new nature needs to be nurtured as well.** Amazingly, we now live in the family of the best nurturer in the universe.

> *What marvelous love the Father has extended to us! Just look at it—we're called children of God! That's who we really are!* —1 John 3:1 (The Message)

So get this: He's given you a new nature, and now, as His kid, He's going to perfectly nurture you so that you can walk in His righteousness. You have the heart. You have the Father. What's left to debate?

My awesome, perfect Father, I receive the love that You are extending to me! Thanks for my new nature in Christ. I entrust it to You now. I give You full access and full permission to nurture me as no human could ever do. Amen.

Keeping in Step with the Spirit

Nothing before, nothing behind: The steps of faith fall on the seeming void, and find the Rock beneath. —J. G. Whittier

I like that short poem. It was a favorite of Hudson Taylor, an English missionary who took a huge step of faith to take the good news about Christ to China in 1854. *"The steps of faith ... fall on the seeming void ..."* Applying a new truth about who you are in Christ is a step of faith like that—it never feels natural. It might even feel like inching out onto ice, or jumping from an airplane, or (as in Taylor's situation) sailing from your homeland into the complete unknown. No, there is nothing natural about the feeling at *first*. But first steps must be taken!

> *Those who belong to Christ Jesus have crucified the flesh with its passions and desires. Since we live by the Spirit, let us keep in step with the Spirit.* —Galatians 5:24-25

The Spirit lives and the Spirit leads! Because of your new nature in Jesus, that means that it is more natural for you to walk in holiness than to walk in sin ... no matter what those first awkward steps feel like. Do you hear me? That's really important. It is more natural for you to make the right choice than to make the wrong one.

When you make the right choice, it's not, "Whoa! Can you believe it? I did the right thing!" It's to be expected now. Yeah, celebrate what Christ is doing through you, but get used to it! It's *normal* now to make the right choice in the power of the Spirit because that's who you are!

How is the Spirit nudging you to take a new step of faith today? Give it a try. It may feel like jumping into an endless fog, but you will find the Rock beneath.

Holy Spirit, by faith, I want to keep in step with You. May the reality of You in me translate into action through me! It feels unsafe and scary, but I trust in You as I learn to walk in new ways today. Amen.

Watching Your Words

The power of the gospel changes him ... and makes them into a new creation ... for the work of Christ sweeps away both his good and his evil and turns him into another man ... it also includes an actual change in the life of the individual. ... a transformation as deep as the roots of his human life. If it does not go that deep, it does not go deep enough. —A.W. Tozer

Words are powerful. Words that label us are some of the most powerful of all ... and all of us have them. The problem is that many of the sinful labels seem to brand us and actually seem to determine what we do:

- I'm an alcoholic
- I'm an addict
- I'm an adulterer
- I'm a liar
- I'm a _____ (fill in the blank)

Simply stated, **you will act as you believe yourself to be.** Well, if you're in Christ, those labels are *not* who you are. Your genetic predispositions were nailed to the cross, too, *dead and buried*. Do you have some issues that you need to work through? Absolutely. We all do. Do you need to get help? Probably.

But never, never forget that if you're in Christ, you are in union with the most truth-telling person in history. **Don't label yourself with anything except the label you have in Christ: an empowered, embraced, adored child of God indwelt with the Holy Spirit.**

Lord, I refuse and reject any label that has been placed on me that is contrary to what Your Word says is true about who I am in Christ! Bring specific truths about who I am in You to my mind today. I embrace Your Truth and reject the lies! Amen.

Do You Greet Grace?

Lord, I crawled across the barrenness to you with my empty cup uncertain in asking any small drop of refreshment. If only I had known you better I'd have come running with a bucket. —Nancy Spiegelberg

We've been studying what it means to be "in Christ," a phrase found in the opening line of Paul's letter to the Colossians.

> *Paul, an apostle of Christ Jesus by the will of God, and Timothy our brother, To God's holy people in Colossae, the faithful brothers in Christ: Grace and peace to you from God our Father. —Colossians 1:1-2*

The opening lines of ancient letters almost always have three elements in them: the sender, the receiver, and a greeting. So if I was writing back in that day, it would have looked something like this:

Pete, a pastor of Christ Jesus by the will of God, to the holy and faithful brothers and sisters in Christ on the internet. Grace and peace to you this morning!

In the ancient Hebrew world, the greeting was almost always *Shalom*, meaning "peace," which Paul chose to use here. The Greeks greeted each other with the greeting *Kairan*, which means "greetings." (Brilliant, I know. Of course, it would have been a lot easier for all of us if they had just used English, like all the aliens in the Star Trek TV series, but that's beside the point.)

But Paul didn't use *kairan*. He used *kairos*, which means "grace." In fact, check out the greeting and closing of every single one of his letters and you will see *kairos*. He was *constantly* reminding people that they are recipients of God's unmerited favor. **The beginning and end of all he wrote challenges us to live in this "grace and peace from God our Father."**

How about you?
- Do you greet grace in the morning as God's gift?
- Is grace what you greet others with as you go through the day?
- When the day is done, have you treated yourself with grace, too?

Father of Shalom and Kairos, by the power of Your Spirit and the truth of Your Word, I receive Your grace for today! May it be the beginning and end of all I do. May it be the theme of all my thoughts. May it saturate all my relationships … may it be my greeting to the world as You live though me. Amen.

Have You Graduated from Grace?

Man is born broken. He lives by mending. The grace of God is glue.
—Eugene O'Neill (1888-1953)

Be nice to nerds. Chances are you'll end up working for one. —**Attributed to Bill Gates during a high school graduation speech**

When learning to read and write, teachers first taught us "sight words." These are basic words like *a, and, big, blue, can, go, jump, little, look, make, me, my, not, one.* Once we get those down, we can forget about them and move on to more adult-sounding words like "antidisestablishmentarianisms" —the longest word in the English dictionary, right?

Wrong. **You can't *not* use them.** They are the glue that holds language together; but **you might be tempted to think you have outgrown them as you grow up.**

Grace is a Christian sight word. It might seem overused sometimes, but it's not! Nothing works in Christianity without it—not even the big Christian words like *soteriology* and *ecclesiology*. Nothing. Because of that, you can be assured of a couple of things:

1. We must always keep grace before our eyes. Our tendency is to want to live out of the flesh. *So we constantly have to remind ourselves that it is grace in which we live.*

2. The evil one hates grace and tries to destroy and distort it every chance he gets.

> *For certain individuals whose condemnation was written about long ago
> have secretly slipped in among you. They are ungodly people, who pervert the
> grace of our God into a license for immorality and deny Jesus Christ our only
> Sovereign and Lord.* —Jude 1:4

Under the influence of the deceiver and the tendencies of the flesh, humans "change the grace of God" into many things: An excuse for inaction, a justification for sin, a smokescreen for unbelief. So we have to constantly remember the pure and powerful meaning and purpose of grace.

Master Teacher, don't let me ever think that I have grown up and graduated from grace! Instead, saturate my soul with its potent presence! Let me see grace as an absolutely indispensable Christian "sight word" that glues everything together. Show me today where I don't see grace as important, then live that grace through me. Amen.

Beyond Grace

A man can no more take in a supply of grace for the future than he can eat enough today to last him for the next 6 months, nor can he inhale sufficient air into his lungs with one breath to sustain life for a week to come. We are permitted to draw upon God's store of grace from day to day as we need it.
—D. L. Moody

Sometimes Christians who are not living in grace have a hard time understanding why the rest of us are always coming back to it. Well, the truth is we should never have left grace in the first place! But, we do. **And the moment that grace leaves my mind, a sneaky form of Christian legalism takes its place.**

It's so subtle. Like when I miss my "quiet time" of Bible study and prayer. In the first ten years of my ministry at Bent Tree, every single Sunday morning I had a quiet time. I didn't miss one, because in the back of my mind I had this thought: *God won't bless my sermon if I don't spend any time with Him.* So my quiet time became my way of twisting God's arm to make sure I didn't lay an egg. See how that works? That's law-thinking. The fact of the matter is God can speak through me as He sees fit, whether I've had a quiet time or not.

Do I want to have uninterrupted time meditating on the Word and praying? Yeah, of course, I do. I usually experience an intimate connection with my Savior, with my King of kings and Lord of lords. But the moment it's not an extension of grace I start to feel that I must have a quiet time so that He'll bless me.

> *Now this is our boast. Our conscience testifies that we have conducted ourselves in the world, and especially in our relations with you, with integrity and godly sincerity. We have done so, relying not on worldly wisdom but on God's grace.*
> —2 Corinthians 1:12

Worldly wisdom says X amount of performance earns X amount of blessings from God. Grace says God just wants our works to be done as an extension of a grace-based relationship. Once legalism creeps in, the relationship gets tainted and the unconditional love of God becomes a theory rather than an experience.

God of Grace, search my heart, Lord. Show me where I have made laws in my own mind, where I have constructed bargains to get Your blessings. Bring me back to pure grace where my works are nothing more than heartfelt overflow of Your Spirit's work through me. Amen.

Is Your Church Off Base?

The law detects, grace alone conquers sin. —Saint Augustine of Hippo
(A.D. 354-430)

Some people are grace-based. Others are not. Some churches are grace-based, others are not. **Every individual and every institution can be works-based by trying to use law and legalism to attain righteousness** (in their own minds at least). But they don't normally advertise this. I have yet to see a sign that says, *Welcome to First Friendly Church of the Law: We will burn you out with a smile on our face! This week's sermon: Self Righteousness Through Self-effort in 237 Easy Steps.*

No, it's much more subtle than that, but law-based individuals and churches can leave you with that feeling you aren't performing the way you should. The conclusion? God's not pleased and you aren't righteous. The church in Galatia was a works-based church. That's why Paul wrote this to them:

> *I do not set aside the grace of God, for if righteousness could be gained through the law, Christ died for nothing!* —Galatians 2:21

Antioch, on the other hand, was grace based.

> *The Lord's hand was with them, and a great number of people believed and turned to the Lord. News of this reached the church in Jerusalem, and they sent Barnabas to Antioch. When he arrived and saw what the grace of God had done, he was glad and encouraged them all to remain true to the Lord with all their hearts.* —Acts 11:21-23

Think about this for a second: **A grace-based church is a family of believers who choose to live not by *rules* but by the *Ruler*.** Their lives are lived through Jesus and His grace! The focus is on Jesus and His grace, not the legalism and self.

Where is your focus today?!

Dear Lord, give me the discernment to recognize the voices of law and legalism around me. Be they coming from my church, my friends or family, or from my own flesh, give me the wisdom and strength to be grace-based with myself and them, too. Amen.

Where Are You in the Picture of Grace?

Grace is given to heal the spiritually sick, not to decorate spiritual heroes.
—Martin Luther

God gives us a lot of pictures of grace in the Bible. Since it's not too cool to have real pictures in our Bibles anymore, God gives them to us in words to keep our attention and to help us see ourselves in His incredible story. Matthew 20 is one of those pictures:

> *For the kingdom of heaven is like a landowner who went out early in the morning to hire workers for his vineyard. He agreed to pay them a denarius for the day and sent them into his vineyard.*

Throughout the day, the landowner kept hiring people until it was almost quitting time.

> *He went out again about noon and about three in the afternoon and did the same thing. About five in the afternoon he went out and found still others standing around.*

So he finally gets everyone working just before the whistle blows. But when they head to the time clock to punch out, something weird happens

> *The owner of the vineyard said to his foreman, "Call the workers and pay them their wages, beginning with the last ones hired and going on to the first." The workers who were hired about five in the afternoon came and each received a denarius.*

And they weren't even with a union or the government! (Sorry, I couldn't resist). Understandably, the guys with blisters on their hands were a little miffed when some of the others haven't even broken a sweat. When I read this, I felt it was really unfair. You probably did, too. My guess is that at least a part of you—maybe a big part of you—identifies with the guys that put in a full day.

But this story isn't about fairness, is it? It's about grace. Do you know the reason why we don't like this passage of Scripture? Because most of us instinctively identify with the all-day workers, don't we? But do you know who we are in this word picture? **We are the eleventh-hour worker, that's who we are.**

O, Lord of the vineyard, reveal my pride and arrogance through Your Word. Humble me by Your grace. Amen.

Where Are You Based?

The great mistake made by most of the Lord's people is in hoping to discover in themselves that which is to be found in Christ alone. —Arthur Pink

After decades of following Jesus and studying His life, I'm still amazed at the graphic contrasts that set Him apart from everything and everyone else. **The contrast between law and grace is one of those black and white distinctions that Scripture magnifies:**

> *Out of his fullness we have all received grace in place of grace already given. For the law was given through Moses; grace and truth came through Jesus Christ. No one has ever seen God, but the one and only Son, who is himself God and is in closest relationship with the Father, has made him known.* —John 1:16-18

If you want to base your life on Law, go with Moses. If you want to base it on grace, go with Jesus. You get to choose. It's one or the other day-by-day!

Law says: God has people on performance-based acceptance, and I must earn His acceptance. That means I must perform in order to earn His acceptance. If I perform well, He'll be happy with me. If I don't perform well, He won't be.

Grace says: God has His people on a Jesus-based acceptance. Because Christ is in me, I am fully accepted. I just need to now appropriate, own, and enjoy that acceptance. A grace-based person always chooses grace, relying completely in Christ and His work. But be warned! The evil one will use anything to deceive you—even Scripture. (Remember, Satan tried to use Scripture to tempt Jesus!)

He loves to see Christians live out of the flesh, and he knows that the flesh and the law go together. So he loves getting you focused on rules, because he knows that law, flesh, and rules lead to death and despondency. **Since Satan has lost you to grace, he'd love to keep you wallowing in law, and he will deceive you any way he can—even using biblical commands to get you to live out law by your flesh, rather than letting Christ live through you by grace!**

God of Grace, I refuse to let Satan put me under performance-based law! Please show me when I fall for this deception. Make all my decisions of obedience based on grace as a natural overflow of Your complete acceptance of me in Christ. Amen.

You and Mephibosheth

To the extent that you are clinging to any vestiges of self-righteousness or are putting any confidence in your own spiritual attainments, to that degree you are not living by the grace of God in your life. —Jerry Bridges, *Transforming Grace*

"Mephibosheth!" No, I didn't just sneeze. That's a name. It's a guy in the Bible. He's one of my favorite biblical characters partly because I love his name so much.

Mephibosheth was the son of Jonathan and the grandson of King Saul, who hated David with a passion. When Saul and Jonathan were killed in the same battle, news got back to the nurse who was taking care of Mephibosheth. He was five years old at the time, and she started to run for fear. She grabbed up the little boy, she tripped, she fell, she landed on top of the boy, and she crippled both of his feet. When David eventually ascended to the throne, he had Mephibosheth brought before him.

I'm guessing that Mephibosheth was pretty sure he was toast. He was a direct descendent of a royal enemy, and David would likely squish him like a bug. But David didn't. David said to him, "I am going to show kindness to you because of your father, Jonathan." Mephibosheth responded, "Why would you show kindness to a dead dog like me?"

This is a beautiful picture of God's grace!

- David represents God giving grace and kindness.
- Jonathan represents Jesus Christ.
- Mephibosheth represents you and me.

Though we are born in sin as descendants of the enemies of God, God shows us kindness because of Jesus. That's a picture of "grace." **Imagine you are Mephibosheth; imagine that you are in this picture of grace ... because you are.**

O Lord, without You, we are nothing more than dead dogs. In Jesus, we are welcome to live in the palace, in the presence of the King. Thank You for Your grace, Heavenly Father. Amen.

God Helps WHO?

The burden of life is from ourselves, its lightness from the grace of Christ and the love of God. —**William Bernard Ullanthorne** *(1806-1889)*

If you've been around Christians much, you've probably heard us mock a very popular motto: "God helps those who help themselves." Yeah, we make fun of it; I mean, it's not even a Bible verse. Not only is it non-biblical, it is *contra*-biblical— the exact opposite of what Scripture teaches. So we laugh at it ... and then turn around and live by it.

Be honest, now. Doesn't something deep down inside you feel that God is more likely to help you, love you, accept you, and deliver you if you are trying your hardest? Don't you fear that He is likely to leave you stranded and alone if you haven't done your best? ... Or am I the only one?!

Listen, I believe that we are destined to be doers of God's Word. We were created to be our part in the Body that is living in grace and sharing His grace with the world (see Romans 10:13-15 for how this works). God's involvement is a given.

For the Spirit God gave us does not make us timid, but gives us power, love and self-discipline. So do not be ashamed of the testimony about our Lord or of me his prisoner. Rather, join with me in suffering for the gospel, by the power of God. He has saved us and called us to a holy life—not because of anything we have done but because of his own purpose and grace. This grace was given us in Christ Jesus before the beginning of time, but it has now been revealed through the appearing of our Savior, Christ Jesus, who has destroyed death and has brought life and immortality to light through the gospel. —2 Timothy 1:7-10

His grace saved us, and His grace calls us to a holy life. One result of this holy life is that I join with others in suffering for the Good News. I want to do that because I want other people to experience His grace. **But it's "not because of anything we have done, but because of his own purpose and grace."**

Who does God help? God helps those who are completely helpless, which, by the way, is you and me and everyone else.

Lord of the Harvest, I come to You helpless today. I give up trying to help myself. Thank You for forgiving me when trying to earn Your help by works. So, I rest in You now. I claim the spirit of power and love You have placed in me. Live a holy life through me by Your grace according to Your purposes. Amen.

Ask Yourself the Question

If you can lose your salvation, you already have. —Tommy Nelson

Being "saved by grace" is a clear doctrine found in tons of passages, like Ephesians 2:8-10. But some people believe that if you don't hang onto Jesus tightly enough or if you commit certain sins, you can actually lose your salvation. You can lose your grip; and you can spend eternity in hell, even though you have been born again. It can be quite confusing because there are a few verses that *look like* they say that, *if* you take them out of the greater context of the whole Bible.

It's important to know that it's not you holding onto Jesus. It's Jesus holding you. For instance, Jesus said:

> *I give them eternal life, and they shall never perish; no one can snatch them out of my hand.* —John 10:28

That's a beautiful word picture. Close your eyes for a second and imagine that: *Jesus is gently holding you in His hands, protecting you. Keeping you secure throughout life so that no one and nothing can separate you from Him.* That's the picture of grace.

The Galatians, however, allowed legalism and the flesh to contaminate the grace of God. So Paul asked them a very important question:

> *Are you so foolish? After beginning by means of the Spirit, after walking in grace, are you now trying to finish by means of the flesh?* —Galatians 3:3

We are saved by grace and secure in grace forever. His love never fails. He is with us and in us always. He is the One who holds us. **Have you become foolish by trying to attain this by your own efforts?**

Unchanging Savior, thank You, thank You for holding me close and never letting me go, ever. I rest in Your love and Your grace. Remind me often of the foolishness of my human effort. I trust in You and the Spirit's work within me for my security. Amen.

Keeping Grace Amazing

He who has not felt what sin is in the Old Testament knows little what grace is in the New. He who has not trembled in Moses, and wept in David, and wondered in Isaiah will rejoice little in Matthew or rest little in John. He who has not suffered under the Law will scarcely hear the glad sound of the gospel.
—R. W. Barbour

Grace is amazing—and I use "amazing" in its truest sense. When we contemplate grace, it should leave us shaking our heads in wonder, and raising our hands in praise. **In pure undiluted form, grace is stunning … yet, I'm afraid that our flesh tends to water it down over time.** A modern rendition of Newton's classic hymn, "Amazing Grace," would sound like this:

"Amazing grace how sweet the sound that saved a pretty good guy like me. I once was directionally challenged, but now I'm found. I once needed some corrective lenses, but now I see."

You probably know how the hymn really goes, and that it is an echo of biblical truth. Grace saved "a wretch like me." Not a "pretty good guy," but a self-centered, independent mess. Scripture is very clear that all our good works in the flesh are but filthy rags, stinking rags in the nostrils of God. I "was lost," not directionally challenged or just a little off track; I was completely wandering in ignorance. My vision wasn't a little fuzzy, "I was blind." Everything was black. I couldn't see a thing, but He opened my eyes and I now see truth.

And, this seeing, this "founded-ness," and this life are a result of His amazing grace.

In 2 Timothy 2:1 the apostle Paul said to his young protégé: *"You then, my son, be strong in the grace that is in Christ Jesus."*

That's a command. It's an imperative. Be strong in that grace. Own it. Appropriate it. **Ponder grace regularly so that it never ceases to amaze you that a just and holy God loves you and embraces you because it is His nature and joy to do so.**

God, keep grace amazing in my soul. May the Spirit prompt my mind to think about it often; may my emotions feel it deeply; and may my will bend to it continually. Amen.

The Power You Need to Overcome Evil

And all the powers of darkness tremble at what they've just heard. 'Cuz all the powers of darkness can't drown out a single word!
—*He Reigns* by the Newsboys

The king of Aram was at war with Israel. Like any decent leader, he had a group of strategists that planned the movements of his enormous army. It should have been a slam-dunk victory. His only problem was that Israel ALWAYS knew what they were going to do before they did it! The king thought he had a leak in his leadership. When he confronted them, they said it wasn't them, but the prophet Elisha who was getting the inside scoop from God about their plans. He told his army to capture Elisha. When Elisha's servant went out to get water one morning, he saw a massive army ready to attack.

> *"Oh no, my lord! What shall we do?" the servant asked. "Don't be afraid," the prophet answered. "Those who are with us are more than those who are with them."* —2 Kings 6:15-16

When the servant's eyes were "opened," he saw that the hills surrounding Elisha were filled with the fiery chariots of God's army. On a natural level, it looked as if all hope was lost. But on a spiritual level, the battle belonged to the Lord.

You face enemies every day. Some are physical, but at least one is spiritual: Satan.

- He and his demons are very powerful.
- He's also wicked.
- He is the king or the lord of this dark world, this present darkness.
- He is the great liar, the great accuser.
- And he hates us—passionately hates us.

Like Elisha's servant, you may be filled with fear today, calling out, "What shall we do?"

> *You, dear children, are from God and have overcome them, because the one who is in you is greater than the one who is in the world.* —1 John 4:4

No matter what Satan has to throw at you today, remember that an army of angels battles *for* you and the Spirit of Christ is *in* you.

God, I'm so glad we're on the same side. Amen.

Your Victory in Jesus

The enemy wants to numb you into a coping kind of Christianity that has given up hope of seeing God's resurrection power. —**Bob Sorge,** *Glory: When Heaven Invades Earth*

Sometimes we visualize God's struggle with Satan like a championship heavyweight boxing match: The contenders are tough and it's gonna be a gruesome fight! Not so. The struggle is more like the Dallas Mavericks playing my 6th grade boys' basketball team. Now, my boys are really, very good. But if they go against the Mavericks, it's "a bit" of a mismatch. (Okay, so they would have no chance at all.)

The evil one, although he is quite powerful, has no chance against the King of kings and the Lord of lords either. There are at least three biblical reasons why we know that the evil one is subject to God:

1. **He is powerful but not omnipotent.** Because he was created, he does not have more power than God Himself.

2. **He is crafty but not omniscient.** He doesn't know everything. He does not know the future.

3. **He is wicked but not omnipresent.** He's in one place at a time. That's why he has to send in demons to do his work.

So if you are in Christ, by God's grace, you are on the winning team. At the same time, you must, must, must live in humble awareness of the fact that **Satan could crush you like the Mavericks would squish my boys' basketball team—if it wasn't for Christ in you and you being in Him.**

> *Finally, be strong in the Lord and in his mighty power … For our struggle is not against flesh and blood, but against the rulers, against the authorities, against the powers of this dark world and against the spiritual forces of evil in the heavenly realms.* —Ephesians 6:10,12

If Christ is in you, the devil can't hurt you because he has essential limitations. He is a created one and he's fighting the Creator of all things. **Just remember, you are strong in the Lord and the Lord alone.**

King of kings, give me humble confidence today. Humble me with full awareness that You and You alone can stand against Satan. Give me the courage to stand confidently knowing that You are in me and I am in You. The battle is Yours, Lord. I rest in You today. Amen.

Living in Victory Every Day

If you see a snake, just kill it—don't appoint a committee on snakes.
—Ross Perot

A South American missionary woke up one morning to find a giant anaconda snake in his little house. Over 25 feet long, right there, curled up. Scared him to death, obviously. He snuck out the window, went and told all his villager friends, "Come and help me!" So they went back to the house with him and looked through the window. Sure enough, there it was.

One of the villagers said, "I know what to do." And he grabbed his rifle, stuck it through the window, and BLAM! He put one bullet right in the head of that big snake. The snake started thrashing around shaking the house violently. They just stood there in disbelief as they heard crashing and shaking and vibrating. Then it started to slow down, and finally it was quiet in the house. When they went inside the house, they saw that the snake had caused incredible damage and chaos inside the little hut.

I know what some of you are thinking, because you're just like me. You're thinking: *Okay, I know the Bible says that Satan, the great serpent, is defeated, but something must be wrong at my house because Satan seems to be wreaking havoc in my life, in my relationships, and with sin struggles and all that kind of stuff.*

We live in the season of the evil one thrashing around after Jesus put a bullet in his head at the cross. Satan's final defeat is imminent. Soon enough, it will be permanent. In the meantime, our struggle with spiritual evil will continue as it attempts to thrash our lives. We are wise to take Paul's counsel:

> *Finally, be strong in the Lord and in his mighty power. Put on the full armor of God so that you can take your stand against the devil's schemes. For our struggle is not against flesh and blood, but against the rulers, against the authorities, against the powers of this dark world and against the spiritual forces of evil in the heavenly realms.* —Ephesians 6:10-12

Holy Spirit, give me faith and wisdom today as I encounter a defeated, dying spiritual enemy. You are in me and You are greater than he that is thrashing my world. I rest in You. I cease trying to fight in my own strength. I trust in You to fight for me and through me. Amen.

Clothing Yourself in God's Armor

The triumphant Christian does not fight for victory; he celebrates a victory already won. —Captain Reginald Wallis

When I was in fifth grade, I had to transfer elementary schools. That doesn't sound like that big of a thing, but for a scrawny fifth-grade boy it was terrifying. The first day I was at school, I was out on the playground minding my own business. All of a sudden, Tom Goodman showed up. Big, redheaded bully.

He walked up to me with all his minions who began to circle around me. "What are you doing?" he asked. "Nothing. I'm just hanging out," I answered as my heart began to beat wildly. "We have a little initiation for all the new boys who come to our school." The boys circled in. But all of a sudden, the circle parted as Nathan Sprague pushed two boys aside and walked in front of me, crossed his arms and said, "You'll have to go through me."

I thank God for the Nathan Spragues in the world, and I thank God for loving the world so much that He sent Jesus into it. **When all seemed lost, Jesus stepped in between us and the evil one … and that changes everything.**

> *Since the children have flesh and blood, he too shared in their humanity so that by his death he might destroy him who holds the power of death—that is, the devil—and free those who all their lives were held in slavery by their fear of death.* —Hebrews 2:14-15

Now don't get me wrong. It's not that we're hiding behind Jesus. Instead, it's that we are enveloped in Him. Even though Satan is the second most powerful entity in the universe, he's second by a long shot. He won't mess with Jesus—he *can't.* Through His death on the cross, Jesus *destroyed* Satan. When we put on the armor of God and walk in Christ, we see the defeat that Satan has already experienced played out before our eyes day after day after day.

Today, be strong in the Lord and in His mighty power. Be enveloped in His power; be enveloped in His armor. We have clothed ourselves with Christ Himself, **because awareness of Christ *in* us and intimacy *with* Him is an enveloping defense against lying spiritual bullies.**

Lord Jesus, thank You for stepping between me and the evil one. Thank You for destroying him through Your sacrifice on the cross. Today, give me a new awareness of who I am in You, of how I am enveloped by You. Amen.

Your Inescapable Appointment with God

I'm not afraid of my death. I just don't want to be there when it happens.
—**Woody Allen**

If you're like me, there are some appointments that you would just as soon not keep. The dentist for a root canal, the accountant for taxes, the doctor for the famous "after 50" physical … Yes, it feels like we should avoid them like the plague.

I think funerals are like that—and not just *other* people's funerals, but our *own*. Wouldn't we just as soon avoid that appointment, too? Maybe; but maybe not. Maybe we're afraid of death only because we aren't certain about what lies on the other side. Maybe if we knew the truth and believed it, it would change our perspective. Let's take a look:

> *Therefore we are always confident and know that as long as we are at home in the body we are away from the Lord. For we live by faith, not by sight. We are confident, I say, and would prefer to be away from the body and at home with the Lord. So we make it our goal to please him, whether we are at home in the body or away from it. For we must all appear before the judgment seat of Christ, so that each of us may receive what is due us for the things done while in the body, whether good or bad.* —2 Corinthians 5:6-10

That's a powerful, loaded passage. And it's kind of schizophrenic, too. Paul is saying that he would rather be away from his physical body and face to face with the Lord, but in the same breath he says that we have to appear before the "judgment seat of Christ." This is a different moment than when believers in Christ will be separated from those who don't believe. Paul is addressing believers in Christ here, saying that everyone who is in Christ will stand before Him and have "the talk." That's one appointment that we have to keep.

Sobering? Exciting? Terrifying? Seem too far away to matter?

We could feel all those things thinking about standing before the judgment seat of Christ. It is definitely "the big moment." It is the summation, the conclusion, the review of our entire earthly life. Are you ready for it?

Lord God, Your Scripture says that You are a righteous judge. But what will it be like to stand before You on that day? Lord, open my mind, open my heart, shape my will as I ponder that inescapable appointment with You. Transform my soul and my mind so that I might worship You with my body in a way that anticipates that powerful day. Amen.

The Christian Four-Letter Word

Do not judge, or you too will be judged. —Jesus

Judgment is not a four-letter word. But if you use it in some Christian circles, people are going to act like you're swearing right there in front of God and everybody. Sure, we all prefer words like *love, forgiveness,* and *acceptance.* Does *judgment* have a place in the Gospel of grace? Yes! Because it's a real, future event. According to 2 Corinthians 5:10, we *will* stand before the judgment seat of Christ, and 2 Corinthians 4:13-15 says that the Father Himself is going to take us there:

> *It is written: "I believed; therefore I have spoken." Since we have that same spirit of faith, we also believe and therefore speak, because we **know that the one who raised the Lord Jesus from the dead will also raise us with Jesus and present us with you to himself. All this is for your benefit,** so that the grace that is reaching more and more people may cause thanksgiving to overflow to the glory of God.*

We will be raised with Jesus. We will be presented to God. That is a remarkable element of our destiny—and it's worth *pondering;* it's worth *imagining;* it's worth *planning.* But most importantly, it's worth putting it into a biblical perspective, because the Bible has a lot to say about it.

One of the things the Bible says—and this probably goes against everything we are inclined to feel—is that this judgment seat of Christ is good for us. It's for our "benefit" and it causes "thanksgiving to overflow to the glory of God." My guess is that those are facets of God's judgment that you never really considered before. But there they are, in black and white in the Bible. *Our judgment will be good for us, our judgment will glorify God.*

But how can this be? Is it because of our successful performance and religious duties? Is it because we somehow purify ourselves and make ourselves worthy? Is it because we somehow avoided the big "no-no" sins successfully through our life?

Not a chance. Check out the verse again. What will make your judgment beneficial and glorifying? It is "the grace that is reaching more and more people."

Jesus, break some of my preconceived ideas right now. In the world, the judgment we receive from other people is never beneficial nor glorifying. Touch my heart right now, so that I might be able to consider Your judgment through the power of Your grace. Amen.

He Will Never Reject You. Ever.

We can never judge the lives of others, because each person knows only their own pain and renunciation. It's one thing to feel that you are on the right path, but it's another to think that yours is the only path. —**Paulo Coelho**

There's at least a little bit of each of us that envies the movie star and the rockstar. We want to be known. But more importantly, we want to be *known and loved.* In the world, we are often *known and rejected*, something that continually keeps us from opening up to other people. More times than not, that fear of rejection gets imported into our relationship with God. We try to hide from Him, too, but to no avail.

> *For we must all appear before the judgment seat of Christ …*
> —2 Corinthians 5:10

The word *appear* means to "be made manifest;" it means "to be turned inside out." As Philip Hughes puts it, to appear is "to be laid bare, stripped of every outward facade of respectability, and openly revealed in the full and true reality of one's character."

That's uncomfortable—worse than those dreams where you are giving a speech and realize you don't have any clothes on. Those dreams are common among humanity, and people that analyze that sort of thing believe they reveal **a common nightmare we all share: Being laid bare, inside out, naked and exposed … and yet that's exactly what is going to happen to us when we stand before Jesus at the judgment seat.** We are talking *fully known* by the Holy One of God. Shouldn't that horrify us?

Nope.

We need to think about this one, need to let the Bible put it in full perspective. Because first of all, that's the way we already are—**we are already appearing before Him. Just because we don't see *Him* doesn't mean that He doesn't see *us*.** He does see us fully, exactly as we are, right now, all the time.

You *are* fully known, and yet, if you are in Christ, you are fully, completely, categorically, unwaveringly, absolutely loved.

Jesus, I grasp onto Your promise that You will never forsake me, nor will You ever reject me. I thank You that You are with me, and in me, today until the end of the age, when I will appear before You, loved, just as I am today, because of Your grace. Amen.

Just You and God

Among the attributes of God, although they are all equal, mercy shines with even more brilliancy than justice. —Miguel de Cervantes Saavedra

Bible passages like 2 Corinthians 5 are packed. They overflow with meaning. Nearly every word can have deep impact on how we anticipate something like the judgment of Christ.

> *For we must all appear before the judgment seat of Christ, so that each of us may receive what is due us for the things done while in the body, whether good or bad.* —2 Corinthians 5:10

For example, consider that the passage says "each of us." But notice what it doesn't say:

- You will not be asked to give an account for your spouse.
- You will not be asked to give an account for your neighbor.
- You will not be asked to give an account for your friends.
- You'll not be asked to give an account for your pastor.
- And no, you won't have a lawyer with you.

At the judgment seat of Christ, it's just going to be you and Jesus. This will be "the big moment." It might lead you to believe that you will be on trial for your sins, but that's not the case. Hundreds of passages of Scripture teach the very simple truth that if you are in Christ, your sins are covered, dealt with, done with, and will not be brought up by Him again. *Hundreds of passages of Scripture* such as Romans 8:1-2:

> *Therefore, there is now no condemnation for those who are in Christ Jesus, because through Christ Jesus the law of the Spirit who gives life has set you free from the law of sin and death.*

No, if you are in Christ, you will not experience His wrath. If you are in Christ, this moment will have nothing to do with your sin. It's just about you and Him … you and Him, alone together.

Lord Jesus, I believe that You are with me now. I believe that Your Spirit is within me. And yet my life is so cluttered by others. I look forward to that day, to that honest moment when no one else will be around, when pure honesty will be shared. Give me a taste today of what the feast will be like. Amen.

Who Are You in the Story?

Whooooooo are you? Who? Who? Who? Who?"—Song by *The Who*
(Who else would it be by?!)

Jesus loved to tell stories. His parables are great because you'll just be reading along in the story, and you think you understand what He's getting at, when all of a sudden, "Smack." He hits you in the side of the head. Matthew 20 is one of these stories—and the "smack" has to do with who you are in the story.

> *For the kingdom of heaven is like a landowner who went out early in the morning to hire men to work in his vineyard.* —Matthew 20:1

The landowner agreed to pay the workers one denarius. Then, every three hours, he went out and hired more workers until it was just about quitting time.

> *"About five in the afternoon he went out and found still others standing around. He asked them, 'Why have you been standing here all day long doing nothing?' 'Because no one has hired us,' they answered. He said to them, 'You also go and work in my vineyard.' When evening came the owner of the vineyard said to his foreman, 'Call the workers and pay them their wages, beginning with the last ones hired and going on to the first.'"* (20:6-8)

This is where the "smack" comes in. The landowner pays the ones who have only worked a few minutes the same amount he pays the guys who have worked a whole day! "Unfair!" you are probably saying. Yes, it is, but it upsets you only because you probably identify yourself with the wrong person in the story.

If you've been working for Christ, diligently doing His work for a long time, you will automatically identify with the guys who worked all day, complaining (probably to yourself) about why the last guys get the same as you. But that's not who you are in the passage. This passage is about the last person hired. Who are you? "Smack!" In this story, *you* are the last person hired, the one who gets far, far more than he has earned. And friends, this is the best news you could ever hear.

> *So the last will be first, and the first will be last.* (20:16)

Gracious Lord, humble me, in the light of Your grace. Deep in my heart give me a keen awareness that every blessing that I have is a free gift from You. When I compare myself with others, convict me that I deserve nothing, and yet, have so richly received everything from You. Amen.

The Moment You Stand Before Christ

I never met a Christian who sat down and planned to live a mediocre life.
—**Howard Hendricks**

Close your eyes for a moment, and imagine into the future. Seriously, close your eyes and imagine. Think ahead to the moment when you will live out 2 Corinthians 5:10:

> *For we must all appear before the judgment seat of Christ, so that each of us may receive what is due us for the things done while in the body, whether good or bad.*

That last little word "bad" probably sends shivers up your spine, and it probably should, at least at first thought. I mean, think about *everything* bad you've done and now you are about to "receive what is due"… yikes.

But remember, we aren't talking about the "great white throne judgment" where those who don't know Jesus are separated and punished. This is where those whose sins are already covered by the blood of Jesus meet Him face to face, and this is what will happen:

> *If anyone builds on this foundation [Jesus Christ] using gold, silver, costly stone, wood, hay or straw, their work will be shown for what it is, because the Day will bring it to light. It will be revealed with fire, and the fire will test the quality of each person's work.* —1 Corinthians 3:12-13

At the judgment seat of Christ, He is going to put everything under the torch and the good stuff will survive and the bad, worthless stuff will go up in flames. Again, imagine it. You are standing there, meeting Jesus face to face and right then He takes a blowtorch to your life. And anything that is worthless (that is what the word translated "bad" in 2 Corinthians 5:10 actually means), anything that was in the flesh, any impure motives, any momentary lapses—even the sin that is already covered by His blood—will be burned beyond recognition for all of eternity.

Wow, the day we stand before the judgment seat of Christ … that is going to be a great day, isn't it?

Jesus, I need You to rewire my brain on this one! Renew my mind about the day I will stand before You in judgment. I thank You ahead of time, and I praise You from the bottom of my heart, that all the worthless things go up in smoke and You greet me with nothing but good. Glory to Your name. Amen.

What God Can Do in and through You

I'm not judgmental; you're just an overly sensitive idiot. —**Bumper sticker**

When we are living by the law rather than by grace, when we are walking in the flesh rather than the Spirit, it is so natural to judge others to justify ourselves. If you want to lift yourself up, why not cut everybody else down? Why not set up your own little judgment seat so that you can categorize other people's stuff as good or bad?

> *You, then, why do you judge your brother or sister? Or why do you treat them with contempt? For we will all stand before God's judgment seat. It is written: "As surely as I live," says the Lord, "every knee will bow before me; every tongue will acknowledge God." So then, each of us will give an account of ourselves to God. Therefore let us stop passing judgment on one another.*
> —Romans 14:10-13

Listen, God's judgment is coming. Not only is it His job to judge perfectly and graciously, but your judgments on other people are going to end up in the "worthless" pile that goes up in flames. Second Corinthians 5:9-10 again puts it in perspective:

> *So we make it our goal to please him, whether we are at home in the body or away from it. For we must all appear before the judgment seat of Christ, so that each of us may receive what is due us for the things done while in the body, whether good or bad.*

What's your focus today, right now? Have you naturally slid into judging others, or are you looking forward to that day when He will judge *your* stuff? Life on earth is hard but knowing the judgment seat of Christ is coming makes it all worthwhile. Don't focus on others, simply respond to the Spirit's work in you and through you!

Jesus, Your Word says that I am "in You" and You are "in me." Open my eyes today, that I might see, moment by moment, the works that You are ready to do through me. Amen.

How You Can Live Life to the Fullest

The steadfast love of the Lord never ceases. His mercies never come to an end. They are new every morning. —**Lamentations 3:22-24**

One morning, I drove my family into the raw beauty of east Texas where a close friend of mine was waiting with a trailer of horses, saddled and ready to go. We climbed on, uncertain at first, not sure of where we were going or what the ride would be like. The horses walked at first, carefully circling. Then we headed into the unknown for six hours.

Through the brush, up over hills, building up speed as we went down into a creek bed, galloping full speed in about six inches of water. In my mind, scenes from that day still play in slow motion, like a movie; water spraying into the deep blue sky, glittering like shards of crystal in the rays of sunlight. Hour after hour with my wife and three kids—it was as near perfection as life can get on earth, I think. Just an amazing day.

I always have a hard time coming up with a vivid picture of what life "in Christ" is like. But that day got pretty close to a life lived in the grace of God. I see that day very much like Kingdom living on earth.

> *For it is by grace you have been saved, through faith—and this is not from yourselves, it is the gift of God—not by works, so that no one can boast. For we are God's workmanship, created in Christ Jesus to do good works, which God prepared in advance for us to do.* —Ephesians 2:8-10

Jesus, the Son, saved us by grace. God, the Father, like my friend, prepares good works in advance for us to do. He gets the horses saddled up for us. And then the Holy Spirit prompts us and pushes us, empowering us and producing fruit through us.

What's your job? Get on the horse. Stay on the horse. Be carried along. Trust… and hang on.

Abba Father, thank You for this day. For a day full of Your mercies that are new this morning one more time. Take me for the ride, Lord. I saddle up, and I hang on, trusting You with whatever this day might bring my way, ready to allow Your Spirit to propel me into any work that You have prepared for me. Amen.

Your Greatest Reward

What meaning have you found? What truth do you claim? For what purpose are you living? Life itself raises these questions. How can anyone help asking "what" and "why" when surrounded by an infinite sky? —Ron James

The horse ride that I had taken with my family through the wilderness of Texas was nearly a perfect day. For six hours I roamed with those I loved through the creation, swept along on a horse of great strength through adventures unknown. When we got back to the camp, we were just about spent. It was almost a perfect day … almost.

What would have topped it off would have been an awards ceremony, for us! Now, that would have been the perfect day. But that's crazy, you say. Why in the world would I get rewarded for something my friend prepared and a horse who did all the work?

Yeah, it would be crazy … but that's what will happen to each of us on "the Day" we stand before the judgment seat of Christ and look into His face for the first time. The good that He has done through us will be our reward. The worthless will be burned away forever.

> *If anyone builds on this foundation [Jesus Christ] using gold, silver, costly stones, wood, hay or straw, their work will be shown for what it is, because the Day will bring it to light. It will be revealed with fire, and the fire will test the quality of each person's work.* —1 Corinthians 3:12-13

> *For we must all appear before the judgment seat of Christ, so that each of us may receive what is due us for the things done while in the body, whether good or bad.* —2 Corinthians 5:10

How could this be? Why do we deserve to be rewarded with anything? Jesus saves us; the Father prepares good works in advance for us to do. The Holy Spirit tells us what they are and then He empowers us to produce fruits through us and then, when all that's done, He rewards US for all that stuff HE did?

It's called grace, my friend. It's called grace!

Father, I thank You for Your biblical truth. I thank You that You did not leave me to guess, that You made things very clear about the day I will stand before the judgment seat of Jesus. I find great joy in the idea of You rewarding me for the work You did through me. Your grace is amazing, Lord. Amen.

How to Avoid Getting Hooked by Evil

Yet the evil still increased, and, like the parasite of barnacles on a ship, if it did not destroy the structure, it obstructed its fair, comfortable progress in the path of life. —**William Banting**

The art of fishing is really all about the lure. If you can lure the fish to the hook thinking he's about to have a meal, he's going to get eaten instead. One of my favorite lures has a "treble hook"—three prongs all in one. If a fish takes it, whamo!

Sin is like a treble hook. Once you take the bait, sin snags you in three ways. Look at the original sin in Genesis when the woman took the bait of Satan's lie.

> *When the woman saw that the fruit of the tree was good for food and pleasing to the eye, and also desirable for gaining wisdom, she took some and ate it. She also gave some to her husband, who was with her, and he ate it.* —Genesis 3:6

What happened then? Whamo! They got hooked on the first hook: **Shame.**

> *Then the eyes of both of them were opened, and they realized they were naked…* —Genesis 3:7

Right after shame, they were pierced by **blame.**

> *The man said, "The woman you put here with me—she gave me some fruit from the tree, and I ate it."… The woman said, "The serpent deceived me, and I ate."* —Genesis 3:12-13

It was a triple blame game. The man blames the woman; he blames God; and she points the finger at Satan. Then finally they got snagged with **consequence.**

> *… with painful labor you will give birth to children … through painful toil … By the sweat of your brow you will eat your food … for dust you are and to dust you will return.* —Genesis 3:16-19

When Satan promises you something, it's just a lure with a three-pronged hook in it—the hooks of shame, blame, and consequences. With what specific temptations are you being baited right now? Do you see the three hidden hooks of sin waiting?

Father, give me insight to see through the lies of sin. Spare me from the shame, blame, and consequences of the sin that so easily entangles me. Amen.

How to Spot a Lie

I'll be there in 5 minutes. If not, read this again. —Text message

Media experts tell us our brains are bombarded with approximately 1,000,000,000 advertisements each day. Beyond that, our lives are filled with text messages, email messages, and phone messages. With all this information headed our way, **why would any Christian ever listen to the evil one?**

Because the Father of Lies knows how to catch people like you and me. He even has a specific strategy. Consider this analogy from Andrew Farley's *The Naked Gospel:*

Imagine you're going to a tropical climate for a vacation. Along the way a parasite crawls into your sandals and burrows inside your foot—so deep you don't even realize it. Eventually, it begins to send pain messages to your brain. You begin thinking, "There's something seriously wrong with *me*." **Not knowing about what lies within your foot you wrongly assume the problem is your foot itself.**

Although not actually physical, the "power of sin" is much like a parasite that has found its way inside your body.

> *What shall we conclude then? Do we have any advantage? Not at all! For we have already made the charge that Jews and Gentiles alike are all under the power of sin. As it is written: "There is no one righteous, not even one."*
> —Romans 3:9-10

When we become a believer in Jesus Christ, we become a new creation in our spirit, and the Holy Spirit comes to live inside us. Yet, **this parasite of sin still lies within us, but it's not us.** When our mind receives a lie from the evil one, "the power of sin" will take that lie and twist it into our own language, and we will think it's our thought—it even feels like it is coming from us. But it's not.

Sin is an imposter. **His strategy is to introduce thoughts into your mind and deceive you into thinking they're yours.** We are righteous in Christ, not in ourselves. The power of sin is still in us, but we don't have to say "yes" to it. When we know who we are in Christ and who He is in us, we can say "no."

Lord Jesus, by the power of Your Spirit and the truth of Your Word, enable me to identify the lies of the evil one that I have accepted as if they are coming from me. I do not want to be a slave to this power of sin. Free me to follow You through grace and truth. Amen.

How to Continually Nourish Your Mind

Nourish the mind as you would your body. The mind can't survive on junk food.
—Jim Rohn

Imagine Eve back in the garden. She's sitting there talking to the snake and she's a little confused. The Father of Lies is creating doubt, he's contradicted what the Father said to her, and yet, she reaches for the apple. Now, imagine what would have happened if she had pulled back her hand and said, "OK, you stay right there. I'll be right back." What if she had called out, "Daddy! Abba! Heavenly Father!" and sat down with Him to have a chat about what the snake had said. "You see that little snake over there? Here's what he told me. What is truth and what is a lie?" If she had done that, do you think the story would have looked differently?

If we're going to recognize the lure of temptation and avoid the three hooks of sin, we have to *know* the truth so that the truth can set us free. This takes place through a dynamic relationship with Jesus, by His Spirit living in us, and *knowing* the Truth. Paul said it this way:

> *For though we live in the world, we do not wage war as the world does. The weapons we fight with are not the weapons of the world. On the contrary, they have divine power to demolish strongholds. We demolish arguments and every pretension that sets itself up against the knowledge of God, and we take captive every thought to make it obedient to Christ.* —2 Corinthians 10:3-5

What does that mean? It means that we grab a suspicious thought and we say, "You're coming with me." We take it captive and we present it in front of Jesus and we say, "Jesus, I just had this thought. Is this a lie or is this Your truth?" And we pray, "Lord Jesus, open my eyes to Your Truth." By His Spirit, He will start to reveal His truth to us as we also compare the thought to what we know from the written Truth of God in the Bible.

Today, when a thought enters your mind, and as soon as you recognize that it might be a lie, take it captive to Jesus and say, "Jesus, what do You think about this?" and then test it with what the Bible says is Truth.

Consider a thought you are wrestling with right now. Take it to Jesus now.

Jesus, You are the Way, the Truth, and the Life. You know all things and Your Word is the test of all things. Search this thought I am bringing to You and lead me in Your eternal way. I trust in Your presence within me and Your Word to live out the truth today. Amen.

How to Identify Fact from Fiction

A lie that is accepted as truth, will affect your life as if it is true, even though it's a lie. —Bill Ewing

Sometimes our strengths can be our biggest weakness. Often our weaknesses can be our biggest … well, weakness (unless, through Christ, we allow Him to be strong through us). Both strengths and weaknesses make us vulnerable to the lies of Satan.

- The perfectionist thinks, *My value is in my performance.*
- The arrogant feels, *I deserve better than this.*
- The leader is certain, *I am more important than the people behind me.*
- The anorexic is convinced, *I am fat.*
- The materialist believes, *If I have a little more, I will be fulfilled .*
- The estranged spouse feels, *I deserve a fling.*
- The gifted know, *I can do it myself.*
- The sexually confused concludes, *I must be gay.*
- The sly is certain, *No one will ever know.*
- The conscientious senses, *I must be guilty.*

What are your strengths? What are your weaknesses? How are they making you vulnerable to accepting a lie as truth? God has revealed His truth to us in Scripture, in the Bible. It's the original, the authentic, the genuine article. Everything else is counterfeit. **And the very best way to recognize the counterfeit stuff is by knowing the real stuff.**

When my Dad was young, he was a bank examiner in England and one of his responsibilities was to find counterfeit money. He had a whole week of training to figure out what counterfeit money was like. They had him study every detail of every bit of normal, real bills all week long. By Thursday he said, "This is ridiculous. When do I get to look at the counterfeit stuff?" And they said, "Oh, you're not going to look at counterfeit stuff. That stuff changes all the time."

When you know the truth, the lies are obvious. When you know the truth, and Satan whispers a lie through the power of sin toward your strengths or weaknesses, you will recognize it for what it is. Then you can choose to allow the Spirit in you to respond in truth.

Holy Spirit, show me today where my strengths or weaknesses have made me vulnerable to a lie. Give me a lifelong hunger for Your Word, that You might implant its truth in my mind, then grant me the willingness to obey it. Amen.

Where Are Your Blind Spots?

You can fool yourself, you know. You'd think it's impossible, but it turns out it's the easiest thing of all. —Jodi Picault, *Vanishing Acts*

A couple years ago I wrote a book based on the Apostle's Creed entitled *Belief Matters.* I liked the double meaning in that title. It dealt with theological matters of belief, but it continually reminded me that what we believe matters tremendously.

A dear friend, Dave, learned this the hard way. During a season when his marriage was "drifting," a lovely young woman came into his office. He met her needs and she fulfilled his desires. Willingly, he was drawn into her seductions. Consciously, he ignored the heartfelt warnings of his friends at church. Intentionally, he decided to leave his wife and two small kids for this younger woman.

The pastor of the church engaged him. Looking across the table at him at a diner, his words were clear and few: "We've got to talk about church discipline, Dave. Until you are walking with Christ again, you're not welcome to worship and fellowship with us. We look forward to seeing you come back."

It was a slap in the face, but the shocking truth woke him up. With no one else to blame, he felt the shame and realized the consequences of everything he had lost. He went home to his wife and begged her to forgive him. By God's grace and in His power, she did. In time, they restored their marriage and have been together ever since.

It's a stunning story, but what stunned Dave was how easily and thoroughly he was deceived by the evil one. He told me, "Pete, I actually got to a place where I thought it was God's will for me to leave my wife for that other woman. I believed it's what He wanted for me ...." He was a living example of 2 Corinthians 11:3:

> But I am afraid that just as Eve was deceived by the serpent's cunning, your minds may somehow be led astray from your sincere and pure devotion to Christ.

Is it possible that you, a believer in Jesus Christ, could be deceived by the Father of Lies too?

Father, humble me. Show me my blind spots. Reveal where I think I can stand on my own. Show me where I am already in sin, where I am already taking control of my life in my own limited strength and flawed wisdom. I surrender to Your loving leadership and Your eternal wisdom again. I trust You in me to do what is right. Amen.

Making Sure You're Ready for What's to Come

In the face of all terror and uncertainty and illusion about the future we gladly point to Jesus and say that he is the future. —Theodore W. Jennings, Jr.

In March of 1942, Pearl Harbor was still in ruins and Japanese forces were tightening their grip on the Philippines. General Douglas MacArthur was following orders by President Roosevelt to leave the islands to "relocate." But it felt like a step in the wrong direction for the seasoned soldier. Perhaps trying to convince himself of the necessity of the move, he would later write, "We are not retreating; we are advancing in another direction." At the end of that month, he uttered the now famous words: "I came through, and I shall return."

Nearly 2000 years before that day, another Man had made a similar promise. He was leaving for good reason, and His promise to come again was even more certain. That man was Jesus Christ. Approximately 300 passages in Scripture allude to Christ's second coming—a return that will be swift, righteous, and unexpected for many. Jesus gave His word that He would be back, and through that promise, we can find tangible hope and clear direction for our lives today.

> *Do not let your hearts be troubled. Trust in God; trust also in me. In my Father's house are many rooms; if it were not so, I would have told you. I am going there to prepare a place for you. And if I go and prepare a place for you, I will come back and take you to be with me that you also may be where I am.* —John 14:1-3

Life can slip away on us quickly. As days turn to weeks and weeks to years, and years turn into decades, it's easy to lose focus on the promise of John 14. Being distracted from this future event, however, can rob us of precious perspective for today.

MacArthur made good on his promise, returning to the Philippines as the Allies pushed back through the Pacific. Jesus will return, too. He is the ultimate promise keeper. When? I'm not sure, but we're at least 24 hours closer to that event than we were yesterday at this time, so … "Don't let your heart be troubled. Trust in God!"

Jesus, open the implications of Your Word to me now. Tell me the truth! In the days ahead, I want to ponder the meaning of Your return and prepare accordingly. Counsel me by Your Spirit so I might live each remaining day with wisdom and purpose. Amen.

Living Today in Light of Tomorrow

The future just isn't what it used to be. —Unknown

The Bible alludes to the return of Christ at least 200 times. Trying to pin an exact date on His return is very difficult. Still, this seems to be an ongoing hobby among Christians. Throughout the centuries, hundreds of predictions have been made, and they all have one thing in common so far: All were wrong.

My favorite example was a little book entitled *88 Reasons Why Christ Will Return in 1988.* By carefully manipulating numerous prophetic verses in the Bible, the author concluded that Jesus would come back in September of 1988. The author sold about a zillion of these little booklets. Where my dad was a pastor, we were constantly getting calls from people trying to get copies from the church's bookstore. As September drew near, the callers kept asking my dad why he wasn't carrying the book. "Call me back in October," he said.

Nobody called.

In Matthew 24, Jesus told the disciples about many of the "signs" that would be seen before He came again. Honestly, it looks like a lot of them are taking place around us here and now. We may have entered the season of the last days of the last days. But putting a date on His return? Jesus made one thing very clear:

> *No one knows about that day or hour, not even the angels in heaven, nor the Son, but only the Father. As it was in the days of Noah, so it will be at the coming of the Son of Man. For in the days before the flood, people were eating and drinking, marrying and giving in marriage, up to the day Noah entered the ark; and they knew nothing about what would happen until the flood came and took them all away. That is how it will be at the coming of the Son of Man.* —Matthew 24:36-39

My concern is that false and foolish predictions have the same effect as the boy who cried "wolf," when the townspeople became numb to the false warnings and were therefore unprepared when the event actually did take place. Instead of fruitless predicting, Jesus calls us to "be on the alert" and make the most of the time we have left for things that matter!

Lord Jesus, calm my mind. Stir up Your Spirit inside of mine and let me truly ponder the implications of Your second coming. Check my priorities, Lord. Expose what I am living for today. Shift my trust to You, and empower me to live by Your Spirit today. Amen.

Where to Find Strength in These Last Days

We are living in the age of the church. It is an age of grace and an age of the spirit in which we have, by God's mercy and love, opportunity to proclaim to the world the good news about Jesus Christ. —Ron James

Let's be honest, aren't we all just a little bit skeptical about Christ's return? It's been almost 2000 years and none of us regularly check the skies to see if His return flight is coming in. Peter's words to the believers of his day are just as relevant today as they were then. They are sober words, words that put it all in perspective:

> *Above all, you must understand that in the last days scoffers will come, scoffing and following their own evil desires. They will say, "Where is this 'coming' he promised? Ever since our fathers died, everything goes on as it has since the beginning of creation." But they deliberately forget that long ago by God's word the heavens came into being and the earth was formed out of water and by water. By these waters also the world of that time was deluged and destroyed. By the same word the present heavens and earth are reserved for fire, being kept for the day of judgment and destruction of ungodly. But do not forget this one thing, dear friends: With the Lord a day is like a thousand years, and a thousand years are like a day. The Lord is not slow in keeping his promise, as some understand slowness. Instead he is patient with you, not wanting anyone to perish, but everyone to come to repentance.* —2 Peter 3:3-9

Noah had been given plenty of warning, but everybody just kept on doing their own thing. Then came a wall of water—whoosh! Today, it's the same thing: Jesus has given plenty of warning, but many who don't know Him go about their way indifferent or unaware He will intervene again in judgment. Plenty of believers are doing the same thing.

It is so, so important to constantly remind ourselves that we are in a very precarious season of human history: We live between the game-winning play (the cross and resurrection) and the end of the game (His second coming). God is taking His time to give us time to play the game through to the end with everything we have!

Lord, I want to use these remaining days, be they few or many, to make an eternal difference. Give me Your heart for those who are perishing. Then live through me in a way that communicates to them Your tangible love. Amen.

How to Make the Most of Each Day

Build me a son, oh Lord, who will be strong enough to know when he is weak, and brave enough to face himself when he is afraid, one that will be proud and unbending in defeat, and humble and gentle in victory.
—**General Douglas MacArthur**

Soccer was my sport as a kid. I grew up in England, so soccer was normal. But there's one thing that isn't normal about soccer: The scoreboard doesn't have a clock. The referee is the one who keeps the time. And when it comes to the future, the Father is the one who keeps the time.

From cover to cover, the Bible contains hundreds of passages that deal with the second coming of Christ. Some of these verses are in apocalyptic literature, including books like Daniel and Revelation. These books are beautifully written and fascinating to read—full of wild imagery and amazing snapshots of future history—but they are very difficult to interpret. Few of the passages are presented in a clear sequence so determining the order of the events that take place around the second coming of Christ is a real challenge.

If you want to be a serious student of this stuff, you'll first have to learn a whole new set of words like *premillennialism, postmillennialism,* and *amillennialism.* Once you're through with the new set of "isms," you'll need to figure out if you're pre-, mid-, or post-tribulation. I have to admit, I've always liked a good debate. But my concern is that we get so caught up in dating and debating that we forget the point.

Imagine you are watching a World Cup soccer match. It starts getting pretty intense, but all of a sudden the guys from one team sit down in the middle of the field and start debating about when the game is going to end. Sure, we could spend a lot of time and energy debating it and trying to convince our own teammates to see our point of view. But what's the point? Paul put it to the Ephesians this way:

> *Wake up, O sleeper, rise from the dead, and Christ will shine on you.*
>
> *Be very careful, then, how you live—not as unwise but as wise, making the most of every opportunity, because the days are evil. Therefore do not be foolish, but understand what the Lord's will is.* —Ephesians 5:14-17

Jesus, come soon, my Lord, come soon. But between now and then, I ask that You will live through me, that I will think as You think, and see as You see. Amen.

How to Navigate the Dangerous Waters of Life

Any ship can be a minesweeper ... once. —Admiral Hornblower

In a hostile world, few things are as dangerous or as terrifying as an explosive mine. Land mines are buried in seemingly harmless areas, killing and maiming decades after being planted. Our seas are full of them. One mine can take down a huge ship. Almost as devastating, the fear of mines can deprive a ship of freedom of movement, paralyzing it in fear of inevitable explosion.

A plume of water, a shuddering throughout the skeleton of the vessel, a chaotic descent into the depths ... Yes, one mine floating beneath the surface can sink a ship—and **one false belief lurking beneath your thoughts can sink your whole life.**

> *The weapons we fight with are not the weapons of the world. On the contrary, they have divine power to demolish strongholds. We demolish arguments and every pretension that sets itself up against the knowledge of God, and we take captive every thought to make it obedient to Christ.* —2 Corinthians 10:4-5

Without even knowing it, many of us are sailing through dangerous waters. Strongholds, arguments, pretensions have been planted in our path. These are the beliefs behind our beliefs, the assumptions behind our assumptions. And in many cases, they are built on lies from the enemy, intent on blowing us to bits.

As part of its anti-mine warfare, the United States Navy flies the largest helicopter in the free world, the MH53. (MH stands for Minesweeping Helicopter). With three engines of over 5000 horsepower each, it can lift a railroad car. But its mission is to fly above dangerous waters pulling an extensive apparatus that identifies and explodes mines.

Just as the Navy uses minesweepers, the Christian today needs a MINDsweeper. Do you know what dangers lurk deep in your mind? Do you know how to get rid of them?

Lord, I ask that You would search my heart and show me my ways. Sweep my mind, Lord. Expose the lies and expectations that lie beneath the surface of my thoughts and actions so that I might live freely and boldly in Your Truth. Amen.

How You Can Stay on the Right Path

Q: How many Unitarian Universalists does it take to change a light bulb?

A: As Unitarian Universalists, we choose not to make a statement either in favor of or against the need for a light bulb. However, if in your own journey, you have found that light bulbs work for you, that is wonderful. Present it next month at our annual Light Bulb Sunday Service, in which we will explore a number of light bulb traditions, including incandescent, fluorescent, 3-way, long-life, and tinted, all of which are equally valid paths to luminescence.
—**From the website of First Unitarian Church, Toronto**

Like mines floating in a bay, ready to sink a ship, several modern philosophies lurk underneath our thoughts, waiting to take us down. One of the dominant mottos of our generation goes like this: "It doesn't matter what you believe, as long as you believe it sincerely." **That's called *universalism*, the dream that everyone will be saved regardless of the choices and decisions they make.** Universalists cling to the truth about God being a loving God but they ignore (or are ignorant of) the fact that He is also righteous and holy.

> *When the Son of Man comes in his glory, and all the angels with him, he will sit on his glorious throne. All the nations will be gathered before him, and he will separate the people one from another as a shepherd separates the sheep from the goats. He will put the sheep on his right and the goats on his left ... Then he will say to those on his left, "Depart from me, you who are cursed, into the eternal fire prepared for the devil and his angels ... " Then they will go away to eternal punishment, but the righteous to eternal life.*
> —Matthew 25:31-33, 41, 46

I wish I could believe that "all roads lead to God," but it's just not true. Universalism is a misguided dream. Jesus said, "No one comes to the Father except through me." If someone accepts His free gift of forgiveness, they are given safe passage into the very presence of God in the future, and are promised the very presence of the Holy Spirit within their spirit today. Only eternity will reveal how amazing that offer truly is. And for today, that's certainly a message worth sharing with others.

Dear Jesus, I believe that You are the Way and the Truth and the Life. Give me great joy in that truth, and use me in any way that You see fit to share that great news with those around me who are wishfully hoping in a misguided philosophy of Universalism. Amen.

Putting Your Hope in the Right Place

The founders of a new colony, whatever Utopia of human virtue and happiness they might originally project, have invariably recognized it among their earliest practical necessities to allot a portion of the virgin soil as a cemetery, and another portion as the site of a prison. —Nathaniel Hawthorne, *The Scarlet Letter*

Applied technology and exploding amounts of information are giving rise to incredible human accomplishments in this world. There is no question that we are experiencing things that our ancestors couldn't even have dreamed possible. But is it resulting in an improvement in the overall human condition? Given enough time, could we possibly create our own utopia?

That's the hope of *Utopianism*—that things will get better and better with time until we have heaven on earth. The problem is that Utopianism is a misplaced optimism, and if we buy into it, it will take us out just like a ship taken out by a torpedo. With all our accomplishments, we have yet to come up with our own solution to the sinful and selfish soul of man. Our world will not end in paradise. Our accomplishments are really just fueling our demise.

> *In fact, everyone who wants to live a godly life in Christ Jesus will be persecuted, while evildoers and impostors will go from bad to worse, deceiving and being deceived. But as for you, continue in what you have learned and have become convinced of, because you know those from whom you learned it, and how from infancy you have known the Holy Scriptures, which are able to make you wise for salvation through faith in Christ Jesus.*
> —2 Timothy 3:12-15

Things are going from bad to worse and this period of history will end in the fair and righteous judgment of Christ who will once and for all set things right. That's not what many hope for, but it's actually very freeing to put our hope and trust in the right place.

Jesus, I place my ultimate hope in You today. Show me where I am trusting in things of this world, things that cannot and will not save me. Rather than scientists, doctors, politicians, or anything else, I transfer my trust to You in all things. I worship You as my Rock and my Redeemer! Amen.

Does What Works Really Work?

The end may justify the means as long as there is something that justifies the end.
—Leon Trotsky, *Communist revolutionary and Marxist theorist*

There probably isn't a single one of us who hasn't at one time, told someone this: *It doesn't matter if you win or lose; it's how you play the game.*

Of course, we only say that to losers, don't we? In our culture "the win" means everything. Our motto is "If it feels good, do it!" We should always pursue the greatest happiness for the greatest number of people. (Sounds like our political "democracy," doesn't it?) Like Trotsky and the early communists, this quickly erodes into the end justifying the means. **It's called** *Utilitarianism,* **a mistaken philosophy that says, "It doesn't matter what's** *right***; it only matters what** *works.***"**

The problem, of course, is that trying to find happiness in circumstances is contrary to finding joy in Christ. **When we pursue pleasure and happiness** *instead* **of God (rather than pursuing pleasure and joy** *in* **God), we immediately make idols out of the things we hope will give us life.** Those idols just can't stand on their own, and Jesus won't stand for them when He returns. The Bible presents an entirely different paradigm:

> *Therefore, I urge you, brothers and sisters, in view of God's mercy, to offer your bodies as a living sacrifice, holy and pleasing to God—this is your true and proper worship. Do not conform to the pattern of this world, but be transformed by the renewing of your mind. Then you will be able to test and approve what God's will is—his good, pleasing and perfect will. For by the grace given me I say to every one of you: Do not think of yourself more highly than you ought, but rather think of yourself with sober judgment, in accordance with the faith God has distributed to each of you.*
> —Romans 12:1-3

Utilitarianism is one of the philosophical mines that is ready to explode and take down your ship. If you head into those waters, only destruction and pain await you and those around you. Thank God, that through His Scriptures, He has told us the truth. He has provided a new and loving way to anyone who chooses a safe course.

Holy Spirit, I believe that You are in me and ready to live through me. I refuse to live by what works, rather than by You. I don't want to be conformed to the world. I present myself to God as an instrument of worship instead—a living sacrifice by His grace through faith. Amen.

Living Life Full Speed Ahead

Damn the torpedoes! Full speed ahead! —Admiral Farragut

Universalism, utopianism, utilitarianism … **With so many "isms" floating around waiting to blow up our ship, is it safe to go anywhere?** How do we navigate through such dangerous waters?

In the heart of the Civil War, Mobile Bay was heavily mined (at the time, tethered naval mines were called "torpedoes"). Admiral Farragut commanded his fleet to charge the bay. When one of his ships was hit, other ships began to retreat from the battle. "Damn the torpedoes!" Farragut shouted. "Four bells. Captain Drayton, go ahead! Jouett, full speed!"

Yes, destructive philosophies are all around us. We have bought into some of those philosophies whether we know it or not. But do we just sit around and do nothing? No. The best thing is to move forward rather than retreat in fear. In my opinion, it is far better to live for the truth than it is to try to hide from the lies. **With the Holy Spirit in us, and with the Word of God in front of us, the lies can be exposed before they cause damage. But a life wasted cowering in fear? That's just a wasted life.**

God has given us such simple and powerful instruction for living in grace and freedom. In response to the lies, we are to aggressively live for truth!

> *Will the LORD be pleased with thousands of rams, with ten thousand rivers of oil? Shall I offer my firstborn for my transgression, the fruit of my body for the sin of my soul? He has showed you, O man, what is good. And what does the LORD require of you? To act justly and to love mercy and to walk humbly with your God.* —Micah 6:7-8

Yes, we need to adhere to the MINDsweeper principle by taking every thought captive. Then it's time to just get on with it! Full speed ahead!

Heavenly Father, I thank You again for the truth of Your Word! I thank You for the power of Your Holy Spirit within me. I thank You that I have been crucified with Christ and He now lives in me. I ask that You continue to reveal the lies that lurk beneath the surface of my thoughts. You have shown me what is good and what is required. I submit to the power of Your Holy Spirit in me right now, and I ask that He would live through me the kind of life that You have called me to today. Amen.

Are You Ready for His Return?

There is nothing like an unexpected guest to get everyone cleaning up the mess.

One Saturday afternoon when Billy Graham was holding a crusade in Milwaukee we got a call from one of his staffers. "Would it be possible for Dr. Graham to retreat to your home for a few hours?" My mother said, "Of course. What day would he like to come?"

"How about in two hours?"… Panic! Mom hung up the phone and assembled all the children. We picked up and primed every inch of the home. She sent us upstairs to shower and dress "appropriately."

When the great preacher arrived, we gathered in the living room where my mom sat next to him. A few minutes later the doorbell rang. My mom popped up to answer it—not realizing that her leg had fallen asleep. Her leg gave way right onto the lap of Billy Graham. In the frenzied preparation, this surprise guest literally had us "falling all over him." It has become a family legend, but here's the point: *Be ready.*

> *Therefore keep watch, because you do not know on what day your Lord will come. But understand this: If the owner of the house had known at what time of night the thief was coming, he would have kept watch and would not have let his house be broken into. So you also must be ready, because the Son of Man will come at an hour when you do not expect him.* —Matthew 24:42-44

Jesus *is* coming back physically, and it could be really soon. How then should we live? In major frenzy to get our "house" cleaned up? If we aren't careful, the ominous reality of the second coming of Christ could frighten us out of peace into a self-propelled panic.

So how then should we live? Paul puts it in full perspective:

> *May your whole spirit, soul and body be kept blameless at the coming of our Lord Jesus Christ. The one who calls you is faithful, and he will do it.* —1 Thessalonians 5:23-24

The truth is that Christ is *already* here, not physically, yet, but His Spirit lives in us. Being aware of that and living in Him is the secret to being ready for the day He comes back to rule and reign physically.

Jesus, thank You that, in You, I will be found blameless when You return. Give me a consistent perspective that looks to THAT day, more so than today. Amen.

How to Be Ready by Being Hopeful

Sometimes, I think we would be better off if we just shut the news off completely. Bad news sells, and we buy it by the truckload. And the price we pay? If we don't keep things in a biblical perspective, it will cost us our hope. When Jesus left the earth the first time, He knew the generations of disciples to follow would have plenty of bad news to deal with. His advice?

> *Do not let your hearts be troubled. You believe in God; believe also in me… And if I go and prepare a place for you, I will come back and take you to be with me that you also may be where I am.* —John 14:1, 3

The promise of the second coming of Christ means that we have the opportunity to live lives of hope in the grace of God, no matter how bad things get.

> *Therefore, since we have been justified through faith, we have peace with God through our Lord Jesus Christ, through whom we have gained access by faith into this grace in which we now stand. And we boast in the hope of the glory of God. Not only so, but we also glory in our sufferings, because we know that suffering produces perseverance; perseverance, character; and character, hope. And hope does not put us to shame, because God's love has been poured out into our hearts through the Holy Spirit, who has been given to us.*
> —Romans 5:1-5

That's a powerful passage. It would be wise to be quiet right now, and just let those words of God speak for themselves. Savor those words, phrase by phrase, and let this living message massage your heart! Jesus is coming back, and therefore, we can live with unbridled hope—that's the ultimate hope. And because the world is going south, His physical return is really the only hope left for the physical world.

May that be where we place our hope today.

Jesus, I place my hope in You today. Let the bad news come and go. By faith, I stand in Your grace, excited about Your glory, embracing Your love which has filled my heart through Your Spirit. I look forward to Your physical return and I thank You for the presence of Your Spirit in my spirit right now. Amen.

Christian theologians sit and think ... mostly sit. —Unknown

Like a thief in the night, Christ will return someday, catching many unprepared. Don't let that happen! These are unprecedented days and they will not go on forever. Christ has shown us through the cross and through His Word how we are to live during these days: *By grace! By trusting in Him to live through us.*

Because Jesus is coming back someday, we are to be helpful everyday. Paul gave us the specifics in 1 Thessalonians 5: *And we urge you, brothers...*

- *Warn those who are idle*
- *Encourage the timid*
- *Help the weak*
- *Be patient with everyone*
- *Make sure that nobody pays back wrong for wrong*
- *But always try to be kind to each other and to everyone else*
- *Be joyful always*
- *Pray continually*
- *Give thanks in all circumstances, for this is God's will for you in Christ Jesus*
- *Do not put out the Spirit's fire*
- *Do not treat prophecies with contempt*
- *Test everything*
- *Hold on to the good*
- *Avoid every kind of evil*

If you were wondering what to do today, this should keep you occupied! Review the list. Consider specific ways to live out a few of the items. I say "go for it" as long as you remember Who is doing the work in you and through you! Paul concludes the list with this reminder:

> **May God himself,** the God of peace, sanctify you through and through. May your whole spirit, soul and body be kept blameless at the coming of our Lord Jesus Christ. The one who calls you is faithful and he will do it.
> —1 Thessalonians 5:23-24

God, You are the one at work in us. By Your Spirit , through Your Word, I ask that You will speak to me clearly now. What specific things do You want to do through me to be helpful today? Lead me. Guide me. I trust You to do it through me. Amen.

Your Key to a Great Marriage ... and Life

A happy marriage is the union of two good forgivers. —Ruth Bell Graham

Marriage is huge. I don't think there is any way to understand how huge it is until you are in it. Good and bad, it spills over into all other aspects of life. It's no wonder, then, that couples always ask, "What's the key to a great marriage? What's *the* secret; just the *one* secret, the one key to a *great* marriage ... What is it?" I always give the same answer, given to me by my close friends:

"A great marriage comes from two people walking in the Spirit, loving one another." The couples almost always respond something along these lines, "Yea, yea, I know that, but tell me something really *practical* that will really make a difference."

And I always answer,

"Oh, now I get your question. Okay then, a great marriage comes from two people walking in the Spirit, loving one another.'"

What's the bottom line?

> *You, my brothers and sisters, were called to be free. But do not use your freedom to indulge the flesh; rather, serve one another humbly in love. For the entire law is fulfilled in keeping this one command: "Love your neighbor as yourself." If you bite and devour each other, watch out or you will be destroyed by each other.* —Galatians 5:13-15

In the pursuit of true love, we can function in the Holy Spirit, or we can function in the flesh. As married couples, if we function in the flesh, this is called "war." If we function in the Spirit, this is called "love." Pretty simple and intensely practical—and it's not just the key for a great marriage, it works for any relationship, and not really just for relationships, it's the key to a great life.

True contentment and life is found in Christ and the abundant life is lived as we live in the Spirit instead of in the flesh. Period.

God, I believe in the truth of Your Word ... in principle. Now, make it practical. I ask that in the days ahead You will open up Your Word, and that You will open up my mind to understand and to be willing to walk in Your Spirit in order to love those around me with all the intensity and purity that You intended. Amen.

How to Turn Your Pain into Gain

Those who believe they believe in God, but without passion in the heart, without anguish of mind, without uncertainty, without doubt, and even at times without despair, believe only in the idea of God, and not in God himself.
—Madeleine L'Engle

When hard times come, it's totally natural to ask, "How do I get *out* of this?!" Life is filled with all kinds of suffering. Some of us are suffering in a bad marriage and our spouses just won't get their act together, and it feels like it's lethal. The fleshly reaction is to get out of the suffering one way or the other. But God has other ideas. In Romans 5:3-4 Paul says,

> *We also glory in our sufferings because we know that suffering produces perseverance; perseverance, character; and character, hope.*

Suffering is a tool that God uses to form us and to mold us to deepen our intimacy with Christ. Rather than the fleshly response of trying to get out, we can chose to ask, "Alright, I'm in this trial and I don't want to waste it. Lord, how are You going to use this suffering to grow me, to deepen my walk with Jesus?"

It's a recalibration of the mindset from flesh to Spirit, and it works in EVERY suffering. Every difficulty we face is an opportunity to become more like Christ and experience Christ more intimately.

But please hear me: God does not expect you to endure physical or sexual abuse in the name of suffering producing growth. If your spouse is abusing you, tell someone in your church whom you trust or another authority who can intervene.

But what if your spouse just doesn't care?

- Ask God to do a miracle, keep asking; He's capable, He can do it!
- Fight for your marriage; don't fall into the temptation of throwing in the towel.
- And, here's the most important thing, *walk in the Spirit.*

Why? **Because the best relationships are between two people walking in the Spirit, loving one another.**

Jesus, be my strength and patience in my marriage and all relationships. Use every difficulty I face to draw me into deeper intimacy with You. Show me what I can learn from these hard times; make me more like Jesus because of them. Amen.

Focusing on Your Father Over Your Flesh

Society drives people crazy with lust and calls it advertising. —John Lahr

Walking in the Spirit, loving one another, is the key to great relationships—particularly that most intense of all relationships, marriage. God's Word tells us that the Spirit, however, is in opposition to our flesh. What exactly is the flesh?

- "Flesh" is that condition where my focus is primarily on myself, self-centeredness to a great degree, as I attempt to live out of my own resources. My resources are the stuff that I can produce on my own or put stock in outside of God like heritage, education, IQ, personality, etc.

- "Flesh" is me trying to live life independently of God, so that I can cope with life. Flesh is trying to produce life on my own rather than in Christ.

I don't know if people realize this, but flesh can actually look good on the outside. Someone can be functioning in the flesh and you might think, "Wow, what a cool person." But listen to what Paul said when he's describing his flesh:

> *If someone else thinks they have reasons to put confidence in the flesh, I have more: circumcised on the eighth day, of the people of Israel, of the tribe of Benjamin, a Hebrew of Hebrews; in regard to the law, a Pharisee; as for zeal, persecuting the church; as for righteousness based on the law, faultless.*

> *But whatever were gains to me I now consider loss for the sake of Christ. What is more, I consider everything a loss because of the surpassing worth of knowing Christ Jesus my Lord, for whose sake I have lost all things. I consider them garbage that I may gain Christ.* —Philippians 3:4-8

Now, you look at all those things and say, "Well those sound pretty good! Moral, passionate, religious, good heritage, aren't those good things?" Paul takes these things, which give him incredibly high status in his culture, and calls them garbage—he calls them "dung" actually. (The literal translation is really a much stronger word than "dung," but we're trying to run a ministry so I'm not going to say it.) The point is that Paul takes the things he's earned in the flesh (titles, earthly possessions, social status, etc.) and says they're worse than worthless compared to Jesus and to living His life in the Spirit.

God, give me eyes that can look past the good performance of flesh and show me how empty it really is. Then move me to focus on You, the One who will always satisfy completely as an individual, as a spouse, and in all my relationships. Amen.

How to Align Yourself with God's Will

He that but looketh on a plate of ham and eggs to lust after it hath already committed breakfast with it in his heart. —C.S. Lewis

A great marriage comes from two people walking in the Spirit, loving one another.

I keep saying this over and over again because it's so important … and I keep saying it over and over again because I also see the worst of the worst. Walking in the Spirit is not just the key to a great marriage—it's the key to protecting yourself and those you love from the very worst expressions of the flesh.

> *The acts of the flesh are obvious: sexual immorality, impurity and debauchery; idolatry and witchcraft; hatred, discord, jealousy, fits of rage, selfish ambition, dissensions, factions and envy; drunkenness, orgies, and the like. I warn you, as I did before, that those who live like this will not inherit the kingdom of God.* —Galatians 5:19-21

Why would someone choose to live this way? In all honesty, I don't think most people who find themselves at this level of fleshly living consciously intended to get there. I don't think anybody walks down the aisle to get married thinking, "I'm going to hate this person, and cause discord and jealousy." No. Yet this is where many of us end up. Why? Because, even though we started with good intentions, we walked in the wrong way.

> *So I say, walk by the Spirit, and you will not gratify the desires of the flesh. For the flesh desires what is contrary to the Spirit, and the Spirit what is contrary to the flesh. They are in conflict with each other, so that you are not to do whatever you want.* —Galatians 5:16-17

Please hear me: One of the greatest gifts of marriage is that it exposes when we are living in the flesh rather than walking by the Spirit. When your flesh fights against those things you really want to do, it *feels* like a war, and you might feel like you have to surrender to your fleshly desires. But remember, the victory has already been won on the cross. The battles will continue, but right now, in Christ, you are alive. In Him, you're free. You have the Holy Spirit living inside you. Surrender to *Him*, and He will lead you through the battle.

Father, I don't like looking at my flesh. Show me where my thoughts are going if they are not lined up with Your Word. Give me willingness to face my flesh, dispel it in Your name! Deliver me from the worst of the worst my flesh could be. Amen.

How to Find Fulfillment in the Fruit of the Spirit

The frustrations of our hearts can be windows into the beliefs of our souls.
—Todd Hillard

Marriage and other close relationships are an amazing gift ... but not always in the way we wish. Go with me for a moment here:

When we asked Christ into our lives, His Spirit really came in, made us a new creation, and took up residence. The Spirit in us wants to produce the fruit of the Spirit in us. Because of Him inside of us, His desires become our desire.

> *But the fruit of the Spirit is love, joy, peace, forbearance, kindness, goodness, faithfulness, gentleness and self-control. Against such things there is no law. Those who belong to Christ Jesus have crucified the flesh with its passions and desires. Since we live by the Spirit, let us keep in step with the Spirit.*
> —Galatians 5:22-25

The twist comes from our flesh. We want the fruit of the Spirit, but our flesh is wired to get it other places. In marriage and other relationships, then, the natural temptation is to seek the fruit in people, rather than in Jesus. If we don't get this right, we are going to expect that the fruit should be given to us by another. We will expect our spouse to give us love, joy, and peace; we will expect that they will treat us with patience, kindness, goodness, etc. ... And we will get angry, frustrated, and hurt when they fall short of these expectations. No, a good marriage comes when we walk in the Spirit, because He can then fill us and provide the fruit.

Yes, marriage *is* an amazing gift. It shows us when we are trusting in people, rather than Christ to experience the fruit of the Spirit.

Jesus, reveal to me right now specific areas where I am looking to my spouse or other people to fulfill my desires for the fruit of Your Spirit. I directly turn to You, right now, and ask that You would live through me in such a way that I can experience these fruit from the inside out, and not from the outside in. Amen.

Getting to Know Yourself Again

There are three things extremely hard: steel, a diamond, and to know one's self.
—Benjamin Franklin

It's fairly easy to get to know your mate. It's a whole lot harder to be honest enough to get to know yourself, and be humble enough to take responsibility for your flesh.

Carol is a counselor who helped my wife and me turn over a new leaf in our marriage. She has talked to so many people about their flesh that she's identified numerous flesh patterns. Which ones might describe your natural bent?

- Performance flesh: The hard worker. Well-adjusted, aggressive, outgoing, positive, motivated, driven, take charge kind of person.

- Religious flesh: The "Good Christian." Passive, nice, sweet, obedient, dutiful, pious, sanctimonious.

- Superior flesh: The "snob," outwardly proud, defensive, conceited, know-it-all. They look down on other people because they're not as bright as they are.

- Comfort flesh: The laid-back easy-going person, cautious, indecisive, unmotivated, and avoids conflict like the plague.

- Victim flesh: Negative, complaining, defeated, self-pitying. They are often unforgiving and blaming.

- Caretaker flesh: The enabler, rescuer, fixer. Often obsessive, nagging, overly responsible, overly protective.

- Pleaser flesh: The nice guy. Compliant, submissive, compromising, self-neglecting. Has a hard time saying no and says yes to too much in order to feel accepted.

- Indulgent flesh: The compulsive person. Obsessive, easily addicted, insatiable, thrill seeker, pleasure seeker.

- Hostile flesh: The abusive antisocial person. Angry, domineering, vengeful, quick tempered, hateful.

Anything sound familiar? (If not, you probably have religious or superior flesh!)

Holy Spirit, make me honest and humble so I can identify the patterns of my flesh. Lead me in the ways of Your love. Amen.

How to Follow God Over Your Flesh

Be nice, have fun, play nice with the other kids. Unless the other kids wanna fight, then you kick the other kids' b---. —Mushu *(with at least a little "hostile flesh", don't you think?)*

Everybody has flesh. On this side of the grave, it's impossible to get rid of it. It comes in many flavors. A few of the most popular include:

- Performance flesh
- Religious flesh
- Superior flesh
- Victim flesh
- Pleaser flesh
- Hostile flesh

Because everyone has "flesh," **you might think it's** *acceptable.* **But it's not.**

> *So I say, walk by the Spirit, and you will not gratify the desires of the flesh. For the flesh desires what is contrary to the Spirit, and the Spirit what is contrary to the flesh. They are in conflict with each other, so that you are not to do whatever you want.* —Galatians 5:16-17

"Contrary to the Spirit" doesn't sound acceptable to me. You might be tempted to shirk off your flesh with a wink, but you don't have to look far to see the devastation it causes in marriages. By now, you should have the mantra memorized:

"A great marriage comes from two people walking in the Spirit, loving one another."

The antithesis is also true.

"A bad marriage comes from two people walking in the flesh, battling one another."

When two people walking in the flesh cross paths, collision *often* occurs, and mutual love *never* occurs. Think about it. What are your flesh patterns? How do they affect your most important relationships?

Holy Spirit, I need You to break in right now. Show me the negative, contrary effects of walking in the flesh. Make me willing to let you take control of these deadly tendencies so that I might walk in Your ways. Amen.

What's Nailed to Your Cross?

Crucifixion ... produced death not suddenly, but gradually ... True Christians ... do not succeed in completely destroying it (that is, the flesh) while here below; but they have fixed it to the cross and they are determined to keep it there till it expires. —Jay Brown

True Christianity is pretty crazy stuff. Its ways are so backwards from the things **we have learned**—so much so, that we might overlook the principles that can free us from the way things work in the world. That's true when it comes to issues of death and life because Scripture says that life only comes through death.

> Galatians 2:20 says, *For I was crucified with Christ and I no longer live, but Christ lives in me.*

That key passage is echoed by numerous others. They all talk about who we are in our spirit, about the transformation that Christ brought about by His co-crucifixion with us, and His raising again to new life so we can be born again. But what about the flesh?

Because the best marriages are two people walking in the Spirit, loving one another; and the flesh tries to get in the way of that. How do we overcome the flesh?

> *Those who belong to Christ Jesus have crucified the flesh with its passions and desires.* —Galatians 5:24

What does it mean to "crucify the flesh?" Well, this is not the same crucifixion that Paul describes in Galatians and Romans 6. Crucifying the flesh is different.

One commentator puts it this way, "**The basic demand of Christian discipleship is that we take up our cross daily and follow Christ.**" As long as we are here on earth, we're never going to be done with the flesh. It's always going to be part of our life, but letting it control us is always optional. When we are "in the flesh," we can respond "in the Spirit:"

- Recognize our flesh and see it for what it is.
- See its effects, and hate them.
- Accept that God's Spirit in us is greater than the flesh.
- Declare that the flesh has no more power over us.
- Turn towards the love and will of God to take its place.

Father, reveal one aspect of my flesh we can deal with right now. Let me affix it to the cross until that day I see You face to face. Amen.

OCT
7

Are You Doing Good for the Wrong Reasons?

The first thing you have to know is yourself. A man who knows himself can step outside himself and watch his own reactions like an observer. —Adam Smith

Recognizing the flesh is easy when it has negative expressions. It's easy to see the junk when "performance flesh" burns us out, when "superior flesh" lashes out, or when "caretaker flesh" perpetuates destructive relationships.

But sometimes the flesh manifests itself in ways that seem positive. Is it wrong to want to please people? Is it wrong to want to perform well? The answer has more to do with the *why* than the *what*.

One of my own flesh patterns is the "pleaser flesh;" I do things for others so they will like me. Back before Libby and I figured out this whole "crucify the flesh" thing, I would sense that she was upset with me, and would try to please her to earn her acceptance by cleaning the kitchen. She'd see it clean and become angry.

Disappointed, I would say, "How could you be mad at me? I just cleaned the whole kitchen!" But one time she said, "I don't know why I'm mad, it just feels yucky." Why did my attempt to please her feel yucky? Because I was cleaning the kitchen to manipulate her, to get her to like me, to control our relationship.

I learned a lot about my flesh from that experience, but I could have just as easily learned it first from the Word and saved us a lot of pain!

> *Am I now trying to win the approval of human beings, or of God? Or am I trying to please people? If I were still trying to please people, I would not be a servant of Christ.* –Galatians 1:10

Anything wrong with cleaning the kitchen? Of course not … IF you are walking in the Spirit. You may get a completely different reaction for the same action. Why? Because in the Spirit I'm serving her to love her; in the flesh I'm serving her to get something. Do you see the difference? It doesn't guarantee that your actions in the Spirit will have the desired effect, but at least it could. Flesh stinks even when doing "good things" and your spouse can sniff it a mile away.

Father, I want to crucify my flesh. If I am doing things for the wrong reasons, change my heart so they would be done without my personal agenda. Amen.

How You Can Get in Line with God's Spirit

He who knows others is wise. He who knows himself is enlightened. —Lao Tzu

Hopefully we've put some meat on the skeleton of "A great marriage comes from two people walking in the Spirit, loving one another." Now I'm going to ask you to take another step.

First, take the list of "flesh flavors" and go away and pray. Say, "Lord Jesus, by Your Spirit, reveal the filth of my flesh. I want to hate it. I want to nail it to the cross."

- Performance flesh
- Religious flesh
- Superior flesh
- Comfort flesh
- Victim flesh
- Caretaker flesh
- Pleaser flesh
- Indulgent flesh
- Hostile flesh

Then get together with your spouse and have a conversation like this: "Here's what the Holy Spirit revealed to me about my flesh." Tell them what He's told you, asking for forgiveness where necessary. The key words here are "my flesh," not "your flesh."

When Libby and I did this I said, "You know what, I've got some 'pleaser flesh' and some 'passive flesh.'" And she said, "Yeah, yeah, I see that." Your spouse will be a wonderful confirmation of what the Holy Spirit is saying to you! We prayed about it and then were able to begin walking together in the Spirit, following the Spirit's promptings in new ways.

That might be a radical step for you to take, but I pray that you will take it in faith.

Since we live by the Spirit, let us keep in step with the Spirit. –Galatians 5:25

The Spirit is in you. Take some time and then get in step with what He is doing.

Spirit, thank You for being a constant presence in my life. Give me the faith to take practical, even radical, action to keep in step with You so that You can love my spouse and others through me in a way that might lead to great relationships. Amen.

Truth to Set Your Marriage Free

Marriage: A legal or religious ceremony by which two persons of the opposite sex solemnly agree to harass and spy on each other for ninety-nine years, or until death do them join. —Elbert Hubbard

Late one night, about five years ago, my wife and I found ourselves sitting in our kitchen. We started talking and it went something like this:

Libby: "Okay, we really need to talk."
Me: "Okay, let's talk."
Libby: "I'm so angry at you I can barely stand it."
Me: "Why?"
Libby: "I'm not even sure why. I'm just seething with anger."
Me: "Well, you know what? I'm angry at you, too."
Libby: "You know, I don't even like you anymore."
Me: "I don't like you, either."

We just stared at each other—silence for the longest time. **It was a defining moment.** We realized that the marriage we had constructed was a poor imitation of what God really had for us. I've learned a lot since then, and I've become more convinced of a simple truth:

Satan divides, and the Holy Spirit unites.

Satan is at work in our marriages, our families, and our friendships, and some of his favorite tools are his lies. If you believe those lies, your relationships can disintegrate before your eyes—at least, that's what happened to us. Paul laid out a counter attack:

> *Have nothing to do with the fruitless deeds of darkness, but rather expose them. It is shameful even to mention what the disobedient do in secret. But everything exposed by the light becomes visible—and everything that is illuminated becomes a light. This is why it is said: "Wake up, sleeper, rise from the dead, and Christ will shine on you."* —Ephesians 5:11-14

That night in the kitchen, we decided that we were going to put in the hard work, learn to be painfully honest, and ask Christ to give us the marriage that He longed for us to have. If you feel trapped like we did, the truth can set your marriage free.

Father, expose the lies of darkness that I have accepted as true. Wake me, elevate me, shine the light of Jesus on my home and my relationships. Amen.

Is Marriage Still Relevant?

Getting married for sex is like buying a 747 for the free peanuts.
—Jeff Foxworthy

The Pew Poll reports that 44% of Americans under 30 believe that marriage is heading for extinction, but 95% of Americans want to get married someday. That's interesting, isn't it? They know there's something dynamic and special about this relationship, but our culture keeps saying, "Marriage was great for your grandparents, but it's unnecessary today." *Time* magazine ran a cover that simply asked, "Who needs marriage?" How would you answer?

Lie 1: Marriage is an archaic institution irrelevant for enlightened modern people. Many believe this lie, the rest of us need to ask ourselves if marriage is worth it.

> *That is why a man leaves his father and mother and is united to his wife, and they become one flesh.* —Genesis 2:24

This is the way God always intended it: One man, one woman coming together, becoming one, enjoying oneness in Christ. It's God's original plan, and it's meant to last. He's never rescinded it. Marriage is simply one of God's great ideas.

I've done dozens of weddings over the years, and I start them all the same way: "Marriage is:

- A holy estate instituted by God.
- Commanded for all who enter it lawfully and in true affection.
- Consecrated by Christ's presence at the marriage feast in Cana of Galilee.
- Set forth as signifying the mystical union between Christ and the Church.
- Ordained for the consecration of union between man and woman so that natural instincts directed aright they might live in purity and honor.
- Ordained for the increase of mankind and that children might be brought up in the fear and the nurture of the Lord.
- Ordained for companionship, health, and comfort.
- Ordained for the welfare of human society which can be strong and happy only where the marriage bond is held highly in honor."

Satan lies. The truth is that marriage is divine, timeless, and significant. Marriage is *part* of God's eternal purpose … and it will be until death we do part.

God, when I begin to doubt the validity of marriage, convict me of Your purpose in marriage for my good and Your glory. Amen.

OCT
11

What Really Makes You Happy?

One is the loneliest number that you'll ever do. Two can be as bad as one. It's the loneliest number since the number one ... —Three Dog Night

Christian colleges can be like meat markets. Church single groups can be the same. Sometimes I wonder if the singles in those classes are into God or into the bod of the person next to them. Are they following the Holy Spirit or their hormones? Sure, there is a natural attraction to get married, but the desire can also be part of a deep emotional deception that lures people out of trust and contentment in Christ.

Lie number 2: You can't be happy unless you're married.

Think you have to be married to be whole and happy? Get this: Paul spends the whole chapter of 1 Corinthians 7 convincing people *not* to get married.

> *Now for the matters you wrote about: "It is good for a man not to have sexual relations with a woman." ... I wish that all men were as I am [Paul was single]. But each of you has your own gift from God; one has this gift, another has that. Now to the unmarried and the widows I say: It is good for them to stay unmarried ... I would like you to be free from concern. An unmarried man is concerned about the Lord's affairs—how he can please the Lord. But a married man is concerned about the affairs of this world—how he can please his wife—and his interests are divided. An unmarried woman or virgin is concerned about the Lord's affairs: Her aim is to be devoted to the Lord in both body and spirit. But a married woman is concerned about the affairs of this world—how she can please her husband. I am saying this for your own good, not to restrict you, but that you may live in a right way in undivided devotion to the Lord.* —1 Corinthians 7:1-1, 7-8, 32-35

Do you believe you can't be happy unless you're married? The truth is this: Singleness is either a *gift* to cherish or a *season* to enjoy.

The loneliest people I know are not single adults. The loneliest people are people I know trapped in a bad marriage. Marriage is not the happiness pill a lot of people think it is. If you want to be happy in marriage, remember that true joy and fulfillment are found only in Christ. Period.

God, Your Word says, "in Your presence there is fullness of joy." I lay claim to that truth right here, right now, no matter what my circumstances might be. Turn my heart towards You, as my source of true fulfillment—filling me until I'm full—in "need" of nothing else. Amen.

Are You Completely Complete?

A man is incomplete until he is married. After that, he is finished.
—Zsa Zsa Gabor

My wife is not Jesus. But even after being raised by a pastor, going to Bible school, and graduating from seminary, I believed she was Jesus. You probably think your spouse is, too. Really. **I lived quite contentedly with Jesus when I was single. But after we married, I expected Libby to do in my life what only Jesus is capable of doing.** It was a recipe for disaster.

Lie 3: Your spouse will complete you.

You can go on believing that fantasy if you want, but the truth is this: **Your spouse will NOT** *complete* you; your spouse will *complicate* you. One of God's purposes in marriage is to use our spouse to reveal our flesh patterns, selfishness, and sin. **If you are looking for true love and affirmation, only Christ will complete you.**

> *For this reason I kneel before the Father, from whom every family in heaven and on earth derives its name. I pray that out of his glorious riches he may strengthen you with power through his Spirit in your inner being, so that Christ may dwell in your hearts through faith. And I pray that you, being rooted and established in love, may have power, together with all the Lord's holy people, to grasp how wide and long and high and deep is the love of Christ, and to know this love that surpasses knowledge—that you may be filled to the measure of all the fullness of God.* —Ephesians 3:14-19

As we come to grips with the love of Christ, we find fulfillment in Him, and **then** we get to delight in the relationships we have been given.

All I can say is that it works for Libby and me. When we walk in the Spirit, rather than the flesh, we really see Jesus as our answer, Jesus as our power, Jesus as our strength, and Jesus as our love. When we see ourselves as completed in Christ, all the pressure is lifted off one another, and we actually start delighting each other.

Father, show me where I am depending on others to complete me, rather than receiving my completeness in Christ. Refocus the expectations I place on others to complete me. I know I was designed to be filled by You! Amen.

Marriage Is a BIG Team Effort

No man is an island, entire of itself. Each is a piece of the continent, a part of the main. —John Donne

People who feel they have strong marriages are 140% more likely to be in a healthy small group than those who are struggling with their marriage. That's a fact. Those who are connected with others tend to be stronger than those of us who are in isolation. But when things get rough in relationships, do you go with the truth or the lie?

Lie 4: You two can handle this on your own. Satan's strategy is to *divide* and *conquer.* He wants you to think that you are the only ones going through this stuff (Ha!). He wants you to feel more embarrassed than you feel motivated to get help. He wants you to avoid the people who speak truth and love into your life. He wants you to disobey one of the foundational principles in Scripture:

> *Let us hold unswervingly to the hope we profess, for he who promised is faithful. And let us consider how we may spur one another on toward love and good deeds, not giving up meeting together, as some are in the habit of doing, but encouraging one another—and all the more as you see the Day approaching.* —Hebrews 10:23-25

You need that. I need that. We need that. It's a lie to think otherwise. It's called loving biblical community.

What's going on in your key relationships? What's up in your marriage? Are you trying to handle it on your own? If you want to go it alone, I suppose you can try, but why? Maybe it's time to flush some pride and ego and get connected like God designed it?

God, I accept that I am not an island. I need You. I need what You provide through others when things are tough. I confess my prideful, independent flesh patterns. Make me willing to accept Your grace, wisdom, and support through others. Show me whom You want me to connect with today. Amen.

Burning Your Bridges

Some people ask the secret of our long marriage. We take time to go to a restaurant two times a week. A little candlelight, dinner, soft music and dancing. She goes Tuesdays, I go Fridays. —Henry Youngman

Winning a war takes devoted commitment to a cause. When an army burns a bridge behind them on their way to a battle, they are cutting off their only possibility of retreat, fully committing to fight for victory, even to the point of death. Today, it's time to burn down a bridge that some people keep as an out in their marriage.

Lie 5: Divorce is an option.

What happened to "till death do we part?" **Entertaining this idea puts a cap on the commitment you're willing to give to your spouse and will allow other distractions to take away concentration from your relationship.** If that little idea's in the back of your mind, it's killing your marriage, guaranteed.

Now, there are allowances in Scripture for divorce in extreme circumstances …

- Matthew 5:32: Jesus said, "Except for sexual immorality." He made an exception for people whose spouses were acting out sexually. In some of those cases, you can move forward with divorce.

- 1 Corinthians 7:12-14: If you become a believer and your spouse is a non-believer, remains a non-believer and they leave you, divorce is allowed.

Just remember: An exception, by definition, is exceptional for extreme cases. It's *normal* for marriage to get tough—even so tough that you don't think you can handle it anymore. But your two options are not "stay in this miserable marriage, or get divorced." Your two options are: 1) disengage, be unhappy, numb, and live separate lives under the same roof, or 2) actively engross yourself in whatever is necessary to bring life to your marriage by letting Christ handle what you can't handle anymore.

Holy Spirit, You are the great Counselor and by Your counsel, I burn my bridges. I'm all in until death do we part. Jesus, I no longer live, but You live in me. I fully surrender to Your leadership. Father, the battle belongs to You. I rest in You and trust in You to bring us to a point of victory over the world, the flesh, and the devil. Amen.

For the Good of Your Kids

I think men who have a pierced ear are better prepared for marriage – they've experienced pain and bought jewelry. —Rita Rudner

God created marriage to strip away our flesh and make us more like Jesus. If we bail on marriage to get away from this pain, however, we actually cause more of it.

Lie 6: The kids will be better if we divorce.

Several studies have proven the devastating effects divorce has on children. There is a negative impact on their emotions, behavior patterns, compliance with rules, and self-image, to name a few. The truth is the kids will be *worse* off if you divorce. Instead of seeing a couple give up on each other, it is far better that children see parents who:

- Focus on Christ – Kids need to see how Christ is conforming their parents to Himself.

- Seek outside help – Kids need to know that it's okay not to know all the answers. They need to see parents seeking out and confiding in others.

- Crucify their flesh – Kids need to see adults look to others with compassion.

- Break old patterns – Kids need a role model that removes their bad habits and focuses on Jesus.

- Forgive forever – Kids need to see parents who forgive and are willing to work on past hurts.

- Trust in Christ – Kids need to learn that Christ is the only one who always provides and always supports us.

  Two are better than one, because they have a good return for their labor: If either of them falls down, one can help the other up ... A cord of three strands is not quickly broken. –Ecclesiastes 4:9-12

Our kids need to live in a home where both parents work through the hardship of marriage together, exemplifying that while marriage is hard, it's so very worth the commitment!

God, for the good of my kids and everyone around me, I place myself in Your hands. Show me how I can be a better spiritual leader to them by walking in Your Spirit today. Amen.

On the Doorstep of What God Has for You

Why does a woman work ten years to change a man's habits and then complain that he's not the man she married? —**Barbra Streisand**

Farmers are scared to death of locusts. A single swarm can cover over 100 square miles and might contain hundreds of millions of ravenous insects that can totally strip land of plant life. The most recent major infestation was in 1915 near Jerusalem—a place where it's difficult to grow food in the best of circumstances. When an enormous swarm of locusts swept through, it caused a major famine, devastated the population, and left a wasteland void of all hope.

Lie 7: Your marriage is hopeless.

Right before marriage blooms into what it's supposed to be, most (if not all) of us come right to the edge of hopelessness. I know. I was there. My wife and I felt bitter anger towards each other, so much that we wished we could be done. Had we not burned the bridge of divorce, it might have been a legitimate option on our list.

In the Batman sequel, "The Dark Night," Harvey Dent said, "The night is darkest just before the dawn. And I promise you, the dawn is coming." Let me say the same thing. If you feel that you are at the end of your marriage, if you've gone to the way of your flesh, or if you look across the table at night saying, "I don't even like you anymore," **you're right on the doorstep of what God has for you. Don't give up now. Reach for the promises of God.**

> *You will keep in perfect peace those whose minds are steadfast, because they trust in you.* —Isaiah 26:3

> *I will repay you for the years the locusts have eaten.* —Joel 2:25

It's a beautiful image! If your marriage is like that utter wasteland, God says, "You see that devastation? I will restore everything that is lost. I will bring it back to life, new life in Me."

God, in the midst of these troubles, I trust in You and You alone. Heal my heart and give me hope for my relationship. I fix my hope on You, focus my mind on You, and depend on You to live through me so that I can walk in Your Spirit today. Amen.

Marriage is DEFINITELY Worth a Klondike Bar

Marriage is an adventure, like going to war. —G. K. Chesterton

Whenever I have a struggling couple in my office, I pitch a very simple vision for them. I tell them to picture themselves sitting on the porch of their house in rocking chairs. Their children are there, grandkids are running all over their yard. They glance at each other, "Boy, remember year 13 when we almost called it quits? Glad we didn't."

Lie 8: Marriage isn't worth the bother.

This lie is really just a sub-lie of one of Satan's other favorite lies that "easy is better than hard." Honestly, easy is seldom better than hard. The truth is that marriage is one of God's best ideas, and a good marriage is an inexpressible joy. Work? Yes … but it's worth it.

> *From the fruit of their lips people are filled with good things, and the work of their hands brings them reward.* —Proverbs 12:14
>
> *He who finds a wife finds what is good and receives favor from the Lord.* —Proverbs 18:22
>
> *There are three things that are too amazing for me, four that I do not understand: the way of an eagle in the sky, the way of a snake on a rock, the way of a ship on the high seas, and the way of a man with a young woman.* —Proverbs 30:18-19
>
> *A wife of noble character who can find? She is worth far more than rubies.* —Proverbs 31:10

I'm asking you to make a new marriage with the spouse you promised to stay with. Engage each other fully to restore and build the marriage that God has for you. As He works in you, look at how you're changing into God's image with your spouse. It will never be perfect, but know that you're in God's will, and that your marriage is worth every bit.

God, renew my mind according to Your Truth. Take my worn-out heart and strengthen it. I can't fix this on my own, so I ask You to be at work in my married life. Use it all, good and bad, to conform me to Your Son and give me the conviction that it is worth it. Amen!

Battling for Truth in Your Marriage

When you get to the end of your rope, tie a knot and hang on.
—Franklin D. Roosevelt

Five years ago, my wife and I realized that we disliked each other. We couldn't get divorced. But we knew we couldn't stay where we were either.

Paul knew about contentment in extenuating circumstances. That's because his joy came from living according to the truth rather than buying into lies. It's the same for you and your marriage. Remember, the secret of marriage is two people walking in the Spirit, loving one another. Let's do something about that, following the pattern Paul laid out in Romans 12:1-2:

> *Therefore, I urge you, brothers and sisters, in view of God's mercy, to offer your bodies as a living sacrifice, holy and pleasing to God—this is your true and proper worship. Do not conform to the pattern of this world, but be transformed by the renewing of your mind. Then you will be able to test and approve what God's will is—his good, pleasing and perfect will.*

For each of the eight marriage lies we've uncovered, there's solid biblical truth of which we can be certain:

- Marriage is not irrelevant. It's divine, timeless, and significant.
- Marriage isn't the only way to be happy. Singleness is a gift to cherish or a season to enjoy.
- Your spouse will not complete you. Only Christ can.
- You two can't handle marriage on your own. You need outside help.
- Divorce is not an option. Only in extreme circumstances can marriage be dissolved.
- Divorce isn't better for your children. Married parents are far better for your kids.
- Your marriage is never hopeless. God offers hope and restoration.
- Marriage is worth it. You'll bring glory to God and blessings to you!

Now, take those truths to the Spirit and ask Him to do the work only He can.

Spirit, show me, right now, the lies that are oppressing my marriage. In the name of Jesus, I rebuke Satan who is the father of those lies. Renew my mind. Reveal to me specific changes that You want to make. Live through me according to Your truth. Amen!

How to Live a Life That Defies Logic

Repent now! Avoid the rush on judgment day! —Church sign

Most of us hope that our Christian faith will get us headed in the right direction, but that depends on which direction you consider normal. **At its core, and in its most vibrant expressions, Christianity is really … well,** *backwards.* Think about it: Jesus lived opposite of what common thinking would expect. He was *counterintuitive.* Not only that, Jesus was *consistently* counterintuitive. Scripture tells us that God's ways are not our ways. When I read the Gospels I look at Jesus and say, "Well, that's not the way I would have done it. Well, that's not what I would have said." Just sayin'!

Take a look at the parable of the Good Samaritan. Instead of making the Jewish religious leaders in his story the *good* guys, he gives credit to the *archenemies* of the Jewish nation! Imagine I'm preaching on the University of Texas campus and I tell a story, and the hero of the story is an Aggie. See the problem!? (If you're not from Texas, take my word for it—it's *bad.*)

Fact is, Jesus sees the world differently than the way the world sees the world. When Jesus was talking to Pilate as He was being tried by the Romans before His crucifixion, He said:

> *My kingdom is not of this world. If it were, my servants would fight to prevent my arrest by the Jewish leaders. But now my kingdom is from another place.* —John 18:36

Jesus defied logical intuition by the way He lived and what He taught. This is evident in the way we will be rewarded by Jesus when we stand before Him at the Bema Seat, when each of us believers will be blessed for our role in Kingdom work on earth. These rewards come from things that are contrary to ordinary.

God doesn't reward us as the world does, so let's look at a few passages in Scripture so you can pattern your life around *that* day, instead of *this* day. **Because, in relation to our world, our Leader is really backwards … and yet, He asks us to follow Him.** He really does—He invites us into a radical philosophy that is contrary to ordinary, leading to a journey that goes in the opposite direction of the world.

Jesus, Your life was an unorthodox one, and yet, I still choose to follow You. As I learn about how You lived Your life in a radically different way from the world, show me how I can apply Your truth to change the way I see the world and change my direction accordingly. Amen.

Serving Those Who Can't Serve You

God, make me the person my dog thinks I am. —Church sign

A number of years ago a family showed up at our church with a little boy named Tanner who was autistic. So we put him in one of the Sunday school classes. Suddenly, Paul, the guy in charge of the class, realized Tanner had snuck out! He was mortified, but after brief panic, we found him. His parents were concerned, and it looked like that could be the last time they came to our congregation.

But our team thought about it and then told them, "We've got a volunteer who would like to minister to your boy one-on-one so you guys can come to church together. Would you be okay with that?" They reluctantly said "yes," and that next Sunday they were back and Tanner was running around our building with Paul running five feet behind him. Sunday after Sunday ever since, Paul has been running after Tanner. It was the start of something special. We've got tons of these precious children in our church now, all of them having someone caring for them each Sunday so their parents can worship together.

I think Jesus and Paul are going to have a great conversation about Tanner at the Bema Seat. When Paul stands face to face with Jesus, Paul will be rewarded for the things he allowed Christ to do through him. That's all crazy talk in the world, but that's what the Bema Seat is all about, so here is one thing that counts on that day:

First, **the B in BEMA stands for benevolence.**

> *Then Jesus said to his host, "When you give a luncheon or dinner, do not invite your friends, your brothers or sisters, your relatives, or your rich neighbors; if you do, they may invite you back and so you will be repaid. But when you give a banquet, invite the poor, the crippled, the lame, the blind, and you will be blessed. Although they cannot repay you, you will be repaid at the resurrection of the righteous."* –Luke 14:12-14

Benevolence is serving someone who can't serve you back. But when you meet Jesus, *He* will reward you. Jesus commends those who love the needy, often in quiet ministries that no one sees. And that counts at the Bema Seat, because our world is full of Tanners.

Son of God, it can be tiring loving on someone who can't serve you back. Show me where I can pour Your love into others like that and give me the strength to do it consistently. Amen.

How to Endure When You Want to Quit

What will people think when they hear that I'm a Jesus freak? What will people do when they find out it's true? I don't really care if they label me a Jesus freak. There ain't no disguisin' the truth! —Jesus Freak by D.C. Talk

I heard a story this week from one of our missionaries about a boy in Iraq, a believer in Jesus. He was pulled off a bus because he was wearing a cross necklace. He was beaten to a pulp right there on the street. No one stopped them. No one helped him. He later died from his wounds.

In the western world, we don't usually suffer physical persecution. But some of you maybe have been fired for your faith. Maybe you've been ostracized by your family. Maybe you've lost profits, unwilling to cross an ethical line in your business. Maybe you stood for Christ at school and you were ridiculed. All that stuff has to do with *endurance*, and that's something that God rewards.

The E in BEMA stands for *endurance.*

> *Blessed are you when people insult you, persecute you and falsely say all kinds of evil against you because of me. Rejoice and be glad, because great is your reward in heaven, for in the same way they persecuted the prophets who were before you.* —Matthew 5:11-12

> *Blessed is the one who perseveres under trial because, having stood the test, that person will receive the crown of life that the Lord has promised to those who love him.* —James 1:12

> *Do not be afraid of what you are about to suffer. I tell you, the devil will put some of you in prison to test you, and you will suffer persecution for ten days. Be faithful, even to the point of death, and I will give you life as your victor's crown.* —Revelation 2:10

Pretty backwards, if you ask me. Shouldn't we stand up for ourselves, defend ourselves, pay others back for what they have done? But He said, "When it happens, just rejoice knowing one day it's going to be worth it. I'm with you and in you. Hang in there. Go the distance!"

Father, give me strength to endure any sort of ridicule or persecution aimed at me because of You. Your love is greater than any insult or injury, and I take solace in Your love, a small taste of the rewards You've made for me in Heaven. Keep me looking forward and up as I move along in my life. Amen.

How to Perform an Impossible Task

Forgive your enemies. It messes with their heads. —Church sign

Our world says, "If people are ungrateful or unkind to you, blow 'em off, let them have it back!" As Christians, we usually don't say that (at least, not at church).

The M in BEMA stands for mercy.

If "benevolence" is serving someone who *can't* pay you back, "mercy" is loving someone who *won't* love you back.

> *But to you who are listening I say: Love your enemies, do good to those who hate you, bless those who curse you, pray for those who mistreat you. If someone slaps you on one cheek, turn to them the other also. If someone takes your coat, do not withhold your shirt from them. Give to everyone who asks you, and if anyone takes what belongs to you, do not demand it back. Do to others as you would have them do to you.*
>
> *If you love those who love you, what credit is that to you? Even sinners love those who love them. And if you do good to those who are good to you, what credit is that to you? Even sinners do that. And if you lend to those from whom you expect repayment, what credit is that to you? Even sinners lend to sinners, expecting to be repaid in full. But love your enemies, do good to them, and lend to them without expecting to get anything back. Then your reward will be great, and you will be children of the Most High, because he is kind to the ungrateful and wicked. Be merciful, just as your Father is merciful.*
> —Luke 6:27-36

Okay, this isn't just counterintuitive, this is crazy! But following Christ leads us away from the logic of the world. Acting like this requires a divine amount of grace-laced empowerment. **And the very same Jesus who calls you to this type of life lives in you. This is the way He wants to live through you,** and at the Bema Seat, Christ is going to bless you for allowing His mercy to flow through you in a way that brings good things to those who don't deserve it.

Alright Jesus, You want to live this way through me? I don't get it; I can't do it—but I'm available. Bring to mind my "enemy" right now—show me someone specific. I surrender my will to You and ask that You would show me how You specifically and tangibly want to love them through me. Amen.

Whose Approval Do You Seek?

Can't sleep? Come hear a sermon. —Church sign

Jesus defied logical intuition by the way He lived. This is very evident in the way we will be rewarded by Jesus when we stand before Him at the Bema Seat, where believers will be blessed for their role in Kingdom work on earth. I don't know if you've seen the theme in these past couple days, but if you haven't, Jesus is going to come right out and say it in Matthew, chapter 6:

> *Be careful not to practice your righteousness in front of others to be seen by them. If you do, you will have no reward from your Father in heaven. So when you give to the needy, do not announce it with trumpets, as the hypocrites do in the synagogues and on the streets, to be honored by others. Truly I tell you, they have received their reward in full. But when you give to the needy, do not let your left hand know what your right hand is doing, so that your giving may be in secret. Then your Father, who sees what is done in secret, will reward you.* —Matthew 6:1-4

The A in BEMA stands for *audience of One*.

Jesus gave three specific examples of how secrecy is rewarded: Giving, prayer, and fasting … but it applies to *everything*. Jesus says we have a choice: We can be praised by people *now*, or we can be rewarded by Him *then*. The actions that elicit people's praise and the actions that elicit Jesus' rewards might be totally the same, but it's the motive that makes the difference. The intent in your heart is what defines your motive.

Make everything you do a thing between you and your Father. Don't flaunt your stuff in front of the world; keep it as a secret between you and Abba. When your heart is seeking God and only God, you're on the right path.

Father, purify my heart, that I would be focused on You and You alone as I surrender to You in me. If I rely on anyone's approval but Yours, make it obvious so I can turn that part of my life to You again. As I start my "secret" life with You, cultivate our relationship and make it something incredible! Amen.

Are You Humble Enough Yet?

Fool me once, shame on you; fool me twice, shame on me. —Well-known
American idiom (not always applied)

A number of years ago our family was at a camp. Of course, there was tons of
stuff for us to do, so my son and I decided to sign up for a paintball version of the
popular children's game "capture the flag." I figured, "What could be the harm?
Kid's stuff. Right?"

The ref blew the whistle and the game started with a rush. I saw an opening to get
the flag and took off running. "Let the old man show them how it's done, right?" I
got *at least* two and a half steps before a searing jolt reverberated through my body.
A direct hit to an unprotected spot. But that was just the start. In the fraction of a
second it took me to hit the dirt and surrender, every enemy gun on the field turned
toward me and unleashed a hailstorm of fire. By the time I limped to the safety of
the sideline, the welts were showing up like relatives after you win the lottery.

New strategy: Forget the flag. Get behind this big honking tree and stand there.

Lesson learned: When you're in a war, having something to shield you from the
enemy's missiles is far better than running out in the open.

Application: In the spiritual war, to avoid taking unnecessary shots that could turn
us into cowards, we need a shield.

> *In addition to all this, take up the shield of faith, with which you can
> extinguish all the flaming arrows of the evil one.* —Ephesians 6:16

**God is our protector. Faith in Him alone shields our souls. I can guarantee you
this: If you trust in other stuff, you will feel the pain. Do it again, you'll feel the
shame.**

Satan's attacks are continual. Each time you run off on your own and take a hit,
thank God for His forgiveness and get back to trusting God and protecting yourself
with the shield of faith.

*Father, there are many places I've tried to find protection from evil—there are so many
ways I run off on my own seeking my own glory and riches, and open myself up to the
attacks of Satan. (Ask the Spirit to reveal something specific!) Today, right now, I put my
faith in You for all my needs. Thank You for saving me from evil as only You can. Amen.*

Arrows Aimed at You from Within

If you tell the truth, you don't have to remember anything. —Mark Twain

Satan's arsenal against Christians is immense. His attacks from the outside are pretty obvious, but did you know that one of his favorite and most effective weapons comes from inside the Church?

There are hundreds of deceptive philosophies and false doctrines competing for our attention, and many of them can come from within the Church.

> *See to it that no one takes you captive through hollow and deceptive philosophy, which depends on human tradition and the elemental spiritual forces of this world rather than on Christ.* —Colossians 2:8

With very little exception, these philosophies and deceptions will distract you from the grace of God and lure you into religious self-effort based on human tradition. It's Satan's favorite ploy, particularly when he can mix in some religion! This subtle attack from within the Church is nothing more than a set of rules handed down from a purely human perspective. Jesus warned about this in a big way:

> *Isaiah was right when he prophesied about you hypocrites; as it is written: "These people honor me with their lips, but their hearts are far from me. They worship me in vain; their teachings are merely human rules." You have let go of the commands of God and are holding on to human traditions.* —Mark 7:5-8

We are taken captive the moment we grasp onto tradition or works. People who buy the evil one's tactics have been diverted from putting their trust in Christ, and put their faith in works rather than grace.

- Do you feel you need to behave a certain way to be accepted by the body of Christ?
- Do you feel God's acceptance is based on what you do?

Inevitably, we need to know where to turn for truth and direction instead of these traditions. God has called His Word and His teaching the only completely true philosophy. If you put your trust in Christ and structure your life around His instruction in the Bible, you'll head down the right path.

God, I know Your Word is the truth. If there is something in my life based on human tradition that takes away from my devotion to Christ, make it apparent so I can ask for forgiveness and reroute my attentions. Amen.

Finding Your Roots

Faith isn't faith until it's all you're holding on to. —Patrick Overton

There's a great big reservoir in northern Texas that has a decent-sized river flowing from it. In the spring, a whole bunch of water is released out of the reservoir into this river. The extra inflow raises the water level and quickens the current, which erodes all the dirt around these huge trees on the banks, exposing their enormous roots. Libby and I were kayaking down this gorgeous river a while back and I was stunned at how deep those roots went. As we drifted by these trees I thought about Jeremiah 17—it's a contrast between "people who honestly put their trust in people" and "people who honestly put their trust in God."

> *This is what the Lord says: "Cursed is the one who trusts in man, who draws strength from mere flesh and whose heart turns away from the Lord.*
>
> *That person will be like a bush in the wastelands; they will not see prosperity when it comes. They will dwell in the parched places of the desert, in a salt land where no one lives.*
>
> *But blessed is the one who trusts in the Lord, whose confidence is in him.*
>
> *They will be like a tree planted by the water that sends out its roots by the stream. It does not fear when heat comes; its leaves are always green. It has no worries in a year of drought and never fails to bear fruit."* —Jeremiah 17:5-8

A tree whose roots go down into the river of life never has to fear. The river is a constant supply of life that is always present, even when bad conditions come with tough times. Choosing to consistently put your faith in God is the same thing. Trust in Him the same way you received Him, by grace through faith and not by works, and He will hold you up, sustain you, and protect you always and forever, no matter what.

Father, thank You for being a constant presence in my life. Your protection of my heart and spirit are total, Your strength encouraging, and Your sustenance refreshing. Show me how I can trust in You even more than I do now, so I can dwell in the prosperity of Your Spirit. Amen.

What We're Really Looking For

What can wash away my sins? Nothing but the blood of Jesus! What can make me whole again? Nothing but the blood of Jesus! Oh, precious is the flow, That makes me white as snow, No other fount I know, Nothing but the blood of Jesus!
—Robert Lowry (1876)

Every once in a while, Hollywood nails it with gripping honesty about eternal truth. It happened awhile ago on TV's "ER." A retired police officer is dying from cancer. Nearing his end, he calls a chaplain into his room, confessing his long-held guilt over allowing a man he knew was innocent to be framed, convicted, and executed.

> Officer: "How can I even hope for forgiveness?"
> Chaplain: "I think sometimes it's easier to feel guilty than forgiven."
> Officer: "Which means what?"
> Chaplain: "That maybe your guilt over his death has become your reason for living. Maybe you need a new reason to go on."
> Officer: "I don't want to go on. Can't you see I'm dying? The only thing that's holding me back is that I'm afraid. I'm afraid of what comes next … You tell me. Is atonement possible? What does God want from me?"
> Chaplain: "I think it's up to each one of us to interpret for ourselves what God wants."
> Officer, staring at her in bewilderment: "So people can do anything. They can rape and they can murder and they can steal all in the name of God and it's okay? … All I'm hearing is some new age 'God is love have it your way' crap. No, I don't have time for this now."
> Chaplain: "I hear that you're frustrated but you need to ask yourself …"
> Officer: "No I don't need to ask myself anything. I need answers, and all of your questions and all of your uncertainty are only making things worse."

Howard Hendricks once said, "In the midst of a generation screaming for answers, Christians are stuttering." Today, may God use us in any way He sees fit to share the simple, powerful heart of the Gospel.

> *If we confess our sins, he is faithful and just and will forgive us our sins and purify us from all unrighteousness.* —1 John 1:9

Gracious Father, in the name of Jesus, by the power of Your Spirit, use my actions and my words to clearly communicate Your truth to desperate souls today. Amen.

Raising the Shield ... Again and Always

No one ever told me that grief felt so like fear. —C.S. **Lewis**

"So what is it?" I asked the doctor.
"Either mono or leukemia," he said.

For twelve days, my prayer life went through the roof, as I struggled to find stability in a situation where I had no control, no certainty, and nothing on earth that could contain my fear. Over and over I begged Jesus to do something, that He would be enough for me. It was my son who was in question, after all. Our elementary-aged Cameron. His life was teetering on the brink of the unknown and there was nothing I could do about it.

Well, maybe one thing:

> *So then, just as you received Christ Jesus as Lord, continue to live your lives in him, rooted and built up in him, strengthened in the faith as you were taught, and overflowing with thankfulness.* —Colossians 2:6-7

During those two weeks I was suspended in the fog of uncertainty and fear. During those days I learned to pray, "Jesus, I trust You with the next 30 minutes. I know a whole bunch of stuff is going to happen, and I give it to you." 31 minutes later I'd add, "Jesus I give you the next 30 minutes ...."

Sometimes, big problems affect my concentration. Instead of just fighting through it, I'll take out my journal and I'll write my thoughts down so I can capture them on the page and take them to Christ. I say, "Jesus, I'm officially giving this stuff to You. Be enough for me and take away my worry. Your will be done."

After twelve days, Cameron's blood showed that he had mono. While we were hugely relieved, I learned again what it means to be fully honest with God.

Satan's arrows will come, but God has given you the shield of faith.

Lord, many are saying of my soul, "There is no deliverance for him in God." But You, O LORD, are a shield about me, My glory, and the One who lifts my head. I am crying to You, the LORD, with my voice. You have answered me from Your holy mountain. Selah. (from Psalm 3:3-4)

Our Boiling Pot

The lack of money is the root of all evil. —Mark Twain

A couple of years ago, someone from the outside warned us. It was one of our church planters from India who'd never been out of his country before. After a week of visiting here, somebody asked him his impression of our fine nation. He said this: **"One thing I've noticed is that the houses you built for your cars are far bigger and much nicer than the houses we have for our families."** That one stopped me cold. Think about it; garages are houses that we build for our cars while millions of people around the world are houseless and homeless. It was fair warning for a subtle but dangerous trend that we don't even seem to be aware of.

Most of us can recognize a dangerous situation when it is sprung on us. But we are susceptible to gradual danger, and unless we're warned, we will fall prey to it. Biologists say that if a frog is placed in a pot of cool water that is slowly brought to a boil, the frog will cook rather than try to jump out. (I've never verified this, I swear.) Sometimes, we need someone who's outside the pot of water to warn us of our situation, because we're oblivious to the danger that's slowly encroaching upon us. Our friend from India did that. He warned us of a big danger that's encroaching upon our entire nation: materialism.

Scripture warns us as well. **Jesus saw money as His primary competition for our heart:**

> *Do not store up for yourselves treasures on earth, where moth and vermin destroy, and where thieves break in and steal. But store up for yourselves treasures in heaven, where moths and vermin do not destroy, and where thieves do not break in and steal. For where your treasure is, there your heart will be also ... No one can serve two masters. Either you will hate the one and love the other, or you will be devoted to the one and despise the other. You cannot serve both God and money.* —Matthew 6:19-21, 24

Have we become so comfortable and complacent in our materialism that we will allow our lives to be boiled away?

Gracious Father, I am going to need a special awareness of Your grace as I address this issue with You. Search my heart, show me my ways. By the counsel of Your Spirit in me, give me the wisdom and the willingness to align my life with the truth of Your Word so that I can serve You in freedom, rather than serve materialism as a slave. Amen.

Are You Being Robbed Right Now?

Honesty is the best policy—when there's money in it. —Mark Twain

"Money can rob you." I know that sounds counterintuitive, but money can steal something very precious from you. *If you find yourself lulled to sleep in a materialistic environment, you will miss untold opportunities to express and experience the love and life of Christ.* The biggest mistake that we make with our money is this: **We trust our money rather than God, and that steals from us the words of life:**

> *The seed falling among the thorns refers to someone who hears the word, but the worries of this life and the deceitfulness of wealth choke the word, making it unfruitful.* —Matthew 13:22

In Jesus' parable of the seeds, the word of God is spread over four different kinds of "soils" representing four different types of responses to the Gospel. The thorny soil represents someone who accepts the Gospel and is initially excited and sacrificial … but then "the worries of this life and the deceitfulness of wealth choke the word," robbing the person of the security, joy, and freedom that can only be found in Jesus.

Can money buy these things?

Security? No. The next dip in the market, the next crooked investment advisor, the next greedy bank can take it all in an instant. Beyond that, even when you do have it, there's the continual *insecurity* that comes from the fear that it could all evaporate tomorrow.

Happiness? Oh sure, little happy moments, but excessive wealth is followed by an underlying *emptiness* because money didn't follow through on the promise it made me.

Freedom? No, again. Actually, quite a bit of bondage. How many of our worries in life are centered around money and things? Honestly, haven't we become *slaves* to all this stuff?

Yeah, someone can steal your money, but the odds are far, far greater that money will rob you instead.

Jesus, gently, but firmly, show me where I have allowed money and materialism to rob me of the richest of blessings that are found only in You. By faith, for my own good, I ask that You would do whatever it takes to refocus my trust on You, to place my hope in You, to serve only You. Amen.

Letting God Guide Your Generosity

The covetous man is ever in want. —**Horace**

"He who dies with the most toys wins." That's what our culture tells us; life is found in the abundance of possessions. The more stuff you have, the better stuff you have, the happier you'll be. Jesus says the *exact* opposite:

> *And he told them this parable: "The ground of a certain rich man yielded an abundant harvest. He thought to himself, 'What shall I do? I have no place to store my crops.' Then he said, 'This is what I'll do. I will tear down my barns and build bigger ones, and there I will store my surplus grain. And I'll say to myself, "You have plenty of grain laid up for many years. Take life easy; eat, drink and be merry."' But God said to him, 'You fool! This very night your life will be demanded from you. Then who will get what you have prepared for yourself?' This is how it will be with anyone who stores up things for himself but is not rich toward God."* —Luke 12:16-21

Yeah, money can rob us of security, happiness, and freedom. **Money confuses us, too.** He gave the world a clear warning in His opening intro to the parable:

> *Then he said to them, "Watch out! Be on your guard against all kinds of greed; life does not consist in an abundance of possessions."* —Luke 12:15

Listen, I need to hear this as much as anyone. Every time I wish I had a bigger garage to store more stuff, this parable should come back to me. **The problem is, I think most of us *want* to be confused and conflicted so we don't have to obey His clear instructions.** How can we tell if we're confused? Ask yourself this: Are you hoarding your possessions for yourself? Or are you giving generously to things that God cares about? Comparing yourself to others doesn't count here. This is between you and God *only*. Are you *really* allowing Him to guide your generosity *day to day*, according to clear biblical principles and the leading of His Spirit in you … or will you die rich and foolish?

God of All, right here, right now, guide my thoughts. I want to be honest: I need You to make me want to be obedient. I need Your Spirit to show me how. I am Yours. Everything in my possession is Yours. Show me the next step of generosity You want me to take with Your stuff right now, then show me the next step, then the next, then … Amen.

Is Money Ruling You?

A great fortune is a great slavery. —Seneca

You probably know the Golden Rule: *Treat others the way you want to be treated.* You've probably also heard the more practical version: *He who has the gold makes the rules.* I've got one Golden Rule to add: *He who owns the gold is ruled by the gold.* Confusing? Let Jesus clarify it with a story:

> *A certain ruler asked him, "Good teacher, what must I do to inherit eternal life?"*
>
> *"Why do you call me good?" Jesus answered. "No one is good—except God alone. You know the commandments: 'You shall not commit adultery, you shall not murder, you shall not steal, you shall not give false testimony, honor your father and mother.'"*
>
> *"All these I have kept since I was a boy," he said.*
>
> *When Jesus heard this, he said to him, "You still lack one thing. Sell everything you have and give to the poor, and you will have treasure in heaven. Then come, follow me."*
>
> *When he heard this, he became very sad, because he was very wealthy.* —Luke 18:18-23

This man was a rich ruler, yet he was really being ruled by his riches. He knew something was missing in his life. Jesus knew the core issue and said, "Sell everything you have and give it to the poor. Then come and follow Me." **But it's the only place in Scripture that I know of where somebody who was truly seeking Jesus left not saying "yes" to Him.**

What ruled this ruler's decision? The same thing that rules so many of our decisions: Money. **Money can rule you.** But Jesus drew the line clearly: "If you want to really follow Me and be a part of what I am really doing, remove the idol from its place of prominence in your life and put Me there instead." And He is still saying that to each of us today.

*Lord Jesus, I want to take You at Your Word—Your Word that is not "as good as gold," but infinitely **better** than gold. I don't want to justify my love of money. I don't want to compromise the simple truths You spoke. Speak to my heart so I can confess my sins in this area. Thank You for forgiving me. I want to be ruled by Your love. Live through me today. Amen.*

When Your Loss Is Gain

It is pretty hard to tell what does bring happiness; poverty and wealth have both failed. —**Kin Hubbard**

I have a friend who has a great story about depending on money. He shared it with our church once, and this is about how it went:

In 1982, I took a job in California. Being young and confident, my wife and I bought another house when we moved. Ten months into that particular stint, I was fired. Now, we had two house payments, and on top of that, our third child had just been born

We were on the edge of declaring bankruptcy when family stepped in to help. The following months were incredibly difficult. It seemed like an endless string of sleepless nights as we begged God for help and tried to figure out what He was up to.

It took about fifteen years to get back on our feet. I ended up CEO of another company in a partnership. But we reached a point when God was prompting us, "It's time to move on." It was a hard decision, but we ended the partnership. Near the end of the deal, my attorney told me, "You need to be prepared to lose everything." I thought, Really? Again?

That night, my wife was anxious to hear how the meeting had gone with the lawyer. I just said, "We need to be prepared to lose everything." As those words tumbled out of my mouth, an enormous peace was driven into my heart. My wife took a deep breath; then she was okay with it too. After 20 years of learning, we were finally at the point where we were ok with having nothing, because in Christ, we had finally learned that we had everything.

What was different the second time around for my friend? He had discovered that perfect security is found in God. What they learned the hard way, we can learn by choice:

- Money can rob us.
- Money can confuse us.
- Money can rule us.

But in Christ we find security, clarity, and freedom in any and every circumstance.

God, thank You for Your perfect security that will never fail. Show me when I trust other things, and when I do, pull me back to Yourself! Amen.

Keeping Your Heart Humble

I'm not a snob. Ask anybody. Well, anybody who matters. —Simon Le Bon

Ephesus was one of the wealthiest cities in the ancient world. If you walk its ancient ruins today, it's still obvious: Wealthy folks with big houses everywhere. That means the believers probably met in one of these big, beautiful, opulent homes. Wealthy and poor all coming together as equals in the body of Christ in that setting—a perfect circumstance for discrimination.

At the very end of Paul's first letter to Timothy, who was in Ephesus, Paul asks him to pass on a message:

> *Command those who are rich in this present world not to be arrogant nor to put their hope in wealth, which is so uncertain, but to put their hope in God, who richly provides us with everything for our enjoyment.* —1 Timothy 6:17

We've got as much to learn from Paul as the Ephesians did. Sure, you might not feel rich compared to fellow Americans, but if you compare yourself to everyone else on the planet, our "middle class" is *very* "rich in this present world."

The first thing Paul tells the rich (us) is to avoid arrogance. Here's a common tendency of the world we often fall prey to:

- When we start to make a little money, we start to think we're a little more important.

- When we start to make more money, we start to think we're more important.

- When we start to make a lot of money, we think we're a lot important.

- When we start to think that people who make less than us are less important than us, we become arrogant—radiating a stench of superiority of the rich over the poor.

Earthly wealth doesn't measure a person's character. On a spiritual level, the rich and the poor are both justified equally in Christ. That is where *everyone* gets their eternal worth, and that's the only place it matters.

Father, with whatever You have blessed me, I pray You keep my heart humble. I recognize my money does not make me superior to those who have less. Amen.

Your Next Step

There are multitudes whose life is nothing but a continuous lottery; who are always within a few months of plenty and happiness, and how often soever they are mocked with blanks, expect a prize from the next adventure.
—Samuel Johnson

If I told you I could push a button right now and transfer a million dollars to your bank account, how many of you would feel a little better? You're probably thinking, "Wow, I could deal with that. I could do this. I could go there. Life would be better if Pete gave me a million dollars!" (I know *I'd* like it if I gave me a million bucks.)

That just shows our tendency to put our hope in wealth. Money makes promises it can't deliver. All I had to do was tell you I'm giving you a million dollars, and you forgot. Here's the daily reminder:

> *Command those who are rich in this present world not to be arrogant nor to put their hope in wealth, which is so uncertain....* —1 Timothy 6:17

Don't put your hope in wealth. It's uncertain and won't be able to fulfill your needs indefinitely. I've got an app on my iPad I check to see what our college fund for our kids is doing. It goes up and down and up and down on the will of a few people on Wall Street. While I'm thankful for the money and what it allows for my kids, I hate watching it fluctuate in ways I have no control over. That app should be a constant reminder.

> *... but to put their hope in God, who richly provides us with everything for our enjoyment.* —1 Timothy 6:17

Where wealth is fleeting, slippery, and weak, God is constant, solid, and sturdy. True security and stability is found in Christ. He promises in His Word that He will never forsake you, that all you have to do is reach for Him and He'll catch you.

The next step is yours. Will you take it?

God, thank You for being constant in my life. I put my trust in You because You will never abandon me. Amen.

Kneading Your Dough into Life

No one has ever become poor by giving. —Anne Frank

We are constantly bombarded in today's culture to spend our money on things we "deserve." But God doesn't necessarily see money as a tool to bless ourselves; He sees money as our tool to bless others.

John Calvin once said, **"A man's opportunities to do good for others increase with the abundance of his riches."** As God gives you more, naturally you have more opportunity to do good in people's lives.

> *Command those who are rich in this present world not to be arrogant nor to put their hope in wealth, which is so uncertain, but to put their hope in God, who richly provides us with everything for our enjoyment. Command them to do good, to be rich in good deeds, and to be generous and willing to share.*
> —1 Timothy 6:17-18

If you are above the American poverty line, you are "rich in this present world." And even giving just a little goes a very long way. Compassion International offers the opportunity for people to feed, clothe, and educate poverty-stricken kids for $38/month! World Vision has a program where you can provide small business loans to families, so they can get the supplies and equipment they need to provide long-term for their basic needs.

God pours blessings and gifts into our lives so we can be blessings to others. Paul just comes out and says, "Be generous and willing to share." But it doesn't end there. Generosity is God's way to bless us:

> *In this way they will lay up treasure for themselves as a firm foundation for the coming age, so that they may take hold of the life that is truly life.*
> —1 Timothy 6:19

God is reaching out, right now, offering a different way to live. The result is a freedom and satisfaction that cannot be matched by anything you could buy. Are you ready to take hold of that which is "truly life?"

God, set my priorities straight. Make my heart compassionate and loving like Yours. Today, show me one special place where the money You have entrusted to me can be a blessing to someone else. I thank You ahead of time for the opportunity to be used in this way. Amen.

The Fight for Your Heart

Perchik: "Money is the world's curse!"

Tevye: "May the Lord smite me with it. And may I never recover!"
—from "Fiddler on the Roof"

I think we can all agree that whenever there is a conflict, it's over something seen as valuable. Sure, sometimes we fight for bragging rights or for mastery of a specific skill, like chess or boxing. Far more often, though, we compete over things or ideas that are more valuable than that.

Jesus and Satan know what is most valuable in the human being; they fight for our hearts.

- Jesus is the best thing for us; in Him we are complete.

- Satan needs to pull us away from that, so he uses materialism to distract us.

As we take Satan's materialistic bait, our hearts begin to covet things that don't last, which pulls us into the trap. **Satan's victory over our souls becomes more and more powerful the more we place our value in the value of our stuff.**

> *Command those who are rich in this present world not to be arrogant nor to put their hope in wealth, which is so uncertain, but to put their hope in God, who richly provides us with everything for our enjoyment. Command them to do good, to be rich in good deeds, and to be generous and willing to share. In this way they will lay up treasure for themselves as a firm foundation for the coming age, so that they may take hold of the life that is truly life.*
> —1 Timothy 6:17-19

We already have life because we have Christ. But we can't waste our wealth completely on ourselves. When spending your fortunes, **avoid arrogance, transfer hope, give generously.** You'll experience *blessing* here, and you'll store up *treasure there.*

The conflict and competition for your heart continues today. Who will win?

Spirit, I know that whatever wealth I have doesn't make me better or worse than those with less or more. Show me where You want me to pour myself and my resources into, so that spiritual wealth abounds in many people! Amen.

Open Your Eyes

We make a living by what we get. We make a life by what we give.
—Winston Churchill

A friend of mine named Bill took his family to Cabo San Lucas, Mexico on vacation a while back. One night, they hired a taxi to take them out to eat. The driver asked if he could come back and pick them up later, so they agreed. After dinner, Bill asked him in broken Spanish how many kids he had. The driver replied, "Cuatro." (Four.)

Bill then asked how old they were. The driver replied, "Cuatro."

"How about the other ones?"

"Cuatro."

At first Bill thought the driver misunderstood. They went around and around until all of a sudden, he realized the man had quadruplets.

Bill, never having seen quadruplets, asked if they could take this man and his family out for dinner. The next day, as the driver and his wife filed into the local McDonald's, Bill and his wife's hearts broke when they saw the last two boys. Their eyes were terribly crossed and they couldn't walk as a result. After a little digging, Bill learned there was a surgery that could fix the little boys' eyes, but a very small window of time was left for it to be done.

The problem? The driver only made $10 per day. There was no way they could afford the surgery. So God moved the hearts of Bill and his family. They looked into it and found a doctor who could perform the surgery. After the kids went through the surgery, both boys' eyes were perfectly straight and they began learning how to walk.

God gave Bill and his family eyes to see the need that was around them. What an awesome way to view the world. Imagine the difference we can make as Christ expresses His life through us. After all, miracles happen when people step out in faith in Him. Will you?

Holy Spirit, I think MY eyes are the ones that are crossed. I'm that one who cannot walk freely as You intended. Correct MY vision. I believe that You will bless me as I allow You to bless others through me. I believe that I'll be storing up treasure in heaven. Amen.

Dropping Your Guard with Jesus

Clothes make the man. Naked people have little or no influence on society.
—Mark Twain

It's the classic nightmare. Imagine you're in the middle of Times Square—completely naked. Feels terrifying, right?

That shame and that drive to "get out of here" is the natural reaction you have when you recognize your unrighteousness before God. Because God is good, I must hide from Him because I am not. This was the natural reaction of Adam and Eve:

> *Then the eyes of both of them were opened, and they realized they were naked; so they sewed fig leaves together and made coverings for themselves.*
> —Genesis 3:7

When you're spiritually naked, you feel the gaze and the stare of God and others with nowhere to hide. The natural human response is to cover up:

- We immerse ourselves in our work.
- We get really religious.
- We try to raise kids who behave in public.
- We try to get rid of the classic outward sins.
- And we really tend to judge others.

"Fig leaves" can sometimes protect us from judgment by other human beings, but they come with a price if we try to hide our sin from God, who is the only one who can redeem us from the fall.

> *But now apart from the law the righteousness of God has been made known, to which the Law and the Prophets testify. This righteousness is given through faith in Jesus Christ to all who believe. There is no difference between Jew and Gentile, for all have sinned and fall short of the glory of God, and all are justified freely by his grace through the redemption that came by Christ Jesus.*
> —Romans 3:21-24

Fig leaves deny this reality and rob you of intimacy with God. But Jesus makes that intimacy always available … no matter how exposed your sin makes you feel.

Jesus, how foolish I am to try to hide behind fig leaves when You know it all anyway … and You forgive and love me always. I drop my guard before You now. I praise You for Your grace. Thank You, thank You for fully embracing me just the way I am. Amen.

Are You a Streaker, a Worker, or a Little of Both?

But then I sigh, and with a piece of scripture tell them that God bids us do good for evil. And thus I clothe my naked villainy with odd old ends stol'n forth of holy writ, and seem a saint when most I play the devil. —Shakespeare, King Richard III

The 1970s was a pretty embarrassing decade. Big hair, tight pants, disco, and the temporary phenomenon called "streaking." It seemed like every time you turned on the news, someone had taken off their clothes and was running naked through public places.

That's actually one of two common responses people show when sin is exposed in their life. **Unable to hide it, some of us just flaunt sin and run with it.**

> *Although they know God's righteous decree that those who do such things deserve death, they not only continue to do these very things but also approve of those who practice them.* —Romans 1:32

But others of us try to hide sin behind good works. It's called self-righteousness: The counterfeit technique of self-focused behavior modification. Quit swearing, go to church, pay your taxes, be associated with the upright crowd …

The goal of the "worker" is to look good on the outside, convincing others, self, and hopefully God, that you are really okay on the inside … at least that you are better than the streakers whose sin is so obvious (or maybe the "streaker" is just more honest than the "worker"?) Anyway, Paul describes the fate of self-righteous people:

> *You, therefore, have no excuse, you who pass judgment on someone else, for at whatever point you judge another, you are condemning yourself, because you who pass judgment do the same things.* —Romans 2:1

Neither the worker nor the streaker responds correctly to the revelation of his sins because neither of them has the grace of God in mind. **Whether you flaunt your sin or try to hide it under good works is really not the issue. God's grace is!**

Jesus, check my heart today. Show me where I flaunt my sin. Show me where I am self-righteous. Replace these fleshly responses with a deep appreciation for all that You have done for me, and then live through me in a way that reflects Your mercy, grace, and love for the world. Amen.

You Don't Have to Live in the Foreshadows

Most of the shadows of this life are caused by standing in one's own sunshine.
—Ralph Waldo Emerson

Like any good movie, God's unfolding story contains foreshadowing. The first foreshadow of His grace came right away, in Genesis 3:15, when God told Satan,

> *And I will put enmity between you and the woman, and between your offspring and hers; he will crush your head, and you will strike his heel.*

This is the first hint of the Gospel ever. This is a foreshadowing of the cross where Satan gives Jesus a hard shot, but in the end Christ crushes Satan.

Another foreshadowing takes place when God took off Adam and Eve's fig leaves and made some permanent skin garments to cover their nakedness—and He had to kill an animal to do that. It's the first physical death in the history of the world. **God showed that through the death of an innocent One, He will put a new garment on you.** It's a theme we see throughout Bible. Take Zechariah 3:

> *Now Joshua was dressed in filthy clothes as he stood before the angel. The angel said to those who were standing before him, "Take off his filthy clothes." Then he said to Joshua, "See, I have taken away your sin, and I will put fine garments on you." Then I said, "Put a clean turban on his head." So they put a clean turban on his head and clothed him, while the angel of the Lord stood by.* —Zechariah 3:3-5

Zechariah, talking about more than clothes, explains how God is going to do this:

> *'... I am going to bring my servant, the Branch. See, the stone I have set in front of Joshua! There are seven eyes on that one stone, and I will engrave an inscription on it,' says the Lord Almighty, 'and I will remove the sin of this land in a single day.'* —Zechariah 3:8-9

Wow. That's pretty clear! And the coolest part? **You can experience today what He foreshadowed in the past. No more shadows needed. The light of Jesus has caught up with the foreshadow of prophecy and you can live in its brightness today!**

My Lord and my God, I praise You, Jesus, for Who You are and what You have done. You have taken off my filth and clothed me with fine garments. What can I do except lift empty hands in thanks and praise to You today? Amen

Got Gunnysack?

A fact is like a sack—it won't stand up if it's empty. —**Luigi Pirandello**

Satan is good at a lot of things. For one, he is the ultimate gunnysacker.

What is gunnysacking? It's pretty simple, actually. When someone says something wrong or does something wrong to you, you don't say anything about the wound. You just take the offense, and store it in a little sack, and go on as though nothing had happened. THEN, later, when you do something wrong and you are called on it, you pull out the painful events you've been storing up and use it to accuse your accuser. We usually do it to deflect responsibility when we feel exposed.

I think we are all pretty good at gunnysacking. But Satan? He's the master.

> *Then he showed me Joshua the high priest standing before the angel of the Lord, and Satan standing at his right side to accuse him.* —Zechariah 3:1

He actually has a gunnysack for every single one of us. He'll see you do something outside of what God has for you and he'll take that thing and throw it in your gunnysack. Then, in a time of weakness, he'll come after you and expose your naked guilt. All of a sudden the accusations start coming fast and furiously … and it sounds true, of course, because it probably is. But it's not the full story.

There is only one way to fight back: Get back in Satan's face with the Truth.

> *Therefore, there is now no condemnation for those who are in Christ Jesus.* —Romans 8:1

> *If we confess our sins, he is faithful and just and will forgive us our sins and purify us from all unrighteousness.* —1 John 1:9

Jesus is the one Who redeems you from the naked shame of sin. And you can celebrate that with all your heart when Satan tries to embarrass you. Don't gunnysack others, and don't take it when Satan tries it on you!

Jesus, I praise You for what You did on the cross. I thank You that I am not condemned, that You continually forgive, and that You have purified me. Thank You, thank You for covering my nakedness with Your righteousness! Amen.

You're Blessed to Be Blameless

Our righteousness is in Him, and our hope depends … upon the fullness of grace and love in Him, and upon His obedience unto death. —John Newton

The best things in life are free.

That's great news to everyone who understands God's grace and walks in His Spirit. But what about those folks who are in Christ, but still living *under* the Law? That usually lands Christians into one of two categories:

> The self-righteous—those who think they must make themselves righteous in their own strength.

> The not-righteous-enough—those who, even though they are righteous in Christ, mistakenly think and feel they are unrighteous as they carry guilt and feel condemned.

Yeah, there is probably an element of one of these in each one of us, isn't there? Daily, we must remind ourselves of the new way God makes for both the self-righteous and the not-righteous-enough:

> *But now apart from the law the righteousness of God has been made known, to which the Law and the Prophets testify. This righteousness is given through faith in Jesus Christ to **all** who believe, There is no difference between Jew and Gentile, for all have sinned and fall short of the glory of God, and all are justified **freely** by his grace through the redemption that came by Christ Jesus.*
> —Romans 3:21-24

Which way will you choose to see your righteousness today? Through the lens of the law leading to self-righteousness or shame, or faith in what Christ did on the cross?

Lamb of God, who takes away my sin, use my sense of self-righteousness and un-righteousness as a teacher today. Use it to lead me to Your grace as the pure, free source of righteousness. By faith, and not my works, I celebrate what You have made me in You: Righteous! I trust in You to live through me today in a way that makes this truth a practical reality. Amen.

Does It Blow You Away?

The greatest enemy to human souls is the self-righteous spirit which makes men look to themselves for salvation. —Charles Spurgeon

I've been studying this "righteousness" stuff for a long time. I'm a professional Christian, right? I even have the big M.Div. seminary degree, which makes some people think I have a higher degree of righteousness! Then why does this topic of "righteousness" still blow me away? Because rightly understood, *our* righteousness comes back to *Jesus*, every time.

> *But whatever were gains to me I now consider loss for the sake of Christ. What is more, I consider everything a loss because of the surpassing worth of knowing Christ Jesus my Lord, for whose sake I have lost all things. I consider them garbage, that I may gain Christ and be found in him, not having a righteousness of my own that comes from the law, but that which is through faith in Christ—the righteousness that comes from God on the basis of faith.*
> —Philippians 3:7-9

God cannot simply declare you righteous if you are still wicked. He can't just *say* you are righteous, and you can't make *yourself* righteous. He must first make you righteous before He can declare you so.

> *God made him who had no sin to be sin for us, so that in him we might become the righteousness of God.* —2 Corinthians 5:21

That's Jesus all the way. He carried our sin to the cross. We were crucified with Him there. He "regenerated us," and He now lives in us ... we have become the righteousness of God in Jesus. Now, each day, we are learning to rest in His righteousness *in* us and trust in His Spirit to live *through* us.

That's the Gospel and after all these years of studying and preaching and teaching, it still blows me away.

Holy Spirit, would You stir up the truth in me today? The truth about my righteousness is in Your Word. Today, make it real in my heart. When the lies of the world, my flesh, and Satan remind me of who I would be apart from You, give me the boldness to proclaim who I truly am in You, because of my faith in You, because of what You have made me to be. Amen.

Rags to Righteousness

Ignorance is not bliss. Bliss is ignorance of one's ignorance. —Unknown

Scripture tells us we can be radically transformed by renewing our minds according to what is true (Romans 12:1-2). That's important, because there is a problem that only Christians can have: We often think we are clothed in sin, when in fact, we are truly dressed in the righteousness of God.

I believe Satan will often try to convince you that you're still who you were before Christ changed you. A sure sign of this is the self-talk that sounds righteous, but is actually based on a lie: *Oh, I am such a sinner. Oh, how could God ever forgive me?* You look at other people and think, *Oh, they are so much "closer" to God than I am.* (Remember, the truth is that you could never get closer to God when He is in you already!)

When Joshua the high priest was standing before God, and Satan was accusing him (Zechariah 3), Satan was pointing at his sinful filthy rags. He probably said something like, "God, look at this miserable slob. How could You love him?" Joshua was listening to all this. How do you think he was feeling? You *know* what he was feeling, don't you? You know what it's like to have your sin pointed out.

But that's when God steps in.

> *The angel said to those who were standing before him, "Take off his filthy clothes."*
>
> *Then he said to Joshua, "See, I have taken away your sin, and I will put fine garments on you."* —Zechariah 3:4

This is exactly what Jesus did to us the day we said yes to Him! **"Take off your filthy rags."** God has made you His righteousness; that's the truth. You *can* renew your mind and be transformed. How? By refusing the lies of Satan and embracing who Jesus made you into. What happened to Satan's accusations when the robes of righteousness were placed on Joshua? Satan went mute. Satan has nothing to say when we stand in the righteousness of Christ.

Jesus, I ask that Your truth would break through my feelings, my experiences, and the lies of Satan and the world that continually remind me of my sins. Thank You for taking away my sin! Thank You for putting the fine garments of righteousness around me. Thank You for what You did on the cross, my Lord. Amen.

Standing Firm in Your Righteousness

Dad, are you naked under all those clothes? —7-year-old Josh to his dad

Satan is smart, and very tricky. If he can get you asking the wrong question, you'll never come up with the right answer. If you are a Christian, the *wrong* question is, "How do I make myself righteous?" But this is the question Satan loves for you to ask, because it distracts you from a fundamental command of God that can seriously protect you from the lies of Satan in many areas:

> *Stand firm then ... with the breastplate of righteousness in place.*
> —Ephesians 6:14

Please note this passage doesn't say to go out and *find* a breastplate of righteousness. He doesn't say to go out and *create* a breastplate of righteousness. If you build your *own* armor, it's going to be flawed and weak. You'll always have to make sure you're doing enough to be protected, enough to be righteous, enough to justify yourself. On top of being extremely exhausting, that is way out of sync with the way it's supposed to be. God wants you to stand firm in the breastplate of righteousness He has made for you. Your job is to put your trust in what *He* has done.

> *Christ is the culmination of the law so that there may be righteousness for everyone who believes.* —Romans 10:4

The breastplate covers the whole chest and abdomen. It covers all the vital organs, the things that keep you alive. You *have* this righteousness in Christ.

Know it and stand firm in this truth! You have nothing to hide from the Father, and Satan can no longer use your guilt to manipulate you. In the Upper Room, Jesus said, *"Satan has no hold on me"* (John 14). Satan had no hold on Him because He was completely righteous. You shared in His crucifixion and resurrection. Everything that He won, you won, too—which means Satan has no hold on you either. That's the truth. The best he can do is to deceive you from the truth by getting you to ask the wrong question.

How will you answer?

Abba Father, I refuse the fleshly instincts to try to make myself righteous. I see Satan's attempt to distract me with the wrong question. I look to You, and You only as the answer and the source of my righteousness. By the power of Your spirit in me, give me the wisdom to stand firm in the breastplate You have provided and made for me already. Amen.

Rejoicing in Your Robes

The hardest people to reach with the love of God are not the bad people. They know they are bad. They have no defense. The hardest ones to win for God are the self-righteous people. —Charles L. Allen

I love those police dramas when one of the police officers gets separated from all his buddies. He's on a dark street and it's night (and of course, the street is always wet for some reason). With gun drawn, he's on the chase for the bad guys. The music starts getting really ominous. Sure enough, the bad guys are waiting and BAM BAM! In slow motion he rocks back, drops his gun, and falls into a twisted heap on the cold pavement.

Game over?

No. Slowly, the officer begins to move! Slowly at first, then stands to his feet. He opens his uniform to reveal a bulletproof vest. Yes! And the slugs are right there over his heart! The vest saves his life … and that modern piece of protection is a picture of the eternal protection God has given us in the breastplate of righteousness.

> *Stand firm then … with the breastplate of righteousness in place.*
> —Ephesians 6:14

If you are living in Christ, you are going to take your shots, too. Satan will do everything he can to convince you that you are not who Christ says you are. Please remember: **The intent of God's breastplate of righteousness is not to perfect you, but to protect you and your heart** today, tomorrow, and every day until that day you finally meet God face-to-face.

> *I delight greatly in the LORD; my soul rejoices in my God. For he has clothed me with garments of salvation and arrayed me in a robe of his righteousness, as a bridegroom adorns his head like a priest, and as a bride adorns herself with her jewels.* —Isaiah 61:10

That's something to truly rejoice in. I don't know of any better news than that.

Heavenly Father, You know my transgressions from my past, my failures today, and my sins of tomorrow. Thank You for protecting me from the accusations of Satan by shielding me with Your breastplate of righteousness. My soul rejoices in You. Amen.

The Big Shift

NOV
17

Think of giving not as a duty but as a privilege. —John D. Rockefeller Jr.

The very basics of Christianity really are backwards from what we would expect. We die to live. When we are weak, we are strong. In most cases, we can look at what the world says and then do the exact opposite and pretty much be spot on. Consider this one: "He who dies with the most toys wins." The more we get, the more blessed we are, right? Nope. The opposite is true.

> *Now I commit you to God and to the word of his grace, which can build you up and give you an inheritance among all those who are sanctified. I have not coveted anyone's silver or gold or clothing. You yourselves know that these hands of mine have supplied my own needs and the needs of my companions. In everything I did, I showed you that by this kind of hard work we must help the weak, remembering the words the Lord Jesus himself said: "It is more blessed to give than to receive."* —Acts 20:32-35

Paul quotes Jesus here. They both agree that it's in *giving* that we are *more* blessed. We hear that so much that it's pretty much cliché. But do we believe it? Honestly, do we really believe there is more blessing in giving than there is in receiving? I'm not so sure.

Paul doesn't say there's no blessing in receiving. There is. Who doesn't love opening presents on Christmas morning? We *love* getting. No problem with that. In fact, a big part of the Christian life is learning to receive from the Father the most intense blessings possible. But it is the wise person who recognizes that the real blessings in life come when we give what we have away.

It sounds backwards, I know. But the key truth is clear: If we want to be blessed *more* than we already are, it will come through giving God's way, not getting the world's way.

Jesus, by faith, I want to explore Your truth about giving. I know this may require breaking fleshly patterns and worldly expectations. Guard my heart from legalism and religiosity as I pursue Your grace and leading. Break me where necessary and make me a conduit of Your generosity that I might receive true blessing. Amen.

Where's Your Heart?

I bought a seven dollar pen because I always lose pens and I got sick of not caring. —Mitch Hedberg

More years ago than I care to count, I traveled to Colombia with a sports team to experience the culture. So naturally, one night we ate at McDonald's. A beggar was sitting by the front door with his hand out. I passed him by at first, but a tug on my heart told me I should give him something. So I bought a Big Mac and gave it to him. I was expecting him to say thank you, but he didn't. Kind of awkward, so I started to walk away when *Poompt!* The Big Mac hit me in the back of the head.

Looked like I was out the price of a burger, but I did learn a valuable lesson: **When you do nice things for people, a lot of times you don't get anything in return, directly.**

God's blessings aren't always what you expect them to be, but they are very, very real. God's Word identifies four blessings that *will* come as we surrender to the Spirit. and allow Him to do this work of giving through us.

Giving blessing #1: A Heart Blessing. When we give in the power of the Spirit, our heart is free to be His.

> *Do not store up for yourselves treasures on earth, where moths and vermin destroy, and where thieves break in and steal. But store up for yourselves treasures in heaven, where moths and vermin do not destroy, and where thieves do not break in and steal. For where your treasure is, there your heart will be also.* —Matthew 6:19-21

Where do you want your heart to be focused? Put your money there *first*, and *then* your heart will follow. That makes sense, if you think about it. If you invest $150,000 in a restaurant, you're going to be pretty eager to make sure that restaurant does well.

Jesus teaches us: Pour your treasure into what I treasure and your heart will be free to treasure Me. That's the "heart blessing" of giving and one of the most important lessons we can learn.

Lord Jesus, right now, in a big or small way, stir up Your Spirit in me, and show me where You want to take my heart. I now ask, by faith, that You would show me how You want me to invest the treasure that You have lent me. I wait for Your leading, Lord. Amen.

An Act of Grace

True understanding of sacrificial brotherly love is letting him take the bathroom first. —George Q. Hauser

The church in Corinth was quite wealthy. The church in Jerusalem was rather poor and for several years, was under a severe famine. Many in Jerusalem were starving to death. So Paul asked some of the wealthy churches to donate money. The church in Corinth said, "Absolutely!" But then, they never did. Paul had some words for them:

> *And now, brothers and sisters, we want you to know about the grace that God has given the Macedonian churches. In the midst of a very severe trial, their overflowing joy and their extreme poverty welled up in rich generosity. For I testify that they gave as much as they were able, and even beyond their ability. Entirely on their own, they urgently pleaded with us for the privilege of sharing in this service to the Lord's people. And they exceeded our expectations: They gave themselves first of all to the Lord, and then by the will of God also to us.* —2 Corinthians 8:1-5

He used the Macedonians as an example to show what giving is like. What did they do?

1. They gave themselves first to the Lord. They made themselves and their resources available to Jesus and placed His desires before their own.

2. They followed through and they gave as the Spirit led them to do.

Part of the "zing" in Paul's message stems from the fact that the Macedonians were an *extraordinarily* poor church, but God had given them grace, and despite their poverty, they took an offering to contribute. This, my friend, is a beautiful summary of new covenant giving. It is an act of grace, born out of authentic love, expecting nothing in return (just like God's gifts to us).

It's what I'll call a "sibling blessing." The Holy Spirit moves us to give and empowers us to do so. As a result, our brothers and sisters in Christ in need are provided for. In His grace, we get majorly blessed, too. There's just nothing like living in sync with God.

O Lord, like the Corinthians, I am often bound up in my giving. I want to be free to give, in grace, like the Macedonians! Right here, right now, today, I give myself and everything in my possession back to You. I will follow the lead of Your Spirit to give where You wish! Amen.

The Unpopular Truth

How well I have learned that there is no fence to sit on between heaven and hell. There is a deep, wide gulf, a chasm, and in that chasm is no place for any man.
—Johnny Cash

To be honest, I really don't like preaching "hell, fire, and brimstone." It always reminds me of red, puffy-faced bald men with neckties that are way too tight.

The problem with that is that the Bible teaches "hell, fire, and brimstone" and we have to be committed to be seekers of true belief … even when the truth is uncomfortable. And while we can avoid the yelling and the red faces and the neckties that are too tight, we can live as gracious warnings to those headed in the wrong direction.

Jesus warned those around Him—as in this unnerving story He told:

> *There was a rich man who was dressed in purple and fine linen and lived in luxury every day. At his gate was laid a beggar named Lazarus… The time came when the beggar died and the angels carried him to Abraham's side. The rich man also died and was buried. In hell, where he was in torment, he looked up and saw Abraham far away, with Lazarus by his side. So he called to him, 'Father Abraham, have pity on me and send Lazarus to dip the tip of his finger in water and cool my tongue, because I am in agony in this fire.'*

> *But Abraham replied, 'Son, remember that in your lifetime you received your good things, while Lazarus received bad things, but now he is comforted here and you are in agony. And besides all this, between us and you a great chasm has been fixed, so that those who want to go from here to you cannot, nor can anyone cross over from there to us.'* —Luke 16:19-26

There are many lessons to be learned from this passage, but the blaring message is this: There is a heaven, and there is a hell, and after death it is impossible to move from one to the other. An eternal barrier is fixed between these two places and the decisions we make on earth will determine where we spend eternity.

Lord Jesus, thank You for the clarity of Your Word. Thank You for telling us the truth. Today and in the days ahead give us grace and mercy and wisdom as we contemplate the eternal future of ourselves and those around us. Amen.

Heavenly Minded AND Earthly Good

NOV 21

Maybe there is no actual place called hell. Maybe hell is just having to listen to our grandparents breathe through their noses when they're eating sandwiches.
—Jim Carrey

Jim Carrey is a good comedian, but an awful theologian. —Pete Briscoe

Is it possible to be "so heavenly minded that you are of no earthly good?" I don't think so, actually. **Having the truth about heaven in our minds puts everything else in perspective.** Throughout the Bible we find various snapshots of heaven:

- A place of joy (Luke 15:7, 10).
- A place of reward (Matthew 5:11-12).
- A place of peace (Luke 16:25).
- A place of righteousness (2 Peter 3:13).

Heaven is *indescribable*. When we step out of the time/space dimension of this screwed up and fallen world, nothing on earth will compare to that. It's everything that is good and beautiful going on forever and ever. The Bible also speaks of a new heaven and new earth that (2 Peter 3:13) will be ours to enjoy and explore. Revelation 21-22 also give a vivid word picture of this place.

But ironically, the Bible actually is most explicit about what heaven will *not* be like: No more pain (Revelation 21:4), no more tears (Revelation 7:17), no more death (Luke 20:36), no more night (Revelation 22:5), and no more Satan. **For those who are in Christ, this certain future up there is great encouragement for living down here.**

> *Since, then, you have been raised with Christ, set your hearts on things above, where Christ is, seated at the right hand of God. Set your minds on things above, not on earthly things. For you died, and your life is now hidden with Christ in God. When Christ, who is your life, appears, then you also will appear with him in glory.* —Colossians 3:1-3

I don't know about you, but this eternal perspective on our future changes the way that I look at today.

Jesus, focus my thoughts on things above, and not on earthly things. May the hope and expectation of heaven, and the fact that my life is hidden with You in God right now, direct my mind, my will, and my emotions today. Amen.

The Truth About Heaven and Hell

It's not that life is too short; it's that eternity is so long. —**Author Unknown**

I could talk about heaven all day long. Hell, on the other hand … not so much. Why not focus on the positive? Well, for one thing, Jesus spoke more about hell than He did heaven, so it sure couldn't hurt to take a look into this unthinkable abyss in order to get a little bit of perspective for living today.

- Hell is torment (Revelation 14:11).
- Hell is darkness (Matthew 8:12).
- Hell is a bottomless pit (Revelation 20:1, 2).
- Hell is continual and eternal (Revelation 14:11).

Hell is the opposite of heaven. Heaven is all good; hell is all evil. **When you're deciding between heaven and hell, it's not like you're deciding between Dallas and Chicago.** The choice is more Maui and a Rwandan refugee camp.

If we truly believe this, then I guess we have to give the red-faced, sign-holding street preachers a little credit. Maybe they're just trying to scare the hell out of people, which is, by comparison, better than sitting by as people unknowingly head there.

> *For God so loved the world that he gave his one and only Son, that whoever believes in him shall not perish but have eternal life. For God did not send his Son into the world to condemn the world, but to save the world through him. Whoever believes in him is not condemned, but whoever does not believe stands condemned already because they have not believed in the name of God's one and only Son.* —John 3:16-18

God sent Jesus into this world on a mission, not to condemn it, but to save it. He now calls us to be a part of the same mission: Sharing a message of salvation rather than pointing fingers of judgment and condemnation. The truth about hell is definitely part of that message. We need to remember that, and by the power of His Spirit in us, we can communicate that to others in a way that points the way to grace, mercy, and hope.

Holy Spirit, through my words and my actions, live through me in such a way that those around me sense the eternal dangers of hell and recognize the incredible gift of Your eternal life. Amen.

Myths About Life, Death and Eternity

I don't believe in an afterlife, so I don't have to spend my whole life fearing hell, or fearing heaven even more. For whatever the tortures of hell, I think the boredom of heaven would be even worse. —Isaac Asimov

I love inventing words. One of my favorites is "mythstake." A *mythstake* is a combination of a *mistake* and a *myth*. I keep checking in Webster's dictionary and they haven't put that word in there yet, but 20 years from now when *mythstake* is in all of the dictionaries of the world, you can say to your sons and daughters, "I remember, back in the day, when Pete Briscoe first used this now famous word in a daily devotional…"

Unlike a mistake, however, a mythstake is not an accident. It's an error that is a consequence of believing a myth (a commonly held notion that has no basis in truth). **Mythstakes can have serious earthly consequences, but some mythstakes impact not only this life, but the life to come as well, what happens beyond the grave, what happens in eternity … as in *forever*.**

That's both exciting and scary, because people believe things about eternal life that are myths. If they buy into those myths, they will make mistakes that last a long, long, long time. If we want to avoid these mythstakes, we need to know more than the facts of life; we need to know the facts about *eternal* life. The most important fact is this:

> *And this is the testimony: God has given us eternal life, and this life is in his Son. Whoever has the Son has life; whoever does not have the Son of God does not have life. I write these things to you who believe in the name of the Son of God so that you may know that you have eternal life.* —1 John 5:11-13

Any myth that causes us to make mistakes by distracting us or diverting us from Jesus is serious. We see these mythstakes all around us. We will take a look at them one at a time in the days ahead and you will be able to recognize them in the people around you. But are you willing to recognize any of these mythstakes in yourself?!

Holy Spirit, burn into my soul the reality of heaven and hell. Search my heart and reveal the myths that have infiltrated my beliefs about everlasting life and replace them with truth from Your living Word. Amen.

The Myth About Getting into Heaven

You may all go to Hell, and I will go to Texas. —Davy **Crockett**

When it comes time to decide how to get off the road to hell and head toward heaven many people base their beliefs on myths and not the word of God. **A lot of people believe that *if you're a good enough person, you'll get to heaven.*** I call this the "good-guy mythstake." The words of Jesus, however, destroy this notion.

> *As Jesus started on his way, a man ran up to him and fell on his knees before him. "Good teacher," he asked, "What must I do to inherit eternal life?" "Why do you call me good?" Jesus answered. "No one is good—except God alone."* —Mark 10:17-18

By human standards, the man that Jesus was talking to was a "good" man. He had kept all the law since he was young—and yet Jesus stopped mid-track and said, "No one is good" (except God, of course). Jesus obliterated the assumption of being a "good guy" before the conversation even got started.

Here's the problem with the "good-guy mythstake:" We compare ourselves to other humans. It's not too tough to find somebody who is more of a scumbag than we are. So in our minds we think "compared to that other guy, I'm a pretty good guy."

Jesus says that if you want to compare yourself to someone, compare yourself to God. He is the ultimate standard of what is good. Hmmm, that's a little tough isn't it? Compared to God, we are *anything* but good. "Good guys" are just an illusion created by human-to human-comparison.

> *For all have sinned and fall short of the glory of God, and all are justified freely by his grace through the redemption that came by Christ Jesus.* —Romans 3:23-24

Listen, if we're honest, we will realize that we are all guilty of this mythstake to one degree or another—that's one of the patterns that just seems to be built into our flesh. Every day, however, we can replace this myth with truth.

Jesus, I want to break free from this mythstake today! By the power of Your Spirit in me, replace my tendencies to judge and compare with a profound awareness of Your grace and the free gift of eternal life that You have given me. Amen.

The Thessalonian Thanksgiving

Whereas it is the duty of all Nations to acknowledge the providence of Almighty God, to obey his will, to be grateful for his benefits, and humbly to implore his protection and favor, and whereas both Houses of Congress have by their joint Committee requested me 'to recommend to the People of the United States a day of public thanks-giving and prayer to be observed by acknowledging with grateful hearts the many signal favors of Almighty God...'
—**George Washington, 1789**

Life is busy. It is and always has been. I know we look back at life 200 years ago as if it were more simple and less demanding, but imagine trying to put together a new country in the ashes of war. Probably required some overtime for George and the Continental Congress, don't you think? Yet, in the middle of the mess, they knew it was time for a day of rest and remembrance, a day to refocus and give credit where credit was due.

Likewise, our days are busy and complicated. No doubt about that. Some of us spend lots of time and energy trying to figure out what the will of God is for our future, (as I'm sure the Founding Fathers did for their country), but when Paul closed his first letter to the Thessalonians, he simplified God's will for us considerably:

> *Rejoice always, pray continually, give thanks in all circumstances; for this is God's will for you in Christ Jesus.* —1 Thessalonians 5:16-18

Is it possible that in trying to figure out His perfect plan for the future, we miss His will for us right now?! Joy. Prayer. Thanksgiving. God's will is that we enjoy Him, talk with Him, and appreciate Him moment by moment.

God of All, I praise You that in Your presence is fullness of joy, that the lines of communication between us are always open. Right here, right now, I give You thanks for all! By faith, I trust You in every circumstance in my life with sincere gratitude. Amen.

Your Holiday Stress-Buster

FORASMUCH as it is the indispensable Duty of all Men to adore the superintending Providence of Almighty God; to acknowledge with Gratitude their Obligation to him for benefits received, and to implore such farther Blessings as they stand in Need of ... It is therefore recommended to the legislative or executive Powers of these United States, to set apart Thursday, the eighteenth Day of December next, for Solemn Thanksgiving and Praise...
—Continental Congress 1777

Giving thanks to God is clearly *appropriate*, isn't it? It's just right to "acknowledge with Gratitude" our dependence on Him for "benefits received." For those of us who are learning and living the mystery of being "in Christ," those "benefits received" are amazing. Why wouldn't we want to thank Him for them all the time?

But giving thanks to God also has *some nice side effects* **for us too:**

> *Rejoice in the Lord always. I will say it again: Rejoice! Let your gentleness be evident to all. The Lord is near. Do not be anxious about anything, but in everything, by prayer and petition, with thanksgiving, present your requests to God. And the peace of God, which transcends all understanding, will guard your hearts and your minds in Christ Jesus.* —Philippians 4:4-7

Giving thanks is a major stress buster. You probably have to experience this to truly believe it; but in the middle of your stress, counting blessings makes a big difference. Hey, I'm really glad that we have a national day of Thanksgiving here in the U.S.—definitely appropriate. BUT, with meals and travel and relatives and all, the holiday of Thanksgiving can cause stress. Remember, the act of giving thanks diminishes that stress.

O God of Peace, I stop right now to give You thanks, not just because You deserve it, but because I need it! As I bring my specific requests to You now, fill my mind with the long, long list of things big and small that are Your perfect gifts to me. Above all, thank You for Your Son, for what He did for me, and that I am in Him! Amen.

Your Antidote for Sin

Thanksgiving is the antidote to sinful behavior. —Philo of Alexandria

Philo was a philosopher who lived both before and after Jesus (20 BC-AD 50)—a brilliant guy living in the most incredible period of all history. I looked up the word *antidote* in the dictionary. It says, "A remedy which counteracts the effects of a poison" or, "Anything that counteracts evil." Hmmm. Do a little philosophizing of your own on this.

Did you know that thanksgiving is an antidote that counteracts evil? I'm not talking about the holiday: I'm talking about the process of giving thanks. Thanksgiving is a sin-buster.

> *Follow God's example, therefore, as dearly loved children and walk in the way of love, just as Christ loved us and gave himself up for us as a fragrant offering and sacrifice to God. But among you there must not be even a hint of sexual immorality, or of any kind of impurity, or of greed, because these are improper for God's holy people. Nor should there be obscenity, foolish talk or coarse joking, which are out of place, but rather thanksgiving.* —Ephesians 5:1-4

The word Paul uses for "thanksgiving" in this passage is the Greek word *eucharisto*—the same word from which we get *Eucharist*, which is another word we use for the Lord's Supper and Communion. Philo would have used the same word when he said that thanksgiving is the antidote for sinful behavior. Interesting! Paul and Philo say that thanksgiving is to be the replacement of sin, and a big part of our thanksgiving is remembering the shed blood and broken body of Christ for our sin.

Quite simply, when we are tempted by (or involved in) immoral sex, greed, or "any kind of impurity," giving thanks can replace it. Thanksgiving is the antidote to sin—one of the ways of escape God has provided out of temptation.

Father of Forgiveness, I thank You for Jesus' sacrifice for my sins! You promise that when I am tempted, You will provide a way out. Replace the lust and greed of my heart with overflowing praise and thanksgiving for all things You have given, especially the personal sacrifice of Jesus for me! Do this again and again each time temptation comes my way. Amen.

**NOV
28**

Give Thanks. Today.

I do therefore invite my fellow citizens in every part of the United States, and also those who are at sea and those who are sojourning in foreign lands, to set apart and observe the last Thursday of November next, as a day of Thanksgiving and Praise to our beneficent Father who dwelleth in the Heavens. And I recommend to them that while offering up the ascriptions justly due to Him for such singular deliverances and blessings, they do also, with humble penitence...
—Abraham Lincoln, 1863

Wow, that about says it all, doesn't it? While the smoke and blood of the U.S. Civil War was billowing and flowing, Lincoln called everyone to a day of "Thanksgiving and Praise"—just as Paul calls those who are in Christ to live lives of continual gratitude:

> *So then, just as you received Christ Jesus as Lord, continue to live your lives in him, rooted and built up in him, strengthened in the faith as you were taught, and overflowing with thankfulness.* —Colossians 2:6-7

My prayers for all of us today echo the words of these men. *May those of us who have received Him, continue to live our lives in Him, offering up the credit justly due to Him for each singular deliverance and blessing with humble penitence and overflowing thankfulness.*

I'll just let you pray this one through on your own, okay?

My God and my Provider, from the depths of my heart, I thank You for ... Amen.

Between the Sidewalk and the Sky

For flowers that bloom about our feet ... for tender grass so fresh, so sweet ... for the song of bird and hum of bee ... for all things fair we hear or see, Father in heaven, we thank Thee. —Ralph Waldo Emerson

Today's devotional comes courtesy of my friend Todd, who recently wrote this...

During bedtime prayers with my little boy a couple of years ago, I was praying my usual words when he jumped in like he does sometimes, "Thank You, God, for the sky, and thank You for the trees. Thank You for the grass. Thank You for the sidewalk." (The sidewalk is where he rides his bike so that's obviously very important to him.) Like you, I was tempted to smile condescendingly at his simple immaturity, but as I sat there thinking about it, I realized something important:

My boy's already praying and thanking God for creation and for life itself. I had never told my boy about that, but **there was something inside of him that knew God was responsible for all of it and that He should be thanked for everything between sidewalk and sky.** Sure, it seemed childlike, but isn't that how we are supposed to come to our heavenly Father anyway? All I know is that this kind of thanksgiving pops up all over the place in the Bible:

> *Give thanks to the LORD, for he is good. His love endures forever ... who by his understanding made the heavens, His love endures forever. Who spread out the earth upon the waters, His love endures forever. Who made the great lights—His love endures forever. The sun to govern the day, His love endures forever. The moon and stars to govern the night; His love endures forever.*
> —Psalm 136:1, 5-9

I'm sure my son will grow up soon enough and learn to pray more about the important stuff—like final exams, job promotions, the stock market, and a 401k. In the meantime, I'll try to pray a little more like him.

Father, open my eyes. Give me the eyes of a child again—able to see You, praise You, and thank You for the simple, essential things in life and the profound gift of life itself. Let me see Your enduring love in everything from the sidewalk to the sky, so that the rest of my "grown-up" years will overflow with praise and thanksgiving. Amen.

Do You Have a Cockeyed View of Hell?

Go to heaven for the climate, hell for the company ... All right, then, I'll go to hell. —Mark Twain

I had a classmate in high school tell me once, "I'd rather party in hell with my friends than go to heaven without them!" If he had known what the Bible teaches us about hell, I suspect his "party cry" would be different. You have to be cockeyed to verbalize this myth but many people do. It can be summarized by a poem on a birthday card:

> *Why worry?*
> *Either you are well, or you are sick.*
>
> *If you are well, you have nothing to worry about.*
> *If you are sick, you only have two things to worry about: either you will live or you will die.*
>
> *If you live, you have nothing to worry about.*
> *If you die, you only have two things to worry about: either you will go to heaven or you'll go to hell.*
>
> *If you go to heaven, you have nothing to worry about.*
> *If you go to hell, you'll be so busy shaking hands with friends that you won't have time to worry! Happy Birthday!*

The cockeyed myth says *hell is going to be an eternal continuation of the party here on earth.* But the truth is we will have a hell of a lot to worry about if we don't go to heaven.

The haunting descriptions we have of hell in Scripture indicate that souls who go there exist in suspended isolation and darkness ... forever (Matthew 8:12, Revelation 20:1-2). If someone says they would rather be in hell with their friends than in heaven alone, ask them *why* they think their friends are going to hell, and *why* they think they are going to be together? They probably won't have an answer.

Heaven is where the party is going to be! An eternal eruption of praise and worship together. No more tears, no more death ... who wouldn't want to be there?!

Lord, use me today, as You see fit, to tell people about the party that awaits in heaven. By Your love flowing through me, invite those around me to join in the eternal dance of grace, together, with You. Amen.

What a Genuine Relationship with Jesus Looks Like

I don't know what I've been livin' on, but it's not enough to fill me up ... I want the best of both worlds an' honey I know what it's worth. If we could have the best of both worlds we'd have heaven right here on earth. Woo! —**Lyrics by rock legend Eddie Van-Halen**

For some, Jesus is just a truck stop on the road of life. They just stop in for a fill-up and get on with life as usual. It's Jesus when you need Him and everything you want on earth, too.

The problem is that Scripture doesn't say that's the way it works at all. Just because you said a prayer doesn't mean that you know Jesus. I call this the *"pass-Him-by"* mythstake. Those who truly know Christ are marked by an inspirational life change.

Eternal life starts the day you believe in Jesus Christ and receive Him into your life. Your life becomes His life, and His life becomes yours (Galatians 2:20). First, this changes your *attitude*.

> *For the love of money is a root of all kinds of evil. Some people, eager for money, have wandered from the faith and pierced themselves with many griefs. But you, man of God, flee from all this, and pursue righteousness, godliness, faith, love, endurance and gentleness. Fight the good fight of the faith. Take hold of the eternal life to which you were called when you made your good confession in the presence of many witnesses.* —1 Timothy 6:10-12

Second, your *behavior* changes.

> *Jesus answered, "Everyone who drinks this water will be thirsty again, but whoever drinks the water I give them will never thirst. Indeed, the water I give them will become in them a spring of water welling up to eternal life."* —John 4:13-14

The person who is comfortable passing by Jesus and then going on with life as normal would be wise to stop and question whether or not they know Him at all. It is far better to search your heart today, rather than live with the consequences of the *"pass-Him-by"* mythstake in eternity.

Holy Spirit, are You in me? Am I in You? Jesus, I embrace You as my Savior and Life right now. From the inside out, transform my attitude and my actions. Amen.

Are Your Priorities in Line?

The safest road to hell is the gradual one—the gentle slope, soft underfoot, without sudden turnings, without milestones, without signposts. —C. S. Lewis

In today's demanding world, priorities and procrastination are a must. **We must choose what's most important, and we must neglect what's less important when there are only 24 hours in a day.** As the procrastinator's motto goes, "Don't put off until tomorrow what you can put off until the day after tomorrow."

But what happens if we procrastinate the most important thing of all, and fail to prioritize our eternal destiny? That leads to what I call the *"standby" mythstake.* It sounds like the words of another man Jesus described:

> *Then he said, "This is what I'll do. I will tear down my barns and build bigger ones, and there I will store my surplus grain. And I'll say to myself, 'You have plenty of good things laid up for many years. Take life easy; eat, drink and be merry.' But God said to him, 'You fool! This very night your life will be demanded from you. Then who will get what you have prepared for yourself?'"*
> —Luke 12:18-20

This mythstake is pretty basic. It says *"Yeah, yeah, I believe that, but I'll deal with it later."* I don't have to explain how foolish this is, do I? "Later" could come in an instant. **If you are living a lie, disaster can strike anytime with consequences that last forever.** Like most mythstakes, this one dissolves with the least bit of thought. *That night* the man lost his life. The Bible tells us the truth: God invites us to live in Truth *today.*

Jesus, I agree that my days on earth are numbered, and I really have no idea when my number is up. I surrender everything I have and everything I am to You right now. I'm trusting You to live in me and through me today to Your glory. Amen.

The Worst Mythstake You Can Make

Christianity is not a formula, but the Person of Jesus Himself. Never think that Christianity is a matter of adjusting behavior, but rather, of letting Christ live through us in His strength and power. —**Malcolm Smith**

No doubt, there are a lot of mythstakes out there about heaven, hell, and eternity. Some are foolish and some are selfish. The last myth on my list, however, is the one that breaks my heart the most: The *"need-not-apply" mythstake.*

Many people believe the "good-guy" and "good-try" myths—but they are honest enough to know that they don't have a chance to make it. They believe that only good people will make it into heaven, and they are smart enough and humble enough to know that they are not good. **Their honesty deflates their hope, for they know they are guilty, a lost cause, a hopeless case, a reject.** *Why even try? There is no point. It's useless. No need to apply for eternal life.*

And they are right … partially.

They have only been told half the truth, the truth about sin and how it separates us from God. The other half of the Gospel is truly Good News to people who know that they are bad. **The message of Christ's love and sacrifice is like a crystal-clear splash of ice water to those dying of thirst in the deserts of sin and shame.** The people who are making this mythstake are often stunned when they hear the rest of the story—what God has done for them through the Person of Jesus Christ:

> *What benefit did you reap at that time from the things you are now ashamed of? Those things result in death! But now that you have been set free from sin and have become slaves to God, the benefit you reap leads to holiness, and the result is eternal life. For the wages of sin is death, but the gift of God is eternal life in Christ Jesus our Lord.* —Romans 6:21-23

That's the Good News, and it never gets old. It's the gift you receive once, but it keeps on giving every breath of every day until you take your last breath and step into eternity with Him forever.

Heavenly Father, how can I praise You for Your lavish grace and unending mercy? On the basis of what Your Son Jesus did, I choose to trust You to cleanse me and enable me to live free of sin, guilt, and condemnation today! No more shame, Lord. I rest in the completeness of Your forgiveness and the presence of Your Spirit in me. Amen.

Hope for Us Thieves

The burden of life is from ourselves, its lightness from the grace of Christ and the love of God. —William Bernard Ullanthorne (1806-1889)

The two men hung together in the midday heat—an unlikely couple, actually, brought together by horrific circumstances. In a matter of hours, Jesus Christ, the sinless Son of God, would breathe His last breath and complete His earthly work. A short time later a thief, a man fully worthy of an eternal hell, would also die.

Consider one of the two thieves who hung on a cross beside Jesus. He was neither a "good guy," nor did he have the opportunity to change his ways and give it a "good try." But, when the man asked for a pardon, Jesus said, "Today, you will be with me in Paradise."

Across the threshold of death Jesus was waiting for him, ready to invite him into everlasting life—just as He is waiting for you right now if you humbly and honestly receive this free gift.

> *Yet to all who did receive him, to those who believed in his name, he gave the right to become children of God...* —John 1:12

Jesus died on the cross for you so that your sins can be removed, so you can confidently enter an everlasting life based on what God has done for you, rather than what you have tried and failed to do for Him.

Yes, the Gospel is truly good news to people who know they are bad. The supernatural and transforming message of truth is like pure oxygen in the lungs of someone suffocating under a blanket of works and religion. That is the eternal hope for our *future*, AND it's actually our living and active reality *today*. Think about it. If we have received Him, we are His children *now*. Eternal life in Christ begins *now*, each and every moment of every day.

That's something we can live with—experiencing Life today—with Christ.

Jesus, I received You as my only hope of eternal life, and I am receiving You right now as my true source of life today. Thank You for giving me the right to be Your child right now, just as I am. Restore to my soul the joy of this radical salvation! Amen.

Questions, Questions, Questions

When the mask of self-righteousness has been torn from us and we stand stripped of all our accustomed defenses, we are candidates for God's generous grace.
—Erwin W. Lutzer

I like asking questions. It's a great way to make people come to conclusions on their own, or, at least, lead them in the direction of truth. I once asked a young woman at a mall the following questions:

"Is heaven a perfect place?" "Yes, absolutely!" she said.

"Do you think you will go there?" "I think I have a pretty good shot. I've tried my hardest," she answered.

"Have you lived a perfect life?" "Well, of course not. Who has? But I'm better than most people I know."

"Well," I continued, "if heaven is a perfect place and you have not lived a perfect life, what makes you think you can go there without wrecking it?"

(Long pause followed by nervous laughter.)

We need to be willing to ask these hard questions of those around us and of ourselves. Are we telling the truth to those around us? Paul really desired we would.

> *... no longer be infants, tossed back and forth by the waves, and blown here and there by every wind of teaching and by the cunning and craftiness of people in their deceitful scheming. Instead, speaking the truth in love, we will grow to become in every respect the mature body of him who is the head, that is, Christ.* —Ephesians 4:14-15

Particularly with eternally important issues like heaven and hell, we need to let the Word be our standard and the love of the Spirit be our guide. We have to believe ... that our good works have zero chance of getting us to heaven ... that hell is a real place ... that Jesus is far too valuable to pass by ... that the decision to choose Him is urgent ... and that the reward for choosing Him is indescribable!

My Jesus, give me a sincere heart for those who are bound for a Godless eternity. Use me to destroy myths and share You with everyone You place in my path. Amen.

Cinching Up the Belt of Truth

Who had deceived thee so often as thyself? —Benjamin Franklin

Have you ever worn one of those weight-lifting belts and cinched it up nice and tight? It gives you a feeling of stability and strength. That's what truth does. It strengthens us at our very core. Maybe that's why the Bible calls us to put on the "belt of truth!"

Truth is reality—things as they really are as opposed to what they look like, as opposed to what they feel like or what you wish they were like. That's particularly important when we're talking about sincerely sensitive issues like heaven and hell. Yeah, it's touchy, emotional stuff, so we need Truth as the undergirding reality that holds everything else up. Jesus' "high priestly" prayer reveals where truth is found:

> *I have given them your word and the world has hated them, for they are not of the world any more than I am of the world. My prayer is not that you take them out of the world but that you protect them from the evil one. They are not of the world, even as I am not of it.* **Sanctify them by the truth; your word is truth.** —John 17:14-17

First, we need to take time to know the truth. When you know the truth of Scripture, lies become obvious. That comes through a lifelong discovery of truth in His Word.

Secondly, take your thoughts captive. If we have a thought and wonder if it's a deception, we present it to Jesus and ask Him, "Jesus, I just had this thought. Is it a lie or Your truth? Open my eyes to Your truth." And by His Spirit, He will.

Thirdly, take your thoughts to community. One of the great joys of living in a community that believes the Bible is that we can sit down with one another and say, "Here's what I'm thinking. Does it sound like a lie to you or does it sound like the truth?" And sometimes just by verbalizing it, we know it's a lie.

So where are you today? Is there someplace you are teetering between Truth and lies? Cinch up that belt of Truth!

Lord, strengthen me with Your truth, protecting me against the lies of the enemy. I bring my thoughts to You now, to be taken captive by You. Thank You for the brothers and sisters around me who are honest and wise. Use them all to lead me in Your everlasting ways. Amen.

A Letter for Your Heart

If God wants you to do something, he'll make it possible for you to do it, but the grace he provides comes only with the task and cannot be stockpiled beforehand. We are dependent on him from hour to hour, and the greater our awareness of this fact, the less likely we are to faint or fail in a crisis. —**Louis Cassels**

Some time ago my mother shared with me a letter that had been found in the office of a young pastor in Zimbabwe, Africa:

> *I am part of the Fellowship of the unashamed. I have the Holy Spirit's power. The die has been cast and I've stepped over the line. The decision has been made. I am a disciple of His. I won't look back, let up, slow down, back away, or be still. My past is redeemed. My present makes sense. My future is secure. I'm finished and done with low living, sight walking, smooth knees, colorless dreams, tamed visions, worldly talking, cheap giving and dwarfed goals. I no longer need preeminence, prosperity, position, promotions, plaudits, or popularity. I don't have to be right, first, tops, recognized, praised, regarded or rewarded. I now live by faith, lean in His presence, walk by patience, I'm uplifted by prayer and labor with power. My pace is set, my gait is fast. My goal is heaven and my road is narrow. My way is rough, my companions are few, my guide is reliable and my mission is clear. I cannot be bought, compromised, detoured, lured away, turned back, deluded, or delayed. I will not flinch in the face of sacrifice, hesitate in the presence of the enemy, pander at the pool of popularity, or meander in the maze of mediocrity...*

The letter was found by the members of the church he led. They were cleaning out his office in the days after his body had been found battered and mutilated. Wow, what can you say about something like that? Can we possibly have that kind of clarity in a country where we do not face the possibility of death for our faith?

The thing I love about this letter is that this young man decided one day that he was fully surrendering to Jesus. **Our words will be different I suspect, our experience will most likely be different, too, but we can all surrender to Jesus.**

My Lord and my God, Your Word says I no longer live, but You live in me. I surrender to You now, and ask that in the big things and the little things my life would be a reflection of the radical Truth about who I am in You. I don't want to make this up. I can't do it in my own strength. I rest in You now and simply ask that You would live through me as You see fit. Praise to You! Amen.

Your Battle Plan for the Week

Nothing less than a whole Bible can make a whole Christian. —A.W. Tozer

Imagine: You are standing on the front lines as a battle of epic proportions is just about to commence. Beside you are your comrades in arms … the faithful brothers and sisters who share your calling. As the enemy marches over the horizon, you can feel your heart pounding beneath your breastplate. You tighten your belt an extra notch and move your shield in front of your face and heart. Your helmet is secure. Now you wait and wait, ready for the inevitable. Finally, your commander shouts down the line, "Ready! Aim! Read!" And your entire army bows to their knees, opens their Bibles, and prays ….

Hmmm, that's not exactly William Wallace-like is it? Not what you would expect from brave hearts? But it's thoroughly biblical. We *are* at war, and Paul shouts the commands:

> *Put on the full armor of God so that you can take your stand against the devil's schemes. For our struggle is not against flesh and blood, but against the rulers, against the authorities, against the powers of this dark world and against the spiritual forces of evil in the heavenly realms.* —Ephesians 6:11-12

Paul goes through a long list of spiritual armor, but when we get to the end, he calls us not to fight, not to charge, but to read:

> *Take … the sword of the Spirit, which is the word of God.* —Ephesians 6:17

And as you face battles of many kinds today, the Spirit is holding it out to you, as an incredible gift, asking you to "Take it up" and read.

Holy Spirit, I thank You for this special weapon of God's Word. By Your power in me, I'll pick up this sword and read it and use it in the battles I face today. I need every piece of armor You have given me to use in my battles today against Satan, my flesh, and the world. Amen.

Your Best Defense

God himself has condescended to teach me the way. He has written it down in a book. Oh, give me that book! At any price give me the book of God. Let me be a man of one book. —John Wesley

The Bible *continually* amazes me. I guess my pride wants to think that once I have a verse figured out, I've got it figured out for good. But that's not the way it works with the sword of the Spirit, God's Word. **The Holy Spirit and God's unchanging Word continually work together to bring us new insights that can transform our day and set us free.** God's Word can be used as a defensive weapon as well as an offensive weapon under the direction of the Spirit in us. We sure see this in Jesus' life. Right after Jesus was baptized, the Holy Spirit descends on Him in the form of a dove.

> *Then Jesus was led by the Spirit into the wilderness to be tempted by the devil. After fasting forty days and forty nights, he was hungry. The tempter came to him....* —Matthew 4:1-3

Satan threw everything he could at Jesus—food, power and recognition, and the wealth of the whole world—but Jesus used the sword of the Spirit to defend Himself every time. Three times He said, "It is written...." Finally, Jesus gets in the tempter's face and says,

> *"Away from me, Satan! For it is written: 'Worship the Lord your God, and serve him only.'" Then the devil left him, and angels came and attended him.* —Matthew 4:10-11

This leads me to believe that Satan flees not only from the name of Jesus, but he flees from the words of Jesus, too. He has no answer to the Word of God—which is why it's important for us to plant some of it in our hearts and in our minds so that wherever we are, we can take it up to our defense.

Holy Spirit, right now, bring to mind unchanging truths from God's eternal Word. Use these words as Your sword to defend me, as well as to make me effective offensively, as You work through me today to glorify God in any way You see fit in this world. Amen.

Cut It Out

Some people like to read so many [Bible] chapters every day. I would not dissuade them from the practice, but I would rather lay my soul asoak in half a dozen verses all day than rinse my hand in several chapters. Oh, to be bathed in a text of Scripture, and to let it be sucked up in your very soul, till it saturates your heart! —Charles Haddon Spurgeon

It cuts both ways, this "sword of the Spirit, which is the word of God." The diversity of the armor that God has given us is truly unending. Yes, the sword of the Spirit can be used both as an offensive and a defensive weapon. **It can be also used as a scalpel, to do self-surgery by cutting out lies and emotions that can grow in our soul like festering tumors.** God's Word, if you "take it up," can be used to cut that stuff out.

Let it do its work through just this one passage today:

> *I remain confident of this: I will see the goodness of the LORD in the land of the living. Wait for the LORD; be strong and take heart and wait for the LORD.* —Psalm 27:13-14

Listen, who doesn't fight against discouragement, despair, and possibly even depression? God's Word is a weapon against that stuff. It puts all of our problems in perspective. The sword of the Spirit can be used today to combat life-sucking lies and faith-draining emotion. I'm telling you the truth on that.

Lord, I'm taking up the truth You have given me in Your Word, and ask that the Spirit would use it as a sword to remove anything that is contrary to the truth of who I am in You and who You are in me. I believe that I will see, and that I am seeing, your goodness while I live here on Earth. I'm waiting for You today. Be my strength. Be my courage. Amen.

Pierced with His Truth

The word of God hidden in the heart is a stubborn voice to suppress.
—Billy Graham

I was a worry wart. Big time ... all the way through my childhood, teenage years, and college. Worry almost seemed to be some sort of a badge of honor, something that gave significance to my life.

And then I married Libby. I had this new beautiful bride, so I had a whole new category of worry. Libby worked in Milwaukee—about a 45-minute drive from our home. On snowy nights I'd be waiting for her to get home ... worrying. This was before cell phones, so she couldn't call me if she was running a little behind. More than once, she would come home and happily bound in the door only to find me in tears of fear and worry. Thankfully, God's Word, the sword of the Spirit, intervened and cut deeply into that situation.

> *Therefore I tell you, do not worry about your life, what you will eat or drink; or about your body, what you will wear. Is not life more important than food, and the body more important than clothes? Look at the birds of the air; they do not sow or reap or store away in barns, and yet your heavenly Father feeds them. Are you not much more valuable than they? Who of you by worrying can add a single hour to his life?* —Matthew 6:25-27

The familiar words cut deeply. Jesus said, "Do not worry," and the Holy Spirit said to me, "Pete, your worry is not some little personality quirk or sign of commitment. If Jesus says 'don't' and you still do, what would that make your worry?"

The conclusion was obvious: Worry is the exact opposite of trust and faith. Worry is a sin to bring before the Lord. It took me to my knees asking, "Jesus, do something about this!" He did. Through the Word and the Spirit, Jesus redeemed me from worry completely. In fact, nowadays I worry that I don't worry enough!

That's God's Word in action. That's the sword of the Spirit which Paul calls us to take up as part of the armor of God in the battles we fight every day.

My battle that day was against worry. What's yours today?

Father God, by the power of Your Spirit in me, and by the truth of Your Word, the sword of the Spirit, I stand aside and ask that You would show me the places where my life is out of line with Your truth. Do something, Jesus. Do something, Holy Spirit. Amen.

The Book That Understands You

I read, and read, and read ... with an indescribable warmth surging within ... I could not find words to express my awe and wonder. And suddenly the realization dawned upon me: This was the book that would understand me!"
—**Emile Cailliet**

Emile Cailliet was born in a small French town and was raised as an atheist. As a soldier in World War I, the horrors he saw set his unbelief in stone. While recovering from a bullet wound that shattered his arm, he married, but informed his wife that no Bible would ever be allowed in their home.

Still, he was a voracious reader and went through everything he could find trying to satisfy the desires of his heart. "I had been longing for a book that would understand me," he said. Unable to find one, he began to write a book of his own. Upon its completion, he sat down under a tree to read his own work, but he was bitterly disappointed. He confessed, "The whole undertaking would not work, simply because it was of my own making."

He was despondent, but God was up to something.

That night, against the household rules, his wife handed him a Bible that she had miraculously found that very day. Instead of rejecting it, he opened it and started to read. And then he read some more. He read long into the night, mostly from the Gospels. The sword of the Spirit began to do its work as the Word of God came alive in his mind and his heart.

"The providential circumstances amid which the Book had found me now made it clear that while it seemed absurd to speak of a book understanding a man, this could be said of the Bible, because its pages were animated by the Presence of the Living God and the Power of His mighty acts. To this God I prayed that night, and the God who answered was the same God of whom it was spoken in the Book."

No wonder Paul exhorts us to "take up ... the sword of the Spirit which is the Word of God." It's not just a book, but it's living and active and in the hands of the Holy Spirit—a powder keg of life transformation and victory over the evil one.

Dear God, I sincerely thank You for giving me "a book that understands me." By the power of Your Spirit in me, stir up these words of Yours in my mind and in my heart so that my life might naturally reflect who I am in You and who You are in me. Amen!

A Challenge to Rethink Your Prayers

If any of you should ask me for an epitome of the Christian religion, I should say that it is in one word – prayer. —Charles Spurgeon

Prayer ... we hear that word a lot. It's all over the place in the Bible. You hear it in passing conversations. It's preached about in sermons galore. When you hear that word, what comes to mind? What do you feel?

At the end of Ephesians 6, when Paul finishes talking about our spiritual armor and spiritual warfare, he concludes the list of our arsenal with this exhortation for prayer:

> *And pray in the Spirit on all occasions with all kinds of prayers and requests. With this in mind, be alert and always keep on praying for all the Lord's people. Pray also for me, that whenever I speak, words may be given me so that I will fearlessly make known the mystery of the gospel, for which I am an ambassador in chains. Pray that I may declare it fearlessly, as I should.*
> —Ephesians 6:18-20

In the next couple of days, we are going to dissect this passage thought by thought. In the process, we are going to blow up some stereotypes and rip out some deeply entrenched misunderstandings. **Looking at prayer from the perspective of who we are in Christ can radically alter our practice of prayer and transform our lives in powerful ways.**

Listen, we have inherited a lot of ideas about prayer—what it is supposed to look like, how you are expected to do it, how often you think you should do it (but probably don't) ... **but when was the last time you really considered prayer as it relates to the other radical things that we know to be true about who we are in Christ and who Christ is in us?**

Jesus, I'm curious! I take prayer for granted and do it according to what I've learned through traditions and the example of others. Renew my mind about prayer according to the truth of who I am in You, and who You are in me. Amen.

A Majorly Wrong Assumption About Prayer

If the spiritual life be healthy, under the full power of the Holy Spirit, praying without ceasing will be natural. —Andrew Murray

It really is hard to see the forest through the trees. We can get so entrenched with the details that we never really consider the big picture. That happens big time with prayer—which oftentimes comes with some monstrous expectations and invisible assumptions.

The biggest assumption is that we're always supposed to pray more than we do! If you don't pray a lot, you obviously aren't serious about God. And if more people, like you, would just pray more, then our world and our nation wouldn't be going to hell in a handbasket, right? Verses like this one might only fuel your struggle:

> *And pray in the Spirit on all occasions with all kinds of prayers and requests.* —Ephesians 6:18

Add this all together, and you might feel like a first-class spiritual loser. Or maybe you try to dodge it by saying, "I don't have the gift of prayer."

What's the problem here? Is God setting us up for failure and condemnation? Not at all. The problem is much more fundamental than that. **Most of our traditions, teachings, and examples miss the simple, pure, liberating essence of prayer:**

Prayer is an intimate conversation with the One who passionately loves you and lives in you.

Erase for a moment, if you can, everything you think you know about what prayer looks like, how you are supposed to do it, and how much you are expected to do it. Consider this simple definition. Really think about it—both what prayer is and also what prayer is not.

What is the big picture? Can you see the forest of prayer possibilities through the trees of your assumptions?

Holy Spirit, I need Your help here. I'm excited about the opportunity to pray without ceasing, using all kinds of prayers and requests. Right now, begin to open my mind to the possibilities of a life praying in You. Amen.

What Real Prayer Looks Like

When prayer has become secondary, or incidental, it has lost its power. Those who are conspicuously men of prayer are those who use prayer as they use food, or air, or light, or money. —M.E. Andross

In Ephesians chapter 6, Paul challenges us to "pray in the spirit." That brings up an interesting question: Is it actually possible to pray "in the flesh?" Could someone actually pray as part of a performance-based system to gain favor with God?

Absolutely! Remember Jesus coming down on the Pharisees? *Don't pray like the Pharisees pray for they stand on the street corner to be seen by everyone.* They were *performing* for people, they weren't *praying*, right? Instead, Jesus told us to get in the closet where no one can see us.

But even in the closet, isn't it quite possible that our prayers are seen as a duty to be fulfilled through self-effort rather than an opportunity to communicate with God?

Let's consider this simple pure definition of prayer again:

Prayer is an intimate conversation with the One who passionately loves you and lives in you. *Prayer is not an action—it is an interaction*—**and that interaction takes place in and through the Holy Spirit.**

Paul says there are going to be times when it's actually impossible for us to pray.

> *In the same way, the Spirit helps us in our weakness. We do not know what we ought to pray for, but the Spirit himself intercedes for us through wordless groans. And He who searches our hearts knows the mind of the Spirit, because the Spirit intercedes for God's people in accordance with the will of God.*
> —Romans 8:26-27

Prayer is not something you do, it's something that the Spirit, who is in you, does through you. We don't even have to use words; in our weakness we might not even know what to say, but God knows the mind of the Holy Spirit in us. If you enter the intimate conversation with the One who loves you, the Spirit in you will intercede and lead you.

Lord, I surrender myself to You in prayer. Holy Spirit, pray through me. According to Your will, lay things on my heart that You want to talk about today. Amen.

Prayer Is an Intimate, Ongoing Conversation

There is a way of ordering our mental life on more than one level at once. On one level we can be thinking, discussing, seeing, calculating, meeting all the demands of external affairs, but deep within, behind the scenes at a profounder level we may also be in prayer and adoration, song and worship and a gentle receptiveness to divine breathings. —Thomas Kelly, Testament of Devotion

Sometimes my family and I hold hands around the dinner table at the end of the day, closing our eyes and bowing our heads, thanking God for a table full of food, a family that loves each other, and a life worth dying for.

On Sundays, I ask everyone to bow their heads, and we ask that God would teach us. At the end of the sermon, we bow our heads again, close our eyes, and ask God to apply what we have learned. And sometimes in my office alone, I get on my knees and raise my empty hands toward heaven, focusing solely on intimate conversation with a God who loves me.

I'm all for structured times of prayer. But "prayer" is in no way limited by the words squished between "Dear God… " and "Amen." **Prayer can be a *never-ceasing* intimate conversation with the One who loves us.** Consider these Scriptural truths:

> *Pray without ceasing … for this is God's will for you in Christ Jesus.*
> —1 Thessalonians 5:16-18

> *Rejoice always, pray continually, give thanks in all circumstances; for this is God's will for you in Christ Jesus.* —1 Thessalonians 5:16-18

> *…the Spirit of him who raised Jesus from the dead is living in you…*
> —Romans 8:11

> *And pray in the Spirit on all occasions with all kinds of prayers and requests.*
> —Ephesians 6:18

> *Walk by the Spirit…* —Galatians 5:16

Just as you walk in the Spirit moment by moment, you can continually pray in the Spirit—always rejoicing, always giving thanks in never-ceasing communication with Him—even as you go about your day and other duties.

Today, I'm not going to close with a structured prayer. Instead, I challenge you to begin a natural, ongoing conversation with God right now! Amen?

The Power of Letting God Lead You in Prayer

Prayer is weakness leaning on omnipotence. —W. S. Bowd

Aaron Boyd was in way over his head. On a mission trip to Thailand, he and his band, Bluetree, played one night in The Climax Bar, deep in Pattaya's red-light district. There, they rubbed shoulders with those stuck in the worst of the worst. There, he and his band discovered what can happen when someone "prays in the Spirit," allowing the Holy Spirit to pray through them, in a way that was natural to them. Aaron remembers:

Everything you can imagine goes on in that place. You see kids as young as 8, 9, 10, just selling themselves, you know?! You see 60-year-old guys walking down the street with two 13- or 14-year-old girls ….

The band was overwhelmed with grief for what they saw around them. When it was time for them to get up and play, words were hard to find.

At one point I just started singing out. I started singing "Greater things …" something along those lines, almost prophesying over the city … slowly this groove emerged ….

The band began to fill in with voices and instruments—praying in the Spirit *with music*. The Spirit's words, flowing through them, began to come together in a passionate intimate conversation with God—the Spirit was writing a new song on the spot:

You're the God of this City. You're the King of these people. You're the Lord of this nation. You are.

You're the Light in this darkness. You're the Hope to the hopeless. You're the Peace to the restless. You are.

For greater things have yet to come. And greater things are still to be done in this City ….

This song, *God of this City*, is now sung worldwide. What is the Spirit going to sing in your heart today? Are you listening to what He is going to pray through you?

Holy Spirit, I'm listening. As we walk together today, lead our conversation. Speak to me and pray through me with all kinds of prayer in all situations. Amen.

Giving Out of Your Nothing

Mail your packages early so the post office can lose them in time for Christmas.
—Johnny Carson

There's a hundred reasons you might be saying, "I don't have anything left to give this Christmas." If that's where you think you are, what's your reason?

- Maybe it's financial. Could even be that you've recently received notice at work—they're downsizing, you got some kind words and a pink slip just in time for the holidays.

- Maybe it's material. You've had to tell your kids not to expect as much for Christmas this year. You've talked about downsizing the home, and they might have to move away from their school and friends.

- Maybe it's emotional. Perhaps your marriage is crumbling but you're supposed to be happily married this time of year so you're pretending on the outside.

Sometimes, we stress about what to give the person who has everything. But what do you do when you're the person with nothing? The biblical account of the first Christmas offers hope and perspective. A quick review of the key players in the Christmas story reveals that most of them had nothing to give.

- A husband without a home.
- An innkeeper without a room.
- A young mother with nothing to cloth her just-born son.

But they discovered that in giving what they did have, they could find joy as they found themselves in God's masterful plan.

> *And he said to me, "My grace is sufficient for you, for my power is made perfect in weakness." Therefore I will boast all the more gladly about my weaknesses, so that Christ's power may rest on me.* —2 Corinthians 12:9

Paul realized his emptiness was an opportunity to experience the fullness of Christ and share that power with others. Is it possible that this was God's intent all along? That His Son should be given to the world through those who had nothing without Him?

Dear Lord, I thank You for all I am: Weak and empty on the outside; powerful and full on the inside. Just as You used Joseph, an innkeeper, and a pregnant young woman, live through me in a way that brings Jesus and joy to the world around me! Amen.

Giving What You Have

Let us not be satisfied with just giving money. Money is not enough, money can be got, but they need your hearts to love them. So, spread your love everywhere you go. —Mother Teresa

I have a great staff. When Christmas rolls around, we like to take them out for a good bash to say thanks for all their service and sacrifice. But, like most of you, we've been keeping things trimmed back these last couple of years. Once, we scrapped our plans and did a service project together as our Christmas party instead.

Seventy-four of us descended on a local middle school and scattered out to help wherever we could. Two of us went to the librarian and said, "We're available for two and a half hours, put us to work, what do you want us to do?" Her little librarian eyes got big, "Would you please just go through the whole fiction section and put the books back where they belong?" Five man-hours later, we got to the Zs. She looked at our work and said, "Oh, you have no idea what a blessing this is." (Honestly, I didn't have any idea, but for her, it was a "blessing" that made her day and saved her a lot of work.) I walked into that school thinking I had nothing to give. I was wrong, not because I had something but because she had a need, and Christ had something to deliver to her through me.

> *Therefore, I urge you, brothers and sisters, in view of God's mercy, to offer your bodies as a living sacrifice, holy and pleasing to God—this is your true and proper worship.* —Romans 12:1

What do you give when you feel like you have nothing left? Listen, it's not that hard. It's not rocket science. You don't have to sacrifice your credit score to give sacrificially. If you are in Christ, you are holy and pleasing to God and Christ is in you. Think about that: Christ is in you. He is your life. Your body is a "living sacrifice" that manifests Jesus to the world today ... just as Mary's did two thousand years ago!

Holy Spirit, open my eyes to the needs around me. Keep me looking for people in our dark, dying, and desperate world who have nothing left to give. Open my eyes to the needs of those who are closest to me. I offer myself as a sacrifice to be used by You. Use me to love them and help them in the name of Jesus. Help me to see that You, loving them through me, are an infinitely more valuable gift than anything money could buy. Amen.

May It Be As You Say

I once bought my kids a set of batteries for Christmas with a note on it saying, toys not included. —Bernard Manning

The Bible doesn't tell us much about Mary. But what I do know impresses me greatly. She had so little to give in the moment. But in the moment, she gave all she had. As a Jew in a devout community, it's safe to assume that the great prophecies and theologies were read to her by candlelight before she went to bed year after year after year.

> *Therefore the Lord himself will give you a sign: The virgin will conceive and give birth to a son, and will call him Immanuel.* —Isaiah 7:14

When the prophecies began to unfold around her, she must have begun to see it for what it was.

> *Do not be afraid, Mary; you have found favor with God. You will conceive and give birth to a son, and you are to call him Jesus. He will be great and will be called the Son of the Most High.* —Luke 1:30-32

Being a virgin, she knew this was a biological impossibility. But after some sincere questioning, she leaned into the truth, choosing biblical truth over biological fact. I believe the Holy Spirit greatly encouraged her in this moment, reminding her of another truth that would have been part of her heritage: *Nothing is impossible for God.*

All God asked of Mary was what she had to give. **What did she have to give? Nothing. No, wait, she had two things, her body and her faith.** And she gave those to Him. In obedience, she laid both before her Lord.

> *"I am the Lord's servant,"* Mary answered. *"May your word to me be fulfilled."* —Luke 1:38

May her faith and obedience be an encouragement to others—like you and me— who find ourselves in places where we think we simply have nothing to give.

Lord, by the power of Your Spirit, give me the faith and obedience of Mary. I truly have nothing to give this world other than what You are already planning to give through me. I am Your servant. May it be so. Amen.

Christmas Every Day

I hate the giving of the hand unless the whole man accompanies it.
—Ralph Waldo Emerson

This Christmas, remember that the true value of a gift depends on how you measure it. Sure, a gift with a large price tag might seem more valuable, but only by the world's standards. As usual, God looks at it differently:

> *As Jesus looked up, he saw the rich putting their gifts into the temple treasury. He also saw a poor widow put in two very small copper coins. "Truly I tell you," he said, "this poor widow has put in more than all the others. All these people gave their gifts out of their wealth; but she out of her poverty put in all she had to live on."* —Luke 21:1-4

If you are feeling like you have nothing left to give right now, that verse is worth pondering. *She gave more; she gave out of her poverty; she put in all she had to live on.* Think about this a little bit—it puts a whole new twist on Christmas when we consider this passage in light of who we are in Christ, and who Christ is in us.

Mary carried Jesus for nine months in order to deliver Him to the world. We carry Jesus for the rest of our lives in order to deliver Him to the world. As living sacrifices, we take Him to mankind so that Christ might literally touch people through our hands, feet, and voices. When we allow Christ to live through us in this way, we are sharing our very life, everything we have, more than anything that can be bought.

Have you ever realized it? Have you ever thought about this? God basically asks us to do the same thing He asked Mary to do. **He came to Mary, someone who had nothing to give, and He basically said, make your body a living sacrifice to me. Entrust yourself to me. And He looks at us and says exactly the same thing.**

Lord, one more time, I willingly and joyfully lay myself at Your feet to be used as the packaging and wrapping of Your gift of Jesus to the world every day, all year long. In the midst of all the holiday noise, give me ears to hear the gentle voice of Your Spirit nudging me toward tangible acts of love. Amen.

God with You This Season

Once again, we come to the Holiday Season, a deeply religious time that each of us observes, in his own way, by going to the mall of his choice. —**Dave Barry**

Learning who we are in Christ is a lifelong process. 24/7/365 … and class doesn't dismiss over the holidays. **In fact, there are facets to the biblical account of Christmas that bring the reality of being "in Christ" to light like nothing else.** Consider the popular yuletide word *Immanuel* (Hebrew for "God with us"). It shows up prophetically in Isaiah 7:14:

> *Therefore the Lord himself will give you a sign: The virgin will conceive and give birth to a son, and will call him Immanuel.*

Fast forward about 700 years to a young girl who is growing up minding her own business. An angel interrupts her placid life in Luke 1:26:

> *In the sixth month, God sent the angel Gabriel to Nazareth, a town in Galilee, to a virgin pledged to be married to a man named Joseph, a descendant of David. The virgin's name was Mary. And the angel went to her and said, "Greetings, you who are highly favored, the Lord is with you."*

The miracle, of course, is not just that the Lord was *with* Mary; He was *in* Mary. The Spirit of God permeated the membranes of human flesh so that the Son of God could dwell in the womb of a woman. A familiar story, but an astounding reality.

Another astounding reality much closer to home is this: If you have come to grips with your sin, thanked God for His forgiveness through the cross, and opened the door of your heart to Christ, the same is true of you as was true of Mary. *You are highly favored, the Lord is with you.*

The miracle, of course, is that the Spirit of God has somehow permeated the membranes of your flesh, so that He isn't just with you, but He is in you, too— your own Christmas story 24/7/365!

O Jesus, this year, fill my mind not only with the awe and wonder of what You did 2000 years ago, but fill my heart with worship for what You did the day I asked You into my life, the day You became Immanuel, God with me, God in me. Amen.

God with You in This Moment

This is the message of Christmas: We are never alone. —Taylor Caldwell (1900-1985), English novelist

Christmas songs tell us this is "The hap-happiest time of the year! With much mistletoeing and hearts that are glowing when loved ones are near!" etc. Psychologists, on the other hand, tell us that it's also "The lone-loneliest time of the year, with many hearts hurting and souls that are yearning when alone and in fear."

Yeah, it can be a hard season, but God speaks into that lonely void with a promise, the same promise He gave Mary nine months before the first Christmas:

> *The virgin's name was Mary. And the angel went to her and said, "Greetings, you who are highly favored, the Lord is with you."*

"The Lord is with you." This is a direct quote from another angelic visit to Gideon during a horrible time for the Israelites. They were trying to make an honest living, but every time they planted crops, the Midianites and Amalekites attacked "like swarms of locusts." They were living on a playground surrounded by bullies, and God didn't seem to be doing anything about it—but He was. God was unfolding a plan that came with a promise:

> *When the angel of the LORD appeared to Gideon, he said, "The LORD is with you, mighty warrior."* —Judges 6:12

Our challenges are probably very different than Mary and Gideon's, but the message of Christmas—the truth about Immanuel—is the same promise that holds true for us today: We are never alone. You see, what God promises is His presence and when we receive the presence of God He takes us from having nothing to having everything that we need.

Lord, I praise You for this promise of Your presence right here, right now. In the midst of the holiday chaos, I ask that You will calm my heart with the true peace that comes only through Immanuel—You with me in this moment. Amen.

The Reality of Immanuel

How many observe Christ's birthday! How few, His precepts!
—Benjamin Franklin

I have to be honest, I really do love the holiday called Christmas. Our church is a beehive of activity. Our home is a menagerie of laughter and friends and family. I love the food. I love the decorations. I love the way Christmas smells. And who can argue with a couple of cool presents under the tree with my name on it!? Not a bad way to observe Someone's birthday.

Yes, the holiday works for me … IF I stay mindful of the core precept behind its observance AND if I'm willing to put that precept into practice. **In that sense, Christmas is really just another day. It's one more special day to revel in the wonderful mystery of Emmanuel, God with us.** The fact is, God is with us, and the command given to Joshua is the command to us as well:

> *Have I not commanded you? Be strong and courageous. Do not be terrified; do not be discouraged, for the Lord your God will be with you wherever you go.*
> —Joshua 1:9

So yeah, I'm looking forward to the holiday. It's another day to release my battles and my fears and my self-righteousness. It's just another day to embrace the incredible love of God and celebrate the reality of His presence in my life. **Yes, Emmanuel, "God is with us." That truth makes every day a celebration!**

Jesus, thank You for this holiday. I praise You for one more day to experience the promise of Your presence. Because You are in me, I trust You to be strong; I trust You to be my courage. Thank you that You are with me wherever I go. Amen.

The Real Spirit of Christmas

Maybe Christmas," he thought, "doesn't come from a store. Maybe Christmas ... perhaps ... means a little bit more." —Dr. Seuss (1904-1991), from *How The Grinch Stole Christmas*

For hundreds of years, the world has been in a culture war for possession of Christmas Day. It's worth noting that December 25 was originally an ancient pagan holiday in northern Scandinavia. The sun completely disappeared during those winter months, and they thought that if they threw a really good party, the sun would be inclined to return in the spring. For thousands of years it seemed to work pretty well so we kept it up. The truth is, we really don't know the date of Christ's birth, yet atheists, Christians, humanists, and polytheists all seem to find new things to fight about every year about who owns this day—and the only ones who really seem to be winning are the big box retailers!

Maybe all the bickering is misguided. I think my dad puts things in an interesting perspective:

> *The spirit of Christmas needs to be superseded by the Spirit of Christ. The spirit of Christmas is annual; the Spirit of Christ is eternal. The spirit of Christmas is sentimental; the Spirit of Christ is supernatural. The spirit of Christmas is a human product; the Spirit of Christ is a divine person. That makes all the difference in the world.* —Stuart Briscoe

As important as Christmas is to many of us as a holiday, shouldn't it pale in comparison to who Christ is in us every day?!

Father, give me the wisdom to choose my battles wisely. Above all things, may the eternal, supernatural, divine Spirit of Your Son, Jesus Christ, overwhelmingly supersede the annual, sentimental, human spirit of Christmas. Amen.

Go Tell It on the Mountain!

To the American People: Christmas is not a time or a season but a state of mind. To cherish peace and good will, to be plenteous in mercy, is to have the real spirit of Christmas. If we think on these things, there will be born in us a Savior and over us will shine a star sending its gleam of hope to the world. —Calvin Coolidge (1872-1933), American president. Presidential message (December 25, 1927).

The Christmas story begins with the message, the message from the angel Gabriel to a young girl with nothing to give except her faith in her body in obedience to the promise of hope of Emmanuel: *God with us.*

> *Greetings, you who are highly favored, the Lord is with you.* —Luke 1:28

Not only was the Lord with her, but the Lord was in her. For nine months she held Him in her room, then fed Him, clothed Him, and held Him by the hand as He began to walk alone and fulfill the destiny given to Him by His Father. Thirty-three years later, she had to say good-bye to Him, twice. The first time, she knelt beneath His feet on soil saturated with the blood that He was shedding for the sins of you and me. The second time she watched as His glorified, resurrected body ascended into the sky leaving her, and us, with a mission and with the same promise that Gabriel had proclaimed to her so many years before.

> *All authority in heaven and on earth has been given to me. Therefore go and make disciples of all nations ... And surely I will be with you always, to the very end of the age.* —Matthew 28:18-20

You *are* highly favored. The Lord *is* with you. Jesus *will* be with you always. That's the beginning and the end of the story—the promise of His presence *with* and *in* those who open their hearts to Him.

Now, go tell it on the mountain!

Jesus, deep in my soul today, I thank You for Your incredible promise to be with me and in me today and to the end of the age. Thank You for the tears and sweat and blood that You shed to bring us to this incredible celebration of what You have done and are doing through us. Set my heart free to worship You for these indescribable gifts and use me in any way You choose to share this love with others. Amen.

A Week for You to Think

The past isn't what it used to be. —Unknown

Congratulations! By the mere fact that you are reading this devotional today, you have obviously negotiated your way through the holiday season without dying. No, you didn't eat so much that you actually exploded. No, none of your immediate relatives actually killed each other by being in the same room too long. The wrapping is crammed in the cardboard boxes on the curb and tree needles are beginning to fall to the carpet. Now all you have to do is figure out how to pay for it all. So it's time to go back to work—or at least *pretend* to go back to work. (I'm not sure that any work really gets done during the week between Christmas and New Year's. So, what's this week good for?)

Traditionally, this is the week that we look back at the past year and then look ahead into the next year, making bold resolutions about what the next 365 days will be like. We also try, in vain, to remember the resolutions that we made *last* year. (BTW, anybody need a very slightly used treadmill? I know where you can find one cheap.)

I'm all for resolution, if it takes place in the biblical context of who we are in Christ and who God is. Let's start with an overarching truth that puts everything in perspective:

> *Now listen, you who say, "Today or tomorrow we will go to this or that city, spend a year there, carry on business and make money." Why, you do not even know what will happen tomorrow. What is your life? You are a mist that appears for a little while and then vanishes. Instead, you ought to say, "If it is the Lord's will, we will live and do this or that."* —James 4:13-15

That's powerful, sobering stuff. **Read it again, if you would.** Think about it. Pray about it. Let it soak in. It's the perspective that keeps our hearts and our resolutions on track!

Lord of Life, my days are truly in Your hands. Every breath and every heartbeat is a gift from You. Open my mind to Your Word. Open my heart to Your voice. Humble me, Lord. I will live only if it is Your will. I will do "this or that" only if it is Your will. Amen.

Whose Will – Yours or His?

New Year's Day … Now is the accepted time to make your regular annual good resolutions. Next week you can begin paving hell with them as usual.
—Mark Twain

The big problem with New Year's resolutions is that they begin with the two words, "I will …" Mustering all of the sincerity and dedication that we are capable of, we determine that we will become something that we aren't and achieve something we have yet to do. "I will …" Fill in the blank with anything you want:

- I will lose the weight!
- I will read the Bible every day!
- I will be courageous!
- I will pay off the credit cards!
- I will fireproof my marriage!

All the good intentions in the world aren't going to get you anywhere when you start with those two words, "I will …" **In fact, when we make any plan according to *our* will, and then try to do it through *our* will power, it's destined to fail.** That's not the way we were designed to live, and that's not the way we were designed to pray.

> *I write these things to you who believe in the name of the Son of God so that you may know that you have eternal life. This is the confidence we have in approaching God: that if we ask anything according to his will, he hears us. And if we know that he hears us—whatever we ask—we know that we have what we asked of him.* —1 John 5:13-15

No, our prayers and plans need to begin with, "If You will, Lord … " and any action must begin with the resolution to allow Christ to live through us, rather than attempting it in our own strength!

Jesus, I am done with "I will." In all the details of my life, I want Your will. My willpower is so limited. Yours is never-ending. Whatever it is that You have planned to do through me this year, I place my trust in Your power working through me. Amen.

What's in Your Account for Next Year?

Good resolutions are simply checks that men draw on a bank where they have no account. —Oscar Wilde

Most of our New Year's resolutions don't survive through Valentine's Day. By then, it's too late to cancel the year-long contract at the gym, the budget is blown by a couple extra dinners out a week, and it looks like it will need most of spring break to catch up on our "read through the Bible in a year" program. We *want* to do what it takes, but it doesn't take long to realize that our accounts are empty. **We don't have what we need in our account to pay for what we have resolved to do.**

Why are we so notoriously poor at fulfilling resolutions? For starters, we tend to be so consumed with outward appearances, with possessions, with our health, and with our finances that we miss the main point of life itself: To know God and enjoy Him forever. Instead, we try to do it on our own.

> *In their hearts humans plan their course, but the LORD establishes their steps.* —Proverbs 16:9

The steps Christ determines for us always lead toward more dependency on His resources, and less on our own. This year, will you rest in Christ and enjoy the promise of His presence moment by moment? Or will you latch onto your agenda and fight for it in your own strength?

Jesus, I hold my plans loosely. Prepare me to be ready to change course, on a moment's notice, as You direct my steps this year! I believe in You and I trust You. I look forward in faith to everything You have planned for me. Give me eyes of faith so that I can see every circumstance (particularly my failed plans) as an opportunity to enjoy You and have deeper intimacy with You! Amen.

Next Year, Listen Up!

A New Year's resolution is something that goes in one Year and out the other.
—**Anonymous**

Researchers have determined that advertisers bombard us with approximately 2,000,000,007 messages a day telling us to buy, buy, buy. Then, there's the news channels telling us to worry, worry, worry. And there's all the other things we hear from teachers, bosses, spouses, kids … Wow! No wonder we have a hard time with New Year's resolutions. **We have so many people telling us what to do, we barely have time to think for ourselves … let alone think about what God thinks.**

So if there is one resolution that I might offer as a valid one for someone who is in Christ, it would be this:

Next year, just listen up.

Ask Christ to create a quiet spot in your soul where just the two of you can meet, and talk, and rest as you go about your days. Sure, reach for the stars and plan for the future if you wish, but ask Him to make His presence a deeper reality as you go about life.

You can claim the same promise that the prophet Isaiah gave Israel during some very difficult and noisy days of their own:

> *Your Teacher will not hide himself anymore, but your eyes shall see your Teacher. And your ears shall hear a word behind you, saying, "This is the way, walk in it," when you turn to the right or when you turn to the left. Then you will defile your carved idols overlaid with silver and your gold-plated metal images. You will scatter them as unclean things. You will say to them, "Be gone!"* —Isaiah 30:20-22 (ESV)

Where might this lead? I have no idea. But God does. If you are aware of who He is in you, and if you reflect on the truth of His Word and listen to the Spirit, all the details will work themselves out step-by-step.

Lord Jesus, I thank You that You are with me, that You are in me. Resolutions might come in one year and go out the other. Open my ears this year, so that I can hear You and enjoy You at every junction, when You tell me to turn right or left. Amen.

The Best Prayer I Can Pray for You

New Year's eve is like every other night; there is no pause in the march of the universe, no breathless moment of silence among created things that the passage of another twelve months may be noted; and yet no man has quite the same thoughts this evening that come with the coming of darkness on other nights.
—Hamilton Wright Mabie

Okay, we are almost done. Next week the holidays are officially over and we get back to life as usual. But first, it's time to flip the calendar—and for some reason, we make a pretty big deal out of that. When you think about it, there's really nothing special about New Year's Eve or New Year's Day. If you were to look down from the heavens, you wouldn't notice anything special at all—just one more twist of the globe. But at the same time, it is a special day, isn't it? It always has been. It's always been a night which calls us to *reflect* and *pray*.

REFLECT. Another year has passed. One of these years, it will be your last. It's not a matter of IF, only WHEN. No sense putting anything off until later. Pour an extra mug of your favorite drink and watch the fire burn down. Take inventory of who you are in Christ. The time to let Christ live through you is NOW.

PRAY. The best prayer I can offer you is the one Paul prayed for one of his church plants:

> *For this reason, since the day we heard about you, we have not stopped praying for you. We continually ask God to fill you with the knowledge of his will through all the wisdom and understanding that the Spirit gives.*
> —Colossians 1:9

Amen.

Happy New Year. See you next year.